Lion Bites

EMMA STARK

WITH DAVID STARK • SARAH-JANE BIGGART
SAM ROBERTSON • JOHN HANSFORD • MICAH HAYDEN

DAILY PROPHETIC WORDS THAT AWAKEN THE SPIRITUAL WARRIOR IN YOU!

DESTINY IMAGE® PUBLISHERS, INC.
P.O. Box 310, Shippensburg, PA 17257-0310
"Promoting Inspired Lives."

This book and all other Destiny Image and Destiny Image Fiction books are available at Christian bookstores and distributors worldwide.

Cover design by Eileen Rockwell

For more information on foreign distributors, call 717-532-3040.

Reach us on the Internet: www.destinyimage.com.

ISBN 13 TP: 978-0-7684-5923-4

ISBN 13 eBook: 978-0-7684-5924-1

ISBN 13 HC: 978-0-7684-5926-5

ISBN 13 LP: 978-0-7684-5925-8

For Worldwide Distribution, Printed in the U.S.A.

1 2 3 4 5 6 7 8 / 26 25 24 23 22

Contents

Introduction

You are living in the days of the birthing and establishing of the purified bride of Jesus Christ, the days of a remnant rising. With this comes a greater clash of kingdoms, as the Kingdom of God and the kingdoms of darkness and of this world face each other. As they do, the differences between these opposing realms will be clearly seen and defined. You will watch the church become aware of how she has partnered with the world in wrong ways. Her contamination will be evident and will be cleaned out because for too long the church has been in partnership with the world, looking toward it to come to its aid. Over many years the people of God have taken on worldly mindsets which have shut down their supernatural cutting edge.

But we, the church, are hungry for purifying fire and transformation. In these days the faithful people of God are boldly reemerging as a countercultural movement, fully submitted to King Jesus and rejecting the ways of the kingdoms of the world. We are responding to His invitation, and we will become a wild, contagious, subversive, courageous *ecclesia* who cry with every breath, "Jesus is Lord!" We are yielded to His leading and have a radical loyalty to His Kingdom—not for domination or our own triumphal self-promotion but to steward with a love and passion all that makes His name famous.

Jesus's power is the power of loving liberation, and it comes to us and works through us in miracles, prophecy, healing, deliverance, encounters, Kingdom strategies, dreams, and visions—all of which will become our new normal. As you wake up to this reality, you will be fully set free and will in turn set many captives free. The cry from our hearts will be that we begin to truly live as citizens of another Kingdom—one that is eternal and not of this world. It is time to be as those *"who have tasted the goodness of the word of God and the powers of the coming age"* (Heb. 6:5).

Jesus, the Lion of the tribe of Judah, wants you to be like a weapon of Holy Spirit–filled, dangerous, dynamite that blows up all the strongholds of darkness, highly tuned in to hear His commands, totally in step with His Kingdom only, and with senses that are trained, alert, and supersensitized to His every move.

LION BITES

For over a decade a team of prophets from our ministry have written and sent out daily prophetic words called Lion Bites to keep believers in step with the Spirit of Jesus Christ and the trajectory that He's moving on throughout the earth. For the book that you now have in your hands, six of us (Sarah-Jane Biggart; my father, John Hansford; Micah Hayden; Sam Robertson; my husband, David; and me) sat down together to listen to God and bring you 365 new, fresh encounters with Him.

The result, *Lion Bites*, is a personal, daily devotional that will build you into someone who is vitally alive and successfully active in a supernatural lifestyle. As you turn the pages, let us take you by the hand into a personal Holy Spirit adventure for the next year. We will submerse you in a culture of seeing in the Spirit, hearing from God, finding freedom, reawakening dreams, and reestablishing the warrior spirit within you!

Each day's reading is not merely a "thought for the day." Every page includes a prophetic word, a passage or verse from Scripture, and an action, prayer, or decree. Occasionally you'll also get a bite-size nugget of pure Bible wisdom when our teachers bring their sharp scriptural insights and wisdom to the table.

A WINDOW INTO OUR WORLD

Here in our house of prophets in Glasgow, Scotland, we are very used to sharpening one another. Our culture is to bring prophetic words and activations to team time, we then outwork them as a group in our conversations, our worship, and our ministry. We live in a community of encountering God together, and really this book is an extension of that. It's a remarkable process when a company of prophets work under a collective anointing! As you read, pray, and activate each day's readings, you will receive a sense of what it's like to sit with us as we lead one another into the heavenly delights that await anyone who yields to the Spirit of God.

When we write together, I lead the team into a time of praise and worship before we begin to note what God is saying by His Spirit. We all sound a little different when we express what we're hearing, with slightly different emphases, but the revelation is from the same place.

The uniqueness in this book is not just that you will read Scripture every day with us but that you will also do the kind of activations that we do in our own lives. Allow us to mentor you in a bespoke, personal way by following these activations (the actions, prayers and decrees that are suggested each day). Let us lead you daily into the spiritual spaces and places that we prophets inhabit together!

Never underestimate the power of a prophetic activation (in other words, something you do, write, pray, or say) that drives a deeper connection with Jesus than you may be used to. This is the relationship with God that you've probably always desired and prayed for! As a house of prophets, these activations are our normal, everyday ways of encounter, experiences that shift us from a head knowledge of Jesus, into a heart connection with Him and into lives transformed by His Spirit.

WELCOME INTO A LIFESTYLE OF REVELATION

We welcome you to be led into a lifestyle of deep revelation as you read *Lion Bites*. We invite you to join with the Holy Spirit to see what we see, hear what we hear, and receive what we receive from our heavenly Father, who loves to give good gifts and to speak with His children.

I bless you as you embark on this supernatural, joy-filled journey! Be empowered by God to see, hear, perceive, and encounter. Be healed, get free, and let the adventure begin!

With much love, and together for His Kingdom,

Emma Stark

P.S. There's more online! Every weekday our team publishes fresh Lion Bites. You can sign up to receive these or read the archive of all of them (there are thousands!) on our website or social media. They're completely free, and there are no restrictions on copying them and sharing them with your friends. Visit www.propheticalliance.com to subscribe and for more information.

CHAPTER 1

Courage Explodes

DAY 1

Security Is Found in Me

Then the angel showed me Jeshua the high priest standing before the angel of the Lord. The Accuser, Satan, was there at the angel's right hand, making accusations against Jeshua. And the Lord said to Satan, "I, the Lord, reject your accusations, Satan. Yes, the Lord, who has chosen Jerusalem, rebukes you. This man is like a burning stick that has been snatched from the fire." Jeshua's clothing was filthy as he stood there before the angel. So the angel said to the others standing there, "Take off his filthy clothes." And turning to Jeshua he said, "See, I have taken away your sins, and now I am giving you these fine new clothes" (Zechariah 3:1–4 NLT).

Come and stand before Me today. Come as you are; in fact, bring your insecurities—every thought of disqualification, unworthiness, low value, and words of "not good enough"—to Me. Stand before Me, and offer these as a sacrifice. Let Me have them; they do not become you. Lay them at My feet. Let Me remove the ones that feel stuck and attached to you.

Let Me in close. In the close proximity of standing face to face, your security is found. Stand close and gaze at Me; look into My eyes. Let Me see you fully, and then take in all that I am. Receive it, soak it in, and let it go deep into your being.

Now, let Me dress you in garments that are washed clean by My blood. Let Me tell you how I see you as I dress you in clothing of righteousness and purity. Listen to My whispers of delight. Experience the joy I feel at seeing you. Let Me adorn you with garments that suit one who is chosen.

I have chosen you and called you by name; now walk securely in Me.

RECEIVE

Spend time with Jesus today by doing the very actions described in this word. And then listen to Him as He tells you how He sees you. Watch as He adorns you. Let what He does go deep down into your being.

Are You Ready for a Fresh Adventure?

Therefore, if anyone is in Christ, the new creation has come: The old has gone, the new is here! (2 Corinthians 5:17)

My child, I have made you for a purpose and for such a time as this. You are blood-bought, a new creation, and I have many incredible, heavenly assignments for you to fulfill.

I am ready for a fresh adventure with you! Are you ready to follow Me down some paths that you have never walked before? There are places that I want to take you that you thought you were disqualified from visiting. But that was a lie! Those paths and places are for you. I have qualified you. You are in Me and therefore the new things are for you.

It is time to rip out the old thoughts that you had about yourself and prepare to be amazed at what you will be able to accomplish when you walk in step with all that I say about you.

DECREE

Pray the following or use your own words: "Father, I am ready for a new adventure with You. I choose to stop thinking that I am not worthy and instead make the decision today that I will believe what *You* say about me. Renew my mind, Lord!"

DAY 3

Rise Up and Break Out!

For God has not given us a spirit of timidity, but of power and love and discipline (2 Timothy 1:7 NASB).

The Spirit of the Lord is putting His hand on the areas of timidity in your life. He is examining every area where you hesitate, where you lack confidence, where boldness seems to be just out of your grasp. Today He wants to address these areas because He did not make you this way. All who are in Him have access to His confidence, His determination, and His boldness.

Just as Jesus knew who He was and what His purpose on the earth was, so He says to you, "Rise up and stand tall! Watch as I put My hand on the core of who you are. Watch as the touch of My hand displaces and drives out that timid spirit. Now, receive and take on My courage and My boldness. I have not given you a spirit of timidity or fear! I have given you power, love, and discipline. Walk in them."

DECREE

Make the following decrees out loud or write them down:

- The Lord God has not given me a spirit of timidity, hesitancy, fear, shyness, or anything resembling these things.

- He has given me power!

- He has given me love!

- He has given me discipline, self-control, a sound mind, and sound judgment!

DAY 4

Timidity Is Broken!

The Lord is my light and my salvation—whom shall I fear? The Lord is the stronghold of my life—of whom shall I be afraid? (Psalm 27:1)

The Lord speaks to you today and says: "Oh courageous one, this is a day for freedom from the lie that you are timid and powerless. In you, I have placed a tenacity and warrior courage that is going to come forth in the days to come. But first, open wide your heart and let Me in as the Deliverer to remove the lying arrows sent by the enemy to convince you that timidity and powerlessness disqualify you from the fight!"

I watched in the spirit as the Lord came rushing into your heart and started to pick out the lying arrows that the enemy had sent to you. He is coming to you with freedom and force, and He is liberating you from the areas in your life that have been held captive by the lies of the enemy. As the Lord rushes in, I hear Him shout over you: "You are not timid but courageous! You are not powerless but powerful! You are not fearful; you are bold!" As He says these words over you, the arrows are pulled out, and they disintegrate, never to return.

So the Lord says: "You are free! You are free from the bondage of the lies of the enemy. You are no longer held captive by timidity and powerlessness. You are free! Today I am infusing you with warrior courage and boldness. Today I am marking you as a power-filled one who already has what is needed for the fight that is at hand. Today, oh courageous one, you will believe that you are courageous!"

RECEIVE

Receive today the freedom that God is coming to deliver. Pray a prayer of surrender and availability, and tell God that you are open and ready to receive deliverance from the lies of timidity and powerlessness. Feel freedom rush through your veins as God comes and liberates you.

Walk with Me
Part 1

Who, then, is allowed to ascend the mountain of Yahweh? And who has the privilege of entering into God's Holy Place? Those who are clean—whose works and ways are pure, whose hearts are true and sealed by the truth, those who never deceive, whose words are sure. They will receive Yahweh's blessing and righteousness given by the Savior-God. They will stand before God, for they seek the pleasure of God's face, the God of Jacob (Psalm 24:3–6 TPT).

I, the God of Jacob, am calling you up My holy mountain. I am calling you into a deeper level of holiness and purity, and I desire that you would be free from all that has caused you to feel stuck at the bottom of the climb.

My child, why are you so discouraged and disheartened? I am for you and with you. It is My desire for you to succeed and to enter into the fullness of life on the earth and in the Spirit that I have at hand for you. Let us climb now.

It is time to reassess your circumstances with Me and see that there is a way to move beyond where you feel stuck. Take My hand as I come now to lift you onto your feet. Stand up and walk with Me. One step in front of the other with Me and we will move up the mountain together.

DECREE

As you respond to Him, speak out loud: "I choose to take Your arm and lean on You, Jesus. I choose to get up out of my place of stuckness and leave all that caused it there. I release my pain, grief, disappointment, and fear here."

Whatever has made you feel stuck, speak it out to God in prayer, using specific people's names if relevant, and then leave it all with Him. Let go of it all. You don't need to carry these things with you anymore as you ascend this mountain.

DAY 6

Walk with Me
Part 2

Who, then, is allowed to ascend the mountain of Yahweh? And who has the privilege of entering into God's Holy Place? Those who are clean—whose works and ways are pure, whose hearts are true and sealed by the truth, those who never deceive, whose words are sure. They will receive Yahweh's blessing and righteousness given by the Savior-God. They will stand before God, for they seek the pleasure of God's face, the God of Jacob (Psalm 24:3–6 TPT).

Yesterday, you chose to get up from the place where you were stuck and began to walk with Jesus, ascending with Him.

"Lean on Me. Take Me by the arm and walk with Me," Jesus continues to encourage you.

He, the Lord Himself, comes now to help you up His mountain. Keep leaning on Him. He has you. Take your first step in faith and determine that you are going to continue with the climb. You are choosing to move forward with Jesus, today and forever.

As you take the hand of Jesus, I can see many other saints walking up the hill of the Lord with you, each on their own walk, yet climbing the mountain together. Some are cheering you and others from the side of the path. Others are singing, and others are on their knees, being helped up, and linking arms with other travelers. They are all walking together. You are not alone.

DECREE

As you respond to Him, be encouraged to speak out loud the following prayer:

I now determine to take that first step and move with You. I gladly join with the saints together to continue my climb. I thank You, Jesus, that I can lean on You and gain strength from You. I receive it today.

DAY 7

See Who You Are

The Lord is my light and my salvation—whom shall I fear? The Lord is the stronghold of my life—of whom shall I be afraid? When the wicked advance against me to devour me, it is my enemies and my foes who will stumble and fall. Though an army besiege me, my heart will not fear; though war break out against me, even then I will be confident (Psalm 27:1–3).

The Spirit clearly says that in later times some will abandon the faith and follow deceiving spirits and things taught by demons (1 Timothy 4:1).

"Did I not call you a coheir and a co-laborer with Me? Did I not seat you beside Me in heavenly places? Did I not bless you with every spiritual blessing according to My riches in glory? Did I not choose you, redeem you, and call you My own?" asks the Lord.

I heard the Lord speak with a commanding force. His words shot out from His mouth as a weaponized war cry. His words devoured the lying demonic spirits that have been sitting on your shoulders and whispering in your ears, speaking invalidation over you and whispering that you are not enough, not worthy, not diligent, not faithful, and not determined enough in matters of spirituality.

The Lord says, "No longer listen to the teaching of demons."

No longer let them weave a story of untruth to you about who you are. No longer keep lying spirits as pets and houseguests who set the tone of your life. For this is a day to be rid of demon voices and hindrances! No longer can you let them shape how you see yourself. For the Lord says that He sees you as "altogether lovely," and His cry of freedom rages against the darkness.

Wipe your shoulders, literally. Where you are, raise a hand and wipe the demons off your shoulders and forbid their return!

ACTION

Ask God to allow you to look in a mirror in Heaven and see your reflection as Heaven would see it. Take time to open your eyes in the spiritual realm. Shift from simply knowing the report of the Lord over your life in your head to encountering the report of the Lord as you see.

This will build you up so you can see good things. Banish your default setting of looking to criticize yourself.

Victorious!

Therefore, since we are surrounded by such a great cloud of witnesses, let us throw off everything that hinders and the sin that so easily entangles. And let us run with perseverance the race marked out for us, fixing our eyes on Jesus, the pioneer and perfecter of faith. For the joy set before him he endured the cross, scorning its shame, and sat down at the right hand of the throne of God. Consider him who endured such opposition from sinners, so that you will not grow weary and lose heart (Hebrews 12:1–3).

Father God is cheering you on today. Like a good dad who cheers as he watches his son or daughter compete in a race, so God is jumping up and down with excitement as you run the race of your life.

He sees you with His spiritual fitness, His strength, and His spiritual muscles, toned and ready to endure what is coming. He sees you qualified to compete; in fact, He knows you were made for this! He knows you were designed to meet every challenge with His strength.

This is your time; this is your season. As He is cheering you on, He says to you, "Ready, set, go! You can do it! You can face all that comes your way for I am with you and I am for you. Nothing and no one can stop you! Run full speed ahead for I have already called you victorious!"

RECEIVE

Sit and receive His strength today. In the areas where you feel tired, weak, or even out of shape spiritually, say out loud: "Father God, I receive Your strength. I allow it to soak into my muscles. I ask You to show me a picture of this word; show me how You cheer me on as I run my race."

Then, watch His face and see what He does. Let the word *victorious* sink deep into your being and begin to see yourself running with His strength. See the victory!

DAY 9

The God of all Comfort

Blessed be the God and Father of our Lord Jesus Christ, the Father of mercies and God of all comfort, who comforts us in all our affliction so that we will be able to comfort those who are in any affliction, with the comfort with which we ourselves are comforted by God (2 Corinthians 1:3–4 NASB).

"Allow Me to have your blankets of security," says Father God. "Give to Me all that you have wrapped yourself in and comforted yourself with that is not Me or from Me. I long to be the source of your comfort and well-being. I desire to bring you solace and relief, contentment and rest. Take off that which you have pulled about yourself to self-medicate for I long to wrap Myself around you. Receive My comfort. Receive My rest. Receive My peace and strength. Allow Me to unravel and pull off of you your own go-to sources of consolation and relief. We will make room for the fullness and completeness of My comfort. I desire to be your only source of true comfort."

I see the Lord unraveling tight bandages. These are like tight blankets of restriction in the spirit around you. He is peeling them back as you give Him access. Lift up your arms as He pulls them off you. Release all that is personal and pertinent to you; it may be alcohol, codependent relationships, sugar, food, exercise, drugs, sexual behaviors, media, or something else. Allow God to remove all those false comforts from you now.

"Allow Me to be your comfort," He says to you, "for I am the God of all comfort." As Father God unravels your historical sources of comfort, He wraps Himself around you in what looks like a snug-fitting duvet, holding all of you, from your head to your feet. Like a babe in its mother's womb, He is holding you; you are safe, and you are known.

RECEIVE

Pray and allow God to come close to you now. Receive the overflow of His reassurance and comfort for you by saying the following pray to Him:

God, I receive the fullness of Your comfort. I choose You and Your comfort above all others. I let go of the empty comforts of this world in this moment. Thank You, Father, that You comfort me for my sake and for the sake of others to whom I will bring Your comfort.

You Are Fearless

For I, the Lord your God, hold your right hand; it is I who say to you, "Fear not, I am the one who helps you" (Isaiah 41:13 ESV).

Today God is releasing the capacity to you to confront fear and call its knees to bow. Just like David stood face to face with the seemingly undefeatable Goliath and took him out with a mere stone, so the Lord is saying, "I have enabled you to stand in the place of battle with what seems like little in your hand to take out the enemy. Though you may feel unequipped or lacking in the necessary tools, I will multiply the power that is in your hands to take fear out."

You don't need to live under the power of fear all your life. It is time to take the authority that is in your hands—even if you think it is small—and use it as a weapon to take fear out. With your authority, you will overcome the enemy and stand more fully in the place of victory over fear.

So, start to move forward. Confront fear and tell it to leave. As you do so, the Lord says, "You are moving into not just boldness but into fearlessness."

DECREE

Make the following decrees. Declare them over your life. Keep them in mind throughout your day:

- I am fearless, not fearful.

- I can defeat fear.

DAY 11

Take Heart! Grab Hold of Courage!

I have told you these things, so that in me you may have peace. In this world you will have trouble. But take heart! I have overcome the world (John 16:33).

As you sit with the Lord, allow Him to search your heart. As He does, He is asking, "Why do you doubt? Why do you doubt that I have called, anointed, and equipped you?

"You only doubt when you focus on *your* ability. Focus instead on *My ability in you*; focus on *who I am in you*. As you focus on Me, My abilities will crowd out the doubts. As you focus on Me, I will boost your courage; I will give you strength.

"As I said to the men and women of old, so I say it again to you, 'Take heart!' Grab hold of courage and do not doubt! I went before you and made a way. I overcame every obstacle and every hindrance so that you would face this life with courage! It is yours for the taking!"

ACTION

Take time to sit with Jesus today and let Him examine your heart. Let Him show you the areas where you have doubt and lack courage. Then, repent of that doubt, and grab hold of His courage!

If this is an area that you know needs a lot of help, take extra time to read through the stories of Moses, Joshua, Deborah, David, or Esther in the Old Testament, and take note of how they grabbed hold of courage.

DAY 12

Don't Look Down

Then a teacher of the law came to him and said, "Teacher, I will follow you wherever you go." Jesus replied, "Foxes have dens and birds have nests, but the Son of Man has no place to lay his head." Another disciple said to him, "Lord, first let me go and bury my father." But Jesus told him, "Follow me, and let the dead bury their own dead" (Matthew 8:19–22).

"Don't look back and don't look down!" Jesus reminds you today to press on, without doubt, trusting Him and focusing on what is ahead. He will guide your feet, and His Word will illuminate your steps. Your provision will not come from what you try to carry for yourself; it will come as you seek first His Kingdom.

Just as expert gymnasts don't look down to find where they want to place their feet, don't be tempted to look down for where your support will come. On this journey, your eyes will be looking straight ahead, as you fix your gaze directly before you (see Prov. 4:25).

Don't trust in your own resources. Follow Jesus and listen to Him. Make plans and dreams that are influenced by God and not what is in your hand. If you are willing to step out and trust, He will support you and guide you.

ACTION

Quiet yourself and spend time with God thinking about your future. Allow the Holy Spirit to fill your mind with big ideas and dreams. If your thoughts waver, become anxious, or you begin to doubt or fear the future, then say out loud: "Lord, today I am fixing my gaze ahead and trusting You for everything."

DAY 13

Step into New Territory

"Come and join me," Jesus replied. So Peter stepped out onto the water and began to walk toward Jesus (Matthew 14:29 TPT).

"Release the fetters! Release the hindrances! I the Lord am speaking over you today to shift you into a place of release from all that has restricted you. Step out of confinement into the place of liberation today as I speak, 'Release!' over you. I release you from all fear and uncertainty of self that is held in your mind. Choose now to step into freedom. I release you from all self-doubt. Choose to move beyond this now."

God is calling you to step over what looks like a shallow ditch before you in the spirit realm. Before it has seemed impossible to you to move beyond this place. The ditch represents how you currently feel stuck or limited emotionally, mentally, and spiritually, particularly concerning how you see yourself and think about yourself today. But God, in this moment, says, "Step over the ditch of self-doubt and all that hinders you from powerfully knowing who you are in Christ. Step over into full knowledge of who you are in Me and erase all self-doubt as you choose to move over that which has hindered you. Come to Me and step over."

"I am breaking you into confidence!" says the Lord. "Step over now! I am breaking you into a new realm of powerful assurance in Me and in who you are in Me. Step into all I have for you today. Move beyond all that has held you back in this moment, and prophetically step over and into this new territory with Me."

ACTION

In faith step over mentally, and the Lord will do the rest. Stand up where you are right now and choose to prophetically "step over" into self-assurance and out of self-doubt. As you do, declare the following over yourself and your life:

- I am leaving self-doubt here and stepping into self-assurance in Christ.

- I am breaking agreement with fear and uncertainty and stepping into a faith-fueled life!

- I am choosing to cross over into all You have for me in this moment, Lord, and I trust You!

Celebrate as you cross over into confidence and assurance today!

DAY 14

You Are Enough

The angel of the Lord came and sat down under the oak in Ophrah that belonged to Joash the Abiezrite, where his son Gideon was threshing wheat in a winepress to keep it from the Midianites. When the angel of the Lord appeared to Gideon, he said, "The Lord is with you, mighty warrior" (Judges 6:11–12).

"As I did with Gideon in the winepress, I have brought you into a place where I am dealing with your insecurities and the lies that you believe about yourself. It is time for 'I'm not enough' thinking to go!"

You may have said some of the following statements:

- I'm not smart enough.
- I'm not trained enough.
- I'm not mature enough.
- I'm not experienced enough.
- I'm not beautiful enough.
- I'm not gifted enough.
- I'm not qualified enough.

But the Lord says, "These are all lies! I have already put within you the capacity to achieve all that is required of you."

Even more than that, God is not so caught up with what you can or cannot do. He is enamored entirely by who you are. He has already made you enough. Beyond your intelligence, your looks, your experience, your qualifications, you are already enough.

You are filled with potential, infused with divine blessings, marked by heavenly beauty, called with a purpose that is alive, created as you are in a way that makes your heavenly Father respond with a "very good!" It is time to tear off the lies, to throw them away and to no longer allow them to cap or limit you.

ACTION

Allow God to bring to your mind the lies that hold you back. Maybe they are some of the ones included in the list above. Write them on a piece of paper and then ask God, "What is the truth I need to believe that will defeat this lie in my life?"

DAY 15

A Fireball Inside You

The Spirit of the Lord will rest on him—the Spirit of wisdom and of under-standing, the Spirit of counsel and of might, the Spirit of the knowledge and fear of the Lord— and he will delight in the fear of the Lord (Isaiah 11:2–3).

I saw the hand of the Lord place a gift deep inside your chest. It had the appearance of a small, bright object, like a ball of fire, burning white-hot. From it came a heat that would melt and destroy anything nearby, and yet it did not harm you as He placed it into your body. It was so blindingly bright that I could not look at it for long.

As He placed this burning ball, Jesus said to you, "I am giving you this gift of fire in your midst that will never burn out. Do not forget that it is there. Whenever you feel your heart begin to freeze with fear, remember Me and allow My Spirit of might to warm your insides and soften your anxiety."

Whenever it gets too dark around you, remember that inside you is a holy light, the knowledge and fear of the Lord, as bright as the sun, illu-minating and transforming you from the inside out. The more you open your mouth with boldness, the more this light will shine from you and illu-minate where you walk. Go forth with newfound confidence and courage because of what is inside you!

DECREE

Pray in your own words:

Jesus, thank You for the gift of Your Spirit inside of me. Help me to be aware in fresh new ways today of the fireball that is inside of me, chang-ing me from the inside out. Holy Spirit, I allow You to explode inside me, that I might be transformed by You and Your wisdom, understand-ing, counsel, might, knowledge and the fear of You.

DAY 16

Fire in Your Bones

The righteous are as bold as a lion (Proverbs 28:1b).

I have come to set the world on fire, and I wish it were already burning! (Luke 12:49 NLT)

But whoever is united with the Lord is one with him in spirit (1 Corinthians 6:17).

The Lord says, "I am setting the inside of you on fire!"

See, the flame of God rises from deep within and takes over. Listen in the spirit realm and hear the Holy Spirit Himself, who lives in you. He is now exploding and crackling as a fire would as it rises and rages with heat, passion, and determination to consume.

Feel the burning and the stirring of God, not descending from outside of you but as an internal detonation of God—inside you—where He is happy to be. In you is His resting place: your body is His temple; your frame is His dwelling; your physical being is His possession. Your God, the erupting, all-consuming fire, who boils you alive with His flame! He restores you right now, as a child of courage and boldness, because you are not just a kindling but a furnace of His life and power.

ACTION

Look in the spirit realm, and see inside you how you are one with the Spirit of God, as First Corinthians 6:17 states. Look and perceive your internal spiritual reality. You are not just fleshly organs. You contain a spirit that is merged with the indwelling Holy Spirit of God, and He is a burning Spirit of fire.

This is a positive thing! It will strengthen you to see the beauty of your spirit and the Spirit of God dwelling in you as one. You got fused with the Spirit of God when you accepted Jesus as Lord.

Write down how what you have seen will impact your life.

DAY 17

Don't Look Back

We know that our old sinful selves were crucified with Christ so that sin might lose its power in our lives. We are no longer slaves to sin (Romans 6:6 NLT).

Do not look back at what was. Stop glancing in the rearview mirror at what you have left behind. Repent and move on, forward into the light.

Pay no heed to the old version of you, for it is time to behave differently. Even when the shadows and habits of your former ways cross your path again, take a sidestep and choose not to be drawn back in. Repent and move on, forward into the light.

If sin has tripped you up, deal with it and leave it behind again. When you catch yourself behaving like your old rebellious self, repent and move on, forward into the light. You are not a slave to destructive behavior. The chains of unfaithfulness have been broken when you accepted Christ's crucifixion for you. There is now nothing to keep you in that dark place. Repent and move on into the light.

DECREE

Pray the following prayer or use your own words:

Jesus, I believe that You suffered and died on the cross for me. Who I once was—my old sinful self—has been crucified with You. I believe that sin no longer has the power it once did over me, and I am no longer a slave to sin. But Lord Jesus, I have messed up. I have behaved badly, and I confess my sin to You. I repent of (name what you've done). This sin has no part of me, and I am sorry for picking it up again. I turn my back on this sin and choose now to walk back into Your light and in the freedom that You have won for me.

DAY 18

Peace That Destroys Anxiety

Let the peace of Christ rule in your hearts (Colossians 3:15).

And he awoke and rebuked the wind and said to the sea, "Peace! Be still!"
And the wind ceased, and there was a great calm (Mark 4:39 ESV).

I watched in the spirit as Jesus stood over your life, and just as He calmed the wind and waves, He decreed "Peace be!" to the storm of anxiety that has often raged inside you. As His hand raised and the words left His mouth, the wind and waves immediately stilled. With authority and certainty, Jesus is speaking right to the core of your being today, to the places where anxiety hides and rules, and He is saying, "Peace be!" No longer are you going to feel like anxiety has incapacitated you from being effective. The days are over when anxiety is the ruling force within.

Now, you are coming to a peaceful place within that empowers you to make bold and courageous decisions in your life. This peace that comes is not frivolous or surface; it's an act of war that disempowers the tools of anxiety the enemy uses against you. As the "Peace be!" cry of Jesus infuses your innermost being, expect there to be a level of consistent boldness that marks your day-to-day; even the most mundane of daily tasks will be marked by a new level of bold decision making and actions.

DECREE

In partnership with Jesus, stand as a prophetic act and lay a hand on your heart. Decree with faith "Peace be!" to anxiety and worry. Watch, feel, and sense anxiety subsiding and peace rising as Jesus delivers and empowers you with these two simple words.

DAY 19

I Long to See Your Face and Hear Your Voice

My dove in the clefts of the rock, in the hiding places on the mountainside, show me your face, let me hear your voice; for your voice is sweet, and your face is lovely (Song of Songs 2:14).

"Stop feeling that you are of little worth to Me," says Jesus Christ to you. Believe Him and do not let what you see on media, in magazines, and on social media play havoc with how you see yourself.

The Old Testament often encourages its readers to *"seek his face"* (Ps. 105:4) and to *"gaze on the beauty of the Lord"* (Ps. 27:4). Continue to do this but know that He is also longing to see *your* face!

He says, "You are My dove, but you are hiding in the clefts of the rock. I long for a deeper and more intimate relationship with you, but you have hidden among the rocks and crannies of the cliff. My dove, you are not visible and have made yourself inaccessible to Me, yet I have longed to see your face and to hear your voice.

"Have you so quickly forgotten how thrilled I am when you speak to Me? Do you not recall how lovely I find your appearance? I know you want to help and please Me, and that is right and good. However, I am talking about *how I feel about you.* I want you to be where I can hear your voice and see your face; your voice is sweet and your face is lovely."

ACTION

Read and reread Song of Songs 2:14 and imagine Jesus Himself saying these words to you today. Don't be distracted by thinking that this cannot be the correct interpretation of this verse. These are words that Jesus Christ is saying to you. Never underestimate His desire for your company, friendship, and expression of your love, no matter how hard you find the latter to do. Thank God you are loved with the ardent affection that you read about in the Song of Songs. It is this truth that establishes your identity and determines your destiny. You are loved with an everlasting love.

The End of False Starts

Return, faithless people; I will cure you of backsliding (Jeremiah 3:22).

"I love your consistent determination to do better," says the Lord. "I even admire your work ethic and the focus of your heart to be the best version of yourself you can be. You have pleased Me with your cries to begin again and start over with renewed energy and repentance. However, you have become stuck in human effort. There are some things that only I can cure. There are some things that need miracle grace and My strong, outstretched right arm. Some things can only come about when My zeal is in operation when you rip open your chest and expose your heart to Me, and instead of applying human effort, you seek My healing. I have supernatural ways that I can cure your cycles and the frail and repetitive, though well-intentioned, human patterns that bog you down.

"Today I am decreeing a day of ending to your false starts, to your patterns of failure, and to boom-and-bust lifestyles. Give Me your work ethic, give Me your determination. Surrender your labor, your toil, your industry, and your sense of duty. Give Me the sweat, effort, and striving. Let Me heal and cure you of false starts."

I will heal their waywardness and love them freely, for my anger has turned away from them (Hosea 14:4).

RECEIVE

Take time to open your heart to God and receive His healing power from human cycles and patterns.

Consider physically kneeing as a sign that you are giving God a deeper access to fix what is broken in you. Take a posture that indicates your need for the supernatural, and today will be a miracle day for you!

DAY 21

Forgive

And whenever you stand praying, if you have anything against anyone, for-give him, that your Father in heaven may also forgive you your trespasses. But if you do not forgive, neither will your Father in heaven forgive your trespasses (Mark 11:25–26 NKJV).

"'Forgive!' is My command to you today. Let go of the wounding that has caused more pain to you and those you love. Forgive those who have caused you hurt and agony; there will be great freedom for you as you do.

"Unforgiveness has gripped your heart and prevented you from mov-ing freely into the future that I have for you. It requires determination and a decision today to say, 'I will no longer partner with unforgiveness'

"I know the cause of your pain, My child, and yet I say to you again, 'Forgive.' Forgive and move past the history and memories. I will release you from the repetitive thoughts of trauma and shock as you liberate those who initiated it by your words of forgiveness. Forgive and be liberated in this moment," says the Lord.

PRAYER

Heavenly Father, I thank You for Your forgiveness even though I do not deserve it. I choose today to forgive (list name(s) here). I repent for part-nering with unforgiveness and bitterness, and I ask You to release and deliver me from those two bondages now. I thank You for Your mercy and patience that allows me to now step into freedom from all pain and wounding associated with these memories. I ask for a reset of all my emotions associated with this event (or these events). I ask for forgive-ness for judging them and release them to Your justice now.

I repent for all my vain imaginings and judging of how they or I could have justice in this situation. I choose to bless them and not curse them; I entrust them to You and pray that Your will for their life and future be fulfilled.

I now move into Your place of freedom for me as I forgive them whole-heartedly. I ask for restitution and restoration over all that has been held up or stolen from me because of my unforgiveness.

If you are struggling to forgive, pray the following each day and wait on the Lord until you can pray the full release above: "Lord Jesus I need Your help to forgive (name the person/people). I choose today to begin the journey of forgiveness, and I say that I desire to forgive (name the person/ people) as You command. Help me get to the place where I can wholeheartedly release forgiveness to them. I do not want to be stuck."

Don't Look to Settle Old Scores

This is what the Sovereign Lord, the Holy One of Israel, says: "In repentance and rest is your salvation, in quietness and trust is your strength, but you would have none of it."…Yet the Lord longs to be gracious to you; therefore he will rise up to show you compassion. For the Lord is a God of justice. Blessed are all who wait for him! (Isaiah 30:15, 18)

He is the Lord your God, and He upholds justice. It is God who will bring the unfaithful to repentance. So put down your thoughts of those who have wronged you. Put away your problems that you have had with leaders, family members, and former friends. Don't look to settle old scores, for these are mere fistfights in the dark compared to the riches that God has for you in the light of His goodwill for you.

Says the Lord: "I have so much for you that is good and that you will enjoy. Where I am leading you is a much better place, full of fruit that will bless you more than anything you could get from fighting past injustices."

Stop going back down those alleyways of offense and bitterness. All you will find down those back streets are fights and battles that will lead to more hurting and wounding. Stop holding accounts of what you think the past owes you. Give those to the Lord, and allow Him to lead you to the place of fruitful joy that He has prepared for you.

ACTION

Ask Holy Spirit to help you write a list of those you are holding in your heart as ones who have wronged you or who you feel still owe you.

Take a few days or even a few weeks to give each person and each situation to God, and trust Him to hold onto these accounts. Forgive each person, just as your heavenly Father has forgiven you.

Breathe Out

Jesus called his twelve disciples to him and gave them authority to drive out impure spirits and to heal every disease and sickness (Matthew 10:1).

And the disciples were filled with joy and with the Holy Spirit (Acts 13:52).

We believe in the miracle of indwelling spirits—specifically the miracle of the indwelling Spirit of God, who has made you His dwelling place (see 1 Cor. 6:17). Today the Lord says, "You have other spirits indwelling that you should not have and that are getting in the way of you being full of Me. They are taking up space from My Spirit fully possessing you."

The Greek word for *spirit* in the New Testament is *pneuma*, meaning "spirit, wind, or breath". In any deliverance and freedom ministry we expect demons to come out on the breath because they are air/spirit in form. Breathe out the demon spirits; they are to be removed from you today, cleanly and without doing you harm. They are removed by your repentance and by breathing them out.

The Lord says, "Come to Me in repentance specifically for your independence and stubbornness that has kept you from the cutting edge of life with Me. At times you are more resistant to My moving than you should be. Let Me have My way and work with Me today to liberate you. I *will* have you as part of the liberated, wild, and courageous remnant, not the self-serving or the self-focused."

ACTION

Repent of where you know you have been self-focused, stubborn, or independent, and then demand that any demon associated with these issues leave you now, in the name of Jesus Christ. Take in a big breath and then breathe out. Do this a few times to get rid of them all. Enjoy the freedom that this exercise brings!

Receive! Open your hands as you invite and receive the indwelling Holy Spirit of God to fill the places the demons vacated. Be filled to overflowing with the Spirit of God.

DAY 24

Feel the Fear, and Do It Anyway

Do not fear, for I am with you (Isaiah 41:10).

Fear is a dreadful enemy. It paralyzes, for it conjures up the worst possible consequences in our imagination. It breaks relationships, for it spends time looking at itself rather than at others. It makes you lie; it believes that the truth will cause unpopularity. It procrastinates, for it convinces that later will be easier. And ultimately, it can destroy a person and all their potential.

Peter to the rescue! The Apostle Peter was prey to fear. Remember when he denied knowing Jesus (see Mark 14:66–72)? That was out of fear. Later, Paul describes Peter (Cephas) as separating himself from the Gentiles, acting in a way that was totally contrary to what he believed, simply because he was afraid. Peter went along with what others wanted to hear because of his fear. So, we can be sure that Peter knows what he is talking about when it comes to fear; he understands the situations we find ourselves in.

But by the time Peter wrote, *"Do not fear what they fear or be disturbed, but honor the Messiah as Lord in your hearts"* he had had a life-changing experience (1 Pet. 3:14–15 HCSB). So much so that he could preach, be in jail, preach again, and face flogging for it—fear was no longer a hindrance to Peter.

So, here is Peter's advice to you when it comes to fear: when your whole being quakes, make sure that Christ, the Son of the living God, is at the center of your heart and is in command there as Lord, where He can bring peace. Jesus said, *"Do not let your hearts be troubled and do not be afraid"* (John 14:27), for He knows that if your heart isn't filled with Him, it will fill with fear instead.

Peter also knew that Jesus at the center of your heart has all power to help you. He was at the tomb to see the resurrected Christ, *"made alive by the Spirit"* (1 Pet. 3:18). And he knows that this same Jesus has all power in Heaven where He commands angels and all authorities throughout the universe (see 1 Pet. 3:22). And this is who is living in your heart!

ACTION

Fear needs to be challenged. It has to be confronted, otherwise, it will hide forever. Let us strengthen and challenge one another not to do anything out of fear, but to live in the openness, courage, and strength that is there even for the most timid of you, in the name and the power of Jesus Christ!

DAY 25

Courage to Help

This is what God the Lord says—the Creator of the heavens, who stretches them out, who spreads out the earth with all that springs from it, who gives breath to its people, and life to those who walk on it: "I, the Lord, have called you in righteousness; I will take hold of your hand. I will keep you and will make you to be a covenant for the people and a light for the Gentiles, to open eyes that are blind, to free captives from prison and to release from the dungeon those who sit in darkness" (Isaiah 42:5–7).

The Lord God has heard your cries for help as you long to be used by Him to help others. He has listened as you have sought Him regarding the injustice you see. He has seen your tears for those who struggle in oppression and depression. He knows that you long to be one with the courage to lead, compassion to heal, and resources to help. He also longs for you to rise up and to be that help.

And so today He says: "I want you to be an extension of Me, to be My hands and feet upon the earth! I love your heart for others! But this is a partnership between you and Me; it requires that you first receive My help. It requires that you first receive My freedom and My strength for what you long to do requires so much of Me. Come, meet with Me and receive!

"For if you will receive a greater revelation of faith, I will give it to you. If you will cry out to Me and ask Me to help you with your shortcomings, I will answer. If you will allow Me to come in and remove the hindrances from your own thinking, I will show you the resources that have been hidden. If you will stand before Me, I will give you the creative solutions required. If you take the time to sit with Me and to draw up the blueprints and the plans needed to accomplish what's on *My* heart, you will be well equipped and rightly motivated to accomplish all that I have put on *your* heart."

RECEIVE

Sit with the Creator today and ask Him what is on His heart for your community, your city, your nation. Ask Him what His dreams and plans are. Sit and hear what He longs to do, and in that space, allow Him to work out this prophetic word.

DAY 26

I Have Not Forgotten You
Part 1

Do not fear, for I have redeemed you; I have summoned you by name; you are mine. When you pass through the waters, I will be with you; and when you pass through the rivers, they will not sweep over you. When you walk through the fire, you will not be burned; the flames will not set you ablaze (Isaiah 43:1–2).

Father God says to you: "Trust Me and do not be afraid. It may seem to you like you are in the most challenging and darkest time of your life. I know that you are tempted to feel that I have forgotten you but know and do not lose sight of the vital truth that I will sustain you through this trial. Allow Me to comfort you in your present situation.

"Remember that I will be with you, whatever happens. You know this truth already but actually sensing My presence and experiencing the comfort it brings is something very different altogether. Years ago, King David wrote that My presence filled him with joy as he took hold of My hand and I led him along the path of life (see Ps. 16:11). I will do the same for you. My presence will take away your fear when you feel you are in over your head and the waters of life are very rough around you. You will not drown (see Isa. 43:2)."

Many people find enormous comfort in Psalm 23, especially the lines in verse 4, "*Even though I walk through the darkest valley, I will fear no evil* [I will not be afraid], *for you are with me; your rod and your staff, they comfort me* [you walk beside me and I feel secure]." There is a nearness to God that David experienced when he felt troubled or distressed, and you can know it too.

ACTION

Read the Book of Ruth and learn all that Naomi went through. Just as God was with her, He is there for you as well.

I Have Not Forgotten You
Part 2

Do not be afraid, for I am with you; I will bring your children from the east and gather you from the west. I will say to the north, "Give them up!" and to the south, "Do not hold them back." Bring my sons from afar and my daughters from the ends of the earth—everyone who is called by my name, whom I created for my glory, whom I formed and made (Isaiah 43:5–7).

Yesterday Father God reminded us that He will be with us, walking with us, whatever happens. He is continuing to speak reassurance and comfort to you today.

"I have a purpose in what you are going through. Your sufferings are not meaningless and your life is not one of random chaos. This is My world, after all, and I will not let a single part of what you are suffering be wasted! Trust Me that I have reasons and purposes in what you are going through, and they are all for your good, regardless of what it looks or feels like."

God's Spirit...knows us far better than we know ourselves, knows our pregnant condition, and keeps us present before God. That's why we can be so sure that every detail in our lives of love for God is worked into something good (Romans 8:28 MSG).

And He says, "Your pain will not last forever. Whatever you are going through, if you are in Me, you can be assured that it will not last forever. There is coming a day when I will make all things new. Until then you will find strength and hope by thinking about what you are experiencing in the light of eternity" (see Rom. 8:18).

Heaven may feel like little comfort when your suffering continues for months, even years, but remember that nothing is outside our Father's ability to redeem beyond your wildest dreams. He knows exactly how long your pain will last, and He always answers prayer. If you are struggling today, remember that He has not forgotten you.

ACTION

Yesterday you read the life of Naomi. Now read Joseph's story in Genesis 37–50; he waited years for God to work things into something good.

DAY 28

True Source

In him was life, and that life was the light of all mankind (John 1:4).

"I am the source of all light and life. I am the source of all hope, peace, and joy eternal. Receive Me as your source today.

"Drink from Me and take fresh life from Me in this moment, for I desire to pour into you the fullness of life that I carry. Open your spirit and your heart to Me now. Fix your internal gaze on Me in this moment and receive an infilling of My light and life.

"The genesis, beginning of all creation, source of life is in Me, and it is My longing to give it to you in unsurpassed measure. So receive and drink. Open up and be filled with a bursting overflow in this moment."

I see the Lord pouring out who He is, as the light of the world and the light of life, over you and into you. As He tips over the fullness of who He is onto and into you, open your spirit and heart consciously and receive the extensiveness and richness of the true source of all life and light.

ACTION

Read the eighteen opening verses of John's Gospel. Meditate on each statement that is made about Jesus, "the Word."

Think about the lines that talk about light and life. As you do, consider that He wants you to drink in this light and life of His.

Respond to Him in prayer; you might want to open your mouth as if you were taking a drink and say, "Jesus, fill me with Your light and Your life."

Elijah and the Path of Confrontation

So Obadiah went to meet Ahab and told him, and Ahab went to meet Elijah. When he saw Elijah, he said to him, "Is that you, you troubler of Israel?"

"I have not made trouble for Israel," Elijah replied. "But you and your father's family have. You have abandoned the Lord's commands and have followed the Baals" (1 Kings 18:16–18).

There is a time for peace, and there is a time for war. There are times when we can sow and reap, build and influence for the Kingdom in the midst of the world's systems. Conversely, there are times when evil so grips a territory that the church has no option but to work underground, spreading the gospel in less overt ways. But there are also times between these two extremes when neither collaboration nor withdrawal represent the path of faith but are instead a surrender of our call.

You must discern the times by the Spirit, for there is a time when the destiny of churches, businesses, and even nations hang in the balance when the battle for the hearts of a whole people is on the knife edge. Then it is time for believers to leave their secret hiding places, be these government offices or monastery cloisters. Then is the time for the path of confrontation. Then it is time for prophetic warriors to arise!

It is a costly path to tread. It means exposure to personal risk and slander. Notice Ahab's words to Elijah, "troubler of Israel." If the enemy cannot take his opponent's life, he will murder his reputation and try to pin the label "traitor" on him. Examples of this abound in the Bible; they tried it on Jeremiah and even on Jesus. The prophet who dares to declare the sins of his or her country in public, as Elijah did, will find themselves accused of being the very cause of the nation's problems. There has been a rise in anger in the West over Christian views on biblical morality. Have you thought, *I'm being made to look like the bad guy here, as if Christianity is suddenly the problem*? Today faith in Christ Jesus is not just one option among many religions to be considered; it is now vilified as the problem.

Nevertheless, choose righteousness over making a peace for yourself. It is a dangerous and costly choice to make, and yet Elijah, one man out of the seven thousand faithful followers of Yahweh, was not intimidated. But what if he had been? What if Elijah had been paying bills at the treasury like Obadiah or singing worship songs in the cave with the sons of the prophets? What if he had not discerned the times and chosen the right path?

DECREE

Ask the Holy Spirit for the ability to discern the times and seasons. And when the time is right, decree: "I am a prophetic warrior, and now is my time to arise!"

Outrageous Expectation

May the God of hope fill you with all joy and peace as you trust in him, so that you may overflow with hope by the power of the Holy Spirit (Romans 15:13).

The Lord says, "Your future is nothing to be afraid of, and today I am enabling you to look forward to what is ahead with hope, expectation, and outrageous joy.

"Just as the Proverbs 31 woman can *'laugh without fear of the future'* (Prov. 31:25 NLT), so My gift to you in this day of deliverance is the ability to stand in expectation of what I have prepared for you in the days that are to come. But first, it is time for freedom. It is time for the demonic spirit of fear of the future to be broken."

I watched in the spirit as the hand of God was outstretched to your head. He lifted off heavy glasses from your eyes that were tinted and foggy and replaced them with glasses filled with luminous color. The former glasses shaded, clouded, and confused your view of the future to make you anxious and unsure of what's to come. But the new glasses bring the ability to look creatively into your future and see potential and opportunity.

So, prophetically act this out to show your willingness to partner with the Lord: take off the "glasses of the fear of the future" and put on the "glasses of outrageous expectation." Decree and declare that the demonic spirit of fear is broken from your life, and welcome a new expectation from the Holy Spirit to mark your vision. Today is freedom day, today is liberation day, today is *new vision* day!

She is clothed with strength and dignity, and she laughs without fear of the future (Proverbs 31:25).

ACTION

Prophetically act out removing the old glasses. As you lift them off say, "Fear of the future is broken in Jesus's name!" Then, lay hands on your eyes and say, "I receive outrageous vision to look at my future with hope and expectation!"

DAY 31

You Are Not a Settler

Have I not commanded you? Be strong and courageous. Do not be afraid; do not be discouraged, for the Lord your God will be with you wherever you go (Joshua 1:9).

I will give you every place where you set your foot, as I promised Moses (Joshua 1:3).

Open your mouth and declare: "I am a Joshua!" When you say this, it means that you affirm: "Where I put my foot I have authority. I am like Joshua, and I will not slip into a mentality of retreat. I am like Joshua, and I will not accept where I am as being my destination. I am like Joshua and reject an assignment to come into agreement with how I am right now."

Today the Lord gives you the gift of a Kingdom of God defiance against the enemy. This is a time to be in open resistance and bold disobedience to what the demons are saying. It is a time to be insubordinate and rebel against the demonic spirits that are grooming you. For these demon groomers would seek to manipulate, exploit, abuse, and establish an emotional connection with you. They want to share their thoughts that you might become a "settler," one who settles for the status quo, one who settles for how you feel, one who settles for how you have been received by others, one who settles for your current level of promotion.

You are a Joshua, and you have authority. When the demons scream, "settle and stay" at you, the Holy Spirit is rising within you and instructing overcoming and movement. You have been in many dress rehearsals for today, and your level of faith is on the rise. You have been prepared, and God has already dealt with your unreadiness. You have been in the classroom of Heaven, learning the heart and truth of your heavenly Father. Today you are released to overthrow!

A savvy agitator rises within you; the revolutionary is switched on. The insurgent formulates a voice in the midst of you, and now you are released to be defiant against dark powers!

ACTION

God is clear that He is a military trainer, and you are in His army (see Ps. 144:1). Stand up where you are right now, and allow God to put new weapons into your hands. Feel the weight and authority of God course through your being. Feel the sharpness of the weaponry you are receiving. Become weaponized by God, emotionally and spiritually, as you stand.

CHAPTER 2

Weaponized by Heaven

Warrior Arise, Alive in Victory!

When you sow, you do not plant the body that will be, but just a seed, perhaps of wheat or of something else....So will it be with the resurrection of the dead. The body that is sown is perishable, it is raised imperishable; it is sown in dishonor, it is raised in glory; it is sown in weakness, it is raised in power; it is sown a natural body, it is raised a spiritual body. If there is a natural body, there is also a spiritual body....And just as we have borne the image of the earthly man, so shall we bear the image of the heavenly man (1 Corinthians 15:37–49).

Warrior arise! Do you know the battle plan? The victorious outcome of the war has already been decided: all things will be put under the feet of Jesus! Do you know your destiny? You have been made righteous by Him and will be part of the incredible resurrection of the dead—when what was perishable will be raised imperishable; when what was sown in dishonor will be raised in glory; when what was sown in weakness will be raised in power; and when what was sown in a natural body will be raised in a spiritual body. You'll shine like the sun, like the brightness of the heavens!

All this is still to come and to be looked forward to. But warrior, know that already you have been raised to a new life with Christ. You already died; your old self is dead! Your life is now hidden with Christ in God. This means that you are dead to sin—praise Jesus!—but alive to God. This means that you no longer have to submit to the rules and regulations of sin and darkness. These things are dead to you. You are now a citizen of Heaven.

So set your heart on things above—the realities of Heaven—where our risen Christ is, seated at the Father's right hand. Meditate on these truths from God's Word about what Christ Jesus's victorious battle of love—His death, suffering, and resurrection—has won for you. Let the truth of His relentless war of love for you compel you into renewed spiritual warfare in this present life of yours.

Warrior arise! Don't spend the rest of your life chasing your desires, those rooted in your old, dead self. Instead, devote yourself to a renewed passion for doing the will of God.

ACTION

Read and meditate on First Corinthians 15 and the other Scriptures referred to in the word above (see Matt. 13:43; Dan. 12:3; Col. 3:1–3; Rom.

6:11; Col. 2:20; Phil. 3:20; 1 Pet. 4:2). How will these truths affect how you live your life from today onward? Are there some new resolutions that you want to make in light of the wonderful reality of who you are in Christ? Write down any decisions you make so that you can keep yourself accountable to them.

DAY 33

Faithful and True

I saw heaven standing open and there before me was a white horse, whose rider is called Faithful and True. With justice he judges and wages war. His eyes are like blazing fire, and on his head are many crowns. He has a name written on him that no one knows but he himself. He is dressed in a robe dipped in blood, and his name is the Word of God (Revelation 19:11–13).

Do you see Him? This is the One who calls you into His army! This is your King!

For today He says to you: "Do you see Me as I am? Do you see Me as the King of kings who is enlisting you into My royal army? I who am called Faithful and True also call you to be faithful and true. Faithfulness and truth are the identifying marks that you bear as one who carries My Word into the earth. I, your King, am faithful to keep My promises; I am trustworthy. And I am truthful; in My truth, I carry justice.

"Many of you face circumstances that cry out for this faithfulness, truth, and justice. Many of you have cried out and asked, 'Lord, where are You in this trying circumstance that I face?' And I say to you that I am here equipping you to face these situations, to war against the enemy as I do, and to take up your calling and identity as a warrior in My army. See Me as Faithful and True!"

ACTION

Take time to dwell on this Scripture and to consider Him as the Apostle John saw Him. And then in that place, present your circumstances to Him and let Him remind you of His faithfulness as He speaks truth into your heart.

Wholescale Shifting

And no one after drinking old wine wants the new, for they say, "The old is better" (Luke 5:39).

When you are transformed, you can transform the world around you. If you do not continually reform, reframe and transform, you become stale and, in time, unpalatable to those in need of Jesus. A lack of reformation makes for boring and wrongly repetitive versions of Christianity. Being a Jesus follower is supposed to be an adventure of being every day molded by Christ until His mind is your mind and His ways are your ways.

Our usefulness to God, our weaponization by Heaven, is always in direct proportion to our ability to crawl onto the altar, over and over; to our allowing the fire of holiness to burn us; to our permitting the shaping of the Potter's hand to be present in our life; to our accepting the challenge of the Holy Spirit that pricks our conscience.

In our resistance to reformation and change, we become dull and small. Being in fresh awe and wonder of God is nourishment to the soul, enabling the new wine to be poured out. Wrongly protecting our inherited orthodoxy and traditions leads us away from delight in the Lord, who does new things, even in deserts and wildernesses.

So, today God is saying to you to shift in how you see church, shift in how you see your role in church, shift in how you interpret Scripture, shift in how you approach prayer. "If you will ask Me to shift you, I will give you My mind—which you need to advance," God says. "Some of My thinking and My solutions that I sent down to you ricocheted off you and could not seed into your brain because you were not in patterns of continual shift and constant reformation."

He says, "There were solutions that you needed to see that I sent, but they did not land because willingness to change was not your normal, default position and attitude."

DECREE

Pray out loud: "I need Your mind, Jesus! I need Your thinking, Your breakthrough, and Your solutions. Forgive me for being stubborn and forgive my own agendas, Father God. Please make reformation and change something I am continually happy with, in Jesus's name."

DAY 35

Mind of Christ

Those who are spiritual can evaluate all things, but they themselves cannot be evaluated by others. For, "Who can know the Lord's thoughts? Who knows enough to teach him?" But we understand these things, for we have the mind of Christ (1 Corinthians 2:15–16 NLT).

Today take the time to consider what it means to have "the mind of Christ." These are not just words; this is the truth that Jesus wants you to possess. Declare it out loud over yourself: "I have the mind of Christ!"

For He says to you, "You are not double-minded, wishy-washy, scattered, foggy, foolish or incompetent. No! I did not create you that way, nor have I called you to walk in any of those. You have access to My wisdom and My thoughts. I have put within you the ability to know and to perceive things from My realm, My Kingdom!

"Make a decision today to put down every excuse, every allowance, every reason that would suggest that you can't think clearly, can't make decisions, can't know My perfect will, and can't understand things in the spiritual realm. Lay these lies from the enemy down at My feet. Then, pick up My truth and declare that you have the mind of Christ!"

ACTION

Take some time to think about or even list out every area where you struggle with your thoughts or in your mind. Go down the list and declare out loud, "I have the mind of Christ and can do all things!" Declare that you are clearheaded. Declare that you make good decisions. Declare His truth over each one!

DAY 36

God's Measure of Faith

The apostles said to the Lord, "Increase our faith!" (Luke 17:5)

Overcome with triumph today, warrior of the Lord, for it is His delight and favor to give you all that you need to face each day and to have victory.

Today the Lord assigns to you the gift of faith in a new measure, to overcome all that is set against you. The gift of faith He gives you is His own measure of faith. Receive this gift, and launch yourself into a fresh way of living, with the assurance of an overcomer and one who knows how to activate their faith in a new measure.

The Lord Himself says to you today: "I give to you now My own faith and My assurance of overcoming all that has come against you. Receive and be charged with My faith today. See that you can surmount all challenges with this gift. I weaponize you with My gift of faith in this moment. Be awakened to a brand-new level of victorious faith. Receive! It is yours."

RECEIVE

Pray: "I thank You, Lord, for Your gift of faith today, and I receive it anew, knowing that it enables me to overcome all challenges. I realize that I can say, 'Anything is possible with God' because of Your gift of faith in me. I make room for Your faith to be awakened in me today."

Take time to sit with an open posture to receive all the Lord wants to give you of His faith today and let Him release and activate it in you.

DAY 37

Perspective Is Everything

God, who is rich in mercy, made us alive with Christ even when we were dead in transgressions—it is by grace you have been saved. And God raised us up with Christ and seated us with him in the heavenly realms in Christ Jesus (Ephesians 2:4–6).

Emma writes: We often go hill walking in Scotland. The beauty of the rugged mountains is truly a powerful way to reset and think new thoughts. The spaciousness of the open hills enables bigger thinking. When your eyes are filled with an expansive horizon, rather than, say, the four walls of your kitchen, something miraculous happens to how you view your own life. Our approach to how we live changes according to how we see.

Therefore, how I see matters massively to how successfully I will navigate life. What I see when walking on the road is hugely different from what I see from the top of a skyscraper. What I see from an airplane is vastly different from what I see seated in heavenly places.

The command "come up here" that Jesus gives to many of His prophets is not just a cry for proximity. Rather, it is a demand He places on them to view things with a comprehensive sweeping eye. It is about not being hemmed in by the battles of the day-to-day. Instead, it is about the freedom to see from a different standpoint.

When Paul in Ephesians reminds us that we are seated in heavenly places, it is not an abstract nicety that massages how I feel in a moment. Rather, it is an invitation to interpret your life the way God does. It is an open door that you are welcomed through to have a new vantage point, a new frame of mind of what is happening to you and through you. This invitation is supposed to give you healing in the tough days.

ACTION

There is an urgency for you to start to see many of your life situations from the correct perspective. The wrong perspective is stunting your ability to find solutions. Lay hands on your own eyes, and contend for the right sight to come to you. As a prophetic act, pull off wrong lenses and trample them under your feet. Do this as a sign of how you will see things moving forward from today!

DAY 38

Your Positional Authority

You yourselves have seen what I did to Egypt, and how I carried you on eagles' wings and brought you to myself. Now if you obey me fully and keep my covenant, then out of all nations you will be my treasured possession. Although the whole earth is mine, you will be for me a kingdom of priests and a holy nation (Exodus 19:4–6).

When a government official is appointed to a ministerial position, they are given much more than just a title and a desk. They are given the authority to make and enforce policies and represent the government at the highest levels. They have full access to all the resources of the department under them, and they have all the "secrets" of that office—records of what has been done in the past.

The Lord has brought you to Himself that you might be a minister of His Kingdom, a director of the affairs of His holy nation. He invites you to take a seat at His cabinet table, to be assigned the priestly responsibilities of bringing Heaven to earth. You have a new position, and with it, you have positional authority.

Stop thinking of yourself as someone who has only just been rescued out of Egypt, out of slavery and bondage to sin and shame. Jesus has made a new covenant for you. You are dressed differently now, and so it is time to behave differently now too. Begin to think of yourself and the positional authority that has been given to you by the King Himself. The more you think of yourself in these terms, the more you will behave with the authority of a priest of the Kingdom of Heaven.

DECLARE

Make the following declaration:

Because the King of kings has carried me out of darkness and into His wonderful light, I am one of His treasured possessions and a minister for His holy nation. I am royalty in His Kingdom, and I will represent Heaven on earth with the authority that the King Himself has given to me! (See First Peter 2:9.)

The Call of a Warrior

Do this, knowing the time, that it is already the hour for you to awaken from sleep; for now salvation is nearer to us than when we first believed. The night is almost gone, and the day is near. Therefore let's rid ourselves of the deeds of darkness and put on the armor of light (Romans 13:11–12 NASB).

I hear the Spirit of the Lord calling. As He calls, your insides are awakening, for this is the call you have waited and longed for. It is the call of the warrior—the call to arise, to put on your armor, to gather your weapons, and to stand tall in your position among the army of God. You can feel the excitement in the air as the army gathers; your heart thrills as you see warriors from every tribe and nation coming together. You join them in eagerly looking to the King as He rides to lead the charge.

In His army, there is no worry of being unequipped or ill-prepared. For each warrior knows that the King has prepared you for such a time as this. Shake off the dullness, shake off the weariness. Put aside any distraction, and set your gaze on the King, the Champion, as He leads you into battle. He is worth following! He is deserving of every sacrifice! And as He goes from victory to victory, so do you!

ACTION

Allow the Holy Spirit to show you what you look like as a warrior on the battlefield. As you look in the spirit, ask Him questions and pay attention to what He shows you:

- Holy Spirit, what does my armor look like?

- What weapons have You put in my hands?

- Holy Spirit, would You show me the angelic army that is around me?

- As you look at the army, do you see King Jesus?

- What does He look like? What is He doing?

- What is He saying to you and your fellow warriors?

Are you ready to raise a new battle cry, to the glory of the King?

The Fire and Voice Within You

The voice of the Lord divides flames of fire (Psalm 29:7 NASB).

There is a fire in you that the Spirit of the Lord longs to release. It is a fire of burning passion for the Father and Son. It is a passion that will set you and those around you ablaze! It is a red-hot fire that the Lord is even now kindling to a new, white heat scorching point. There is a fire within you ready to be released.

There is also a rallying shout within you that is made to join the call of "Advance!" of the army of God from Heaven and on the earth. I see that, in His hands, Father God is marrying your powerful and anointed internal shout with your core personal fire. He is taking them in each hand and combining them to be a fusion of fire and voice. This powerful blend is about to come out of you in a fresh, forceful way. It won't be in some half-hearted or testing toe-in-the-water kind of way but in a thundering force, affecting change and transformation to all around you as you release it.

Your shout brings down our enemies in one blow. Your fire scorches unholiness on the earth, eradicating enemy encampments so that they will never return. Your voice becomes a weapon that nothing can stand against. So now release your voice and release your shout!

The Father says to you, "Allow Me to reach into you now and marry your fire with your voice in this moment. For I will have you like a burning one who speaks. I will have you like a fiery one with a powerful voice. So announce your shout and discharge your fire today."

DECREE

Lord, I give You access to my voice and declare anew my passion for You. Let me burn more for You, my Lord. Increase my desire for You—I need more of You, Lord. I long to burn with an intensity that does not let up.

I give You access to my voice and give it into Your hands. Have Your way with my voice, Lord, and let Your fire in me be married to my voice so that it can be released at the right time, in the right place, to bring change and transformation.

DAY 41

Father's Mighty Warrior

When the angel of the Lord appeared to Gideon, he said, "The Lord is with you, mighty warrior" (Judges 6:12).

The Father says to you today, "I am molding you and making you into a new shape by My own hand. I am causing you to be one who knows how to war in My name. Today I am speaking over you the words I spoke to Gideon.

"You are My mighty warrior. and I have plans for you to overthrow the enemy in My name. So now, My Gideon, arise for this time!

"There is a victory shout and a war strategy that I will give you as you wait on Me to overcome the enemy in your own life and circumstances.

"Kneel before Me and receive your orders, My Gideon. Receive orders instructed by My hand as I give you a fresh word of battle strategy today. This will be a new sword in your hands to wield against the enemy at this time.

"Then arise, Gideon, and take up your sword! Speak My word and overcome your enemy, for it is time to take back what has been stolen and to rise up in confidence and courage. Take heart, for I am with you, and I am giving you strategy. Ask Me and I will release it freely to you now."

DECREE

Decree and declare over yourself: "I am a mighty warrior!" Kneel and stretch out your hands as a sign, a prophetic act, to God that you are ready to receive your sword and fresh battle strategy. Then, stand up, arise and tell God that you are ready for battle against the enemies of God!

DAY 42

Your King!

Blessed is the king who comes in the name of the Lord! Peace in heaven and glory in the highest! (Luke 19:38)

On his robe and on his thigh he has this name written: king of kings and lord of lords (Revelation 19:16).

Worship Him as King!

So much of what you struggle with and what you long for will be sorted and answered when you become one who bows low before the King. Kneeling before Him in a posture of humble reverence and adoration is far more powerful and effective than you have realized. It is in the surrendering and the submitting to the Lord's kingship and His authority that your own authority is found. When you bow down and recognize His authority over your life, you begin to carry the authority needed to break the oppression and the demonic hold over your life. You also begin to see yourself as you were made to be.

Therefore, as one who is a conqueror and a coheir with Christ, it is vital that you practice the lifestyle of bowing low before Him. Just as any mighty warrior would know the privilege of serving a mighty, majestic, conquering champion king and would easily bow to that king, so is it for those who desire to be warriors in the army of the King of kings.

ACTION

Kneel before your King today! Spend time kneeling before His throne in worship and adoration because of who He is! He is worthy!

DAY 43

Weaponized with Favor

Then Abraham rose from beside his dead wife and spoke to the Hittites. He said, "I am a foreigner and stranger among you. Sell me some property for a burial site here so I can bury my dead."

The Hittites replied to Abraham, "Sir, listen to us. You are a mighty prince among us. Bury your dead in the choicest of our tombs. None of us will refuse you his tomb for burying your dead" (Genesis 23:3–6).

"My favor is on your life as a weapon. You have not always been aware of this mighty gift, but it is present in your life. My favor opens doors for you. My favor predisposes men and women to bless you. My favor enables you to possess what is yours. You can embrace it or you can speak negatively about your life with words that undermine your own journey and shut off My goodness.

"Thank Me for My favor and cease words that would seek to speak in opposition to Me blessing you," says the Lord.

In the unusual Bible story where Abraham is negotiating with the Hittites for land to bury his dead wife, Sarah, he is seen as having God with him. The visibility of God with him enables him to negotiate advantageously, then own and take full possession of the land.

There are some things you are supposed to own and have access to, to possess, to inherit, to have in your hands. God says, "I am weaponizing you with My favor that you might take what is meant for you. As you do, you will see some, who you think might be hostile to you, make a way for you today.

"My favor will enable hearts, minds, and wills to work with you and not against you, especially when it comes to having ownership. Possess your possessions!"

DECREE

Decree and declare your gratitude to God for marking you with His favor. Then, act; go and have the conversations you need to have with business leaders, employers, banks, colleagues, and family members, and see the favor of God go ahead of you, making a way!

DAY 44

Warrior in Training

Praise be to the Lord my Rock, who trains my hands for war, my fingers for battle (Psalm 144:1).

I see angels coming today to dress you in your new battle clothes in the spirit. I see the training wear of a warrior being put on you and fastened securely in this moment. These clothes look like chain mail, which goes under the hard, professional soldier armor that you will receive later. It consists of a chain mail tunic, gloves, and leggings—full-body under armor. This protects you and provides free and easy movement as you practice your battle moves in this training season.

The Lord is saying that it is time to make the moves of a warrior, to practice your stance as a soldier of the Lord, and position your heart as one who knows that this is part of their identity. You are a warrior. You are one of Heaven's troops on the earth called to fight.

Take the battle stance each day. Practice your exercises, confident in knowing who you are. Ask the Lord for the specific prayers and scriptures to release today for the area He has called you to war over; perhaps it is for your family, your workplace, your community, or even for your nation. Ask and listen to what the Holy Spirit is saying to you. Step into your entry-level soldier movements as you practice advancing God's Kingdom with His Word.

DECREE

Make these decrees daily as you train:

- I am a warrior of the Lord.
- I am part of His army on the earth.
- I am called to fight and hold my ground as a warrior.
- I have weapons of warfare available from Heaven in my mouth and my hand.
- I will use my voice and release my weapons and not hold back.
- Train me in warfare, God!

DAY 45

You Are Made for Confrontation

The weapons we fight with are not the weapons of the world. On the contrary, they have divine power to demolish strongholds (2 Corinthians 10:4).

Do you know that you are made by God for confrontation? In you is the capacity to confront and overthrow the plots, plans, and purposes of the enemy as part of the expansion of the Kingdom of God on earth. Today the Lord is waking up your confrontational warrior call! He calls to you and says, "Shake off the lies of weakness and stand in your call to confront the powers of darkness to see them defeated. You have been born as a warrior into a war, and you already have what you need to defeat the already defeated foe.

"Do not allow the enemy to confront you or to catch you off guard; do not allow him to convince you that confrontation is his game. You are called to forcefully extend My Kingdom by eliminating the tactics of the enemy and releasing the purposes of Heaven. Do not hold back or dilute what I have put within you. Do not allow your inner warrior to be dampened, removed, or silenced. Instead, call for the confrontational warrior in you to wake up!"

ACTION

Repent for diluting your inner warrior. Lay hands on your mind, and call for the warrior inside you to wake up!

DAY 46

The Shield on Your Left Arm

In addition to all this, take up the shield of faith, with which you can extinguish all the flaming arrows of the evil one (Ephesians 6:16).

Warrior, it is time to press back against the enemy. I heard the cry go up in the spirit, "Lead with your left and advance!" You are armored with a great shield of faith, strapped tight to your left arm; in your right, you wield the sword of the Spirit. Now you must go and extinguish the wicked and evil fires that are burning.

Don't think of your shield as small, the size of a dinner plate! No! Your faith shield is meters high and surrounds you. You are protected, like a well-equipped firefighter, who rushes toward a burning building without fear of his own safety.

There are evil fires burning in the spiritual realm that threaten to destroy families and lives. Get up, faith-filled warrior, advance, and quench those flames! Snuff out everything that the enemy throws, and prevent him from spreading wickedness in the areas that God has given you to protect. Do not fear, take up the shield of faith, lead with your left, and ADVANCE!

ACTION

Make a list of the areas that God has given you influence in, for example, your home, workplace, school, college or university, church, neighborhood, city, and online and social media spaces.

Whenever you are in those spaces, ask Jesus, "Are there evil fires burning here, or are arrows on the way?" These could be situations or simply words spoken by others. Make a note of these, and then ask Him, "How can I behave in a new faith-filled, fearless way that will extinguish the evil from this place or situation?"

DAY 47

Take On the Identity of a Warrior

The Lord is a warrior; the Lord is his name (Exodus 15:3).

I see, in the spirit, seeds of the word of God falling into your mind in this moment. As the Lord drops His words of war and battle-ready weaponizing into your brain, He is telling you that it is time to receive His words and be established in His truth; you are a mighty warrior, just as He is a Man of war.

The Bible is full of verses about spiritual warfare. There is a call of God to let the truth of these Scriptures of war penetrate and permeate your thinking; decree and declare all of these weaponizing Scriptures out loud over yourself each day, believing that this is who you are. It is time to shape your thinking and mindset as one made for war.

As you do, the seed word of God is set in your thinking, affecting how you act and live. Be activated in these war words of Scripture and be one who has the identity of a warrior from this day forward. Declare and be transformed.

ACTION

Build yourself up by reading what Scripture says about spiritual warfare and your authority as a spiritual warrior. See the appendix for more verses to encourage you on this theme.

Praise be to the Lord my Rock, who trains my hands for war, my fingers for battle (Psalm 144:1).

Behold, I have given you authority to tread on serpents and scorpions, and over all the power of the enemy, and nothing shall hurt you (Luke 10:19 ESV).

"No weapon formed against you shall prosper, and every tongue which rises against you in judgment you shall condemn. This is the heritage of the servants of the Lord, and their righteousness is from Me," says the Lord (Isaiah 54:17 NKJV).

Master and Subdue

God blessed them and said to them, "Be fruitful and increase in number; fill the earth and subdue it. Rule over the fish in the sea and the birds in the sky and over every living creature that moves on the ground" (Genesis 1:28).

See, I have chosen Bezalel son of Uri, the son of Hur, of the tribe of Judah, and I have filled him with the Spirit of God, with wisdom, with understanding, with knowledge and with all kinds of skills—to make artistic designs for work in gold, silver and bronze, to cut and set stones, to work in wood, and to engage in all kinds of crafts (Exodus 31:2–5).

Christ Jesus says to you, "I want you to master what I have put into your hands. You are to be a master."

Consider those who are masters of their art, craft, or profession. They are never phased or alarmed by what they are given to deal with. They work with the materials or the situation that crosses them, and they subdue it and make it do what they need it to do.

For the master builder or the master craftsman, there is never an impossible project. They are confident in their gifts and knowledge, and they are committed to their work. A master sportsperson is never fazed by the opponent's experience or abilities; they approach each game or tournament without fear, only considering what is in their own hands to deliver and make happen. They know that whatever shot or move they face, they have something in their armory to turn it to their advantage.

It is time to master what has been put into your hands. You were not born into this world at this time to be passive or to go with the flow of the world. People of the Kingdom, followers of King Jesus, it is time to master and subdue. It is time to reshape what the enemy has formed and remold it into something good and pleasing to the Lord. Go and be a master!

RECEIVE

Spend time with God, and ask Him for downloads and blueprints. Pray for a reawakening of the gifts and talents that He has put within you. Where you have doubted or feared, listen to what Jesus says and receive a new mastery of what you thought would not amount to anything. Be ready to make notes and action points from all that you hear, and receive when you pray with Him about this.

In the Meantime

Since everything will be destroyed in this way, what kind of people ought you to be? You ought to live holy and godly lives as you look forward to the day of God and speed its coming (2 Peter 3:11–12).

John writes: I can't remember a time in my life when I have so deeply longed for the return of Christ. I have wanted Jesus to come back and put an end to the brokenness and sin in our world.

I'm ready for Him to vindicate truth and to put things right; I look forward to His wonderful recreation of a new Heaven and a new earth. I want Jesus to return to be glorified and exalted and seen by everyone as the true Lord and King of the universe.

What will it be like to experience joy, God's very presence, true goodness, and the beauty of holiness after the warped and tainted life here?

But this picture is one that should cause us sober thinking and a determined focus on how we should live in the meantime as we ready ourselves for Jesus to return. No more excuses and no prevaricating.

DECLARE

Carefully read and take time to consider these words, found among the papers of a young pastor in Zimbabwe after he was martyred. When you are truly ready to make them your own, read them aloud:

> *I'm part of the fellowship of the unashamed. The die has been cast. I have stepped over the line. The decision has been made. I'm a disciple of His, and I won't look back, let up, slow down, back away or be still. My past is redeemed. My present makes sense. My future is secure. I'm done and finished with low living, sight walking, tamed visions, mundane talking, cheap living, and dwarfed goals.*
>
> *I no longer need preeminence, prosperity, position, promotions, plaudits, or popularity. I don't have to be right, or first, or tops, or recognized, or praised, or rewarded. I live by faith, lean on His presence, walk by patience, am uplifted by prayer and labor by Holy Spirit power.[1]*

That's what we need to set our hearts on today!

NOTE

1. Found in slightly varying versions on many websites. Original source unknown.

DAY 50

Are You Ready for a Perspective Change?

But God, being rich in mercy, because of His great love with which He loved us, even when we were dead in our wrongdoings, made us alive together with Christ (by grace you have been saved), and raised us up with Him, and seated us with Him in the heavenly places in Christ Jesus (Ephesians 2:4–6 NASB).

Are you ready to have your perspective tweaked today? Jesus asks, "Will you allow Me to make small adjustments to your thinking?"

He wants to remind you that you are seated with Him in heavenly places, and because of that positioning, your perspective, or view, is primed to see the full picture. It is not a view of one who is seated down in a valley or a dark, shaded place from the hardship of circumstances. But it is a view that is over and above life's circumstances! It is the same view that Jesus has! For from this vantage or viewpoint, as one seated with Him, He can show you what He sees. He can bring the right things into focus while also highlighting where your vision has become distorted.

He says: "If you will come regularly to sit with Me and look at life from this perspective, you will find that these tweaks that I make will change much more than perspective. They will shift your whole outlook and attitude toward life. You'll even see yourself differently as you will then see as you were always meant to—as one who is seated with Me in the heavenly realms."

ACTION

Activate your spiritual sight by trying the following exercise:

- Sit with Jesus and ask Him what your "heavenly places" seat looks like.

- Now, sit in it and take in the view.

- After you have looked around, ask Him to show you what He sees. Allow Him to give you the full picture.

DAY 51

Your Voice Carries My Authority

The voice of the Lord is over the waters; the God of glory thunders, the Lord thunders over the mighty waters. The voice of the Lord is powerful; the voice of the Lord is majestic. The voice of the Lord breaks the cedars; the Lord breaks in pieces the cedars of Lebanon (Psalm 29:3–5).

My voice is around you, My voice is over you, My voice is within you. Hear My voice, know My voice! I have anointed you by My Spirit as one who speaks for Me, as one who listens to Me, and as one who makes My voice known on the earth. When you speak for Me, your words carry My authority.

So why then are you silent? I have given you My Spirit so that you might speak out against the forces that rage against all that is good, pure, and righteous. Just as My voice shatters the very pride of Lebanon, so I need you, My warrior, to speak to strongholds of pride and declare that I am the Lord God Almighty.

You have seen injustice and whispered in your heart, "This is not right." But now it is time to speak up and speak out. Though you doubt your voice and doubt your influence, know that it is I, the Lord, who will sustain your words and who gives authority to what you say for Me. I am leading you into a situation where you will need to speak up for the innocent. I will put a thundering power on your voice so that it is heard and so that it will break even ancient strongholds. Do not be silent!

ACTION

It's time to get into practice so that you're ready to speak up when God needs you to. When you're outdoors, for example, walking or driving, begin to speak out against things that you see that are broken and command them to be fixed.

So, if you see a barren tree, call it to bear fruit; if you see a derelict building, command it back to life, ownership, and purpose; if you see a dry riverbed, declare the rains; if you see a flooding river, speak peace to the waters and protection to lives and property; if you see the effects of vandalism, speak God's blessing to the perpetrators and declare that cleansing will come to the area. Practice speaking with spiritual authority!

DAY 52

A Warrior Under the Command of Jesus

For the Lord Most High is awesome, the great King over all the earth. He subdued nations under us, peoples under our feet (Psalm 47:2–3).

You have been grafted into the army of God, equipped as a warrior under the command of Jesus. He has dressed you in heavenly armor, trained you with Kingdom techniques. His name is on your sword, and you fight with weapons of warfare that are not of this world. You have been commissioned by *Yahweh Sabaoth*[1] to fight as part of His victorious army.

God is shifting your mindset today from civilian to soldier, from spectator to participator, from inactive to active. This power shift in your mind will change how you hold yourself, how you look at yourself, what you think about who you are, and how you react to the situations you face. No longer shall you back down when the enemy comes near because you will understand that you have been trained and commissioned by the Lord of hosts to fight and win, to subdue the enemy and defeat his tactics.

As you read this word today, the Lord is disintegrating the mindset that makes you shrink back and partner with fear. He is liberating you into the fullness of the Kingdom military mindset.

RECEIVE

Receive this mindset shift today. Align yourself with the biblical truths that you have been grafted into the army of God and equipped to expand His Kingdom territory wherever you go!

NOTE

1. *Yahweh* is translated "LORD." *Sabaoth* means "armies" or "hosts." This name denotes that He is commander of the angelic armies and the stars. See First Samuel 1:3.

DAY 53

Mobilized

So God created mankind in his own image, in the image of God he created them; male and female he created them (Genesis 1:27).

God saw all that he had made, and it was very good (Genesis 1:31).

Recognize your area of greatest strength, and focus your actions where you have the capability. Acknowledge that you have specialist attributes, honed skills, and expertise. Silence the voice that says, "I don't do things well" or "I am an underperformer and underachiever."

The Lord says, "You are no use to Me if you are blind to the skills that I have put within you. You are very little good if you do not see the level of My power that I have trusted you with.

"Do not underestimate what being made in My image has achieved in your life. As a reflector of Me, as My image bearer, you have attributes of authority, leadership, peacemaking, negotiation, and strategy."

Today the Lord is speaking a word of mobilization over you. You are being readied for more fruitful active service. God is mobilizing you to be outstanding at what He has called you to do. He wants you to feel the reward of doing things well. This mobilization will require you to review how you spend your time. To fully honor God and step into the days of your high call, some things will need to be left behind. In this moment of mobilization and empowerment, drop all that your hands are not supposed to touch. Feel liberty to partner with the nature of God, who is both Alpha and Omega, Beginning and End. This means that He starts and finishes. It means that He knows when to step away and call time on an action.

No longer speak of yourself as a person of *future potential* only, as someone who one day in the future *might* fly high. You are a threat to the powers of darkness *today*! Now, go be one!

ACTION

Sit and write a new list with God, asking Him to help you see and collate the things in which you have a specialist capability. Ask God what He put in you when He created you that you are good at. Then, thank God that He has not made you empty-headed or empty-handed.

DAY 54

Your Weapons of Warfare

The priest replied, "The sword of Goliath the Philistine, whom you killed in the Valley of Elah, is here; it is wrapped in a cloth behind the ephod. If you want it, take it; there is no sword here but that one." David said, "There is none like it; give it to me" (1 Samuel 21:9).

I heard the Lord say, "I am returning what has been forgotten through battle weariness and putting your sword back into your hands. It is time to remember and pick back up the weapons I have called you to fight with. I have designed a sword specifically for you, a weapon that only you can wield by the power of My Spirit."

No matter how far you feel like you have fallen from where you are supposed to be, God is putting your sword back in your hand. No matter how sluggish and worn out you feel, God is returning your weapons to you. No matter how distracted or busy you have been, God is reminding you of who you are. The Lord says, "I am putting back in your hands what is already yours and reminding you this day of the history of victories that are behind you as I stir your faith for the successive victories that I have prepared ahead of you. Get your sword back in your hand, stand up straight, and get ready for war!"

Some of you have forgotten that you're immensely creative; some of you have forgotten that you're called to help heal hearts. Some of you have forgotten your entrepreneurial flare, and others of you have forgotten your call to worship. So much has been forgotten, yet so much is being restored today. Let God remind you of what rightfully belongs in your hands.

ACTION

Ask God: "What have I forgotten about me? What weapons have I forgotten that are rightfully mine? Remind me, oh God, and I choose to pick them back up!"

DAY 55

The Ending of Control

Then God blessed them, and God said to them, "Be fruitful and multiply; fill the earth and subdue it; have dominion over the fish of the sea, over the birds of the air, and over every living thing that moves on the earth" (Genesis 1:28 NKJV).

At man's formation in the garden of Eden, God gave him *dominion*, which is the ability to subdue and to be fruitful. It is a place of power and delegated authority. It is the skilled exercising of influence. It is the ability to build the Kingdom of God and to recognize the flourishing and well-being of all mankind as *our* responsibility.

He did not give you *domination*, which is the ugly and unbiblical version of dominion that we sometimes fall into. Domination is a grotesque entitlement that seeks to control or master others, where we desire to conquer and command, rather than serving and enabling the thriving of many. The need to feel and be in control has dogged the church for generations. The demonic spirit of control and domination is rampant in church history. God wants it removed.

Today if you have been controlled and unrighteously and severely squashed, God is healing your heart from the repression of previous years.

Today if you tend to control and enforce ferocious order, God is liberating you from this inappropriate mindset. No longer use control as a weapon against others and yourself. Break agreement with it. Out loud, make this statement: "I don't want to control; I want to liberate."

Control is a demonic burden that will ultimately hurt you and limit how you interact with others. In this moment, switch your thinking from *domination* to *dominion*; switch from being in control to enabling increase. Switch from limiting others and yourself to mass fruitfulness and (sometimes messy) multiplication!

RECEIVE

Having dominion is not something you work up to. It is something you are born with as one made in the image of God. You have been made with the capacity to responsibly bless and release others into fruitfulness. Receive afresh this Genesis 1 mandate: you can flourish and you can let that happen for many others. You are already blessed by God to thrive and to blossom. This is who you are by birthright!

His Supernatural Power Reveals His Love for You

And I pray that you, being rooted and established in love, may have power, together with all the Lord's holy people, to grasp how wide and long and high and deep is the love of Christ, and to know this love that surpasses knowledge—that you may be filled to the measure of all the fullness of God (Ephesians 3:17–19).

You cannot consciously experience the love of God for yourself, except by the enabling of God's supernatural power. Only by divine power can you know what it is to be loved by Him!

Why? This "knowing" of His love surpasses knowledge (see Eph. 3:19); therefore, the love of God surpasses the power of our human minds to comprehend and the powers of our human hearts to experience. It goes beyond what you can do, which is why you need to pray, like the Apostle Paul did, for God's power.

May God give you the power and strength of heart and mind so that you will know, with rich certainty, Christ's wide, long, high and deep love—today.

RECEIVE

Kneel in humility before the Father and read Ephesians 3:14–21 slowly and carefully. Make Paul's prayer into *your* prayer for today. Stretch out your hands, your arms, to show that you need His power. Receive a new powerful revelation from the Holy Spirit of how much you are truly loved by Christ!

DAY 57

The Mundane Is Becoming Powerful!

So David triumphed over the Philistine with a sling and a stone; without a sword in his hand he struck down the Philistine and killed him (1 Samuel 17:50).

In a vision, I watched as outside a blacksmith's workshop a large line began to form. People from far and wide brought with them seemingly mundane and banal household objects and equipment into the shop. The blacksmith received them, refashioned them into weapons, and gave them back to the owners. Those items that looked as though they possessed little or no warfare significance became essential armor and weaponry, fit for battle in the hands of the owner.

The Lord says: "You are equipped already with skills, abilities, and talents in your hands that seem mundane and worthless: creative art, music, cooking, hospitality, singing, movement, building, teaching, researching, writing, and more. They seem insignificant, but in and through My hands they can become weapons of victorious warfare that become mighty for battle. Cooking skills can carry deliverance as you gather those that need freedom around your kitchen table; your writing can produce breakthrough in the life of those who read; art, music, movement, building, and more, all these things by My Spirit can become weapons that enforce My victory on the earth.

"Do not underestimate what is in your hands! Don't discount what appears mundane! Don't disqualify yourself by assuming there are no weapons for effective battle. You have what you need, just surrender it to Me and watch as I take the mundane and make it powerful and effective for battle!"

RECEIVE

As you sit in response to this word, invite the Holy Spirit to reveal to you what is in your hands that He wants to transform into weapons for war. Ask Him to show you how to use it for warfare and battle, what it looks like, and how you are you respond.

DAY 58

"With Christ" and "in Christ"

And God raised us up with Christ and seated us with him in the heavenly realms in Christ Jesus, in order that in the coming ages he might show the incomparable riches of his grace, expressed in his kindness to us in Christ Jesus (Ephesians 2:6–7).

Imagine you are sitting in an airplane that is just about to race down the runway to take you on the vacation of a lifetime to beautiful Scotland! Up, up above the clouds you will fly, until the pilot reaches the desired altitude of forty-five thousand feet. If a fellow passenger asked, "Are you flying to the UK?" you would answer, "Yes." If he then asked, "Are you flying over the Atlantic Ocean?" you might also answer, "Yes." Both your answers are truthful and correct, but of course, it is not actually *you* who is flying. The airplane is flying, and therefore you can say that you are flying over the ocean because you are seated in the plane.

In Ephesians 2 Paul uses two different prepositions "with" and "in" to describe our position to Christ Jesus. Both make the same point that what happened to Christ has happened to those who are in Christ. Paul has written that God *"made us alive with Christ"* (Eph. 2:5). Now he takes us a step further and wants us to understand that God has also raised us up with Christ and seated us with Him in the heavenly realms. In a way, this is simply a continuation of Paul's prayer for us in the previous chapter, that we might know the same power that God exerted when He raised Christ from the dead and seated Him at His right hand in the heavenly realms (see Eph. 1:19–20). Paul now says that we have been raised up and are seated in Christ. Why has this happened? Because God has placed us in Christ. So, everything that happened to Christ has happened, is happening, and will happen to you and me. This is a wonderful truth!

When Paul speaks of us seated with Him in the heavenly realms, he is obviously not talking about us being physically present there with Him right now. We will know that experience when Christ returns and we receive our new bodies. Instead, he is saying that right now we have been exalted with Christ to a position of authority over evil spiritual forces, far above all rule and authority, power and dominion (see Eph. 1:21). Your body is still here on earth, but your spirit is already where one day a new body will join it, in the heavenly realms! In His name, we can now minister boldly to people because we share Jesus's position of authority. We are no longer governed by a spirit of fear or under the dominion of the devil whose power may have previously enslaved us. Hallelujah!

ACTION

Why don't we more often describe ourselves using the actual language of the New Testament? The word *Christian* is found only three times in the Bible, whereas Paul's letters use the phrase "in Christ" around 100 times. Knowing what it means to be "in Christ" gives you a completely new self-understanding, outside of yourself. Try it!

DAY 59

Up and In

And God raised us up with Christ and seated us with him in the heavenly realms in Christ Jesus (Ephesians 2:6).

Look around you just now. What do you see? Is there furniture: a bed, a sofa, a coffee table or a TV? Or are you outdoors, surrounded by hills and trees, or roads and buildings? What about in the spirit? What are you surrounded by in the realms of the spirit?

The Lord says to you, "Though you are surrounded by the material, do not forget that you are positioned from the eternal. I have called you up and in, up and into My throne room where angels abound and My presence is overflowing. It is this place, where supreme victory is upheld and released, where you are called to fight from.

"Do not get caught up in the natural battles that occupy the spaces that surround, but see Me where I am and fight with Me from where I am! You are seated with Me in heavenly places and carry the essence of a Kingdom warrior within. You are not far off, distant, disqualified, or pushed aside. You are positionally seated in the place that offers you the resources to win every battle before you even set a foot in the ring.

"Shift your mindset today, mighty warrior! Stand as one who knows they are positioned with Me in My realm. Do not allow the enemy to convince you that you are far off and alone. You are with Me and you fight with Me and My angelic hosts. So stand assured that you are seated with Me in heavenly realms, and watch as the atmospheres and situations around you shift and align because of how you start to hold yourself."

DECREE

Make the following declarations out loud:

- I am seated with Christ in heavenly realms!
- God has called me up and into His throne room.
- I fight *from* victory not *for* victory.
- I am seated in the most powerful place in Heaven and earth.

CHAPTER 3

Release Your Roar

DAY 60

Purified Desire

Follow the way of love and eagerly desire gifts of the Spirit, especially prophecy (1 Corinthians 14:1).

God desires you! He is not absent of emotions. He has longings, jealousies, passion, and determination. You, created in His image, are also jam-packed with emotions. God did not create you to meet Him just in your head. Rather, your life with Him is to be woven together, emotionally and spiritually: your heart and your head, your strength and your might.

Today God wants to bless you by purifying your desires. He does not want you to switch off key emotions, He wants them cleaned and refreshed, and then pointed in the right direction.

God is increasing your appetite today for the things that matter to Him. He is giving you permission to eagerly desire spiritual gifts, spiritual blessing, and spiritual authority, and to claim your birthright of hearing His voice. First Corinthians 12:31 and 14:1 urge you to eagerly desire revelation (be zealous for it, earnestly desire it, or covet it. You can even be ambitious for the gift of prophecy!).

The level of desire that God asks us to demonstrate for the prophetic, for revelation, for His voice, can appear to us as being "over the top" or even unbalanced in its ferocity. Yet the Apostle Paul is exceptionally clear that from you should rise a focus and tenacity to have revelation as a key part of your life. Paul pushes us to go after the ability to prophesy beyond other gifts. The cry of our hearts today must be, "I cannot live without Your voice! Lord, I come determined to be able to communicate what You want to be said."

ACTION

Allow the fire of God to burn inside your being and to incinerate wrong desire. Confess your fleshly desires, and allow the Holy Spirit to upgrade you so that your feelings might now align with Heaven. Where you have been emotionally numb, allow God to resuscitate your feelings. God will walk with you in these refreshed emotions to ensure they become a blessing and not a hindrance.

Wherever you are sitting or standing turn around as a prophetic act of pointing your desire in a new, right direction. Now open your mouth and decree: "I desire an increase of revelation, God. I desire, according to Your Word, the ability to prophesy in a way that I never have before."

DAY 61

Listen and Hear Him

My sheep listen to my voice; I know them, and they follow me (John 10:27).

I have put the gifts of My Spirit inside you, My child. I have given you the gift of knowing and hearing My voice. You dwell in the proximity of My words and voice always. You are close to Me. It is not difficult for you to hear My voice. You are next to Me, and you hear My whispers of love, My declarations, My commands.

I have placed the gift of hearing My voice inside you. You are one with Me, and you know Me just as I know you. You know My tone. You know My heart; hear My affirmation of you in My every breath. It is not hard for you to do this. Breathe and listen.

Breathe.

Listen.

I am speaking to you now. Hear My voice. See what I am saying to you. Receive My affirmations of love to you today. Welcome My words of encouragement and edification. Catch My words of strategy for life and work. Accept My words and embrace them. I long to build you in strength and truth. Hear My heart for you and be edified today.

ACTION

Take time each day to quiet yourself and listen for God's voice. He is speaking to you throughout every day. Start a new notebook and write down in it what He is saying to you.

Practice the "art of listening" each day. It will become easier and more natural the more you repeat this exercise. You may even want to draw what you see, alongside what you hear.

In time you will begin to hear God speaking when you haven't deliberately silenced yourself. Repeat the practice daily, asking the questions: "What do You want me to hear from You today, Lord?," "What do I need to hear?," and "What are You excited to share with me?"

It's Bubbling Up

The words of the mouth are deep waters, but the fountain of wisdom is a rushing stream (Proverbs 18:4).

I saw a rounded rock on a dry, sandy plain. The ground was desertlike, and nothing had grown there for a long time. The rock was smooth and dusty and it blended into the monochrome landscape. The scene was the last place one would expect to see life and fruit.

Then, I saw a line appear on the surface of the rock. The line became darker and darker, and it widened. As it did so, I could see that the line was caused by water coming from within the rock. The water began to spread across the surface, making the rock wet. The stone began to glisten in the sunlight. Soon bubbles began to form, as the water pressure from within the rock increased. Water began to pour from the rock at a greater and greater rate. Little jets of spray became fountains. I stepped back as the water from these fountains began to rain down all around me. Now the landscape looked completely different—colorful, green, and teeming with life. Fruit exploded on tall trees that reached toward the sky, and bright flowers leaped from every new bush that sprang up from the ground.

And the Lord said: "Child, begin to prophesy. Speak forth My words, let them bubble up from within you. Let the words flow up and out of your mouth. Let them wet your lips and pour down your chin. Become soaked in your own prophetic words that come from My Holy Spirit in you. You might feel like a young child being weaned, with messy words tumbling everywhere, but do not despise the gift that I have given you. Get used to how it feels to speak forth prophecy and allow it to explode from that deep well of revelation within you."

ACTION

You can practice prophecy anytime, anywhere. If you're in bed, speak to the ceiling and fill your bedroom with words that will cascade back down over you. If you're washing dishes, prophesy about your home, your family, or what you see out of your window. If you're at work and not able to prophesy out loud, keep a stack of notes beside you that is reserved for quick-fire prophetic words, one word, a phrase, a sentence, or a whole page of revelation!

Qualified

Moses said to God, "Suppose I go to the Israelites and say to them, 'The God of your fathers has sent me to you,' and they ask me, 'What is his name?' Then what shall I tell them?"

God said to Moses, "I am who I am. This is what you are to say to the Israelites: 'I am has sent me to you'" (Exodus 3:13–14).

The Lord says: "I have brought you to a burning bush moment as I did with Moses. Just as I delivered him of his insecurities regarding what to say and how to say it and sent him with a full mouth, so your insecurities are about to disintegrate by the blistering hot heat of My deliverance fire."

You may feel unqualified to use your voice for the sake of the Kingdom for a myriad of reasons. Yet the Lord reminds you today: "It is My words in your mouth. All I'm looking for is a surrendered heart and an open mouth so that I can fill you up with My words of power."

The Lord continues: "When I created you, I put inside you the capacity to speak My words. When I formed you, I created the skill to steward revelation. Don't allow insecurity and the lie of disqualification to make you feel that you're not qualified and handpicked to speak My words.

"You are qualified to speak! You are qualified to roar! You are qualified to prophesy! You are qualified to decree! You are qualified to release words of power! You are qualified!"

RECEIVE

Receive freedom today from the lies of being unqualified that the enemy wants to use to bind your voice. We break these lies off of you in Jesus's mighty name! You are free today.

DAY 64

You Are Approved!

Fear of man will prove to be a snare, but whoever trusts in the Lord is kept safe (Proverbs 29:25).

My beautiful child, My mighty warrior, for far too long you have struggled under the bondage of approval addiction. I come to you today to free you from the fear of man and to set you loose from the need for approval.

I *approve* of you!

I stamp "APPROVED" over your life. I take off the chains and the ties of man's words and man's criticism. I throw them into the pit and leave them there! Receive this freedom and the new identity that I am giving you!

Come to Me *first* when you wonder if you are doing the right thing. I will tell you! Come to Me when you feel insecure and unsure. I will steady you, build you up, and speak truth to you.

Come to Me when you need validation or need to know your value. I will speak to you about what I see. I want to fill your heart like no other can. I satisfy. But will you believe Me and come to Me today?

RECEIVE

Repent before the Lord for taking on any of man's criticism and allowing it to define you. Repent for partnering with words that have been like curses upon your life. Ask Jesus to wash you afresh and to make His word "APPROVED" come alive to you today.

DAY 65

A Prophet in the Making

How long, Lord, must I call for help, but you do not listen? Or cry out to you, "Violence!" but you do not save? Why do you make me look at injustice? Why do you tolerate wrongdoing? (Habakkuk 1:2–3)

God challenges you today to begin to think like a prophet, seeing things from His point of view, not yours. It is time to stop thinking that He is there to meet your needs when you are here to bring God what He wants!

God is looking for prophetic people who will say, "Jesus, let me see things from Your point of view; let me hear what You are thinking; let me feel what You are feeling in your heart. Lord, You have allowed me to sit in the heavenly realms in You; let me see things from there as You see them."

He asks you today: "Will you stop being preoccupied with your needs, your desires, and your problems? Will you become so preoccupied with Me that you begin to see things from My perspective?"

The prophet Habakkuk gives us an example of how not to begin! He started his prophetic life by telling God what he saw and giving his opinion on what was happening: violence and a law that was paralyzed, increasing breakdown in society. Before he could be a true prophet God had to change his outlook, his perspective. Habakkuk had tunnel vision, and so he only complained to God about what he saw in his nation. God let Habakkuk know that he should be watching the nations instead of just looking at his own little country, Israel. Habakkuk needed to get a bigger view and see that God is the God of the nations. Only then, when he saw the full prophetic context, would he understand what God was doing in his nation.

Look at the nations and watch—and be utterly amazed. For I am going to do something in your days that you would not believe, even if you were told (Habakkuk 1:5).

ACTION

Read the complete prophecy of Habakkuk; it's a short book of three chapters. Note how God helps Habakkuk get a longer view of Babylon and her future. Though God uses Babylon, she too will be judged for her cruelty and inhumanity.

DAY 66

I Am Destroying Silence

So I will not be silent; I will sing praise to you. Lord, you are my God; I will give you thanks forever (Psalm 30:12 GNT).

I see the Lord sending a destroyer angel to your side to violently and determinedly rip from your mouth demonic black tape that has forced your mouth closed and silenced you. The black masking tape I see in the spirit represents historic word curses of silence from people in authority over your lifetime. People in authority in your life such as parents, teachers, bosses, church leaders, perhaps even abusers, who said, "Be quiet!" and "Be silent!" over you. When they said that you can't or won't have an opinion, you agreed to be silent and suppress your language (perhaps for your safety, out of fear, or simply for an easy life). You may have had another reason that you agreed to be or wanted to be silent. The Lord says to you today, "My child, let Me release you from the silence. Allow Me to release your opinion from you once more."

The Lord adds: "You have believed that you must be quiet and even mute to survive and succeed in life, but I now come to tear off silence and release back to you your strong voice. I give you back your determination and your resilience to be able to speak and hold ground. Release your beautiful voice and viewpoint with both power and passion. Your words have power and sustenance for you as you hear yourself speak as well as for others who hear and receive your words. Allow Me to tear off all limitations of silence from you today."

Break agreement with those word curses of silence and muteness now and allow God to release both your inner voice and heard spoken words.

PRAYER

Repent of and break agreement with silence, using these words or your own:

I ask for Your forgiveness, Father God, for when I agreed to be silent over my lifetime thus far and when I have partnered knowingly and unknowingly with muteness. I choose now to forgive those who silenced me and release them from any judgment I have held against them. Forgive me, Lord, where I judged them in any way.

I now renounce and break agreement with silence in all its forms. I now choose to allow my voice to be released, and I give You access to tear off from me all curses that have silenced my voice. I want my voice to be heard again.

Satan Is Listening, but Your Tongue Is a Weapon

Have you ever given orders to the morning, or shown the dawn its place, that it might take the earth by the edges and shake the wicked out of it? (Job 38:12–13)

God governs with His voice. God legislates with His commands. God creates order in chaos by speaking. He does not "think" creation and then expects it to form. Rather, He becomes a vocal craftsman and speaks creation into being (see Gen. 1:1; John 1:1–3).

He who calls Himself *"the Word"* (John 1:1) has designed things so that what you say also creates. This is why satan has battled you for years to limit your sphere of influence by hijacking your vocal opinion. At every opportunity, he seeks to wrap thorn bushes around your neck to minimize your impact and to stop you from creating breakthroughs by your decrees.

You were made with a remarkable, built-in, anointed weapon—your tongue! Your tongue is a weapon so strong that the enemy is in fear of even the slightest use of it.

The Lord asks you, "Why are you not commanding your days? Why are you not speaking order as you rise in the morning? Why do you try to think your way through a crisis, rather than speak for a way to be made open?"

God takes us back today to His interactions with Job in Scripture, where He explains how He commands the morning, that the wickedness might be shaken out of it. As we reflect on our Maker's words, there is the need to speak over our days as we prepare to fully enter them. Even if this is done on the move, amid the hustle and bustle of daily life, you will still see significant changes to what unfolds in your life, as solutions move from your mind to your mouth for declaration.

Today angels are flying to where you are as you read this, and they are unwinding the cords of constriction from your neck area. There is vocal freedom and healing that is resting upon you so that you will no longer battle to secure an impact.

The Lord says to you today, "Speak, My child, for satan is listening. He wants to know whether you will crush him by your decrees or whether you will empower him by your silence. Satan is attentive to the movements of your mouth."

ACTION AND DECREE

Work with the angelic hosts by unwinding hindrances from your throat. Then stand and make a minimum of eight decrees of things that need to shift in your life. List out loud the solutions, rather than rehearsing the problems.

DAY 68

Yield

My frame was not hidden from you when I was made in the secret place, when I was woven together in the depths of the earth. Your eyes saw my unformed body; all the days ordained for me were written in your book before one of them came to be. How precious to me are your thoughts, God! How vast is the sum of them! (Psalm 139:15–17)

In every area of life, I desire yieldedness. Not because I am a controlling God, but because I see all and know all. I know your end from your beginning. I know best because of who I am, and I want the very best for you!

I have seen your struggle to speak up, to be decisive, and to choose a path to take. I know how to help you in these areas, but it first requires yielded submission. It requires a heart that bows low before Me. It requires one who will say, "Lord God, you know what I should say, what I should do, and which path to take. I choose to follow Your lead. I choose to yield to your lordship of my life."

In that place and that posture of heart, I can then lead you into the very best. When you place your voice into My hands, I will equip you to speak. When you seek Me regarding the decisions to make, you can then act with decisiveness. When you let Me lead your way, the path will become clear.

ACTION

Spend some time meditating on the three Scriptures below. Do you know any others that you could add to this list? As you meditate on them, list to God the decisions and future fears that you are committing to Him. Be honest with yourself. Are you able to fully commit, yield and trust Him yet? If your answer is no, not really or even nearly, then there's still work to be done in prayer with Him.

> *Commit to the Lord whatever you do, and he will establish your plans* (Proverbs 16:3).
>
> *Commit everything you do to the Lord. Trust him, and he will help you* (Psalm 37:5 NLT).
>
> *In the fear of the Lord there is strong confidence, and his children will have refuge* (Proverbs 14:26 NASB).

Tongue-Tied or a Ready Tongue?

My heart is overflowing with a good theme; I recite my composition concerning the King; my tongue is the pen of a ready writer (Psalm 45:1 NKJV).

I heard the Lord say over you today, "You are skilled!" Over and over again, He declares, "You are skilled! You are skilled!" As these words were uttered, I watched them go into your atmosphere and do a bizarre thing. God used these words to untie a knot that had formed in your tongue!

The Lord says: "I am untying your tongue. I am undoing the knot of silence and of confusion that causes you to feel tongue-tied and ill-equipped for speaking forth the words of My Spirit. You are skilled, and your tongue is ready to speak. The words that will come forth from your life will carry divine resonance and melody; though they may seem insignificant to you, upon their release, the full weight of Heaven shall back them up."

As you read this, the significance of this moment is not to be missed. The Lord is turning some things around on your behalf in dramatic ways. I saw those who struggle with reading and writing becoming skilled to produce prose and poetry, and novels and short stories. Those with stage fright are coming into a new boldness for public speaking, and some who have battled stuttering and speech impediments are being liberated by the power of God even now. The Lord says, "You are not tongue-tied! Your tongue is ready to speak My words!"

RECEIVE

Take whatever area that you have felt impeded by to Jesus. Repent of partnering with limitation, and receive from Him all that you need. Now, how are you going to test this word in your life and turn it into a manifest reality?

You Have a Voice

Out of my distress I called on the Lord; the Lord answered me and set me free (Psalm 118:5 ESV).

I hear the Lord shout this word over you with force: "Liberation!"

He is speaking freedom over you. Yesterday your tongue was untied, and today He is loosing your voice from every hindrance, caution, and restriction. All bondages that have tied up your words are being shattered.

In this moment courage and boldness that you have never had before are coming to help you release what the Lord puts in you. His song, His word, His desire is being put in your mouth. His fire and His burning are being set on your tongue and inside your lips.

He is asking you to agree with Him by saying out loud, "I have a voice!" as He roars, "Liberation!" over you. As you do, increasing your volume, agreement, and determination, you will find that your courage and boldness will grow. Your voice will sound different—even to your ear—clear, strong, and purposeful. "I have a voice!" will become your battle cry.

The Lord now says, "Open your mouth and I will fill it."

As you respond with, "Put Your words in my mouth, Lord," an exchange will happen in you. Be amazed as you go from timidity of speech to a bold truth-telling, from reticence in releasing the word of God to confidence and assurance that you are now releasing God's voice.

ACTION

Pray and ask God to put words in your mouth. As you do, open your mouth in a prophetic act, demonstrating that you are ready to allow Him to liberate your voice and fill it with His words. You might find yourself yawning or coughing as you do this; don't resist anything that accompanies the new freedom that the Lord is giving you.

DAY 71

Strength to Your Voice

You who bring good news to Zion, go up on a high mountain. You who bring good news to Jerusalem, lift up your voice with a shout, lift it up, do not be afraid; say to the towns of Judah, "Here is your God!" (Isaiah 40:9)

"I am releasing a new strength to your vocal cords. No longer will you regard your voice as weak and not worth being listened to because now you will have the ability and the opportunity to roar with justice over situations where once you would have watched in silence from the sidelines. I am increasing your capacity to hold a war cry over oppression until situations shift. I am calling you to raise a shout of renewal over places where the enemy has brought disgrace and ruin.

"Your tongue will carry My words with a new razor sharpness that cuts through any spiritual chains and fetters and sets captives free. As you follow Me and begin to use your voice in new ways, you will discover that you have a new ability and opportunities to shout freedom over prisoners and captives, who have until now only heard the belittling, enslaving words of the deceiver. Now I am going to use you to cut through all other noise and speak words of life."

This new empowerment to your voice is by the Spirit of God, and you will find new freedom to your physical body too, as you get used to speaking with more volume, more words. Do not be silent, even when you're alone. Sing! Shout! Praise the Lord with all your newly strengthened vocal abilities! Get used to being a strong voice.

DECREE

Make this declaration: "I decree that I will not be silent anymore. I declare that I am a warrior with a strong voice. What I say is worth hearing because of He who is in me and who has set me free to shout, sing and roar!"

DAY 72

Prophetic Power

The voice of the Lord is over the waters; the God of glory thunders, the Lord thunders over the mighty waters. The voice of the Lord is powerful; the voice of the Lord is majestic. The voice of the Lord breaks the cedars; the Lord breaks in pieces the cedars of Lebanon. He makes Lebanon leap like a calf, Sirion like a young wild ox. The voice of the Lord strikes with flashes of lightning. The voice of the Lord shakes the desert; the Lord shakes the Desert of Kadesh. The voice of the Lord twists the oaks and strips the forests bare. And in his temple all cry, "Glory!" (Psalm 29:3–9)

God's voice is powerful! When He speaks everything changes. Do you know that this is the weight of power that you are meant to steward when you prophesy?

The Lord says: "I have marked you with prophetic power, to speak forth My word and see My Kingdom come in astonishing ways. When you speak My words, the earth must tangibly respond: nations change, bodies are healed, captives are released, prison doors fling open and the dead are raised. *I am only scratching the surface!* One word from Me spoken by you with boldness can cause catastrophic damage to the camp of the enemy and release unimaginable transformation into the earth.

"So why hold back? Why keep to yourself what I have called you to release? Determine 'no more!' as of today! No more holding back; no more timid speaking. Stand tall and boldly speak the words I have given to you. Stand with your shoulders back, and begin to prophesy by My Spirit and watch as astonishing things begin to unfold."

ACTION

You can do this at home or out in any open space: Stand up tall, with a confident posture, and begin to prophesy into the atmosphere of your home and territory. Make declarations about who God is and what He is going to accomplish. Allow the Holy Spirit to rise within you and propel your words. Don't worry if you get tongue-tied or stumble over your words; it can be hard for our bodies to keep up with the Spirit! When you feel your words drying up, go again and again. Dig deep and ask Jesus what He is declaring over your territory. Train yourself to speak out only what the Spirit gives you and not your own desires or prayers (although these may already be in tune with what is on God's heart). Then, as you continue with your day, keep your senses alert to the changes that follow based on what you spoke out.

DAY 73

A New Clarity

For the word of God is alive and active. Sharper than any double-edged sword, it penetrates even to dividing soul and spirit, joints and marrow; it judges the thoughts and attitudes of the heart (Hebrews 4:12).

He made my mouth like a sharpened sword, in the shadow of his hand he hid me; he made me into a polished arrow and concealed me in his quiver (Isaiah 49:2).

"Seek Me each day, and I will give you the words to speak to bring clarity to your family," says the Lord.

Where there has been confusion, misunderstanding, or even some deliberate misinterpretation of past words and conversations, it is time for a prophetic voice to speak. You are that prophetic voice! Spend time with God each day; allow Him to fill your thoughts and your mouth with new words, new phrases, and new ways to approach broken situations and dysfunctional relationships. As you listen to Him, things will become clearer, crisper, and more focused. You will hear the prophetic words that need to be spoken. They won't necessarily sound like, "Thus sayeth the Lord..." prophecies, but be confident that as you listen to Him, you will carry the weight and sharpness of revelation from Almighty God that is required to shift situations and personalities.

Be ready for the Spirit to lead you into some unexpected circumstances that He will ordain so that you can say what needs to be said. Have confidence that the Lord will fill your mouth with the right words for the right time.

RECEIVE

Spend time asking God to give you phrases or conversation starters that can be used in broken or difficult relational situations. Ask Him for names, and make note of what you hear. Be open to hearing things that are unexpected or are new to you.

DAY 74

Speaker of Truth

Instead, speaking the truth in love, we will grow to become in every respect the mature body of him who is the head, that is, Christ. From him the whole body, joined and held together by every supporting ligament, grows and builds itself up in love, as each part does its work (Ephesians 4:15–16).

I call out to those who would be bold firebrands of truth! This is your time; this is your season!

To those who have stored My Word in your hearts, it is now time to let it loose. To those who have set your face upon Mine and have looked into My eyes to feel the piercing of My fiery gaze, now is the time to release your roar.

I have put a sound within you. It is a noise that pierces through atmospheres. It is a truth that breaks through deception. It is a voice that partners with those of like heart to release My sound upon the earth. As each of you releases the roar that comes up from your belly and out of the time spent on your face before Me, a new sound will arise across the earth. It will cause the enemy to tremble for he will know that his time is short! It will also let the world know that a warrior bride has indeed risen and she is standing tall in her rightful identity!

Do not hold back! Do not be timid or quiet any longer! Your sound will be uniquely yours, but it is perfectly made to be in beautiful harmony with the Body. Stand up and let it loose!

RECEIVE

Take some time to sit and listen to birds singing or a piece of music performed by an orchestra. Note how each bird or each instrument has its own, unique sound. Listen to the variety of the individuals. And then listen to the harmony of sound that is produced by the individuals coming together. With this in mind, ask the Father to reveal to you what your sound is. Then, ask Him to show you how to release it.

DAY 75

God's Flood Tide

See, the enemy is puffed up...he is as greedy as the grave and like death is never satisfied, he gathers to himself all the nations and takes captive all the peoples (Habakkuk 2:4–5).

Do not be shaken by what you see in the world around you, as empires and kingdoms of men rise with increasing wickedness. Resist partnering with fear as you watch and read news reports. Know that God is over all things.

As the mighty Babylonian empire conquered the nations of the earth, they set about establishing their dominion with great building projects that were built by forced labor: *"Woe to him who builds a city with bloodshed and establishes a town by injustice"* (Hab. 2:12). It mattered little to the Babylonians whether the dirt-shoveling workers lived or died; they were expendable. They thought they were building for posterity, expecting their empire to last a very long time. As great conquerors, they seemed to possess fearsome, unstoppable power. But God had a prophetic word for them—and us and all of history. It's a single sentence tucked amidst five "woe" statements in Habakkuk 2. Something amazing is coming:

> *For the earth will be filled with the knowledge of the glory of Lord as the waters cover the sea* (Habakkuk 2:14).

Even as blood from the fallen workers flowed from Babylon's building projects, so one day something else will flow across the entire earth. From the throne of God will sweep His glory, like a great, surging roar of water, pouring over the entire earth. Not a single part will be left untouched, for water seeps into every crack and crevice. It rises, imperceptibly filling the earth, until the whole world is flooded with God's power, majesty, and glory. Creation will stand amazed. Compared to the real King, the Babylonians were only playing at being kings. With the King will come a washed earth, cleansed by floodwater. The great cities will be forgotten and licked up as fuel for the fire (see Hab. 2:13), gone without a trace.

The world arrogantly schemes and builds, and we look on, watching a wave of ugliness, hostility, and corrupt values. But we can revel in God's magnificence as we stand by His side and resist, knowing that His tide will cover us all with His fame and reputation, and the earth will be full of His glory!

DECREE

Remember, if you have tunnel vision, if you only look at your nation, your people, your denomination, then you will miss the bigger canvas that God is painting on. To understand what He is doing with your nation and your people, you need His perspective over *all* the nations. Begin to decree against the flow of the world's news reports. Give God praise.

DAY 76

Drivenness Removed

For you created my inmost being; you knit me together in my mother's womb. I praise you because I am fearfully and wonderfully made; your works are wonderful, I know that full well (Psalm 139:13–14).

You are gloriously peculiar, strangely wild, and determinedly different. I did not make a mistake in fashioning you to be unlike anyone else. Let go of the pain of earlier years where you did not fit in. Let go of the measurements and criticisms of others, as they are beginning to really stifle you.

You have one eye on Me and one eye on others. This is not right! If you keep one eye on others, you will begin to build and plant things that are shaped to please men rather than please Me. I want to give you some remarkable blueprints. I have architectural plans for your life that are uniquely specific to your gift mix and will delight you. However, I have withheld them because you are beholden to your past, and you are tied up in your present because of the criticism you have received from others.

It is time to separate yourself from a spirit of perfection and an unhealthy driven work ethic that was never given to you by My hand. Some demons shadow you and cause you to need to perform for approval. They support you in your desire to look good to others. My liberation comes today so that your creative flair may rise unhindered! I know how to do things well. What My hand touches I can decree that "it is good." It is easy to lose your sense of joy in the completion of tasks and to lose your self-worth in your work because you measure yourself more forcefully than I would in your place.

This means that it is often hard to be in your head and to reflect on your journey, because you have an internal stick that you beat yourself with because you do not often believe that you have done enough or are being enough. You tend to believe that you fail in some way every day. This is not the report card I have of you. My hand is healing you today, and I am giving you a gift of remembering the person I made you to be. There will be a greater ease of knowing when to stop. There will be a greater joy in reflecting on your work output. There will be a greater sense of achievement, affecting each and every area of your life. Your own sound is coming forward, and your unique flavor will become established without the tarnishing of others' thoughts about you.

RECEIVE

Sit and receive the oil of ease and acceptance that Jesus has for you today. Allow it to cascade over your entire being. Liberate yourself from the ways people have boxed you in. See yourself saturated in the acceptance of God; you are an acceptable sacrifice, and you have been made righteous by Jesus Christ.

You Have a Sound

And I saw the glory of the God of Israel coming from the east. His voice was like the roar of rushing waters, and the land was radiant with his glory (Ezekiel 43:2).

You carry a sound and a unique resonance. God fashioned and formed you to specifically resound with your unique sound and voice. Yours is an individual reverberation of creation that the Lord has placed in you from your mother's womb. The exclusive and irreplaceable character of your expression and particular expression of God is found in you alone.

As God is the voice of many waters, you represent a portion of His great and mighty voice. You reflect both its power and beauty. You release a tone that synchronizes with others to reflect a portion of the voice of God in its multifaceted nature like the sound of many waters.

You are part of the voice of many waters on the earth. Your sound, your song, and your words need to be released and heard with the unique resonance God has given you personally and exclusively.

Feel and recognize the connection to the voice of God that is "many waters" in you; allow the flow of the voice of God to come forth in you and from you. Release your unique sound, your perfect expression formed by God Himself in you. It is time to allow the voice of God on the inside of you to be released. Liberate your sound. Free your voice, and allow its reverberation to come forth.

ACTION

Let your sound out! Allow yourself to shout, roar, and sing in ways that you might never have dared to before. Do this at home, in a local park, or even at your church. What does His new sound in you sound like? Have fun discovering it!

DAY 78

Your New Prophetic Song

The Lord your God is with you, the Mighty Warrior who saves. He will take great delight in you; in his love he will no longer rebuke you, but will rejoice over you with singing (Zephaniah 3:17).

God sings—and He sings over you! Do not be surprised that whenever the Spirit of God moves there is an explosion of new music and other creative arts as people respond to Him. This was one of the signs the Spirit was moving in the second half of the twentieth century. From all around the world there were new songs and musical settings of Scriptures, accompanied by renewed exuberance, movement, and dancing. The music of these renewal movements has been used in worship and evangelism ever since.

But now there is another sound that is ready to burst out from us, a new musical movement of prophetic worship. It has a name that you've probably never heard before: *shigionoth*.

You'll find it in the last chapter of Habakkuk: "*A prayer of Habakkuk the prophet. On* shigionoth" (Hab. 3:1). According to the *Illustrated Bible Dictionary, shigionoth* "denotes a lyrical poem composed under strong mental emotion; a song of impassioned imagination accompanied with suitable music; a dithyrambic ode." It could be considered to be deep, stirring, wild, enthusiastic, and *prophetic*. It is certainly not superficial, and it will impact you, the worshipper, increasing your capacity to feel, enlarging your vision of God, and contributing to the health of your soul. We need prophetic music, songs that come from deep within, to help us focus on God. Prophetic music will be for this moment and will never be the music of past generations. Get ready to sing your prophetic song to God, even as He sings over you!

ACTION

Take time to get quiet and listen to God's songs over you. What is He singing over you today?

Whether you are musical or not, whether you are part of a worship group or not, ask God to give you more *shigionoth*. Ask Him to give you stirring music that is as big and as deep as His vision and His songs over you. Remember, when the Spirit gives you a song, you will still have to work at shaping it, practicing it, singing it out!

Alleluia! for the Lord God omnipotent reigns! (Revelation 19:6 NKJV)

He Will Place a Burning Heart Within You

But if I say, "I will not mention his word or speak anymore in his name," his word is in my heart like a fire, a fire shut up in my bones. I am weary of holding it in; indeed, I cannot (Jeremiah 20:9).

The Lord says, "I am putting a fire inside of you, a fire deep into your belly." And as Jesus said these words, I saw Him pushing what looked like a flaming heart, a fireball in the shape of a heart about the size of a large fist, into your stomach. When this happened you bent over and roared into the ground. As you straightened up again, the heart on fire was still burning, but now the flames had also spread up the windpipe and down both arms, to the tips of the fingers. And the Spirit of the Lord said, "This is a fire for communication. Fan it into flame in intercession, then use it and be changed."

Jesus is igniting you so that you will speak and write in new ways. He has put the fire of His passion deep within you, and you will fan the flames with your cries of intercession to Him. This fire reaches your fingers because you will write and type with a renewed zeal. The flames of this fire also reach to your mouth, so that you will speak with fire.

No longer are you to be silent; you are to talk and write with a fire, a fire that comes from the place of intercession, the place of crying out to God with an authentic roar. There is an invitation from the Lord to kneel before Him, or even stand, doubled over, and allow your roar to come out. As you do this, He will purify your voice and ignite it with fire, so that you will be formed into one who communicates boldly, passionately, and truthfully—a prophetic warrior!

RECEIVE

Find somewhere private that you can go regularly to kneel or stand before God. It could be a closet, a room, or even the shower! After praising and exalting God, begin to receive His fire. Pray, "Lord Jesus, I receive Your fire, and I allow You to put a burning fiery heart deep within me."

Ask Holy Spirit to show you where Jesus is placing that fireball in your midst. What does it feel like? What does it look like in the Spirit?

Allow the Lord to do something within you and do not resist if you feel like crying out, shouting out loud, or roaring. Don't try to subdue or control what happens but don't force things. The Spirit will guide you at His pace. If this is unfamiliar territory for you, you may need to repeat this prayer until you begin to become aware of what He is doing in you.

DAY 80

Pure Stream

"Woe to me!" I cried. "I am ruined! For I am a man of unclean lips, and I live among a people of unclean lips, and my eyes have seen the King, the Lord Almighty." Then one of the seraphim flew to me with a live coal in his hand, which he had taken with tongs from the altar. With it he touched my mouth and said, "See, this has touched your lips; your guilt is taken away and your sin atoned for" (Isaiah 6:5–7).

I am drawing you into My fire today, as My mercy is outstretched to purify your voice and your mouth. This is a sobering but liberating moment as I set your voice and mouth on fire to carry words of life and not death.

Gossip and slander, hatred and criticism, profane language and unwholesome talk—these all have no place in you, My mouthpiece. So today take heart and know that there is liberation for you from any places where you struggled when it comes to how your voice is used. Do not stay bound in the patterns of the flesh. Instead, come and speak from a heavenly point of view. There is freedom for those who answer, "Yes!"

> *Then the Lord reached out his hand and touched my mouth and said to me, "I have put my words in your mouth"* (Jeremiah 1:9).

ACTION

A moment of repentance is needed in response to this word. Use the following as a guideline prayer:

> *Father God, I'm so sorry for each and every way my mouth and voice have not been used to glorify You. I acknowledge that this is not the best of me. I repent for (list anything the Spirit brings to mind), and I ask for Your forgiveness. Father, I ask that You would give me the strength to stand strong and stay pure. Strength to use my voice for magnifying Your name and not for tearing others down. I yield my voice, my thoughts, and my mouth to You afresh and declare that I will live and speak with purity in my heart, in Jesus's name.*

DAY 81

My Conquerors

No, in all these things we are more than conquerors through him who loved us. For I am convinced that neither death nor life, neither angels nor demons, neither the present nor the future, nor any powers, neither height nor depth, nor anything else in all creation, will be able to separate us from the love of God that is in Christ Jesus our Lord (Romans 8:37–39).

Did you know that creation is longing for you to realize who you are (see Rom. 8:22)? You who were bought with such a high price, the blood of Jesus, awaken to your true identity and calling! When you stepped into the Kingdom of God as a son or as a daughter, you were marked as a Conqueror! You were made into a victorious one because He who is victorious dwells within you! It is not wishful thinking or nice, inspiring words. This is the truth!

Jesus, who intercedes before the Father on your behalf, is coming to place His hand on your insides to stir up the revelation of this truth within your very core. You were made to live as a conqueror. You were made to walk in and with His authority. You were made to know that the Champion fought sin and death and WON so that you would live as His co-heir—one who inherits all that He has!

Today the Spirit of God is stirring you up, and He's calling out to you: "Awaken to your true identity! Strip off the hesitancy, the sluggishness, the excuses, and the words of disqualification! I qualified you! I call you My own! I just need you to believe Me and to walk by faith in your true identity. 'Weak,' 'confused,' 'mute,' 'without purpose or meaning'—I have never called you any of these things! Take them off today! Draw a line across each word that you have allowed to define you and say to each one that you will no longer call yourself by those identifiers.

"My son and daughter, I have brought you into My royal bloodline. You are called by My name now! Everything that I have is yours. Grab it, hold on to it, and live as the conqueror that I have called you to be!"

ACTION

Sit and read Romans 8:18–39. Highlight it, take notes, and write out confessions from this passage. If you have struggled with labels that you've put upon yourself or that others have put on you, write those words out, then cross them out, and write over the top of them who you truly are according to this passage of God's Word.

DAY 82

His Sword Will Set Your Voice Free

On my account you will be brought before governors and kings as witnesses to them and to the Gentiles. But when they arrest you, do not worry about what to say or how to say it. At that time you will be given what to say, for it will not be you speaking, but the Spirit of your Father speaking through you (Matthew 10:18–20).

The Lord comes with a sword to release your lips. His blade will cut through all that has bound your mouth and silenced you. He says to you, "You are My witness and I will use your voice to speak out the good news of My Kingdom!"

The Lord's sword is mighty and will cut through all demonic hindrances, ties, tape, and staples that are keeping your lips closed. Though the knife edge is sharp and destroys every demonic cord, it will not harm you at all.

Where words from others have made you silent, Jesus says, "I want to hear you speak."

Where the spirit of fear has clamped your jaws shut, Jesus says, "I love you and I will fill your mouth with songs of joy."

Where circumstances and the prejudices and traditions of others have persuaded you that your voice is not worth hearing, Jesus says, "I will fill your mouth with words of My Spirit."

Where the spirits of religion and control have put locks and chains on your lips, Jesus says, "Be loosed! You are free!"

Believe that the one who loves you and sets you free has set you free indeed. Open your lips wide, raise your voice, speak forth in confidence. Do not worry what to say, for I will speak through you!

DECREE

Make declarations out loud:

- I declare that I have a voice and that my voice will be heard.
- I declare that I will speak before leaders, authorities, and anywhere else that God gives me favor and influence.
- I declare that I do not have a spirit of fear. I am loved and have a sound mind. I believe that my voice is worth hearing and that I

hear from God. No demonic spirit will control or shut my mouth because Jesus Christ has set me free from all bondage!

- I declare that the Spirit of God will speak through me.

Prophecy Is Not the Mystery You Think It Is

The Lord would speak to Moses face to face, as one speaks to a friend (Exodus 33:11).

God is honest! He is a truth teller. God is not difficult or awkward. God does not twist and turn to try to stay out of reach. God is not into making your life difficult. God is not under-skilled relationally, impatiently tapping His fingers on the arm of His throne and rolling His eyes in frustration that He has to interact with you. God is not poorly connected to you!

Yet when it comes to hearing His voice, when it comes to the prophetic, we can believe that we are lacking something or that we have missed out on some secret that only a few get to know, some kind of connection with God that only the "specialists" are in on!

We tend to overcomplicate listening to Him, wondering if we have failed in some, as yet unrevealed, way to us. We ponder our inadequacies and, in the process, we allow lies to form deep in our hearts that we will never be prophetically truly great. And that there might always be something *substandard* connected to our usage of spiritual gifts.

Emma writes: As a senior church leader, I would like to repent and say sorry today for all the times and all the ways that we, as leaders, stood on platforms and held microphones and hid behind our insecurities and in doing so, made spiritual matters look more mysterious than they are. I'm sorry where we as leaders promoted ourselves and, instead of pulling others up around us, demoted and limited freedom of development in spirituality.

I'm sorry for the training courses that were not clear in speaking the simple truth that *prophecy is friendship with God.* And also that friendship with God is conversation. And that conversation with God is delightful, joyous, easy, and healing! And that you are *not* second rate and missing something. I'm sorry when we were not clear that *you* were made to steward much revelation—*you* were made to hear the voice of God, to know heavenly rhythms, and to walk as one who is in the light (not one who has to squirm in the shadows, *trying* to hear).

ACTION

Breathe deeply today. As you exhale, eject the lies that there is something defective in you and your spirituality. As you breathe in, receive the clean, fresh, air of ease of revelation that comes from conversing with your friend, God.

DAY 84

Strong Words in Your Mouth

"Is not my word like fire," declares the Lord, "and like a hammer that breaks a rock in pieces?" (Jeremiah 23:29)

God is saying to you today that He has placed His "hammer word" in your mouth. The strength, weight, and power of God's Word is inside you and on your tongue poised and positioned; ready to be released.

There is a force of what God is speaking now in your mouth. You are the deliverer of the prophetic voice of God in this moment. Open wide your mouth and discharge the word that has been released to you. Declare and release the word. As you do, the force of it smashes every rock into pieces, into dust.

ACTION

You may be asking, "What is the word you have put in my mouth today, God?" Take time aside to quiet yourself before the Lord. Attune your inner focus and gaze toward God and listen. Speak what Samuel the prophet spoke in your own prayer and let God know you are available to hear and receive what He is speaking to you today.

The Lord came and stood there, calling as at the other times, "Samuel! Samuel!"

Then Samuel said, "Speak, for your servant is listening" (1 Samuel 3:1).

Wait on the Lord and then write down what you hear Him say and release it from your mouth by speaking it out loud.

Sing! Fly! Be Free!

But whenever someone turns to the Lord, the veil is taken away. For the Lord is the Spirit, and wherever the Spirit of the Lord is, there is freedom. So all of us who have had that veil removed can see and reflect the glory of the Lord. And the Lord—who is the Spirit—makes us more and more like him as we are changed into his glorious image (2 Corinthians 3:16–18 NLT).

My beloved, I am coming today to give you eyes to see and discernment to know when the enemy is trying to trip you up and hold you back. For far too long, you have faced opposition of every kind and have thought that you were the cause of it. You thought that your failures and mistakes were holding you hostage; you have felt like a bird trapped in a cage with no voice and no freedom to fly. That ends today!

Look and see, for the cage is not real! Discern with My Spirit what is truly holding you hostage! For just as I set the man possessed by Legion free from living among the tombs (see Mark 5), free from the daily torment, free from all that was oppressing him, so I do for you! Come into your right mind, *My mind*, and see that I made you to sing! I made you to fly! I have given My all for your freedom! Do you see it? Do you consider it the truth?

Step out of captivity and into freedom today. It's yours!

ACTION

What is holding you back? Do you feel free to speak, to sing, to express what you know the Lord God has put within you? If not, then it's a good day to step into that freedom. Begin by reading Mark 5:1–18 and think about what areas in your life need freedom. Picture Jesus coming to you and setting you free. To then activate this truth in your life, write a newspaper headline about your freedom. Put it in big, bold letters! Then describe your freedom. Write as though your current opposition was yesterday's trial and the good news of your freedom is being announced today!

DAY 86

Seek God, Not Entertainment

A Message from God-of-the-Angel-Armies: "Don't listen to the sermons of the prophets. It's all hot air. Lies, lies, and more lies. They make it all up. Not a word they speak comes from me. They preach their 'Everything Will Turn Out Fine' sermon to congregations with no taste for God, Their 'Nothing Bad Will Ever Happen to You' sermon to people who are set in their own ways. Have any of these prophets bothered to meet with me, the true God? bothered to take in what I have to say? listened to and then lived out my Word?" (Jeremiah 23:16–20 MSG)

"Examine your motivations," says the Lord. "Do not seek Me out for your entertainment and do not seek out those who will say only what you want them to hear."

Beware those who preach or prophesy only what entertains their listeners. Question prophecies that are only for gains, likes, shares, or financial reward. It is not a prophet's job to make the church happy!

When the prophet Jeremiah arrived in Jerusalem from his simple country life, what he saw shocked him enormously. As a young man transported into a big city, he was confronted by so much that was false, unreal, and untrue. His first surprise was to find that the political leaders were corrupt. More worryingly, when he went into the temple and looked at the priests, the religious leaders, he declared that they had turned the temple of God into a den of robbers. However, there was a third group of men, prophets, in whom he hoped to find integrity and he was going to join them (these were professional prophets who had been trained in the schools of the prophets). But when Jeremiah met them, he was so shattered by what he found that he said: *"My heart is broken within me, all my bones tremble; I have become like a drunken man"* (Jer. 23:9). (He did later find some who were true to their calling.) When he listened to what these so-called professional prophets claimed to be the word of God, he said, "That's not the message of God. They are dreaming it up!" These men were telling the people what they wanted to hear because that is the way to popularity.

It is very easy to please a congregation by never challenging them, but a true prophet who really cares for the Shepherd and the sheep will challenge and rebuke when necessary. Jeremiah listened and looked to God before he spoke. That is why he was a true prophet. He was prepared to listen and ask, "God, what do *You* want me to say?" He didn't tell the people what *they* wanted to hear, He told them what *God* wanted them to hear.

ACTION

Thank God that where there are false prophets, that means there are also true prophets! Do you need to examine who/what/why you listen to certain things; are you looking to be entertained? Are you seeking prophecies just to confirm what you want to hear, or do you truly want to know what is on God's heart? When you pray and listen to the Holy Spirit for yourself, do you actually stop to listen, or do you go ahead with what you always intended to do, no matter what God might be saying?

Fire Words That Make You Burn!

"You prophets who do nothing but dream—go ahead and tell your silly dreams. But you prophets who have a message from me—tell it truly and faithfully. What does straw have in common with wheat? Nothing else is like God's Decree. Isn't my Message like fire?" God's Decree. "Isn't it like a sledgehammer busting a rock?" (Jeremiah 23:28–29 MSG)

The prophets were telling the people, "I had a dream! I had a dream!" and that sounded terribly impressive. Jerusalem's professional prophets were saying to one another, "Have you heard any good dreams lately?" Someone would share something, then they would all preach it, even though they had dreamt nothing of the kind! But even the pagan prophets of pagan gods used to give their oracles through dreams. In the ancient world, it was a favorite way of imagining that the spirits had spoken. Jeremiah 23 is a devastating revelation of what was going on among the prophets, lying and stealing each other's messages just to entertain the masses and give them what they wanted to hear. God exposed them with a declaration:

> *Let the prophet who has a dream recount the dream, but let the one who has my word speak it faithfully. For what has straw to do with grain?* (Jeremiah 23:28)

When God's Word is truly passed on, you can tell by two things: You will get burned, and you will be broken by it.

> *"Is not my word like fire," declares the Lord, "and like a hammer that breaks a rock in pieces?"* (Jeremiah 23:29)

After Jesus talked with two of His followers on the road to Emmaus, they agreed, *"Did not our hearts burn within us?"* (Luke 24:32 ESV). The Word is fire, and it should make your heart burn within you, exposing and destroying shame and igniting passion for Him.

Be discerning of who and what you listen to. Those who give false comfort may make you feel safe but leave you no better off in the end; they are of no benefit. Embrace the fire and hammer words—by them you will be truly blessed!

ACTION

How do you react when a prophet, leader, or teacher preaches unpalatable words? Do you take offense or do you let God's Word do its sometimes painful work? Are you submitted to leaders who have permission to be "editors" in your life? Are you yielded to the fire, or do you prefer cozy comfort? Be honest with yourself and take these tough questions to God.

Don't Let Your Silence Wound You

But if I say, "I will not mention his word or speak anymore in his name,"
his word is in my heart like a fire, a fire shut up in my bones. I am weary of
holding it in; indeed, I cannot (Jeremiah 20:9).

We live in cycles of receiving the blessing of God, His provision, and His abundance, followed by times of receiving His correction and discipline, where He sharpens and grows our character. There are rhythms we walk that are deeply biblically based, rhythms of reaping and sowing, and then of undeserved mercy.

Some days we have to walk out the consequences of our actions; this is the walking out of a judgment, where we can only be taught by God in the thorn bushes of repercussion and ramification. Walking out a judgment can be, for example, when we behaved financially presumptuously, and then had to work to undo overstretching ourselves; or it could be the time we took the wrong job but had to somehow make it work, even though there was limited blessing in it.

I heard the Lord say, "Be careful that you do not walk out a judgment when you make decisions to be silent when in fact I have asked you to speak." You can walk into a place of containment, limitation, and correction by your lack of courage that becomes a partnership with silence.

When Jeremiah tried to suppress the word of the Lord, it became like a burning fire inside him. This fire in his bones was a physically painful consequence of not speaking when he should have. Have we ever considered that our silence may have wounded us and done more harm to our physical frame and emotional stature than just mere indigestion?

Today it is time to partner with the blessing of God and not the rebuke of God. Today you have a choice: God needs your sound and your willingness to speak often, even in the most uncomfortable of moments. He wants to know today if you are wholly available or if you will seal your lips shut when it costs you to speak.

DECREE

Lord, I want to roar for You! I want to open my mouth and let the full
spectrum of what You sound like, God, cascade out of me. I will not
resist You by shutting my mouth, Lord. Instead, I will be a vocal vessel
for however and whatever You want to communicate.

DAY 89

It's Good to Ask God

Ask and it will be given to you; seek and you will find; knock and the door will be opened to you. For everyone who asks receives; the one who seeks finds; and to the one who knocks, the door will be opened (Luke 11:9–10).

From time to time we all need fresh incentives to pray. Here are some incentives to motivate you to ask God for things:

We pray to glorify God. He is glorified in many ways; prayer is one of them and an important one at that. Think about it; if we don't pray, God will not be glorified:

> *And I will do whatever you ask in my name, so that the Father may be glorified in the Son* (John 14:13).

We pray and then experience the fullness of joy:

> *Until now you have not asked for anything in my name. Ask and you will receive, and your joy will be complete* (John 16:24).

If we don't pray, we will go without. James wrote that *"you do not have, because you do not ask God"* (James 4:2b). Remember, if you don't pray for something that He has promised only to give in answer to prayer, God will not give it to you. This includes healing! If we don't pray, the sick will not be healed:

> *Is anyone among you in trouble? Let them pray....Is anyone among you sick? Let them call for the elders of the church to pray over them and anoint them with oil in the name of the Lord. And the prayer offered in faith will make the sick person well....Confess your sins to each other and pray for each other so that you may be healed* (James 5:13–16).

If we don't pray, the demonized will not be set free. Do you remember when Jesus explained to His disciples why they were unable to set the boy free? He told them that *"this kind* [of demon] *can come out only by prayer"* (Mark 9:29).

ACTION

What do you need to ask God for in Jesus's name?

- If you don't ask, it won't be given to you.

- If you don't seek, you won't find it.

- If you don't knock, it won't be opened!

And don't forget, we can be certain that God will hear and answer our prayers because in Luke 11:11 (ESV) Jesus asks, *"What father among you...?"* Read Luke chapter 11 and be encouraged!

Give It a Go!

I have put my words in your mouth and covered you with the shadow of my hand—I who set the heavens in place, who laid the foundations of the earth, and who say to Zion, "You are my people" (Isaiah 51:16).

I heard the Spirit of the Lord say that you have been holding back from prophesying because you feel you don't have the experience. However, by holding back you stop yourself from getting the experience you need! The Lord says to you instead, "It is time to give it a go. It is time to relinquish the fear of getting it wrong, mixing up your words, not sounding skilled enough, not having lots of words to say, and to just give it a go!"

It's time to relinquish the "but what if?" mindset that holds you back. It's time to cut it off and remove it from your life.

What if I get it wrong? What if I don't know what to say? What if I sound stupid? What if it doesn't make sense?

All these "what ifs" are set up to stop you from stepping into your prophetic destiny. They hold no power anymore, and it is time for them to go!

God says: "As you step out and begin to give it a go, know that I will turn up and give you the words to say. I, your God, am a faithful God who will provide you with the words and the language at just the right time. From your insides, powerful words will bubble up and burst forth, but for this to happen, you first need to start—and give it a go."

ACTION

Find a willing volunteer, such as a good friend, who will let you practice prophesying. Make sure you have their permission and that they know that you are practicing. Prophesy into an area of their life that you don't know much about to encourage them, comfort them, and build them up. Be brave and push yourself to speak for at least three minutes. Laugh with each other if you mess up, and then try again. Ask for feedback. Keep practicing. Enjoy exercising the Holy Spirit's gifts to you!

CHAPTER 4

Revolutionized by Love

DAY 91

Seeds of Thanksgiving

Praise the Lord! I will give thanks to the Lord with all my heart, in the company of the upright and in the assembly. Great are the works of the Lord; they are studied by all who delight in them. Splendid and majestic is His work, and His righteousness endures forever. He has caused His wonders to be remembered; the Lord is gracious and compassionate. He has given food to those who fear Him; He will remember His covenant forever (Psalm 111:1–5 NASB).

Look back over your life and remember the prayers that the Lord your God has answered. Look back and thank Him for the times of His provision. Look back and see when He carried you and brought you through hard days. As you look at these moments, offer Him your thanksgiving.

- Thank Him for His faithfulness.

- Thank Him for His generosity.

- Thank Him for His constant presence.

- Thank Him for who He is.

Let this thankfulness become an offering that you present before Him each and every day. On the difficult days, even those filled with pain, choose to remember what He has done in order to remind yourself of what He *will* yet do. For He says to you, "If you will be one who plants seeds of thanksgiving daily, I will cultivate and nurture these seeds. They will then produce an ever-flourishing harvest of contentment, joy, strength, and faithfulness in your life."

ACTIVATION

Make a list of what Jesus has done for you, and then go through the list and thank Him for each one. Keep the list in a safe place or memorize it so that you can refer to it on the difficult days. Make thanksgiving a regular part of your devotional life.

DAY 92

You Have a Spirit Dwelling Inside of You!

But whoever is united with the Lord is one with him in spirit (1 Corinthians 6:17).

When you came to Jesus and chose to surrender your life to Him, His Spirit took up residence inside you and you became *"one with him in spirit."*

We often glibly speak of Jesus "living in our hearts" because we understand the need for relational connection. However, biblically this is not an entirely accurate description of what happens. At your salvation, the Holy Spirit becomes *one with your spirit*. Then, at the point of your earthly death, your body will decay and go back to the dust, but your spirit, woven together with God's Holy Spirit will go to be with Jesus.

Your internal reality is that you have an indwelling Spirit. The Holy Spirit does not abandon His post or leave you for day trips! His indwelling is a continual truth. The Holy Spirit desires not to be caged within your spirit alone but that He is allowed to explode within you, taking over your thinking and touching your heart.

The Apostle Paul prays for this to happen most eloquently in Ephesians chapter 3. Paul intercedes that the Spirit of God who is in your inner being may also dwell in your hearts, that you would know how much you are loved and become established in love (see vv. 14–19). Make this prayer for the Ephesians become *your* prayer!

ACTION

Read Ephesians 3, especially verses 16–20. Start to study, meditate on and memorize the words of Paul's prayer. Make them your own, for example, pray, "I pray that out of His glorious riches He may strengthen me with power through His Spirit in my inner being." But it's not enough to simply "know" these words; this is a power transformation by the Spirit of God. Allow Him to work inside of you and be transformed!

DAY 93

Permission to Feel Loved

And I pray that he would unveil within you the unlimited riches of his glory and favor until supernatural strength floods your innermost being with his divine might and explosive power. Then, by constantly using your faith, the life of Christ will be released deep inside you, and the resting place of his love will become the very source and root of your life. Then you will be empowered to discover what every holy one experiences—the great magnitude of the astonishing love of Christ in all its dimensions. How deeply intimate and far-reaching is his love! How enduring and inclusive it is! Endless love beyond measurement that transcends our understanding—this extravagant love pours into you until you are filled to overflowing with the fullness of God! (Ephesians 3:16–19 TPT)

Yesterday we considered that the indwelling Holy Spirit does not want to simply be caged within your spirit alone but wants to be allowed by you to explode within you.

The Holy Spirit of God wants greater access to every part of your insides! He wants to stretch out and to be given permission to radically alter how you feel. The Holy Spirit wants to make an emotionally impacting move. The Holy Spirit wants you to have a different internal experience of Him. He is seeking to heal your emotions and His request right now is, "Give Me permission to enable you to feel loved."

He does not merely want you to have a "head knowledge" in your mind of how loved you are. He wants you to feel and experience, to a new level, the love of God.

The Holy Spirit is asking you today, "Will you give Me permission to do something you cannot do for yourself? That is, to create within you an emotional wholeness and heart stability that is able fully to receive the emotions of the love of God."

RECEIVE

Give permission today for the Holy Spirit to do more in you than ever before.

After permission is granted, watch Him move from unity with your spirit only to now also taking up residence in your head space and heart space. As you go about your day, keep measuring the transformation of your mind and your emotions.

DAY 94

Intentional Pursuit

"Though the mountains be shaken and the hills be removed, yet my unfailing love for you will not be shaken nor my covenant of peace be removed," *says the Lord, who has compassion on you* (Isaiah 54:10).

"I am pulling you in close today, right into the depths of My love. My love is not a surface kind of love or a friendly kind of love. My love is a radical, deep, overwhelming, and never-ending love that invades the depths of who you are and transforms you from the inside out. Will you create space to receive this from Me?"

The Lord is inviting you to build an intentional pursuit of His love into your lifestyle in the coming weeks, a space where you're going to go after the One who is pursuing you fervently.

I heard Him say, "Create 'love space' in your week; carve out time in your diary and dedicate prolonged encounter time to responding to and receiving My love."

ACTION

Get practical with this!

Get your diary or calendar out, whether it's on your phone, in a book, or on your wall, and start to mark out times where you are going to intentionally pursue the love of God. It doesn't mean that you can't pursue God at any other times, but it shows that you are serious about dedicating yourself to this endeavor. Go deep with God, and invite Him to let you feel His deep love. Say to Him, "I let You love me," and sit and wait for Him to overwhelm you.

DAY 95

His Beautiful Embrace

His left arm is under my head, and his right arm embraces me (Song of Songs 2:6).

I see Lord Jesus Himself embracing you in this moment. I see His arm moving around your shoulders, gently, yet firmly drawing you into His embrace. He is pulling you in with strong love and adoration.

Jesus says to you: "Let Me hold you, My loved one, in this moment. Allow My embrace to rest on you, and allow yourself to rest in My embrace. For there will be a divine exchange for you as you let Me hold you. Close your eyes. Trust that I have you and will not let go. Rest in My arms."

I see Jesus now closing His eyes as He simply enjoys this precious time with you. He is imparting His amazing, deep love for you as He draws you ever closer. Do not resist this profound love that He has for you—this beautiful embrace. Receive His love; relax into the arms, the hold, of your Savior and faithful love. He longs to hold you; His hold is always and forever.

ACTION

If this invitation makes you feel uncomfortable or upset in any way or you are finding it difficult to receive the embrace and love of Jesus, then the following prayers will help.

Pray something like this, adding your own words, "Jesus, I want to receive Your love and embrace, but I am finding this really tough. Please help me to feel relaxed and good about You holding me and help me fall into Your arms. I want to love You and receive Your love, Jesus. I want to trust You in that love. Please help me get there."

When you are ready, ask Jesus to come closer to you, and as you are aware of Him doing that (you may sense His proximity or you may actually see Him), ask Jesus to move closer until He is standing right beside you. Then, when you are ready, say, "Jesus, I am ready for Your embrace." Stay with Jesus in that moment for as long as you are able to do so.

Go back to this invitation regularly, and during each session allow Jesus to embrace you for a longer period of time. When sitting or relaxing or when readying for sleep, welcome Jesus to hold you and rest in His arms. You will feel transformed surrounded in His great love for you!

DAY 96

Held by Your Father

You will look in vain for those who tried to conquer you. Those who attack you will come to nothing. For I hold you by your right hand—I, the Lord your God. And I say to you, "Don't be afraid. I am here to help you" (Isaiah 41:12–13 NLT).

I am holding you, My precious child. My hand surrounds all of you and shall protect you for all eternity. No one and nothing can tear you from My palm (see John 10:28–29); you are safe in My embrace.

Though you have been told that you are alone and isolated, the very opposite is true: you are in the very midst of My love, and for as long as you choose to remain here, you shall never be far from Me and from all that I whisper to you. Do not listen to the lies of the enemy. He seeks to twist your perception of reality around you with thoughts of vulnerability and despair. His words of hopelessness are like banners twisted around you, bill posters stuck on you, carrying lies and destructive messages.

But satan's lies about you could not be further from the truth. You are mine forever! Remember that *"those who know your name trust in you, for you, Lord, have never forsaken those who seek you"* (Ps. 9:10). I, the Lord Almighty, your Father who loves you, will never forsake you, abandon you, fail you, or leave you.

Choose today to tear off those banners, posters, stickers, and sashes that have become attached to you. Rip off those lies and repent of believing them. Press yourself back into the arms of Father God, who loves you, surrounds you, and keeps you safe—forever.

ACTION

The best way to fight the enemy's lies is with Scripture; that's how Jesus resisted satan when he came against Him. Spend some time making note of some Bible verses about how God never leaves or abandons His people. The Psalms are a great place to begin your search, for example, Psalms 9:10; 34:4; 37:28; 91:14; 94:14. Whenever you have thoughts, feelings, or words of despair, isolation, or hopelessness, grab your list of verses and begin to decree and declare them until they drown out the lies.

Dive into My Love

As the Father has loved me, so have I loved you. Now remain in my love (John 15:9).

"Dive into the ocean of My love," invites Jesus, your Lord and Savior.

There is an encouragement today from the Lord to dive into the depths of His amazing love. Be inspired by Him to acknowledge the truth that there is no end, no bottom, no edge, or completion to God's ineffable love; see and know that it is truly unfathomable.

Just as a free diver would take a series of deep breaths and then push under the surface of the ocean, determinedly pressing on to see how far they can go into the depths of the waters (training themselves to hold their breath for long stretches of time), so today God invites you to dive deep into the vastness of His love.

"There is no end," I hear Him say, "There is no limit. Come deeper." God is drawing you into the deep, cavernous volume of His affection and adoration. He is saying to you, "Be immersed and saturated in My love. Allow Me to baptize you afresh in My love. Allow My love to flood you and surround you. Dive into My love today, My child."

RECEIVE

Imagine you are in the ocean. Take a deep breath and intentionally confess with your mouth out loud: "I am diving into Your love today." In that moment, allow your spiritual senses to begin to feel the pressing of God's love tangibly on your body, surrounding you from your head to your feet; begin to recognize what it feels like to be immersed in the waters of God's love.

Prophetic act: If you are able, run yourself a full bath, and as you get into the water, make the same declaration: "I am diving into Your love today, God. Baptize me in Your love." Allow yourself to become completely immersed in the bathwater, and as you do, ask the Holy Spirit for a super sensitization to all the facets of His love. Ask for your eyes to be opened to a new revelation of His love, your skin to feel His complete surrounding of you, and your ears to hear the sound of God's love for you.

The God Who Walks with You

The Lord is my shepherd, I lack nothing. He makes me lie down in green pastures, he leads me beside quiet waters, he refreshes my soul. He guides me along the right paths for his name's sake. Even though I walk through the darkest valley, I will fear no evil, for you are with me; your rod and your staff, they comfort me (Psalm 23:1–4).

You may be one who is walking through a dark, dark valley where hope seems nowhere to be found. If that is you, then the Lord God says, "I am here! I am right with you! I know that you feel that you cannot see or find Me, but I am here. Just believe Me. Reach out and feel Me. Reach out and grab hold of My confident strength. Take hold of My love. Receive My peace. I am walking with you step by step; you are not alone. You are not helpless. Trust Me."

Whether you know it well or you don't remember reading it before, let Psalm 23 become yours today. Let it permeate your being. Let it not be just memorized in your head but is written on your heart. For David was a man who penned this out of his own experience; he walked and lived this psalm. Yet in the wisdom of God, it was written down so that generations of believers could also live out its truths.

ACTION

This Psalm is a great one to activate your spiritual senses. Take some time to sit with Jesus and look at Him as the Shepherd. As you do, ask yourself questions like:

- How is He dressed?

- What does His rod look like?

Let Him guide you to the still waters and listen to how peaceful it is. Allow Him to lay you down in green grass, and in that space look at the heavens. Tell Jesus what you see.

If you are in a deep, dark valley, and the action above is too much to begin with, then start by reaching out and feel His emotions. Feel His great love for you. Ask Him how He feels when He looks at you.

DAY 99

I Do Not Miss a Moment

You have searched me, Lord, and you know me. You know when I sit and when I rise; you perceive my thoughts from afar. You discern my going out and my lying down; you are familiar with all my ways. Before a word is on my tongue you, Lord, know it completely. You hem me in behind and before, and you lay your hand upon me. Such knowledge is too wonderful for me, too lofty for me to attain (Psalm 139:1–6).

There is not a single moment that I miss. I am intentionally engaged with every moment of your existence. I am fascinated by you and always looking toward you to shine My grace, My favor, and My mercy down. You are My favorite occupation, and there is nowhere I would rather be than with you right now. Turn your face toward Me as I turn My face toward you. Do not hide from Me or run away. I want to be with you! I really do.

The deceiver would have you believe that you are a burden, a nuisance, and an inconvenience to Me. But this could not be further from the truth. You are My delight. As you turn your face toward Me, I am dissolving the lies that the enemy tells you to make you feel distant or make you feel like an outsider. I have pulled you in close, and nothing the liar says or does can change this.

RECEIVE

Spend some time to focus on the nearness of God—the God who sees you and sees all. Allow yourself to grow in awareness of His presence with you. Start to tell Him "thank You" for all the different emotions and feelings that are rising out of your encounter with Him.

Pray: "Jesus Christ, I let You near me, and I recognize Your nearness. I am growing in awareness of Your nearness. Thank You, Lord, for being the One who comes near, that You're never far from me or difficult to find. You are the right-here-with-me God, always present and always close."

Angels Have Been Sent to Heal You
Ministering Angels
Part 1

Are not all angels ministering spirits sent to serve those who will inherit salvation? (Hebrews 1:14)

In the spirit realm, I saw angels with basins and towels and salves and balms walk into the room where you are today. They had been dispatched to bring immediate restoration to battle scars and wounds of the previous few months.

They were anointing you and soothing ragged emotions and bringing healing to your battle weariness. This was not surface-level ministry but a very deliberate deep dealing with your exhaustion and healing you from the rigors of willing yourself to stay strong.

Emma writes: Personally, for years I would not have been able to survive the demands of being a soldier in the army of the Lord without the Hebrews chapter 1 ministry of angels.

The beauty of this Scripture is that they have *already* been sent; you are not waiting for one day in the future for an angelic dispatch to come and minister to you. They have already been dispatched; they have been in active service for years. Angels are continually sent to further your well-being and to assist you in walking out your salvation with fear and trembling.

These angels are not awaiting the command of God but have already received the command of God to support you and to perform tasks in your life that are acceptable to the all-holy God. Theirs is a remarkable role of service and ministry; they function to benefit you. Don't miss out on this remarkable gift of God to you today.

RECEIVE

Lie down and rest, or sit back in your chair—even if it is only for a few moments—and let the ministry package of God heal your battle weariness. Receive Heaven's salves and balms as they are poured into your wounds, and be restored.

Healing to the Wounded Warrior Ministering Angels Part 2

In you, Lord, I have taken refuge; let me never be put to shame; deliver me in your righteousness. Turn your ear to me, come quickly to my rescue; be my rock of refuge, a strong fortress to save me. Since you are my rock and my fortress, for the sake of your name lead and guide me. Keep me free from the trap that is set for me, for you are my refuge. Into your hands I commit my spirit; deliver me, Lord, my faithful God (Psalm 31:1–5).

Good news! If you feel wounded from war and battle-weary, God has a gift for you today.

I watched as the Lord dispatched a host of angels from the heavenlies into the earth. They were dressed in scrubs and medical attire and carried with them all manner of tools and provisions. The Lord turned to me and said, "These are My healing and nurture angels that I am sending to the earth. I'm healing the wounded warriors and restoring the battle-weary."

You may feel wounded from a particularly nasty war you just walked through or wearied from battle after battle after battle. Yet God has sent His host of healing angels to minister to you and make you well. Your wounds are being healed, your weariness is being lifted as God gets you ready to war as part of His victorious army.

As God heals your wounds and delivers your weariness, I hear Him say: "No longer will battle frighten you! Your previous experience will not prophesy into your future, and you are going to know a remarkable new boldness as you look forward to the battles at hand knowing that you are healed and set free!"

So receive healing today—be free! Let the angels minister deeply to you and heal your wounds and your battle weariness.

DECREE

- My wounds are healed by the blood of Jesus!
- My battle weariness is lifting in the name of Jesus!
- I am being made whole for war!
- I am being healed for battle!
- My weariness is lifting in Jesus's name!

DAY 102

Kintsugi

Where sin increased, grace abounded all the more (Romans 5:20 NASB).

John writes: Recently a few of my friends asked me if I knew anything about the Japanese art of *kintsugi*. They had read a story about this old Japanese practice of mending broken pottery. *Kintsugi* means "golden joinery." It is the art of joining broken pieces of pottery with a liquid resin that resembles gold. The result is a bowl or vase that is more beautiful, more aesthetically complex, and more valuable than the original piece.

I think that is amazing! The new piece with golden seams became so popular among Japanese art collectors in the fifteenth century that some were even accused of purposely breaking pottery in order to repair it with gold.

What a beautiful illustration of the grace of God! His grace takes what is broken—each of us—and puts it back together in such a way that it is more beautiful and more valuable than it was before.

ACTION

The Bible is full of stories of flawed, broken people who God uses in remarkable ways. Ponder this question: If you were in Scripture, what would the chapter and verses say about you? What story from your life would be recorded there?

Be sure to thank God for His grace.

DAY 103

Angels Will Minister to Your Wounds
Ministering Angels Part 3

If you say, "The Lord is my refuge," and you make the Most High your dwelling, no harm will overtake you, no disaster will come near your tent. For he will command his angels concerning you to guard you in all your ways; they will lift you up in their hands, so that you will not strike your foot against a stone. You will tread on the lion and the cobra; you will trample the great lion and the serpent (Psalm 91:9–13).

"I have seen how you have been wounded by others, wounded by words, wounded by repetitive actions, and wounded by experiences from long ago. I have seen the strips that have been torn from you, even cuts that have gone deep, beyond the skin and into your flesh. You thought that these flesh wounds, because of how deep they went, would remain open, exposed, and sore forever. These cuts cause echoes of pain that vibrate through your whole body and limit the fullness of life that you want to live and that I have for you.

"But I can close up those wounds, and I can soothe the pain. Even now I have assigned two angels to minister healing to you and to nurse you to wholeness. One angel will apply a soothing balm to ease the pain. The other will bind the wound together, covering and sealing up where you have been torn," says the Lord.

Praise Jesus! As you allow these ministering angels (see parts 1 and 2 on Hebrews 1 "Ministering Angels") to carry out their assignments, you will be able to come to Him and receive in ways you could not before. You'll find yourself able to forgive—and be forgiven—like you could not before. You'll receive new freedom, new life, and new joy.

Are you ready to let Jesus and His ministering angels tend to your wounds?

RECEIVE

Pray (add your own words and be specific if you can be): "Jesus, I receive Your healing now. I allow You and Your angels to minister to those places and parts of me that have been deeply hurt and wounded. I am ready for the process to begin. Thank You for loving me, Jesus my Savior."

DAY 104

His Kindness

The Lord is compassionate and merciful, slow to get angry and filled with unfailing love. He will not constantly accuse us, nor remain angry forever. He does not punish us for all our sins; he does not deal harshly with us, as we deserve. For his unfailing love toward those who fear him is as great as the height of the heavens above the earth. He has removed our sins as far from us as the east is from the west. The Lord is like a father to his children, tender and compassionate to those who fear him (Psalm 103:8–13 NLT).

Take some time today to think about how the Lord cares for you. Is He kinder to you than you are? Many times His kindness and faithfulness are longer, wider, and more freely given than we even realize.

Today He wants to minister to the areas where you have been hard on yourself. He says this to you: "You have beaten yourself up over things that I forgot a long time ago. You have carried self-punishment like a ball and chain wrapped around your ankle. As you try to walk, it has caused you to be ever aware of your past sins and mistakes. Are you ready to allow Me to remove that ball and chain?

"I forgave you and cast that sin into the ocean of My goodness! It cannot be found, so let Me remove that chain today! Receive the gift of My forgiveness and My kindness. Soak it in and let it wash over you. Receive My compassion, and watch as I unhook that ball and chain from you. Watch as I throw it as far as the east is from the west! It's gone! You are free!"

RECEIVE

Lord God, I repent for carrying my sin instead of giving it to You. I ask You to forgive me once and for all. I ask You to come and remove this weight of self-punishment from me. Take this ball and chain! I receive and accept Your forgiveness today.

Open Wide

I am the Lord your God, who brought you up out of Egypt. Open wide your mouth and I will fill it (Psalm 81:10).

In the spirit, I see you like a little bird being fed in the nest by your parent today. Your Father God is feeding you by His own hand, sustaining and strengthening you in this moment. This repose of mouth wide open and your heart cry of "feed me, Father" is not only for today but these days and weeks ahead, as the Lord desires to "feed you up" with rich nourishment by His Word and His Spirit.

There is deep nourishment for you in this time. Rich nutrients will be given to you to strengthen you and provide a robustness to who you are. I see a solidity coming to you as you feed from the Lord's hand. There is a sense of you needing to take time to sit and receive that nourishment daily. "Open wide your mouth and I will fill it," says the Lord.

Your "daily bread" is coming from your Father's hand. Your daily sustenance and diet from the Word and the Spirit are coming to give you all you need in this moment. The Lord says to you, "Take the time to feed from My hand this month. I am raising you and sustaining you in these days. There are fresh bread words to fill you and satisfy you, as well as to bolster and consolidate what is already in you. Take and eat."

RECEIVE

Take intentional time to sit and "feed" from the Lord's hand this month. Carve out a specific time for this. Let the cry of your heart be, "Feed me, Lord!"

Devour the rich food of the Word, and ingest the food coming to you by the Spirit of God. This is the time to feast and devour the Word and the Spirit of God in a fresh way. Take time to eat!

Reflect and Celebrate

He who overcomes [the world through believing that Jesus is the Son of God], I will grant to him [the privilege] to sit beside Me on My throne, as I also overcame and sat down beside My Father on His throne (Revelation 3:21 AMP).

Our lives are a woven tapestry of our successes and our failures, our strengths and our weaknesses. Our lives paint a picture and tell a story of all the places we've been, of the cultures that shaped us, the childhoods that we wrestled to grow up in, and the friends whose lives rubbed along with ours. We are a walking picture that speaks of the richness of the human experience.

We have all learned to admit that, although we would perhaps prefer to be in vacation mode, on a sandy beach with the sun gently warming, a cold drink in our hand and water repetitively lapping on the shore, the places where we have actually learned the most and felt the most alive were the harsh winter days, with the cold gnawing at our bones and the snow hitting our faces.

It was in the wrestling and the testing, in the uncomfortable and the unpleasant, that we grew and were refined. Though there are many moments we would not want to rehash and revisit, we know that where we are grown by God more fully into the image of His Son was when we were in the dirt, taking decisions that cost us, the times we pushed ourselves to choose well even though it was painful.

Today the Lord says, "You have had more successes than failures. You have had more victories than defeats. You have lived more as an overcomer than as one overwhelmed by the world." For God measures you today, not in what you own or by your level of fame, but by the content of your character and the attitude of your heart. Even though there are more trials yet to come, the pattern you have established of knowing how to endure and win in the ways that really matter will continue to mark your life. For God has purposed that you would receive the rewards in eternity assigned for those who overcome!

ACTION

Right now God asks you to spend time listing your victories. Write them down and reflect and celebrate. Whether they might be navigating challenging relationships, overcoming abuse, gaining an education against the odds, living contentedly in the midst of rejection, or staying a Christian after undergoing spiritual abuse, you have had a multiplicity of victories. Today is the moment to overflow with gratitude and see your life through the lens of Heaven. God speaks over you and says, "Victorious one, well done!"

Run Back to Fortress God

Whoever dwells in the shelter of the Most High will rest in the shadow of the Almighty. I will say of the Lord, "He is my refuge and my fortress, my God, in whom I trust" (Psalm 91:1–2).

"I am your fortress!" shouts the Lord your God over you, "run to Me, come and shelter beneath My shadow, and you will find the deep rest that you need. Run to Me. Flee everything else; leave it all behind. Ignore and shut your ears to all other influences for they will steal the rest that I have to give you."

Do not resist or ignore this call of God for you to press back into His place of nurture and care. It is not weakness or lack of confidence to return to His shelter. Even great warriors need their rest and refuge. Soldiers return to their fortress, where they regroup, recover, reequip and receive their instructions. Fighters know that they can't just keep on running and punching; at some point, it is necessary and good for them to return to their corner.

There is so much vying for your attention, such as social media, games, entertainment, food and drink, employment, and the pursuit of money. These are not your shelter or fortress. Do not retreat into them. Do not try to hide there for you will not find your rest there. Instead, hear the shout of the Lord and trust Him for everything. Run to Him, for He is a strong tower and in His shadow you will be safe (see Prov. 18:10).

ACTION

Repent (use your own words): "Father God, I am sorry for trying to find rest, shelter, and escape in other things, such as (speak those things that come to mind). I repent and choose today to run to You. I commit to retraining myself to choose to trust Your loving arms as my first place of refuge and not these other distractions. I am Your warrior and You are my Lord. You are my strong tower, my mighty fortress, and I love You because You love me and are always there for me."

Hold Him!

Simeon took him in his arms and praised God (Luke 2:28).

John writes: I have a wonderful painting *Simeon's Moment* by Ron DiCinanni in my study. It's of the aged prophet Simeon holding the infant Jesus in his arms at His presentation in the temple. For a number of years, it has been a source of inspiration, especially Simeon's joyful facial expression of hope fulfilled, which seems to be inviting me to mirror Simeon—to spiritually take Jesus in my arms and hold Him closely.

When I consider the character, it is as though Simeon wants me to know what he has seen and heard in this rich moment of salvation history (the name Simeon means "hearing" in Hebrew). He had been told by the Holy Spirit that he would not die before he had seen the Lord's Messiah. So, moved by the Spirit, he arrives in the temple and holds in his arms the Lord Jesus, God in flesh and blood (the name Yeshua [Jesus] means "deliverer" or "savior" in Greek). Then, Simeon's seeing turns into believing:

> *For my eyes have seen your salvation, which you have prepared in the sight of all nations: a light for revelation to the Gentiles, and the glory of your people Israel* (Luke 2:30–32).

Having first been offered to God at this presentation in the temple, this baby would, thirty-three years later, hold my sin and yours tightly to Himself on the cross and there present Himself as an offering for sin. No wonder His arms were wide open in death by crucifixion! He could not have given a wider invitation or warmer embrace to those who see in Him their salvation and eternal destiny.

Maybe your arms once held Jesus near but other things have filled your heart and arms today. Be like Simeon, and take Jesus in your arms and hold Him closely once more.

ACTION

- Do you feel the need for the assurance of a love that will not let you go? Hold Him close.

- Are you gripped by loneliness, confusion, or fear as you face the future? Hold Him close.

- Do you long for an *"inexpressible and glorious joy"* (1 Pet. 1:8) to fill the emptiness of your life? Hold Him close.

It matters that Jesus is near to you.

Celebrate with Your Proud Father

But we had to celebrate and be happy, because your brother was dead, but now he is alive; he was lost, but now he has been found (Luke 15:32 GNT).

The Lord reminds you today, "Look how far you have come!" He is a proud Father, reflecting with you on all that you have overcome, all the obstacles that you have navigated, and every time you said yes to God and no to temptation. Make this a celebration day, and see the things in your life that He is rejoicing in with you.

At the same time, God is smashing every demonic mirror which would want to reflect back to you distortions and lies about your journey thus far. These mirrors want you to focus on the negatives. The voice of the enemy would highlight the shadows, saying, along with what he wants you to focus on, "Well, you could have done better. You didn't do very well did you?"

But in this moment Father God smashes those evil mirrors and allows you to see your life's passage as He sees it. God is saying to you, "Let us celebrate together the truth of what you have accomplished and conquered by faith. I am proud of your yeses, and I celebrate you today."

So we smash those demonic mirrors and reflections together; we disperse every demonic shadow, and we agree that you will only see and celebrate the things that the Lord is celebrating over you and your life.

ACTION

Take time to reflect with God on the past few months and year. Allow the Holy Spirit to show you where you have reasons to celebrate, even the "small wins" but also the huge decisions of faith that enabled great forward movement. Rejoice and give thanks over personal, relational, and financial decisions that enabled you to be a better steward of all that the Lord has given you, all those good life choices and biblical value choices that you have made. Write them down and celebrate each one as God says to you again, "Look how far you have come!" Well done, you!

DAY 110

The Expanse of My Love

I pray that out of his glorious riches he may strengthen you with power through his Spirit in your inner being, so that Christ may dwell in your hearts through faith. And I pray that you, being rooted and established in love, may have power, together with all the Lord's holy people, to grasp how wide and long and high and deep is the love of Christ, and to know this love that surpasses knowledge—that you may be filled to the measure of all the fullness of God (Ephesians 3:16–19).

Take in the expanse of My love for you. Truly take it in! Sit and look at it in the spirit. Look at how deep, how wide, how high it is! Swim in it! Plumb the depths of it! Look at the color of it. Tell Me what you see. Do you believe Me?

My love for you is endless; it cannot be contained. My thoughts of you never stop. My desire to be with you cannot be quenched! My pleasure and My delight over you cannot be changed.

I tell you today to get to know the extent of My love for you. This revelation will change your life as nothing else can. It will absolutely transform you from the inside out. It will affect your life as nothing else can. Even if you have only known My love for a short while, or for a very long time, come and take in more. Come and bask in it today.

ACTION

This action will help to activate your spiritual sight.

Grab some colored pens or pencils and paper. Then, sit and ask God to show you what His love looks like. Ask Him to show you the size, the color, the nature of it. Draw what He shows you until you can see it clearly. You don't have to be a great artist to do this! Don't be tempted to draw a red heart and then stop there! You may draw multiple pictures, scribbles, or doodles as the Holy Spirit begins to show you more about His wide, long, high, and deep love for you.

As you work with your pencils or pens, you are seeing what the Holy Spirit wants to show you; your spiritual sight is being activated. Then, as the word above says, swim, bask, soak in what you have seen—His great love for you!

DAY 111

You'll Never Find the End of His Love!

Yesterday we returned to a wonderful passage of Scripture that has appeared already a few times in this book, activating our spiritual sight to see what the Father's love for you looks like. Today we continue to push yet deeper into His love. Don't let your new familiarity with this verse switch you off to the wonders still to be discovered:

> *And I pray that you, being rooted and established in love, may have power, together with all the Lord's holy people, to grasp how wide and long and high and deep is the love of Christ, and to know this love that surpasses knowledge—that you may be filled to the measure of all the fullness of God* (Ephesians 3:17–19).

You will never find the end of My expansive love for you; it is an unmappable and endless ocean. My love for you is not frugal, scarce, rare, or limited. It does not come and go or change with the season. My love is never-ending, all-consuming, ever-present, and always available. My love is not a "petal-picking" kind of love, where I love you one day and then love-you-not the next. My affection for you is constant and consistent in every way, without a trace of wavering or shifting or changing.

As My love for you pours out, will you let yourself be loved by Me? Will you give Me access to your innermost parts, the places that sting and that are uncomfortable, and let Me fill you with affection? Will you swing wide the doors of your heart and let Me in?

The level of love you *feel* is not dependent on the level of love that I have for you but instead on the level of *access* that you give to Me. Do not be closed off to Me or selectively open small parts of you for My love. I am a jealous God, jealous for *all* of you and not just part of you. I long to saturate every molecule of your body, every thought in your head, every emotion in your heart, every hair on your head, your skin, your bones, and your cells with My undivided affection. Let Me love you, My child!

DECREE

Because of our past experiences, sometimes we believe that we are unworthy of the love of God or we resist being loved by Him. It's important to pray these key phrases out loud:

- I let You love me.

- I give You access to all of me so I can receive all of You.

- I am worthy of Your love because You say so.
- Your love for me is not dependent on how I feel.
- I let You wash me with Your affection.
- I receive Your lavish outpouring of love in my life today.

DAY 112

A Contented Heart

Peace I leave with you; my peace I give you. I do not give to you as the world gives. Do not let your hearts be troubled and do not be afraid (John 14:27).

I heard God cry, "Here comes a piece of Heaven!" At this, the heavens were torn, and I saw the hand of God coming, like a precision-specialist surgeon, to target your heart today. God pushed through the skin barrier and fully rested His open hand on your heart area; His fingers glowed with electricity, and divine energy flowed, bringing an immediate reset. New life came into your body. This connection between the divine and the human established a new rhythm and disseminated around your body a sense of ease and contentment.

Then I heard God say: "My Son walked this earth and maintained a settled inner rhythm that was not overturned or undermined by the significantly serious situations that He faced. I want your rhythms to match His so that a new sense of inner relief and tranquility may take up a perpetual place inside you."

God is seeking to end the days of emotional boom and bust, ending the patterns of being tossed around by every wind of change that blows in. This is a day of receiving inner stability and inner certainty for you are not bereft of hope or devoid of a secure future. The certainty of your eternal home now speaks inside you and has the dominant voice that drowns out other sounds that drive and rule you.

He says: "This ends the days where you had to pretend that you were doing well. For there were times that you spoke and looked like all was going well but internally you were jam-packed with doubts and significant stress."

This peace that is being deposited on the inside of you is stitched into you by God with the words, *"Peace I leave with you."* Be still and know that something that will endure has been infused into you today.

DECREE

Declare: "From today I number among those who have had heart surgery from God and my insides receive Heaven's peace. I let it merge with all that I am. My whole frame welcomes the peace of God and chooses to not eject it but to allow it to fully become who I am."

Your Redeemer Has Sewn You a Fine Robe

He told them this parable: "No one tears a piece out of a new garment to patch an old one. Otherwise, they will have torn the new garment, and the patch from the new will not match the old" (Luke 5:36).

I saw the Lord sewing together a garment of bright chain mail. The robe that He was fashioning was made of precious metal, finely woven together. It was made to be light to wear and moved freely with no hindrance. He was stitching it together to fit you perfectly—a made-to-measure garment that would cover you from head to toe. Despite being made of strong, protective metal, it was easy to see that it would hang lightly from your shoulders; this is not a suit of armor that will weigh you down.

As He looked down at His handiwork, still carefully putting the chain mail links together, the metal glistened in the bright light that shone from His face. This strong and precious robe reflects His light.

When He came to dress you in this robe of bright, light armor, Jesus tore off every layer of clothing that you had been wearing before. Nothing of the old remained, and He covered you completely with His brilliant, new robe. As He stepped back to admire how you looked, He beamed a huge, warm smile and declared, "That's better!"

As I watched from the sidelines of this vision, I couldn't help but blurt out, "That must have cost a million...no, a billion!"

Jesus smiled and said, "The new covenant was established by My blood, not paid for by money." As He spoke His next line, He looked straight into *your* eyes and said, "I made it for you. I am your God, and you are Mine. I have forgiven your sin and redeemed you. Know Me."

Beloved, you are part of a new, complete, faultless covenant that your Redeemer has made for you. It is bright and strong and will not fail. You have not simply been patched up. Wear your new life well!

ACTION

Read more about the new covenant that Jesus made for you by reading the following passages:

- Jeremiah 31:31–34

- Luke 22:14–20

- Hebrews 8–9

DAY 114

Love Bombs

Your love, Lord, reaches to the heavens, your faithfulness to the skies. Your righteousness is like the highest mountains, your justice like the great deep. You, Lord, preserve both people and animals. How priceless is your unfailing love, O God! People take refuge in the shadow of your wings (Psalm 36:5–7).

There are explosions of God's love that He desires to release out of the midst of you. You are fully loaded with explosive power, a force of passionate, uncontainable love that is ready to be unleashed to do some incredible reversing of damage. You are a bomb of love, ready to detonate!

Strongholds will come down with this "supernatural love dynamite" that is going to be released from you. Strongholds in your own life and those of your family and your community and places of work will be destroyed. There is a force of love that is set to repeat detonation in you.

There is a force inside you that God now is releasing. Be explosive! Be the force of love. Allow the catalyst of love inside of you to be released.

ACTION

Ask the Lord where you are to release and detonate this "love force" that is inside you. There will be a variety of places and people God brings to your mind by His Spirit. Ask the Lord what the release of this will look like. There is a range of ways that His love will be manifested, such as practical acts, prayers, releases of worship, demonstrations of faith, physical gifts, and unique actions. All these are available to you as the Lord inspires you.

Every time you initiate these there will be an explosion of forceful love that takes out enemy strongholds and releases captives. Release your love weapons; they never run out!

DAY 115

Refined Gold

In all this you greatly rejoice, though now for a little while you may have had to suffer grief in all kinds of trials. These have come so that the proven genuineness of your faith—of greater worth than gold, which perishes even though refined by fire—may result in praise, glory and honor when Jesus Christ is revealed. Though you have not seen him, you love him; and even though you do not see him now, you believe in him and are filled with an inexpressible and glorious joy, for you are receiving the end result of your faith, the salvation of your souls (1 Peter 1:6–9).

I am the God who tests the hearts of men. Do not despair at this, but take heart! You have been through difficult seasons; you have been through hidden seasons. Each one is and has been an opportunity to come out as pure, refined gold. For you do not live for this temporal world or for what blessings may come tomorrow, but I created you to live with eternity branded upon your heart.

With eternity in mind, you endure just as Jesus endured the cross. With eternity in mind, you allow Me to do the work that needs to be done in the hidden places. With eternity in mind, you look forward to being one who has become pure gold, refined in the fire. Know this—I work all things out for the good of those who love Me (see Rom. 8:28), those who call upon My name, who walk with Me in the dark valleys. Walk forward knowing that there is joy ahead!

If you are in a hidden place, yield to My hand. If you are in a dark, difficult valley, allow Me to guide you. If you are in a winter season, allow My love to cultivate, nurture, and prepare the soil of your heart for the day of flourishing.

RECEIVE

If you are able, sit in a dark closet or a dark space, and pray about the darkness in your life. Pray about what has been hidden or if you have felt hidden, ask Him why. Pray about the areas where you feel confined. Give these things to the Lord, and ask Him to show you what is ahead.

Ask Him to show you how Jesus endured the cross for the joy that was set before Him (see Heb. 12:2). Allow the Lord to renew your vision, your strength, and your hope so that you can grab hold of an eternal perspective. And then, open the door of the closet, step out, and walk into the light, free from all confinement. Do this as a prophetic act but, as you do, you are spiritually stepping into a greater sense of freedom and openness today!

Trauma Healed

He will cover you with his feathers, and under his wings you will find refuge; his faithfulness will be your shield and rampart. You will not fear the terror of night, nor the arrow that flies by day, nor the pestilence that stalks in the darkness, nor the plague that destroys at midday (Psalm 91:4–6).

I saw the Lord take you into a refuge, a place of safety and healing. As He brought you in, the Lord started to minister to your memories and the places of your mind where you feel trapped. And He said, "I come today as wonderful Counselor to renovate your mind and release you from the power that trauma has had over your daily life. This is a day of significance, of significant healing, where trauma shifts and in its place a hope for the future comes.

"I am drilling deep—not you! I am doing the healing—not you! I am releasing your mind from bondage—not you! Do not strive or try and make this happen. Let Me do what I do best: heal you! Sit back, open up and let Me heal you. Sit back, open up, and let Me set you free. All you need to do today is be still and say yes!"

This is an Exodus 14:14 moment when *"The Lord will fight for you; you need only to be still."* Find a still place and let God minister to you today, healing you from the inside out. Watch trauma flee as freedom rolls in!

RECEIVE

Pray: "Father God, I recognize that there have been moments in my life that have caused me pain and trauma. Yet, I recognize that You are the Healer. I declare that You are my Healer! Today I open up and receive Your healing oil to come to the sore places, the painful places, the areas of my heart that are loaded with trauma or fear or shock. I choose to let You in, and I give You permission to heal as You wish. Lord, heal me today as I glorify You and lift Your name up."

DAY 117

Eternity in Your Heart

He has made everything beautiful in its time. He has also set eternity in the human heart; yet no one can fathom what God has done from beginning to end (Ecclesiastes 3:11).

One of the absolute wonders that is gifted to us at our creation is the ability to grasp the *reality of eternity*. Not that we *pretend* to understand it, but rather that we are to be settled in our ordinary, everyday life, because we truly, really understand eternity as a secure reality. In other words:

- It *is* going to happen.
- It *is* hidden in my heart.
- From its position in me, my whole life can be framed around the security and certainty of my heavenly eternal home.

I heard the Lord say today, "Cast your anchor forward; pick up your hope and throw it with force into the certainty of your forever future!" We are to anchor ourselves outside of this world and into the promise of eternity. Our security does not come from our determination to build well here and to provide for our retirement on planet Earth. Rather, if you can hurl forward an anchor outside of the framework of this finite planet and into the security of the infinite Kingdom of God, you will thrive with an enhanced level of understanding that is necessary for you to live securely *now*.

Throwing an anchor into eternity means that your stability comes from those things which will last forever, rather than anything in this temporal space. Once you see a glimpse of the eternal, you can weather very brutal storms here below. Casting your anchor forward is God's way of enabling you to be so balanced and stable that you can navigate, without mental shattering, what must happen as God shakes nations. Casting your anchor forward is about securing a mindset that means you can be in the world, but not subject to its desire to unravel you.

DECREE

I am exceptionally certain that my forever home is in resurrection with God. I decree that my hope is placed fully on the promises of God that a room has been prepared for me in my Father's house (see John 14:2). I anchor myself into that future reality. I bless my heart to grasp the stability and security of Heaven. I anchor myself in my forever home in the new Heaven and new earth (see Isa. 65:17; Rev. 21:1).

DAY 118

You Are Lovely

Dark am I, yet lovely, daughters of Jerusalem, dark like the tents of Kedar, like the tent curtains of Solomon (Song of Songs 1:5).

Don't be in two minds about who you are to God. He sees you as lovely; He sees you as worthy.

The Shulammite woman who sings in Song of Songs wrestles with who she is. On the one hand, she seems to feel shame at her tanned features (weather-beaten from working in the fields), but then she reminds herself that she is lovely because she's heard her lover, the shepherd king, tell her so.

She flips back to unworthiness, describing herself as like the dusty, dark tents of the nomads of Kedar before changing her mind again, telling her friends that she's like the tent curtains of Solomon (who, as the richest ruler on earth, surely had the finest linen tapestries in the holy temple).

You are not dirty, dusty, or unworthy. You are not a nomad, wandering in the dry desert. Jesus, the Shepherd King, found you, sang His song over you, washed you clean, and called you His holy tabernacle, His dwelling place. He made you worthy, and He called you "lovely." Don't flip-flop about who you are; find your identity in Him.

How beautiful you are, my darling! Oh, how beautiful! Your eyes are doves (Song of Songs 1:15).

RECEIVE

Thank Jesus for loving you, finding you, rescuing you, washing you clean by His blood, making you worthy, making you lovely. Give thanks to Him as a besotted, head-over-heels lover would.

Depending on your life experiences, you may need to work hard to do this, putting aside any uncomfortableness and awkwardness at expressing vulnerable emotions to Jesus. Really push yourself to get over any discomfort. It will be worth it!

Do You Know Jesus Loves You Deeply?
Part 1

Five times in John's Gospel he describes himself as the disciple Jesus loved:

> *One of them, the disciple whom Jesus loved, was reclining next to him* (John 13:23).
>
> *When Jesus saw his mother there, and the disciple whom he loved standing nearby, he said to her...* (John 19:26).
>
> *Mary Magdalene went to the tomb....She came running to Simon Peter and the other disciple, the one Jesus loved...* (John 20:1–2).
>
> *Then the disciple whom Jesus loved said to Peter...* (John 21:7).
>
> *Peter turned and saw that the disciple whom Jesus loved was following them* (John 21:20).

Have you ever thought that this phrase is rather boastful? When John first calls himself this, we might excuse its implied favoritism, but to go on repeating it seems like the height of arrogance!

Perhaps when you read these verses, you struggle more with feelings of resentment: "Jesus seems to have His favorites and I don't feel like one of them!" This can lead to an awful sense of insecurity in us and even jealousy of our brothers and sisters. We then uselessly strain ourselves to try to gain Jesus's love!

We must remember that Jesus did not love John any more than He loves you and me. The only difference is that John *knew* he was loved. The title John gave himself was not him being arrogant but was instead an indication of his sense of assurance. John never thought he was any more loved than the other disciples. (In chapter 11 we read John writing that Jesus loved Lazarus and his two sisters as well!) John's identity was secure in the love of Christ.

We all need to be able to say about ourselves, as a statement of joyful truth: I am (insert your name), the disciple whom Jesus loves!

ACTION

Do you know that Jesus loves you? Do you really know? You can know more by doing the following:

- Meditating on Calvary and especially the verse, *"Greater love has no man than this: to lay down one's life for one's friends"* (John 15:13). Jesus has already loved you to death!

- Experience the witness of the Holy Spirit. It is the Spirit who pours out the love of God into our hearts (see Rom. 5:5). Ask someone to pray with you.

Do You Know Jesus Loves You Deeply?
Part 2

When John, the disciple whom Jesus loved, wrote his first pastoral letter to the church, he addresses the believers in the same way six times:

> Dear friends, I am not writing you a new command but an old one, which you have had since the beginning (1 John 2:7).
>
> Dear friends, now we are children of God, and what we will be has not yet been made known. But we know that when Christ appears, we shall be like him, for we shall see him as he is (1 John 3:2).
>
> Dear friends, if our hearts do not condemn us, we have confidence before God and receive from him anything we ask (1 John 3:21–22).
>
> Dear friends, do not believe every spirit, but test the spirits to see whether they are from God (1 John 4:1).
>
> Dear friends, let us love one another, for love comes from God (1 John 4:7).
>
> Dear friends, since God so loved us, we also ought to love one another (1 John 4:11).

When he says "Dear friends," he uses the same title that he used of himself when writing his Gospel. He says *agapētos*—deeply loved disciples.[1]

Your Bible translation may have it as "Dear friends" or perhaps "Beloved," but the point John is making should be very clear to us: the description that he used for himself is also the description he applies to us, the church. We are the same as he is, *deeply loved disciples*.

ACTION

- Reread the verses above, only this time instead of *"Dear friends"* substitute *"Deeply loved disciples."*

- Now add your name, for example: "Deeply loved (first name), now we are children of God."

- What impact does this way of reading the Word of God have on you?

- When you think about yourself today, why don't you add "deeply loved disciple" to your thoughts and see how your thinking is transformed!

NOTE

1. With the words "Dear friends" John addresses his letter to *agapētoi*, also translated as "beloved" (plural). Throughout John's Gospel he refers to himself as "the disciple whom Jesus loved."

CHAPTER 5

Miraculous Power

DAY 121

A Breakthrough Anointing

So David and his troops went up to Baal-perazim and defeated the Philis-tines there. "God did it!" David exclaimed. "He used me to burst through my enemies like a raging flood!" So they named that place Baal-perazim (which means "the Lord who bursts through") (1 Chronicles 14:11 NLT).

The Holy Spirit is imparting new strength to you for breaking others through. This "breakthrough anointing" is for the purpose of helping others to progress where they have become stuck or reached an impasse. Believe in Him and the strength that He gives you. This is a supernatural strength that achieves things for other people that would otherwise be unlikely, too difficult, or even impossible.

Where someone, it could be a friend or it could be a stranger, is strug-gling with a problem, challenge, or desperate situation, you must apply your prayers with a new faith and with a sure and certain belief that the Lord God Almighty will break through even the most seemingly helpless of situations.

Picture a weak and tired person trying to open a door that is jammed tightly shut. They are exhausted from their efforts to push it open. Now a second person arrives on the scene. Even though they don't look any stronger than the first person, when they apply their shoulder to the door, it spectacularly bursts open.

You are that second person who will push through for others. Believe in the strength that the Spirit will give you for the right situations. Be on the lookout for those who need a prayer warrior to break them through. Your simple obedience will bring miraculous freedom into a myriad of complex situations that people are facing. Be ready!

RECEIVE

Pray: "Holy Spirit, thank You for this new strength that You are giving me. I am ready to receive it. Help me to be on the lookout for situations that need me to be Your agent of breakthrough for others. I refuse to part-ner with the doubt and despair of the people who I encounter but instead choose to be obedient to You, trusting that You will enable me for times like these. Lord, renew my mind, that I might know what it is to be a strong solution, even when it seems to be impossible. Lord, I believe and trust in You. Amen."

DAY 122

Our God Is Able!

When was the last time you thanked God for being able? I cannot think of anything that would be more depressing than if I were to believe in a God who did *not* have the power to carry out His plans and keep His promises!

The Apostle Paul often celebrated the ability of God and His limitless power to act on our behalf:

> *Now to him who is able to do immeasurably more than all we can ask or imagine, according to his power that is at work within us, to him be glory in the church and in Christ Jesus throughout all generations, for ever and ever! Amen* (Ephesians 3:20–21).

Again, in his letter to the Romans:

> *Now to him who is able to establish you in accordance with my gospel, the message I proclaim about Jesus Christ…to the only wise God be glory forever through Jesus Christ! Amen* (Romans 16:25, 27).

And one more in the Book of Jude:

> *To him who is able to keep you from stumbling and present you before his glorious presence without fault and with great joy—to the only God our Savior be glory, majesty, power and authority, through Jesus Christ our Lord, before all ages, now and forevermore! Amen* (Jude 24–25).

Our God is able! Why is this so important to grasp? It is vital because your spiritual growth is governed by the greatness of your God. If your God is small in your mind, you will be small spiritually speaking. If His power is limited, so will yours be. It is of great consequence that we know and celebrate *the God who is able* because your spiritual maturity will be in proportion to the greatness of the God you know.

ACTION

According to Daniel 11:32, the people who know their God shall be strong and do exploits. What exploits for God are you going to do today in celebration of the truth that our God is able?

DAY 123

The Mindset of My Abundant Power

There's more to come: We continue to shout our praise even when we're hemmed in with troubles, because we know how troubles can develop passionate patience in us, and how that patience in turn forges the tempered steel of virtue, keeping us alert for whatever God will do next. In alert expectancy such as this, we're never left feeling shortchanged. Quite the contrary—we can't round up enough containers to hold everything God generously pours into our lives through the Holy Spirit! (Romans 5:3–5 MSG)

And behold, I am sending the promise of my Father upon you. But stay in the city until you are clothed with power from on high (Luke 24:49 ESV).

There is more in you than is currently being revealed; there is more power to flow from you, more healing to be released by you, more revelation to be spoken through you, more miracles to be seen by your hands. There is more!

I heard the Lord say: "It is time to tear the mindset of rationed power off your life. I do not give you My power in small portions at set times of the day. You *always* have the fullness of power within you, dormant and ready for you to act in order for it to be released. So do not think that I am stingy or frugal in the distribution of My miracle-working power to My people. I give it all to you, and I watch and wait to see what you will do with it."

The Lord is training in you the mindset of abundant power. This mindset empowers you to live life, always knowing that you carry miracle-working ability from God on your insides. Where low-level expectation has tried to cloud your faith and reduce your impact, the Lord says, "Throw it off and run into the waters of the 'more' that I have made available, in and through you."

And so the Lord says: "Lay hands on your head and decree unbelief to shift. Decree expectation to increase! Decree that you have faith for the more! Decree that you carry explosive miracle-working power on your insides! Decree that there is abundant power at your disposal by My Spirit in you. Decree it and believe it!"

ACTION

Make a "faith list." What are you believing for? Write out a list of promises and dreams, and start to stir your faith to see the impossible made possible.

The Heroic Example

And now, compelled by the Spirit, I am going to Jerusalem, not knowing what will happen to me there. I only know that in every city the Holy Spirit warns me that prison and hardships are facing me. However, I consider my life worth nothing to me; my only aim is to finish the race and complete the task the Lord Jesus has given me—the task of testifying to the good news of God's grace (Acts 20:22–24).

The apostle considered his life worth nothing to him. For so many who desire to walk in the spiritual gifts, Paul, through whom *"God did extraordinary miracles"* (Acts 19:11) was one who rightly understood where these gifts originate. His only goal and motivation were to see Christ glorified and, out of that place, came the miracles.

Today I hear the Lord asking His devoted ones, "What are you holding on to? Is it your reputation, your family, your home, your finances, your plans, or your dreams?"

It's like we've gathered these earthly treasures, and we've put them deep down in our hearts to keep them safe. Yet He's asking if each one of us will take those well-loved things and place them at His feet. Will we entrust them to Him? Is He worth our trust? Is He worth our lives?

Those in relatively comfortable, wealthy, and free nations have not yet faced the persecutions and extreme opposition that the Apostle Paul did, yet he still teaches us through his example. For in the laying down of his life, he was then filled with the life of Jesus. In counting his own life worth nothing, he was able to fix his eyes and set his purpose on expanding the Kingdom of God. Those signs and extraordinary miracles were then the natural outflow of one who lived for the glory of Him—our Lord Jesus.

And He challenges you today: "Will you let Paul be just a hero and a good story to read, or will you follow his example and live as he did?"

ACTION

A word like this requires time to process through journaling, prayer, and meditation on these Scriptures. A good place to start would be to list those things, people, and places that you hold so dear to your heart. Ask the Lord if you have held them so tightly that it is now holding you back? Ask Him if there is anything that you love more than you love Him? Ask Him what these things, people, or places look like when He is rightly prioritized.

Dive In! Open and Experience Your Gifts!

There are different kinds of gifts, but the same Spirit distributes them (1 Corinthians 12:4).

In the spirit, I saw some partially unwrapped gift boxes at your feet. One or two were torn enough that the present inside had been taken out. Other gift boxes close to you have had their wrapping peeled back, enough to glimpse at what's inside, but then have been forgotten and discarded. Still, others are slightly off to the side and are as pristine as they were on the day they were given to you. They remain untouched.

Following this image, the Lord asks, "Why have you not opened and experienced what I have gifted to you, My child?"

There has been a palpable sense of anticipation from the Lord, as He waits for you to open and experience the gifts He has wrapped and laid out for you. God is patient as you take your time to open and experience each one. And yet, He is also eager with anticipation, desiring for you to grab each box and rip open the wrapping paper like an excited child would open a gift—not carefully taking their time, just desperately trying to get to the present!

Apprehend all the spiritual gifts God has given you today. They are all yours! What are you waiting for? Dive into the spiritual gifts that are laid out and available before you.

ACTION

The nine gifts of the Spirit given to each one of us are listed in First Corinthians 12. Consider each one and speak to God about them in turn. Apprehend every gift God has given you; unwrap each one in your prayers. Tell the Lord that you gladly receive each one of the spiritual gifts available to you and that you know that you have received each one by faith. Ask the Lord for opportunities to utilize and activate each gift at the right time. Practice using each one as you recognize it in your life:

- A message of wisdom
- A message of knowledge
- Faith
- Healing
- Miraculous powers

- Prophecy
- Distinguishing between spirits
- Speaking in different kinds of tongues
- Interpretation of tongues

DAY 126

A Force Inside You

But you will receive power when the Holy Spirit comes on you; and you will be my witnesses in Jerusalem, and in all Judea and Samaria, and to the ends of the earth (Acts 1:8).

Perhaps one of the greatest tragedies of the Spirit-filled church is her measurement of what hosting the Spirit of God looks like. For years we have elevated the gift of tongues to be the sign of our baptism in the Holy Spirit. We seem to have made the gift of tongues our ultimate measurement in terms of being spiritually awake. Then, when altar calls for the baptism of the Spirit are made, we demand tongues as the sign that something has happened. And yet Scripture gives us a very different rhythm and measurement of the Spirit's work.

Jesus explained that we would receive power when the Holy Spirit came. Jesus's measurement of your hosting of His Spirit has always been that you *move in power*! The New Testament Greek word for *power* is *dunamis* (from which we derive the modern word *dynamite*), but the primary meaning of *dunamis* is actually "force." Therefore, "You shall receive *a force* when the Holy Spirit comes" is perhaps a better way to interpret Acts 1. We are supposed to pulsate with power and radiate that power as an everyday part of our Christian experience!

This power is not for the domination of other people, but it is to be radically used for the invasion of the kingdom of darkness! Your call is to be a forceful, invading child of God, where you take territory from satan by forcefully and deliberately exuding the Spirit of God.

- Healing miracles are a forceful invasion of satan's kingdom of infirmity.

- Deliverance ministry is a forceful invasion of satan's kingdom of human oppression.

- Prophetic ministry is a forceful invasion of satan's kingdom of lies, where people have believed falsehoods about themselves. Prophecy reestablishes truthful destiny.

- Worship ministry is a forceful invasion of satan's kingdom where idols proliferate.

- Prayer ministry is a forceful invasion of satan's kingdom, pushing back demonic blueprints.

Are you biblically forceful about spiritual matters? Are you biblically forceful whenever and wherever you see satan's kingdom of darkness in action? Do you *think* forcefully with an invasion mindset when it comes to aspects of life that need transformation?

ACTION

Give yourself permission to believe that you are a carrier of the forceful invasion capabilities of God's Spirit! You are trusted to hold the full weight of the force of God. Allow that to marinate in your spirit and captivate your heart, thus ending the days of intimidation that have so rampantly knocked you out!

Retrained with a Royal Warrior Mindset

The person with the Spirit makes judgments about all things, but such a person is not subject to merely human judgments, for, "Who has known the mind of the Lord so as to instruct him?" But we have the mind of Christ (1 Corinthians 2:15–16).

It is time to train yourself to believe, live and speak like one who has the mind of Christ. Have you been guilty of speaking ungodly beliefs about yourself or situations? Evidence of ungodly beliefs can be found in sentences that begin with something like the following:

- I will never manage this.

- This is impossible.

- I'm going to be sick or die.

- I'm destined to fail or I'm a failure.

- This situation is beyond hope/irredeemable.

- Nobody loves me, cares for me, or listens to me.

These are not the words of a royal warrior in God's Kingdom army! Don't speak these words over your life. Resist them when you hear them and be wary of coming into agreement when others whisper them. Let the Holy Spirit be like an alarm bell that sounds a warning when an ungodly belief is expressed or you begin to put on a mindset that is man's, not God's, way of thinking.

But be aware that right now you are probably desensitized to these things, numb to them because of how exposed you have been to the thinking that is all around us in the fallen world. Train yourself to be sensitized to ungodly beliefs and mindsets when you speak them or hear others express them. Invite the Holy Spirit to help you discern when something has been said that you need to break agreement with.

This will take practice and discipline so that you can hear and see when the Spirit's warning buzzer sounds and His red light flashes to warn you! Repent and speak the opposite when you catch yourself falling into satan's trap. You are on an accelerated journey with Jesus, and so it won't be long until Kingdom thinking, not stinking thinking becomes natural to you!

ACTION

If you've been partnering with ungodly beliefs, you may have formed bad habits in your speech or actions. Pray and ask the Holy Spirit to help you recognize when you're acting or speaking in this way. Then, be sure to correct yourself out loud so that you can begin to retrain yourself in the speech, actions, and habits of a royal warrior! Use Scripture where you can, for example, if you say, "I will never manage this..." then speak out the opposite using biblical truths such as, *"I can do all things through Christ who strengthens me"* (Phil. 4:13 NKJV).

DAY 128

Learning a New Dance

But the fruit of the Spirit is love, joy, peace, forbearance, kindness, goodness, faithfulness, gentleness and self-control. Against such things there is no law....Since we live by the Spirit, let us keep in step with the Spirit (Galatians 5:22–25).

A growing believer's life is essentially a reflection of the character of God Himself. We are growing into the likeness of His Son, Jesus Christ. That is why it is only possible to be like Him if His Holy Spirit is resident within us. His Spirit produces His fruit.

Some of us may be temperamentally quite patient, and others of us find it easy to be gentle, but the total package of spiritual fruit is grown when God works in us, in our least-like-Him areas. It's remarkably easy to congratulate ourselves on the qualities in the Galatians 5 list of fruit that we *already* have, whilst glossing over the areas where we are weak. But God grows *all* this fruit on the same tree, and the real sign of the Spirit's indwelling is a marked change in our areas of personal weakness.

This fruit does not come so spontaneously as to be without our cooperation and human effort. We are to crucify the sinful nature and *"keep in step with the Spirit"* (Gal. 5:24–25). Both of these are active commands. Keeping in step with the Spirit suggests watching Him very carefully and following, putting our feet where He puts His feet, much like learning a dance routine. Where He walks, we go; how He moves, we move. It's a close and cooperating partnership, fluid harmony, not wrenching effort. Eventually, it becomes second nature—quite literally—for we have a new nature now that our old nature has been crucified with Christ.

The fruit of the Spirit is at the core of what spiritual growth and maturity are all about. It will inevitably come in your life as you abide in the Spirit of Jesus (see John 15). So the good news is to stay in the vine; keep receiving the unceasing flow of life and nourishment from God.

ACTION

Pray: "Lord, I know which fruit of the Spirit I'm not manifesting well. I bring that area to You and commit myself to cooperate until Your Spirit produces real change in me. I decide to be among the 'abiders' from today on."

DAY 129

Marked for Miracles

Very truly I tell you, whoever believes in me will do the works I have been doing, and they will do even greater things than these, because I am going to the Father. And I will do whatever you ask in my name, so that the Father may be glorified in the Son. You may ask me for anything in my name, and I will do it (John 14:12–14).

And God was doing extraordinary miracles by the hands of Paul (Acts 19:11 ESV).

In the Spirit, I watched as parts of you started to glow bright white with the power of God: your mouth, your hands, your feet. They all started to glow under the power. As I watched this, the voice of God spoke: "I have marked you for miracles! I have marked your mouth to decree words that break chains and set captives free. I have marked your hands to release healing and wholeness to the sick, the ill, and the dying. I have marked your feet to release vibrations of My miracle-working power into every room, geographical location, and place you tread. Do not underestimate the weight of power that I have already marked you with."

So this is the day to stretch forth your hand and believe that healing will be released! This is the day to speak forth with boldness as chains break and captives are liberated. This is the day to tread with confidence and to walk forth knowing that with every step the Kingdom is being manifest.

As your hands, mouth, and feet continued to glow brighter, the Lord began to laugh, not in a mocking way but in a joyous way. And as He laughed, He continued to say: "Do not underestimate the measure of My power that I have put in you. I have marked you for miracles! I have marked you for miracles! I have marked you for miracles!"

ACTION

Therefore, in light of what God has said to you, discard your thoughts of inadequacy or the self-questioning "Can I or can't I?" Decree with God that "I am marked for miracles!" and start to make bold faith decisions that release the power of God that you already carry the capacity to perform.

Through Faith

I do not have time to tell about Gideon, Barak, Samson and Jephthah, about David and Samuel and the prophets, who through faith conquered kingdoms, administered justice, and gained what was promised; who shut the mouths of lions, quenched the fury of the flames, and escaped the edge of the sword; whose weakness was turned to strength; and who became powerful in battle and routed foreign armies. Women received back their dead, raised to life again. There were others who were tortured, refusing to be released so that they might gain an even better resurrection. Some faced jeers and flogging, and even chains and imprisonment. They were put to death by stoning; they were sawed in two; they were killed by the sword. They went about in sheepskins and goatskins, destitute, persecuted and mistreated—the world was not worthy of them. They wandered in deserts and mountains, living in caves and in holes in the ground (Hebrews 11:32–38).

The world was not worthy of them! These men and women of faith did mighty exploits for the Kingdom through faith! They sought a better Kingdom for they received the promise of the Messiah, and by faith, they lived in expectation of Him!

"Oh, My sons and daughters, you are living in that better Kingdom! You are called to join your faith with the faith of all who went before you and to do these same exploits! The men and women in this list were not more exceptional than you are! They faced difficulties, challenges, fear, insecurity, and loneliness, just as you do. Yet you have the privilege of knowing Jesus and having the indwelling of My Holy Spirit! You have daily empowerment! You have daily access to this life!

"So, as you read this, look to Me and cry out for more! Do not be satisfied with the life you have led so far. For the same Spirit that raised Christ from the dead dwells in you, so have faith! Believe My Word and step out. Listen for My voice and have faith; I will do what I have said. Through faith begin to boldly conquer the things that come against you to hold you back from being who I have called you to be—one who walks by faith! Through faith begin to see yourself as one who is equipped with the life and power that comes from Me! See yourself as one who operates in the gifts of the Spirit, one who hears My voice clearly, and one who is not dismayed or deterred by difficulty. See yourself by faith!"

DECREE

Read through the entire chapter of Hebrews 11. Underline the parts that thrill your soul and write out the sections that inspire you! Let this truth go deep within you, and then declare out loud: *"The Spirit of Him who raised Jesus from the dead dwells in* [me], *He who raised Christ Jesus from the dead also gives life to your mortal bodies through His Spirit who dwells in* [me]!" (Romans 8:11 NASB).

With your spiritual eyes, your eyes of faith, see Him living and dwelling on the inside of you!

DAY 131

Miraculous Powers

This salvation, which was first announced by the Lord, was confirmed to us by those who heard him. God also testified to it by signs, wonders and various miracles, and by gifts of the Holy Spirit distributed according to his will (Hebrews 2:3–4).

"My child, I have put the ability for miraculous power on the inside of you, and I long to make a withdrawal from you in these days ahead. There is a supernatural *dunamis* force and energy that is primed and ready to flow from you. Feel that force and acknowledge its power on the inside of you today. It is surging through you and ready for an outlet. You are ready to explode with supernatural intensity and life at this moment. Feel My supernatural power on the inside of you now; allow Me to surge in you and release My life force through you."

I see the Lord inviting you into a repeated exchange of receiving more of His miraculous life force and then allowing a release of it from you again and again on repeat. This divine exchange comes as you allow the Holy Spirit to reveal to you more of who He is tangibly on the inside of you. Becoming more aware of God and of feeling His force and power, that through you, He will be glorified.

ACTION

Pause and be open to the Spirit, praying: "Holy Spirit, I want to feel Your power and life force flowing on the inside of me in this moment. Please allow me to feel the extent of who You are in me right now."

As you pray, feel for the surge of energy and life that is moving through your body, rising and coursing through all of who you are. Once you are aware of the pulsating energy of the Spirit, begin to ask the Lord, "How and where would You like me to release Your supernatural, miracle-working power?"

Wait on the Lord. You may see it or hear it, or He may give you strong impressions of who, what, and where He would like you to begin to release His miraculous power. Take note. Then, pray into the people and contexts that the Lord has highlighted; speak the words of life that flow from you over them and into those situations. Ask the Lord if there are any other actions required. You may have practical gifts to send, written words to release, decrees to speak, or prophetic acts that the Lord may highlight for you to do. Take note of these, and ask Him when you should action these.

Once you have fulfilled these prayers and actions, expect transformation and testimonies of healing and deliverance to come!

Make this a regular exercise until releasing who God is on the inside of you becomes so natural that you don't even have to think about the process anymore! To Him be the glory!

You Are a Missionary

He told them, "The harvest is plentiful, but the workers are few. Ask the Lord of the harvest, therefore, to send out workers into his harvest field" (Luke 10:2).

God is reactivating your missionary DNA. In you is the ability to cry with a loud voice, "Father God, give me souls!" and then to see this cry become a reality. Your ability to lead people to faith in Jesus Christ is about to radically increase.

We are so easily tempted to pray more about ourselves than for a harvest of souls in our nation. Our self-focus has hindered revival in our nation; at times we want God to move so that *we* feel better, rather than contending for an increase in the family of God so that *everyone* feels better for all eternity. Our temporary focus on the immediate life that we are living today has hijacked our eternal understanding of what will happen to those who don't believe. We fixate on the small, transient rhythms of life, rather than embracing long-reaching understandings of strategic planning for harvest in a nation.

We do not tend to want to think about anything negative in the afterlife, but we must have a more robust understanding of the reality that many do not have the promise of being with Jesus forever to hold onto.

Today God is touching your tongue so that you might be reinvigorated to contend for the harvest and to call it in. God is saying, "Decree a shift in the church back into its missionary mode, for the church has forgotten that she is a missionary movement."

The only way to save nations is with the church becoming once again a mission-focused, outward-looking, advancing movement. God is undertaking a significant course correction in His people so that they easily "gossip the gospel" and display the miraculous power of God with signs, wonders, and miracles. The power of God is not simply given to impress the people already in the church; it is given as a dominant signpost for who God is to those who do not yet know.

As much as you contend for the power of God to course through your veins, you must equally contend for the lost to be witnesses of that power. I heard the Holy Spirit groaning in lament today. He said, "The harvest nets are untouched. It is time to mend the nets, even to remember that you have a net, and then to cast your net." I felt the church in birthing mode, bringing forth a fresh harvest-thinking and missionary-minded generation.

ACTION

I heard the Lord say: "Jump up, jump up high! Stretch your arms in the air and indicate to Me with your physical body that you are all into being reinvigorated as a missionary and reactivated in your missionary DNA."

Set Apart to Do the Impossible

I have given them your word and the world has hated them, for they are not of the world any more than I am of the world. My prayer is not that you take them out of the world but that you protect them from the evil one. They are not of the world, even as I am not of it. Sanctify them by the truth; your word is truth. As you sent me into the world, I have sent them into the world (John 17:14–18).

"I have called you to be set apart and different," says Jesus. "You are not of this world anymore. Its values are not My values and so they must not be yours either. What the world calls a problem or impossible is never too great for Me. Neither should it ever be too great for you."

Don't duck away from situations that require you to bring a heavenly answer and a solution. You are not of this world anymore; you are a commissioned ambassador of the Kingdom of Jesus Christ. It's no longer a time for you to stay silent or look away in embarrassment. You are not here by accident; you are here to be different. It is time for you to go against the flow and speak the opposite of what those who have a worldly mindset say.

Where you once didn't want to stand out like a sore thumb, now you are being encouraged to stand up like a bright beacon—a beacon of hope, creative solutions, and miracle answers. It is time to be a sign and a wonder. Initially, this might feel very awkward as you grapple with the nerves that naturally come when you lift your head above the parapet for the first time. But there has to be that first time, and then the second time, and then the third.

It was the same for the disciples, for Peter, John, and the others. They all had their first attempts of going against the flow and of stepping up to work their first miracle. For you, make today that first time, or if you've tried this before, make today your "next time."

RECEIVE

Pray: "Christ Jesus, I believe in You, just as Your disciples believed in You. Fill me with the fullness of Your Spirit, the same Spirit and power by which You and Your first followers demonstrated Your Kingdom with signs, wonders, and miracles. I'm ready to be different. I repent of my fear of man and what other people think. Fill me with fresh boldness and courage to do all that You have commissioned me to do."

The Spirit's Power

My message and my preaching were not with wise and persuasive words, but with a demonstration of the Spirit's power, so that your faith might not rest on human wisdom, but on God's power (1 Corinthians 2:4–5).

Sometimes the Holy Spirit of God can actually be seen! He made Himself visible when, as a dove, He settled on Jesus at His baptism. As a result, Jesus returned to Galilee *"in the power of the Spirit"* (Luke 4:14). At other times He made His presence visible in different forms, such as when tongues of fire rested on each of the disciples at Pentecost. That was the Holy Spirit in person. Other times, we *feel* His presence rather than *observing* Him. You'll notice a different feeling when the Spirit is empowering you! Jesus and Paul both felt it.

When the Spirit is involved, extraordinary results happen, beyond what mere human words would do. You find words coming into your mouth that you didn't know were about to come out:

> *This is what we speak, not in words taught us by human wisdom but in words taught by the Spirit, explaining spiritual realities with Spirit-taught words* (1 Corinthians 2:13).

The Spirit makes things turn around in unexpected ways, and His presence gives believers a firm footing so that they know afterward that they haven't just been persuaded by clever words:

> *So that your faith might not rest on human wisdom, but on God's power* (1 Corinthians 2:5).

As if that were not enough, He tells us things that we didn't know before! He is a revealer of what God has in mind. And He clarifies things that we were confused about:

> *"What no eye has seen, what no ear has heard, and what no human mind has conceived"—the things God has prepared for those who love him—these are the things God has revealed to us by his Spirit* (1 Corinthians 2:9–10).

He gives us lots of "Aha!" moments, when things fit into place and make sense:

What we have received is not the spirit of the world, but the Spirit who is from God, so that we may understand what God has freely given us (1 Corinthians 2:12).

The Holy Spirit is constantly busy, invading the lives of Christians who want to be effective servants of God, connecting Heaven to earth, bringing the very Spirit of Jesus Himself into our lives.

RECEIVE

Pray: "Lord Jesus, I want all these things that the Spirit can give me—every one of them—so that I don't miss what You want me to do in the Spirit's strength."

DAY 135

Deep Prayer and New Tongues

When the day of Pentecost came, they were all together in one place. Suddenly a sound like the blowing of a violent wind came from heaven and filled the whole house where they were sitting. They saw what seemed to be tongues of fire that separated and came to rest on each of them. All of them were filled with the Holy Spirit and began to speak in other tongues as the Spirit enabled them (Acts 2:1–4).

Today God is setting your mouth on fire! Burning hot with new languages of the Spirit that will enable you to communicate with Him and to pray in step with His heart. I hear the Holy Spirit say: "Expect new tongues today! Expect expansion to your current prayer language, and expect to go deeper as you use it. This is an era of praying in the Spirit, where I am calling you to press in, to press in deeper into Me, My heart, My ways, and My realm. Your prayer language and the new languages that are coming to you will help pull you into My deep places. So use them and pray with a fervent pursuit of My deep places as your goal."

Deep calls to deep in the roar of your waterfalls; all your waves and breakers have swept over me (Psalm 42:7).

As you contend and go deep by praying in the spirit, you are going to find an ease of access to the Spirit of God. Like a slipstream or a slide, you will find yourself very quickly flowing deep into the presence of the Holy Spirit, a place where you are overwhelmed and saturated, and you will emerge with resources and power to go and extend the Kingdom. These new tongues carry power for healing, insight for prophecy, wisdom for decision making, warfare for breaking oppression, and more!

RECEIVE

So, be brave and step out! Welcome God. Allow the Holy Spirit to explode within you! Physically open your mouth and begin to let new prayer languages flow out over your tongue from deep within you.

DAY 136

My Gifts

There are different kinds of gifts, but the same Spirit distributes them. There are different kinds of service, but the same Lord. There are different kinds of working, but in all of them and in everyone it is the same God at work (1 Corinthians 12:4–6).

I hear the Spirit of the Lord asking, "Why do you strive for the gifts? Why do you strive or compete to be seen or heard before men? Why do you eagerly seek out the gifts in order to show others that you have arrived?"

"These gifts are exactly that—GIFTS. They are given to the Body in order that I would be glorified! They are given to the earth in order that I might work in and on the earth! These gifts are for bringing more and more of the Kingdom into the earth in order to displace and destroy the works of darkness. They are never, ever meant to be worked for, compared, or looked at through a lens of achievement.

"And not only that, but they are also not meant to be left unopened. I give gifts so that they will be used, for there are many, many in need of My supernatural power. There are many waiting for you to lay hands on them so that My power might enter and heal their bodies. There are those who need their loved ones raised from the dead because they died before their time. And there are those who just need a word that reveals that I know the secret places of their hearts for they long to be known.

"Yet who will speak that word to them? Who will step out in faith and say, 'Lord, I'm here to be Your vessel! I give You permission to use me in whatever way You desire. I will lay hands on the sick; I will give a word of wisdom. I will open my mouth and give both a tongue and its interpretation so that the Body might be edified.' This is the type of heart I love to see. This is the one to whom I desire to give gifts. Will you be that one?"

ACTION

Allow the Lord to examine your heart to see if you fall into striving or ignoring the gifts as described above. If you need to repent for striving, do so. If you need to study the gifts again in order to stir them up and to make use of them, then spend some time in First Corinthians 12 again today. Speak to Jesus about which gift He'd like you to operate in, and then begin to be diligent in growing in it and making use of it.

DAY 137

Working Closely with Angels

Then the devil left him, and behold, angels came and were ministering to him (Matthew 4:11 ESV).

For he will command his angels concerning you to guard you in all your ways (Psalm 91:11).

The Lord is inviting you into a close working relationship with the angels who minister (see Heb. 1:14). There is a clear call from the Lord to be aware and acknowledge the angels, ministering spirits, who serve and release strength and healing to the members of the Body of Christ.

God is first bringing healing to your own body by angelic impartation, which will impact you personally and help you become more aware of the angelic at work for you and those around you. Then, as you begin to pray and intercede, become more aware of the angelic. As you do, you will learn how to work with the angels who are under God's command in the context of releasing ministry prayers for others. Angels release strength and healing to the Body of Christ. Be aware of how they minister and make yourself available to work with them as the Holy Spirit leads you.

The Spirit of God is urging you to come into alignment with the work of the angels serving under Jesus Christ, Captain of the hosts, as their work intensifies in this era. We, the people of God, should not simply acknowledge their existence but should also understand how to work effectively with them.

ACTION

There is a speed and alignment with Heaven in this that comes when we pray, "I align with You, Jesus Christ, Captain of the heavenly hosts. I come under Your authority. I choose to co-labor with You, Lord, and with the angelic hosts who work for You. Please make me more aware of the angelic in this time so that I can be more effective in working with these supernatural ministers of Yours."

DAY 138

Elisha's Capabilities

Elisha, the prophet who is in Israel, tells the king of Israel the very words you speak in your bedroom (2 Kings 6:12; see also 2 Kings 6; 5:19–27).

Elisha had a remarkable ability, given by God, to not just hear the voice of God but to hear the schemes and plans of men—even in their own bedrooms! God permitted him to know of the private military strategy conversations of the king of Aram. Previously he had demonstrated this when he knew what Naaman and Gehazi had spoken about in private. He was given momentary, specialist capabilities to hear unrighteous conversations so that he could then intervene and bring justice.

God wants to bring righteousness to the earth through you. God is including you in His plans for the justice and judgment priorities that He is out working. The Spirit of the Lord says, "You will not just stand by and watch and hope that I do something sovereign, but you will become spiritually alert and alive, and you will hear and know the schemes of man so that you may, like Elisha, overturn unrighteousness. I have made you in My image and I am spirit. Just as Adam and Eve knew no boundaries to seeing and perceiving the spiritual dimension, so you are going to now come into remarkable understandings. Like Elisha and Elijah, you will navigate the spirit realm differently from your previous experiences. I call you into My plans. I call you to understand what is happening on the earth.

"You will know and hear what sex traffickers are plotting. It will be revealed to you what extremist terrorists are proposing. You will know the location of missing children. I will allow you to hear of unrighteous business practices that are being schemed about in secret back rooms."

God welcomes you today to His "clean up" team and to a level of responsibility and revelation that is remarkable. Once you hear these unrighteous plans, God will empower you to action and to communicate so that intervention can happen to halt the decimation of society.

RECEIVE

The Lord asks you to get on your knees in fear and trembling, that you may receive a level of spiritual ability that Elijah and Elisha knew but that has not been well stewarded in recent decades. On your knees, soberly and seriously receive this weighty spiritual prophetic blessing, that you would perceive in the spirit, as God biblically ordained.

DAY 139

You Are a "Solutionary"

Jesus gave them this answer: "Very truly I tell you, the Son can do nothing by himself; he can do only what he sees his Father doing, because whatever the Father does the Son also does. For the Father loves the Son and shows him all he does. Yes, and he will show him even greater works than these, so that you will be amazed" (John 5:19–20).

I heard God call you a "solutionary"! You are someone who brings solutions where it seems like there are none. He is commissioning you to go into places where those without hope need a word, a prayer, or a manifested miracle to bring about change.

You won't have to look hard to find situations that need Heaven's solutions. Neither will you have to travel to a dark corner of the globe in order to be a solutionary. Every new room you walk into, every person you encounter in the street or at the store, every client or customer you serve, every time you read a social media update are all opportunities waiting for you to bring hope, encouragement, a Scripture truth, a word of revelation, a declaration of faith, or a creative solution.

Don't be too hasty to respond from your own knowledge or opinion. Instead, get used to turning to the Holy Spirit first in every situation. A quick prayer, "Holy Spirit, what do You want me to say or do in this moment?" can be said in the blink of an eye. Then be obedient to what you hear next. Don't overthink it and don't question God, just go for it and watch what He does. This is something you'll mature into until it becomes second nature.

Everything Jesus did came from watching His Father. It's time for you to look to Him, not to yourself, when an answer is needed. It's time to practice being a solutionary!

ACTION

You may not be able to predict all of the situations that Father God is going to lead you into today, but it's still good to be prepared in advance. Write down where you'll be going and what you'll be doing—work, school, a friend's house, shopping, talking on the phone, or sending an email. Then write beside each one a simple decree: "Be a solution." Talk to Jesus about each one, and ask the Holy Spirit to prompt you. A short time of preparation for the day ahead will reap massive rewards for the Kingdom!

DAY 140

Jesus in the Temple
Part 1

It was Passover time and the population of Jerusalem had increased to ten times its normal size, with huge numbers of visitors having to camp out on the surrounding hills. Thousands gathered around the temple area to pray, to offer their sacrifices, and to pay their tithes. More than 250,000 lambs were required for Passover in first-century Jerusalem!

This is the setting for what we call the triumphal entry of Jesus into the city. The people were impatient for Jesus to do something and called out, "Save us now!" (in modern worship "Hosanna!" now means "Praise Him!" but it did not then) and put their garments down in the road for Jesus and His disciples to walk over (see Matt. 21:1–11). (Something similar happened centuries before when Jehu was appointed as the king to destroy the house of Ahab and dethrone his queen, Jezebel [see 2 Kings 9].)

For the crowd in Jerusalem, it was a display of sheer nationalism, and their shouting "Hosanna!" was just like it would be to sing a freedom song today. Jesus entered the temple court and, in an amazingly violent outburst, "drove out" the merchants (the phrase is the same as is used to describe the exorcising of demons). Jesus overturned their tables, leaving everyone stunned and in awe. Is this Jesus, who rides into the city on a donkey—a sign of His humility and gentleness—capable of such righteous indignation and holy anger? The Son of Man brought judgment down on those who were selling religion for a profit.

Not only was this act reminiscent of Jehu's driving out of Jezebel, but Jesus's actions in the temple courts may also have been an act of prophetic symbolism, a foreshadowing of what would happen in AD 70 when the Romans under Titus utterly destroyed both city and temple.

ACTION

Spend time reflecting on Jesus. Is the Jesus you are familiar with like the one of Matthew 21:1–14? Do you normally think of Him as meek, gentle, and peaceful or do you most often consider Him a warrior king? He is both and much more! Whichever is your default, ask Him to show you new aspects of His character that renew and expand your thinking about who He is, our Prophet, Priest, and King. Spend time with Jesus.

DAY 141

Jesus in the Temple
Part 2

Yesterday we visited Matthew's account of Jesus causing havoc in the temple courts, upending tables and benches everywhere, releasing doves from cages, and sending coins rolling all over the floor. Jesus is obviously someone not to be trifled with! Suddenly, in verse 14, we are confronted with a story that seems completely misplaced and inconsistent with what has just occurred:

> *The blind and the lame came to him at the temple, and he healed them* (Matthew 21:14).

We might think, *Surely this is not the moment one would expect to see such tenderness and love? Surely this is not the scene to show such compassion and mercy!* Perhaps if *we* had been there instead of Jesus, we would have said to the sick and disabled, "Sorry, but you need to come back later. I need some time to process what's just happened. Please talk to my disciples and arrange with them a time later in the week when we can get together."

But no. Jesus is not like that. Jesus is at the same time holy *and* loving; just *and* kind; powerful *and* tender; filled with wrath *and* love. Think about those sick folks. They had just seen an extraordinary explosion of righteous anger. Did they worry that they would be hit rather than healed? Why didn't they run away from the scene? Why weren't they frightened of Jesus? The answer is that they saw in Jesus and sensed in their hearts that Jesus was someone who hated sin but loved sinners. They saw a beauty in Jesus. This is the reason He is so worthy of our praise!

This amazing event has much to speak into our approach to healing the sick. Who of us would have stopped to pray for the sick in that moment? Perhaps we have a tendency to think that God is more likely to heal if the atmosphere is conducive, the music is soft, and the right people are present. But not Jesus! For Him there are no such things as inappropriate places, unapproachable people, and awkward times.

Do we ever think of praying for the sick in the supermarket or healing people at work? Do we pray for our neighbors while standing with them in our front gardens? Worshipful music, peaceful atmospheres, and church services are great, but they are not necessary to manifest the Kingdom of God. Let's not use the awkwardness of time or place as an excuse to not pray for healing!

ACTION

Have you strayed from your first love for Christ and those early bursts of love for your neighbors and sick friends? Do you need to repent and ask for new courage? What might a return to radical (normal!) Christianity look like for you?

Training Your Faith for Increase

Truly I tell you, if you have faith as small as a mustard seed, you can say to this mountain, "Move from here to there," and it will move. Nothing will be impossible for you (Matthew 17:20).

For we live by faith, not by sight (2 Corinthians 5:7).

I saw you in a boxing ring, punching the air and skipping from foot to foot, as you began to work up a sweat and get yourself ready. As I watched you, I heard the Lord say, "It is time to train your faith for increase."

The Lord has brought you into a practice ring, a zone where He is inviting you into a faith-training and faith-stretching regime. This is somewhere your faith can increase to believe for all that God asks of you. This intense training regime is about choosing to believe, even when something in you doubts. It is about choosing to say, "I know God can heal that illness!"—even if you're not really sure yet if He can!

You increase your faith by stretching your faith beyond what you think is possible. Increasing your faith is both about choice and action. It's about saying, "I choose to believe and I will act accordingly!"

DECREE

Making these declarations regularly will help you to raise your faith in God.

- My faith is increasing.
- I believe You are the God of the impossible.
- I believe mountains move at Your name.
- I believe mountains melt like wax before You, God!
- I believe that with one touch You change everything!
- I decree the mountain of (_____) is shifting.
- I decree the mountain of (_____) is melting.

DAY 143

My Power in You

For God is working in you, giving you the desire and the power to do what pleases him (Philippians 2:13 NLT).

"I come to remind you today that you carry My power on the inside of you. You have My Spirit dwelling with and in you; therefore, you are never powerless! It is *My* Spirit working deep within you that gives you the will to do what pleases Me. You do not have to force it or make it happen because it is *My* Spirit working within you. Yield, yield, yield!

"Let *Me* do this work. Let *Me* have My way. I know you long to be one who is filled with might and power. I know you tire of the endless battles, the oppression, the depression, and everything that would try to hold you back. My strength is here to cover these things. My grace is sufficient. My power is at work deep within you."

What God says to you cannot be emphasized enough! You are not powerless. Today it is time to begin to truly believe that the all-powerful One lives in you and is doing a mighty work that He will complete! Yield today!

"Not by might nor by power, but by my Spirit," says the Lord Almighty (Zechariah 4:6).

RECEIVE

Pray this prayer today: "Lord Jesus, I choose to believe that Your Spirit is at work in me! He is completing that good work that He began on the cross. He is giving me the will to do what glorifies You! My insides are strengthened as He stirs up His power within me. No weapon formed against me will prosper, because You enable me and give me the grace to do all things. I stand firm upon these truths today!"

Now may the God of peace—who brought up from the dead our Lord Jesus, the great Shepherd of the sheep, and ratified an eternal covenant with his blood—may he equip you with all you need for doing his will. May he produce in you, through the power of Jesus Christ, every good thing that is pleasing to him. All glory to him forever and ever! Amen (Hebrews 13:20–21 NLT).

DAY 144

Repenting of Lies About Miracles

Jesus Christ is the same yesterday and today and forever (Hebrews 13:8).

You are a force of power! You are a determined, explosive *dunamis*, dynamite power! You have been let loose! Jesus has released all the fetters of religion and oppression that have made you believe you have nothing to give and nothing to offer the world. There is a strength inside you that releases the Lord's life and light everywhere you discharge it and it never diminishes. In Him you are a potent energy for change. Be released! You are filled with the life that was surging when all creation was created by the force of God's word and life. That power is unstoppable and untamable.

We see where the enemy, the words of the world, and even some in the church have tied you up and shut you down. We come to decree that all chains and fetters of words, curses, and locks are broken off you. All hooks of religion and uncertainty are broken and pulled out of you, in the name of Jesus Christ. Walk free, released from all hindrances and ties of the enemy and the world. Live in the fullness of the power that God has placed inside you!

ACTION

Pray out loud: "Father God, in the name of Jesus Christ, I repent and say I am sorry, Lord, for believing and partnering with the spirit of religion and all words that have said that miracles are not for today. I repent for any way that I have believed that the supernatural power of God died out with the early saints. I repent for agreeing with the world in any way, consciously or subconsciously, that the only supernatural power is of the devil and found outside the church and should be avoided by the people of God. I renounce and break agreement with all lies that I have believed in relation to Your miraculous power not being for me or for today."

At this point take time out with the Holy Spirit and ask Him to show and highlight every way that you might have done this. Then repent and break agreement with each area He highlighted.

Now declare aloud with faith: "I choose to break agreement with these lies and agree with You, Lord, that You are the same God yesterday, today, and forever and that who You are and how You manifest in healing, supernatural signs, and wonders has not stopped. I declare that in this era of the church You are manifesting supernaturally in increasing measure! I choose to step into that truth and expectantly say, 'Lord, please activate me in miraculous signs and wonders as I step out in faith and begin to pray for the sick and the broken.' Allow my expectation of Your supernatural ways grow. I now expect supernatural manifestations of Your Spirit and Your ways. God, I welcome You, with Your wonderful signs, to be revealed in my own life and the life of my household. I make room for You to reveal Yourself in our daily lives. Come and reveal Yourself, Lord, at this time. We expect You to move, God!"

DAY 145

The Gift of Faith
Part 1

Now to each one the manifestation of the Spirit is given for the common good...to another faith by the same Spirit, to another gifts of healing by that one Spirit (1 Corinthians 12:7, 9).

There are three types of faith in Scripture. First, *saving* faith is activated at the moment you come to Jesus and believe in Him. By this act of faith you are saved; by faith you become part of the family of God (see Hab. 2:4; John 20:31; 2 Tim. 3:15).

Secondly, there is the *measure* of faith (see Rom. 12:3). This is faith that grows as you prove the goodness of God consistently in your life. You move from a level of faith to a greater level of faith as you journey through life. Expectation continually develops, and your history with God enables you to believe for more.

Emma writes: When we first started out in ministry and started to rent ministry buildings, we had a measure of faith for finances. As we saw God pay the bills, our measure of faith increased for larger buildings that came with greater bills. God had proven Himself, and we learned how to believe in Him in increasing increments.

Thirdly, there is the *gift* of faith. You do not work for it or earn it. It is received from the Holy Spirit as part of His package of spiritual gifts. It is exceptionally potent and a necessary part of living supernaturally, success-fully. This one gift has the ability to revolutionize your insides, to shoot down the demons of doubt, and to bring inner stability and security that will anchor you better than you have ever been before.

ACTION

Open your hands and receive the gift of faith. It is that simple. Allow the Holy Spirit to bring a deposit of the gift of faith, and watch in the spirit realm as it is handed to you and is seeded into your being.

The Gift of Faith
Part 2

My message and my preaching were not with wise and persuasive words, but with a demonstration of the Spirit's power, so that your faith might not rest on human wisdom, but on God's power (1 Corinthians 2:7, 9).

When you prophesy, you have the words *of God* in your mouth. When you rebuke a demon, you have the authority *of God* in your commands. When you heal the sick, you have the power *of God* in your words. When you speak in tongues, you have the language *of God*. And when you use the gift of faith, you apply the faith level *of God*. The gift of faith is the faith of God, the belief that God has that something will come to pass!

You can access the faith level of God by receiving the gift of faith. That means that you can have an internal assurance that comes from a supernatural Holy Spirit empowerment to believe, not because of how hard you work. This faith, at the level of God, can be applied to any breakthrough that you need.

Emma writes: I have a faith gift when it comes to ministering to infertile couples. This means that the gift of faith outworks in my life through an ability to pray for children to be gifted to those who are struggling to conceive, and I am therefore able to believe for this at the faith level of God. It is a gift from Him, for His glory!

ACTION

Yesterday you asked and received a seed of the gift of faith. Spend time with the Holy Spirit and ask Him what areas of unbelief for which He is giving you a supernatural faith. Are there already things that you feel a strong belief or faith for that others are doubtful or dismissive about? Have you stepped out and applied your gift of faith in this area yet? There may be people waiting for you to come with your gift of God's faith!

DAY 147

The Fullness of Healing

Praise the Lord, my soul; all my inmost being, praise his holy name. Praise the Lord, my soul, and forget not all his benefits—who forgives all your sins and heals all your diseases, who redeems your life from the pit and crowns you with love and compassion, who satisfies your desires with good things so that your youth is renewed like the eagle's (Psalm 103:1–5).

Oh, how I desire that you would walk in wholeness and life! I have given you every spiritual blessing and that includes healing. I am the God who heals you from the inside out. I desire your emotions to be as healthy as your physical body. In fact, there is nothing that I cannot heal. Do you believe Me?

I am *Yahweh Rapha* (see Exod. 15:26). I have the desire, the power, and the ability to heal your past and your present. I am here to heal you from sickness and disease and to make you emotionally whole. There is nothing I cannot do!

Will you give Me access to the broken places of your heart? Will you let Me heal your past? Look and see that I am with you and for you. I do not put trauma or disease on those who love Me; that is not who I am! I gave My Son so that you would have life, and with His death and resurrection, He brought complete freedom and healing. Do not allow the enemy to kill your body; do not allow him to rob your emotions any longer! This is not My will for you.

RECEIVE

If you are struggling with physical illness or emotional brokenness, spend some time in the Gospels reading the accounts of Jesus as He healed with compassion all who came to Him for healing. Two good places to start:

> *When Jesus landed and saw a large crowd, he had compassion on them and healed their sick* (Matthew 14:14).

> *Jesus went throughout Galilee, teaching in their synagogues, proclaiming the good news of the kingdom, and healing every disease and sickness among the people. News about him spread all over Syria, and people brought to him all who were ill with various diseases, those suffering severe pain, the demon-possessed, those having seizures, and the paralyzed; and he healed them* (Matthew 4:23–24).

Impossibility Bows Low

The Lord reigns, let the earth be glad; let the distant shores rejoice. Clouds and thick darkness surround him; righteousness and justice are the foundation of his throne. Fire goes before him and consumes his foes on every side. His lightning lights up the world; the earth sees and trembles. The mountains melt like wax before the Lord, before the Lord of all the earth. The heavens proclaim his righteousness, and all peoples see his glory (Psalm 97:1–6).

For the kingdom of God does not consist in talk but in power (1 Corinthians 4:20 ESV).

God is power! Pure, unfiltered, and undiluted power. Power emanates from Him, destroying the works of the enemy and advancing the purposes of His rule. His name is above every other name and all things are under feet. Because of Jesus, impossibility now bows low and concedes defeat.

The Lord says: "I am changing your relationship with the word *impossibility*. In previous seasons you viewed it as a deterrent, the mark of an immovable situation or problem. But now you shall hear the word *impossibility* as an invite to manifest the fullness of My power. For when impossibility calls your name, you will instead call My name and that which has raised itself against you must bow low. Do not partner with fear over what may seem impossible, immovable, unretractable, or undefeatable. Instead stand in outrageous, bold faith that believes everything must shift at My name."

This is a day to stand firm in the *possible* of God. What is the possible of God? Jesus said that the possible of God is "all things"! Specifically, *"Jesus looked at them and said, 'With man this is impossible, but with God all things are possible'"* (Matt. 19:26 ESV). It is time to change your relationship with the word *impossible*. Shift from viewing it as a deterrent to seeing it as an invitation. Don't let it push you back, instead let it be something that stirs you to act in the unstoppable power of God! Nothing is impossible with God!

ACTION

Take one situation that seems impossible and start to ask the Holy Spirit to reveal His perspective of the situation to you. Just like a mountain seems unconquerable from its foot but is minuscule when viewed from an airplane, so your situation may feel unconquerable right now but from God's perspective will seem like a speck, easily blown away by the wind!

Write it out: "This is how I see my situation..." and on the other side write, "This is how God sees it..." Start to pray according to God's perspective.

DAY 149

Be Expectant!

So it is said: "Wake up, O sleeper, rise up from the dead, and Christ will shine on you" (Ephesians 5:14 BSB).

Be expectant for the amazing signs and wonders that the Lord is releasing to the earth at this time. These are signs and wonders for all, but particularly for His church in this hour there are signs and wonders of destruction and tearing down, planting and building up; signs and wonders that can be explained and those that cannot be explained because they hold the mystery of God.

He reminds you: "I am a supernatural God! Expect the unexpected supernatural signs and wonders that I am sending to you in this hour."

Signs and wonders in the natural earthly realm coming from the Kingdom of God are being revealed to you, as you allow God to increase your expectation for them. These are signs that will make you wonder and mysteries that point you to Jesus and His everlasting Kingdom. Expect to see signs such as heavenly dust, fragrances, gems, and markings on your body. Or look for signposts in the physical that manifest in the spirit: keys, doors, natural signs like trees and waters, weather patterns, and visitations. These will enable you to step through into another level of the spiritual reality of God's manifest ways as you become aware of them and hear the Lord's invitation through them. Be expectant!

"Watch for My signs and wonders," says the Lord, "for I long to make you a supernatural Bride who understands My heavenly language and the signs and demonstrations of My Kingdom in this hour."

Expect to see the following miracles:

- Broken bones being straightened.

- Hair growth where previously there was none.

- Growth in height where there was restriction before.

- Shape changes that point to His Kingdom and His ways.

- Signs that will make you wonder.

"Be expectant, My Bride, My love, as I move in and through you. Look for Me and My Kingdom always. Do not miss the signs. Do not fail to wonder."

RECEIVE

Pray: "I praise You that You are a supernatural God with ways I do not fully understand. I acknowledge today that You are the Lord of mysteries and will reveal them to me at the times and ways that You choose for Your own purposes. Lord, I am expectant and ready for the demonstrations of Your Kingdom and Your ways! In response to Your call, I make room in my life, my home, and my workplace for You to break through at the time and with the method of Your choosing. I say, 'I am expectant, Lord!'"

DAY 150

Bitter Roots

See to it that no one falls short of the grace of God and that no bitter root grows up to cause trouble and defile many (Hebrews 12:15).

We are the temple of the Holy Spirit, His dwelling place. Our bodies must be pure and undefiled. The aim is that nothing internally happens in our thinking or emotional processing that does not happen in the heart and mind of God. This is a high call indeed! We are to have His mind, to think as God thinks, to steward the mind of Christ, and to reflect emotions in the way that Jesus would have processed emotions.

Our insides must be clean, clear, spiritually bright, and illuminated; supple, soft, and yielded, without any dark spots of contamination lurking there. Do you know what it is to feel internally emotionally clean?

God wants to do something remarkable inside of you today. He wants you to experience the feeling of what His Son's blood bought for you. This is more than praying repentance prayers. This is saying sorry but also touching the emotions of how it feels to be forgiven and made righteous. The miraculous power of God doesn't just bear the burden of your sin but allows you to emotionally connect with a sense of righteous well-being. You can feel the well-being of Heaven become established on the inside of you.

"But first," I hear the Spirit of the Lord say, "you have a dark spot that I want to dissolve and remove from you. It is a blemish on your internal landscape. It is a bitter root."

At this I saw the Lord release a cleansing balm, like a waterfall cascading internally that refreshed but also brought the removal of the resentment that has hidden inside of you.

Bitter roots are judgments, resentments, anger, harshness, hatred, and even irritations that we have with others. They can range from a simple, internal eye roll to outright rage, from dislike to disdain. They are the unhealed portions of us, and they mean that we often want an unhealthy form of retribution for ways that we have been treated.

ACTION

Say sorry to Jesus for the judgments and resentments you have held against others. Break agreement with bitter roots that have become like stones that weigh down your emotions. Take your time to list and be specific with the ways that others irritate, frustrate, and absorb your thinking time. Acknowledge that these thoughts are errors that have tarnished you. Then, allow yourself to receive the emotions and the sensation of restoration. Ask God to bless you with the ability to emotionally connect with restoration and the feelings of being clean.

DAY 151

Walking in Faith

For in this hope we were saved. But hope that is seen is no hope at all. Who hopes for what they already have? But if we hope for what we do not yet have, we wait for it patiently (Romans 8:24–25).

We walk by the Spirit, live by the Spirit, are led by the Spirit, and keep in step with the Spirit (see Gal. 5:16–25). We also walk by faith, not by sight (see 2 Cor. 5:7). These Scripture truths reveal that our life must be one spent moving, acting, and loving in light of God's promises and all that is unseen and eternal.

We don't walk, act, live, or move according to the flesh or according to what our physical eyes can see. That means that we don't make decisions based on the media, what our friends post online, what politicians say or do, or what our bank balance is. We live by faith, a waiting, expectant faith, and we must activate that faith daily. That means practicing our faith constantly, taking "faith leaps" into the unknown, trusting and believing in God's promises. Be faithful and obedient to God, even in the little steps, and within a short time you'll be taking bigger and bigger jumps and leaping off metaphorical cliff tops, knowing that you're in His perfect will.

But this kind of bold, audacious Spirit living takes training. Your faith will be tested, over and over again. Your faith will be put through the wringer or waiting and patiently enduring until you almost can't bear it anymore. You will learn the difference between presumption and promise, between recklessness and secure confidence in God.

As you go on this faith journey, make sure you do your "faith exercises" to build up your faith muscle. *"So faith comes from hearing, and hearing by the word of Christ"* (Rom. 10:17 NASB). Increase your time spent hearing the Word of Christ, reading and listening to others read and expound Scripture. Also *"pray in the Spirit on all occasions with all kinds of prayers and requests"* (Eph. 6:18) and activate your praying in the Spirit, which will build up your faith (see Jude 20).

ACTION

Do you need to increase your hearing of the Word of God? Is it time to build more time for reading or listening to the Bible during the day? If reading is problematic, consider using an app for your phone to listen to Bible readings as you walk, commute, exercise, work, or rest. Fill your ears with the Word of God and activate your faith!

CHAPTER 6

The Kingdom of God

DAY 152

King Jesus

He sits enthroned above the circle of the earth; its dwellers are like grasshoppers. He stretches out the heavens like a curtain, and spreads them out like a tent to dwell in. He brings the princes to nothing and makes the rulers of the earth meaningless (Isaiah 40:22–23 BSB).

There is a King on the throne! Jesus your Savior has overcome and is seated above all—all circumstances, concerns and worries, challenges, expressions, and determinations of your heart and life.

He calls to you today to see Him as that powerful, majestic King, who is high above all things created, seen and unseen. He calls you to raise your gaze and to look above what is in front of your mind's eye and see Him as He is now. Not One in the manger. Not One who is still hanging on the cross. Not One who is restricted by any earth realm or heavenly principality or power. No! He is all-powerful, sitting in all authority on that throne, with all rule and reign beneath His feet and under His name: King Jesus!

See your King today! Jesus Christ, the almighty One is mighty and formidable, commanding in His kingship over all creation, known to us and unknown to us.

Bow before Him and acknowledge His rule and His majesty. See Him clothed in His royal robes, and acknowledge His supreme royal authority. Nothing compares. Nothing stands against. No one and no thing is greater. Jesus is King!

RECEIVE

Gaze upon Jesus the King. Take the time to focus your heart and all your senses, physical and spiritual, on Him as He reveals Himself to you afresh as the King of all kings and the all-powerful authority over all things. There is a fresh revelation and encounter of King Jesus for you today. How will you respond to Him?

The Gates of Hades Will Not Overcome

When Jesus came to the region of Caesarea Philippi, he asked his disciples, "Who do people say the Son of Man is?"...Simon Peter answered, "You are the Messiah, the Son of the living God." Jesus replied, "Blessed are you, Simon son of Jonah, for this was not revealed to you by flesh and blood, but by my Father in heaven. And I tell you that you are Peter, and on this rock I will build my church, and the gates of Hades will not overcome it" (Matthew 16:13–20).

Contained in this Scripture is perhaps Jesus's most powerful prophetic challenge and declaration to the demonic world. He made it in northern Galilee, in the shadow of Mount Hermon, about two thousand years ago.

The area near Mount Hermon was a place of pagan worship, with many shrines and pagan carvings devoted to Baal. It was a depraved, occultic high place, renowned for its demonic and erotic excesses. One ancient text claims that Mount Hermon was the place where Baal had his palace on earth. It stood in complete defiance of the God of Israel.

At the base of this mountain was the town of Caesarea Philippi where a Roman temple to the god Pan had been built next to a huge cave known locally as the Gates of Hades. It was here before the very hordes of hell that Jesus Christ publicly acknowledged that He is the Son of God and our Messiah. Here, in the most depraved place on earth, He declared, *"I will build my church, and the gates of Hades will not overcome it."*

And the Spirit of Jesus Christ reminds you today that "it was where satan held sway that I chose to stand and show him who is truly Lord of all. There I chose to humble the hosts of evil spirits at their own gateway. This means that you can be confident that there is no evil, however great, that I will not confront and be victorious over."

Today you can be sure that there is nothing that you face, no matter how evil, corrupt, ungodly, or demonic that it might seem, that cannot be overcome by the power and authority of Jesus Christ.

ACTION

Rejoice with Zechariah who called Jesus the *"king over the whole earth"* (Zech. 14:9) and with Paul and John who gave Him the title of *"King of kings"* (1 Tim. 6:15; Rev. 19:16). Take time to praise Him as He deserves, the name above all others.

DAY 154

Heavenly Perspective

"For my thoughts are not your thoughts, neither are your ways my ways," declares the Lord. "As the heavens are higher than the earth, so are my ways higher than your ways and my thoughts than your thoughts" (Isaiah 55:8–9).

He replied, "Because the knowledge of the secrets of the kingdom of heaven has been given to you, but not to them" (Matthew 13:11).

I have pulled you into My Kingdom as an ambassador. From My Kingdom you can view and transform the world that surrounds you. You are called, created, and sent to usher in the "now" reality of My domain into every situation, place, and zone that I have called you into. As a Kingdom ambassador, you are motivated to bring change by seeing from Heaven's perspective.

Do not look at the earth from an earthly perspective; do not get caught up assessing your situations from a worldly point of view. These pursuits are worthless and fruitless! Instead, choose to look from My point of view. Choose to see what I see, to see *how* I see, and then to respond as I would respond.

Even as you look and see from My point of view, solutions and innovations are going to spring up from within. Rather than trying really hard to crack that hard situation, there will be an ease to overcome by My Spirit as you choose to live from My vantage point and not the earth's. So, be strengthened and see! See from My perspective, and do not allow what is around you to form a response of fear. Instead, act as a Kingdom ambassador and overcome by My Spirit.

ACTION

Lay hands on your head and pray, "Lord, shift my perspective from earthly to heavenly. Show me how to live from a Kingdom of God mindset and not a worldly mindset." Then, lay your hands on your eyes and ask, "Release to me the capacity to see as You see, God, and not as the world sees."

DAY 155

He Reigns!

Yahweh now reigns as King! Let everyone rejoice! His rule extends everywhere, even to distant lands, and the islands of the sea, let them all be glad. Clouds both dark and mysterious now surround him. His throne of glory rests upon a foundation of righteousness and justice....For you are King-God, the Most High God over all the earth. You are exalted above every supernatural power! (Psalm 97:1–2, 9 TPT)

I watched in the realms of the spirit as the heavenly hosts started to dance, shout, and sing around the throne of God in response to every act He made. As God stretched out His hand to release order into a nation, the hosts of Heaven responded with dancing, singing, and shouting. As He stretched forth His staff to align His church, again they responded with dancing, singing, and shouting. With every sovereign act that the Lord made, the hosts of Heaven would respond with ever-increasing adulation and exaltation. They sang: "He reigns, He reigns, He reigns, and He is good!"

Over and over again they sang, danced, and shouted this statement, and out it went over the nations of the earth. I watched as the hosts then turned to you and they asked you, "Does He reign in your life? Will you let His rulership be established in the midst of your heart?"

The Lord is seeking to establish His rule and reign in your life with greater force than ever before today. He says to you, "Every idol must bow as I occupy your heart with My lordship. Will you submit to My reign? Will you bow low to My lordship? For as you do, you shall find life, and as you submit, you will find freedom. For My reign comes and destroys every pretender to the throne, casting off every entanglement and fear. I reign over the nations of the earth, but shall you let Me in to reign in your heart?"

ACTION

Welcome the King in prayer: "Lord Jesus, I recognize You as King and welcome You to come and establish Yourself on the throne of my heart. I am sorry for where other pretenders have occupied the chief position in my life, and today I evict any other who has taken up this place. You alone are God, You alone are King, and I enthrone You once again—this time forever on my heart. Take Your place, Jesus, and may all the other names now fade away."

DAY 156

Our Cultural Lenses

Those who cling to worthless idols turn away from God's love for them (Jonah 2:8).

How we view and navigate the world around us is massively influenced by our culture. The way we see things depends on our life experience, the culture of our upbringing, the geography of the nation that we were born in, how we were educated, and our current standing in society.

Emma writes: "I grew up in Northern Ireland during 'the Troubles,' which was our version of a civil war, fought between Catholics and Protestants/Republicans and Unionists. This experience gave me a totally skewed version of what constituted being Christian. 'Those on the opposite side could not possibly know God, could they?' we doubted. My local culture taught me suspicion, caution, and even hatred of those who did not align completely with our worldview. We siloed off and learned that all conversation with 'them' was to be avoided so that we could maintain defensiveness and purity of our position."

My experience, though dramatic and with deadly consequences, is probably not much different from yours. Just substitute Unionist or Republican with the names of the political party in your country that you feel most aligned to and then substitute the other name for the political party that is on the end of your greatest suspicion. Your upbringing and life experience will be responsible for your political indoctrination and cultural perspective. You need to be very aware that this exists. We see through a backyard perspective, and we are shaped by our culture before we even think to question it.

The great danger of this is that we see God as *we* are and view Him through *our* perspective. And yet the Bible expresses that we see dimly (see 1 Cor. 13:12). In other words, we are prone to idolatry. We must therefore constantly renounce cultural idolatry as part of our lifestyle. We must wear Jesus Christ–shaped lenses and see the world through His eyes, not ours.

ACTION

Make a good habit of regularly repenting of cultural and political prejudice: "Jesus, I take off my cultural lenses and repent of how I have made my cultural identity an idol. I repent of filtering Scripture through my political preferences. Lord, I want to see the world as You see it. I'm sorry for where I have assumed that You see things as I see them. Wash me clean of my prejudices. I commit to worshipping You alone, forsaking all others. Give me Your perspective, Lord."

If reading this word or praying this prayer caused you to bristle with offense, then take this as a sign that you still have wrong alignments that you need to submit to Jesus, your Lord. Realign yourself with Him above and before all others.

DAY 157

God's Representatives

Now when Joshua was near Jericho, he looked up and saw a man standing in front of him with a drawn sword in his hand. Joshua went up to him and asked, "Are you for us or for our enemies?"

"Neither," he replied, "but as commander of the army of the Lord I have now come." Then Joshua fell facedown to the ground in reverence, and asked him, "What message does my Lord have for his servant?" (Joshua 5:13–14)

Yesterday we repented of when we have tried to fit Jesus Christ to our perspective and committed to seeing the world through His eyes, not ours.

Jesus is not us on our best day—the best, most good version of us. Jesus is not us whitened up. Jesus is the King of His own Kingdom, and He does not bow His knee to our culturally indoctrinated opinions.

When Joshua meets the angel of the Lord, his first question is, "Whose side are you on?" The commander's answer is, "I am on no one's side! God is only on God's side!" We biblically fail when we assign God to a "side" or one political party or another because that means that we assign righteousness to a political party, a movement, a strong man or woman, or an ideology. Political parties and ideologies are not the *ecclesia*; they are not the church; they are part of the world's system and are not the righteousness of God. As blood-bought citizens of the Kingdom of God, we are supposed to be representatives of the government of God, His ambassadors. Whether you politically lean to the left, right, or somewhere else completely, make sure your feet are firmly planted on the solid rock of Jesus Christ!

ACTION

Think of someone you disagree with, someone you know personally or a political leader or another type of leader. Pray for them with love; pray God's blessings for them and their family. Don't pray your agenda for them (in other words, don't pray that God would change their mind so that they agree with you) but ask Jesus to encounter them, save them, and transform them as He wills.

As a practical action, is there someone or a group you disagree with? Perhaps they are from another political persuasion or simply believers from another denomination persuasion. Ask Jesus to give you a Kingdom strategy for how you can work with them to advance His purposes on earth. You don't need to join them or even agree with them, but what one thing would God have you do with them that would be *"on earth as it is in heaven"* (Matt. 6:10)?

DAY 158

Do You Know Who You Are?

Jesus Christ is King over an everlasting Kingdom, and you are one of His holy people:

> *Then the sovereignty, power and greatness of all the kingdoms under heaven will be handed over to the holy people of the Most High. His kingdom will be an everlasting kingdom, and all rulers will worship and obey him* (Daniel 7:27).

Declare this truth over yourself today: "I am one of the holy people of the Most High! I have responsibilities in the everlasting Kingdom of Jesus Christ my King!"

You are adopted into His family, a very special family, a holy nation of royal priests:

> *But you are a chosen people, a royal priesthood, a holy nation, God's special possession, that you may declare the praises of him who called you out of darkness into his wonderful light. Once you were not a people, but now you are the people of God; once you had not received mercy, but now you have received mercy* (1 Peter 2:9–10).

Declare: "I am chosen. I am God's special possession. I am one of the people of God, and I am part of His holy nation!"

You are a part of a Kingdom, freed from the sins of your past, and now you serve as a priest to God the Father:

> *...Jesus Christ, who is the faithful witness, the firstborn from the dead, and the ruler of the kings of the earth. To him who loves us and has freed us from our sins by his blood, and has made us to be a kingdom and priests to serve his God and Father—to him be glory and power for ever and ever! Amen* (Revelation 1:5–6).

Declare: "All my past allegiances are worthless. I am no longer a slave to anything in this world. I am now a priest serving in the royal household!"

The Bible is clear about your future. You are destined to reign on the earth, in service to God:

> *And they sang a new song, saying: "You are worthy to take the scroll and to open its seals, because you were slain, and with your blood you purchased for God persons from every tribe and language and people*

and nation. You have made them to be a kingdom and priests to serve our God, and they will reign on the earth" (Revelation 5:9–10).

Repent of thinking too lowly of your destiny and purpose. Thank Jesus for His blood and what it purchased! You reign with King Jesus. Reigning is what royal rulers do!

If we died with him, we will also live with him; if we endure, we will also reign with him (2 Timothy 2:11–12).

DECLARE

With conviction, make this declaration: "I am a royal priest. I rule and reign with my King, Jesus Christ!"

DAY 159

Citizen of Another World

But we are citizens of heaven, where the Lord Jesus Christ lives (Philippians 3:20 NLT).

You are a citizen of Heaven! You are one gifted with anointing from the King Himself, and you rule and reign with Him.

In Him you are no longer a normal, mortal being. You are one infused with the same power that raised Jesus Christ from the dead. Authority has been given to you because of His victory on the cross. You are alive in Christ. You are alive in Him! There is a call and a determination in you that is alive and forceful. It is the life of the eternal Kingdom. The perspective of your heavenly home has been given to you for now and for today.

You are marvelous in the eyes of your Father and your Savior, King Jesus. You are born of the Spirit, born of the Kingdom of God, and infused with light, life, hope, and immeasurable possibility.

I hear the Lord say to you today: "Acknowledge the power and life that I have placed inside you. It is potent and explosive. You are one fashioned in Heaven by My hands. You do not only have a purpose, you have eternal impact. Recognize who you are today and see that nothing can overwhelm My Kingdom within. Shine! Be awakened to the potency of My life force and power within you today."

RECEIVE

Take time to think about this word over you. Pause and reflect on the words describing who you are and what is inside of you. Reread yesterday's Scriptures. Sit with the Lord, and let the reality of who you are as a citizen of the eternal Kingdom of God take hold and grip you. Be assured that this is not some mere hopeful thought; this is the reality of who you are. You are born of the King and marked for a powerful purpose, with a Kingdom force on the inside, ready to be released.

Listen to what the Holy Spirit is speaking to you based on this word. Pause in quiet and breathe. Allow yourself to hear and see what the Lord is saying to you as you wait on Him about who you are. Write down what you hear; write it somewhere that you can return to and read again what He said to you. Meditate on the truth of your divine nature and origin. Allow that truth to permeate your mind, your thoughts, and your physical body as you think on these things.

The Kingdom of God Is Higher Than My Nation

But you are a chosen race, a royal priesthood, a holy nation, a people for his own possession, that you may proclaim the excellencies of him who called you out of darkness into his marvelous light (1 Peter 2:9 ESV).

We must love the Kingdom of God more than we love our own nation or tribe.

When we get this right in our hearts, we begin guarding the Kingdom of God, rather than guarding a national, cultural, or political agenda. We must be more aligned with God than with our political opinion. We are predominantly and primarily citizens of the Kingdom of God before we are British, or Canadian, or Chinese, or Kenyan, or American, or French, or European, or even Western. We are in the nation of God before we are anything else. We don't just follow a Savior; we follow a King. You are now part of a civilization headed and led by Almighty God Himself!

We, therefore, have more in common with a believer living in Asia or Africa (or anywhere else in the world) than we do with a nonbeliever living in the house next to us. We have more in common with a Christian in an opposing political party to us than we do to one whose politics we agree with. We, as followers of Christ, are the family of God together, the Kingdom of God working to spread the Gospel and change the planet by making it more like Heaven.

Therefore, being a patriot first or pledging allegiance to flags, documents, earthly structures and systems, or having strong nationalistic tendencies can be a place of dangerous unseating of the premier place that the King and His Kingdom should have in your hearts. This doesn't mean we don't love our nations and pray for them (and all the nations), but we certainly must make sure that they are secondary in our hearts to the Kingdom of God.

DECREE

Jesus, help me to love Your Kingdom more than I love my nation, tribe, culture, or earthly identity. Lead me into the righteous reordering of my heart. I am sorry for overdoing my nationalistic tendencies and therefore any resulting partnership that I have with suspicion or fear of other nations that are not mine. I recognize today that I have family, Your family, in those nations that also love You. May Your Kingdom come and Your will be done, on earth as it is in Heaven.

DAY 161

Choosing Your King

Then Jesus said to his disciples, "Whoever wants to be my disciple must deny themselves and take up their cross and follow me" (Matthew 16:24).

On his robe and on his thigh he has a name written, King of kings and Lord of lords (Revelation 19:16 ESV).

Jesus is Lord and He is King. But it is important that we understand what happened to us at the point of our salvation when we repented and turned to Jesus. We didn't *make* Jesus Lord at that point. The Gospel of the Kingdom is not about your somehow making Jesus Lord of your life. He is *already* the crowned ruler of Heaven and earth! So the issue isn't about you having to make Jesus Lord or King. He's already Lord! No, the issue at salvation is about you *submitting* to His lordship, the lordship He already has.

At salvation we should not pray something like, "Jesus look after me and You can have the throne of my life," as if we were making some sort of deal or contract with God! We must not have the idea in our hearts that "if You save me from death, I will make You King."

Rather, we should pray, "Jesus, I *surrender* to Your universal and complete rulership." This is the difference between the mistaken "Gospel of personal salvation," where I try to make Jesus my personal Savior, and the actual, biblically true "Gospel of the Kingdom of God," where I submit to Him as the ruler of all, including me and my life.

You don't just have a Savior; you choose to follow a King, the King with a holy nation and the government of God upon His shoulders. When you repent and follow Him, you become a part of this Kingdom and are subject to it before and ahead of anything else.

DECREE

Nothing you say or do will make Jesus any more Lord or King than He already is, but perhaps for your own realignment you need to reacknowledge His lordship with your mouth and heart, forsaking all others and giving Him the first place in everything. Paul's words to the Romans are a good template for doing this:

> *If you acknowledge and confess with your mouth that Jesus is Lord [recognizing His power, authority, and majesty as God], and believe in your heart that God raised Him from the dead, you will be saved* (Romans 10:9 AMP).

Repent of putting anything else as King or Lord in your life ahead of Him.

DAY 162

Build, Build, Build!

*Then Haggai, the Lord's messenger, gave this message of the Lord to the peo-
ple: "I am with you," declares the Lord. So the Lord stirred up the spirit of
Zerubbabel son of Shealtiel, governor of Judah, and the spirit of Joshua son
of Jozadak, the high priest, and the spirit of the whole remnant of the people.
They came and began to work on the house of the Lord Almighty, their God,
on the twenty-fourth day of the sixth month* (Haggai 1:13–15).

The Spirit of the Lord says to you: "I am with you, equipping you and
readying you to build with Me. On this day I am stirring within you innovations, creative ideas, solutions, places, administrations, organizations,
and more that, I have called you to build for the cause of My Kingdom. Do
not doubt yourself at this time, for I am with you!"

God is putting around you, in the spirit, a tool belt filled with all manner of building equipment. This tool belt has everything necessary for you
to complete the building works that God is inviting you into. You are not
one tool short, or one tool overpacked. You have exactly everything that
is needed. The Lord says: "You are ready. You are ready to build because I
am with you and have equipped you. This is not forcing something out of
your will or by thinking really hard. This call is not about trying really hard
or overplanning. Building in My Kingdom is about a partnership with Me,
the chief builder!"

For every house is built by someone, but the builder of all things is God
(Hebrews 3:4 ESV).

So what are you going to partner with God to build? What project is He
inviting you into? What plans has He approved for you to facilitate?

ACTION

I heard the Lord speak specifically, but not exclusively, into a partnership for building Kingdom solutions in the following areas at this time:

- Restoration in family relationships
- Financial strategy for personal financial freedom
- Organizations for the care and freedom of "the least of these"
- Miraculous and supernatural ministries that release signs of
  wonders and miracles
- New businesses and small enterprises

- Charities to steward the well-being of masses

- Evangelistic activities for souls to be saved, healed, and delivered

- Creative exploits stewarding art, music, writing, painting, etc.

And many more areas! Perhaps He has spoken to you about another area? Remember, you are ready, prepared, and called. It's time to partner with God to begin building. What first steps can you take today to begin to make this a reality?

The Finger of God

"This is the finger of God!" Pharaoh's magicians exclaimed when they witnessed the God of the Israelites strike Egypt again and again (see Exod. 8:19). Many centuries later, Jesus used the same phrase:

> If I drive out demons by the finger of God, then the kingdom of God has come upon you (Luke 11:20).

On this occasion, the crowd was amazed when Jesus drove a demon out of a man who was mute and afflicted by an evil spirit (see Luke 11:14). Matthew also records that Jesus healed him so that he could both talk and see (see Matt. 12:22). However, some religious leaders, the Pharisees, who were present wondered by what power Jesus had been able to perform this miracle over the powers of evil. Had the promised Messiah come and was He beginning to establish God's reign? Many of them didn't like that idea. "He is not doing this by the power of God," they argued, "Jesus is driving out demons by the power of the king of demons!" (See Matthew 12:24.)

Jesus shows how illogical they are being. His power over evil spirits is clear evidence that God is at work by His finger. The Kingdom of God had already arrived.

What comes into your mind when you read the phrase "the Kingdom of God"? An important part of the story in the Gospels is the spiritual conflict and cosmic battle that takes place when God comes to reign. The powers of evil will fight back ferociously but will be decisively defeated. *"The reason the Son of God appeared was to destroy the devil's work,"* wrote John (1 John 3:8).

The miracles of Jesus are a wonderful visual picture that satan's cause is lost. He may do a lot of damage, as any army can, but he has lost and is now being crushed. Someone stronger has come—Jesus! And on the cross He completed the victory.

DECREE

Read the story of this miracle in Luke 11:14–22 and be encouraged. Take time to reject and resist the evil one. Make some decrees and declarations out loud if you are able:

- Affirm and celebrate satan's downfall.

- Rejoice in the victory Christ won for you.

- Claim Paul's promise that *"the God of peace will soon crush* [satan] *under your feet"* (Rom. 16:20).

DAY 164

A Citizen at Home

That's plain enough, isn't it? You're no longer wandering exiles. This kingdom of faith is now your home country. You're no longer strangers or outsiders. You belong here, with as much right to the name Christian as anyone. God is building a home. He's using us all—irrespective of how we got here—in what he is building. He used the apostles and prophets for the foundation. Now he's using you, fitting you in brick by brick, stone by stone, with Christ Jesus as the cornerstone that holds all the parts together. We see it taking shape day after day—a holy temple built by God, all of us built into it, a temple in which God is quite at home (Ephesians 2:19–22 MSG).

Over the next few days, the Lord God wants to deal with the struggle of not belonging and not fitting in. Many of you have battled with doubts about how well you fit in the family of God. You seem to think that you're the black sheep of the family, the odd one out, the one who is just different, or the one who missed something that everyone else knows. None of that is true; all of it has come as lies from the enemy of your soul. You were perfectly made, and you fit into the living stones that He is building together.

So, listen closely as He wants you to hear and receive this.

"I am coming to silence the voice of the enemy who continually whispers doubt in your ear. Do not let him tell you that you don't belong or fit in My Kingdom! You belong with Me as one of Mine. You are a fully fledged citizen with every right to be a part of My Body. No one can take this away from you! I silence the voices and the repetitive words that you've heard in your head over and over; I take those words and I shred them with My TRUTH! You are Mine! I have fit you into My household, into My dwelling place. You are HOME with Me!

"Pick up your sword and join Me in shredding the words that have come against you. And then replace them with My truth and declare over yourself these words: 'I belong to God's Kingdom as part of His family! The Lord God is fitting me into His building, and I am at home in Him. I am His, and I cover myself with His truth, His acceptance, and His view of me. I am perfectly made and perfectly fit in as a living stone!'"

ACTIVATION

Write down those negative words that you've heard over and over, the words that keep you from fully being a part of His Body. Then take your spiritual sword and partner with the Lord; the two of you shred those words by declaring what He says over you! If you need to, shred those words, and then write, "I belong! I'm home! I am a valuable member of God's household. I fit perfectly in His family." Let them all sink in as they are the truth!

DAY 165

Find Your Place

And he said to them, "Truly, I say to you, there is no one who has left house or wife or brothers or parents or children, for the sake of the kingdom of God, who will not receive many times more in this time, and in the age to come eternal life" (Luke 18:29–30 ESV).

Have you felt burdened and not sure of where you belong? The Lord is highlighting to you today that you are not alone. Your inheritance in Christ means you are part of an extensive Kingdom family. You belong to a company of Kingdom citizens. There is identity and acceptance in this company of heavenly citizens on the earth which will be realized in your life. Listen to what the Spirit of God says about this.

"You are made to fit in My Kingdom. You, My child, are fashioned to perfectly fit next to your brother and sister in Me. You have been hewn and shaped by My hand to belong and rest in exactly the right place. You are not an anomaly. Neither are you strange, odd, or imperfect. Your Kingdom shape is at My hand and I have made you to belong. I have made you to fit in the perfect place for you.

"Ask Me who your people are. Ask Me where I have made you to fit and find your temporary home on the earth until you are with Me forever in My everlasting Kingdom. For I have a place that you can call home on the earth until your due time of crossing over, a place of peace, for My glory and your joy. It will be a place where you maximize your potential in life and relationships and where you will come most alive in Me and in your life. Ask Me where your people are and where your home on earth is to be. I will surely answer."

RECEIVE

Take quiet time to do as the Lord asks, asking Him the questions that He poses today and listening for the answer. If you are not hearing any-thing specific, or you feel that it may be your heart speaking and not the Lord, pray the prayer below. Ask the Holy Spirit for clarification by His Word, through dreams, and through others you trust in your life to sharpen you. If you feel God is asking you to move geographically or change your church family, ask Him for more confirmation before you commit yourself to that move. Weigh it in prayer and come back to it in a few weeks or months. You will get your confirmation from the Lord if it is right. Listen also to your heart and pay attention to what it feels and says to you as you hear God's answers. He said there would be joy!

A prayer you can pray: "Lord help me to know who my people are and where my optimum place in this world is. Lord, I will go anywhere and do anything for You. I long to be in the place You have prepared for me and with who You have prepared me for as 'my company' and 'my people.' Thank You, God, that at the right time You will reveal this to me and confirm it by Your Spirit. I welcome being rightly positioned in my Kingdom company on the earth."

DAY 166

No More Isolation

So then you are no longer strangers and aliens, but you are fellow citizens with the saints and members of the household of God, built on the foundation of the apostles and prophets, Christ Jesus himself being the cornerstone, in whom the whole structure, being joined together, grows into a holy temple in the Lord. In him you also are being built together into a dwelling place for God by the Spirit (Ephesians 2:19–22 ESV).

I hear the Spirit of the Lord continue to press on you, "I have a family, a Kingdom, where you belong. Do not think of yourself as one isolated life; do not consider that you are a nomad, drifting from one place of loneliness to another. When you said no to darkness and death and yes to Me, I pulled you in and formed you as part of My Body and My Bride—My church, My *ecclesia*—and now you belong.

"As part of a company of Kingdom people you are made to advance as one, and like an arrowhead, I will form you to move forward together, not isolated or disconnected, but as one people. For My Kingdom does not gather around politics, race, gender, theory, or geography, but My Kingdom gathers around Me. Your belonging is not dictated to you by these earthly external factors but is extended to you by your accepting Me as your Lord and as your Savior."

RECEIVE

For many of you these words will be healing because you have felt isolated for years. To those who feel this way, we release healing into your heart and an ability to trust people again, in the name of Jesus. Others of you will say yes to this word but still feel desperately disconnected. To you we release an ability to know where to connect, who to connect to, and how to connect. But for all of you we release a joy and a knowing that you are not an isolated life but you are part of a *"kingdom of priests"* who serve God (Rev. 5:10; 1 Pet. 2:9).

DAY 167

Building with Broken Stones

As you come to him, the living Stone—rejected by humans but chosen by God and precious to him— you also, like living stones, are being built into a spiritual house to be a holy priesthood, offering spiritual sacrifices acceptable to God through Jesus Christ....But you are a chosen people, a royal priesthood, a holy nation, God's special possession, that you may declare the praises of him who called you out of darkness into his wonderful light. Once you were not a people, but now you are the people of God; once you had not received mercy, but now you have received mercy (1 Peter 2:4–5, 9–10).

Forget the temple! Magnificent as it was, it is obsolete. Imagine those gigantic stones, the priests in their robes, so hushed and important, the sacrifices of animals that everybody had to bring. It is finished!

The Lord says to you: "From now on you and I are the temple! I am at the foundation, as the main cornerstone, ensuring that what is built on top will be firm and secure. You are one of the living stones that this new temple is built of—misshapen stones, chipped stones, broken stones. I know you are worried about this idea, but do you recall that Nehemiah rebuilt the walls of Jerusalem with burnt and broken stones, using his tools to rebuild what looked like useless rubble? Likewise, I will make use of you, and you will not be left out. I am the strong and precious stone that you can stand upon; build your life on Me, knowing that I am utterly solid and reliable."

Now you are a priest! Unlikely as you might think you are, every living stone is part of a holy priesthood because of Jesus's sacrifice. No animal sacrifice is necessary anymore, just your loving, committed, holy life. And now you do not just get to come into the temple, you are the temple!

ACTION

If these concepts of being the temple are new to you, then Paul has a few verses that will help you:

- Read Ephesians 2:19–22 where Paul gives a more detailed picture of temple imagery.

- In another letter he uses temple imagery again when he asks, *"Don't you know that you yourselves are God's temple and that God's Spirit dwells in your midst?"* (1 Cor. 3:16–17).

- And later he uses the same image to describe individual believers: *"Do you not know that your bodies are temples of the Holy*

Spirit, who is in you, whom you have received from God? You are not your own; you were bought with a price. Therefore honor God with your bodies" (1 Cor. 6:19–20).

From Living Stones to Flowing Water

You also, like living stones, are being built into a spiritual house to be a holy priesthood (1 Peter 2:5).

Peter's use of the term "living stones" would have stirred up images of the Exodus in the minds of his Jewish readers. Their ancestors experienced two events of living stones, at the beginning and the end of their wilderness wanderings. In the first year after leaving Egypt, the people complained of thirst. God instructed Moses to strike a rock; he did and water came out for the people to drink (see Exod. 17:5–6). In the fortieth year, the people grumbled and complained against the Lord, and He again gave them water from a rock. This time Moses was told to *speak* to the rock rather than strike it (see Num. 20:1–13). Look at how the Bible emphasizes the personal identity of the rock, as if it were a living stone: "*Speak to that rock before their eyes and it will pour out its water*" (Num. 20:8). But Moses, in his frustration with the people, instead struck the rock twice. Water still came out, but Moses's disobedience resulted in him not being allowed to enter the Promised Land.

Much later, Ezekiel was among the exiles in Babylon who had witnessed the destruction of the temple in Jerusalem. His message to those in exile was that God was over the nations and His ultimate plan to dwell among His people would not be overturned by any earthly kingdom. In a vision, Ezekiel takes us to the heavenly temple where he sees water coming out from under the threshold toward the east (see Ezek. 47:1). From the stones of the holiest place came the water of life. The water leaked out of the heavenly temple and became a fuller, deeper stream that brought life to everything it touched.

We take up the story again at the Feast of Tabernacles (see John 7). In this seven-day feast the focus was on celebrating that despite living in tents in the wilderness, God had wonderfully met Israel's needs, especially in giving them an ongoing supply of water. So, each day of the festival the priests would draw water from the Pool of Siloam and pour it out by the altar in the temple, with the climax on the last day of the feast. On that great day, Jesus stood up and declared in a loud voice, "'*Let anyone who is thirsty come to me and drink. Whoever believes in me, as Scripture has said, rivers of living water will flow from within them.' By this he meant the Spirit, whom those who believed in him were to receive*" (John 7:37–39). Jesus is the stone that gives living water. As we believe in Him, we are born again of "*water and the Spirit*" (John 3:5) and are remade into living stones that are so filled with the presence of God that we cannot contain His work in us. It flows out of us and brings life to our family, friends, and the rest of the world!

DECREE

If this is new thinking for you, decree it over yourself: "I am a living stone, and living water flows out of me!"

Who Will You Run With?

Other Benjamites and some men from Judah also came to David in his stronghold. David went out to meet them and said to them, "If you have come to me in peace to help me, I am ready for you to join me. But if you have come to betray me to my enemies when my hands are free from violence, may the God of our ancestors see it and judge you."

Then the Spirit came on Amasai, chief of the Thirty, and he said: "We are yours, David! We are with you, son of Jesse! Success, success to you, and success to those who help you, for your God will help you." So David received them and made them leaders of his raiding bands (1 Chronicles 12:16–18).

The Lord God designed you to run with a company of believers. He created each one of us to be linked with others of like heart and mind for the purpose of sharpening, strengthening, and building. No one can survive isolated, disconnected from relationships, for we were not made to be alone.

He says to you today: "Ask Me about relationships. Who should you run with? Who were you meant to build with? I have divine connections and alignments for you, but I want you to seek Me in order to hear My instructions. I am the master builder; I have blueprints, teams, and projects that I designate and delegate. I want you to play your part in this, and I want to give you people to journey with.

"When you attempt to build, labor, or journey on your own, you are quickly tired and easily picked off by the enemy. But when you come together to work for My success and My glory, all ego falls to the ground and you become one. Come and I will show you what I am planning and what I want for you. Come and see that you are better together; you thrive when you are in the right place with the right relationships."

ACTION

Ask the Holy Spirit to show you those who you can serve or serve alongside. He may show you faces, names, or simply roles or positions that you could slot into. Don't second-guess what the Spirit shows you; you may recognize some people, others may be surprising or unfamiliar. Then, ask the Lord for a prophetic revelation of this group in the future, five or ten years hence. Ask Him for discernment to see your tribe as they are, before, during, and after their Kingdom breakthrough. What beginning steps would they be taking alongside you? Ask Him to show you what you need to lay down and pick up and what you need to say and do to begin to run and build with your company.

Beware the Yeast of Politics

"Be careful," Jesus warned them. "Watch out for the yeast of the Pharisees and that of Herod" (Mark 8:15).

Jesus tells us to be on our guard for the dangerous viruses of the religious spirit and the political spirit. Those demonic spirits were prevalent when He walked the earth, and they are rampant around the world today. Don't let them infect you; don't let them have any place or foothold in you. You can love politics and even steward a call to influence in this arena, but be careful that you never begin to believe that politics carry the dominant solutions to humanity's well-being.

God's Kingdom can never be fully implemented at the political level because the political system is part of the world system. Politics can and should be influenced for good, and we should do all we can to call our civic leaders and systems to a higher standard of God's justice. But political ideologies do not exalt Jesus Christ or bring Heaven to earth, and they are not the Kingdom of God. Therefore, do not place your hope in them.

ACTION

Renounce and repent of any ways you have knowingly or unknowingly taken on board any "yeast" from politics or religion: "Jesus, You are my rock. In You I trust. You alone bring life, justice, and righteousness. I renounce any ideologies, methodologies, systems, or rules of men that I have trusted in and put ahead of You. That even includes any man-made church traditions and rules that have become dominant in my life. I repent of choosing legalism over grace, and salvation by my effort, and works rather than by faith in Christ alone. I refuse to allow anything to come between me and You, Lord."

DAY 171

Salvation Is Not Found in Politics

The law is only a shadow of the good things that are coming—not the realities themselves. For this reason it can never, by the same sacrifices repeated endlessly year after year, make perfect those who draw near to worship (Hebrews 10:1).

When leaders set the laws of the land and vote in measures that set some national standards for your country, remember that no matter how good these laws might be, your access to the Kingdom of Heaven has never been granted on the basis of lawmaking and law-keeping.

The message of Jesus Christ does not come with a heavy-handed "take-over" mandate that enforces rules and codes of morality that everyone must abide by, whether they truly want to or not. The people of a nation are not saved by which political or religious leaders they have at the top of the system. The law never saved anyone. It may be a reasonable measurement of a wholesome society, but it is not the core of the good news. We are saved only by the sacrifice of Jesus, and the new covenant that He made for us is in our hearts and written in our minds by His Spirit.

This word is good news also to those who live in nations with ungodly leaders who set corrupt laws and celebrate immorality. Rejoice that these leaders and their laws will not stop the spread of the Gospel and the knowledge of the glory of God (see Hab. 2:14).

DECREE

Choose to recommit yourself to Jesus and reacknowledge Him as your Lord and Savior: "Jesus, You alone are the way, the truth, and the life. You came into the world to seek and save the lost. I was one of those lost sinners, and You died for me. There is no other name under Heaven—no man, no leader, no political party or system, no law, no ideology or system—by which I can be saved."

See Your Tribe!

After this I looked, and there before me was a great multitude that no one could count, from every nation, tribe, people and language, standing before the throne and before the Lamb. They were wearing white robes and were holding palm branches in their hands. And they cried out in a loud voice: "Salvation belongs to our God, who sits on the throne, and to the Lamb" (Revelation 7:9–10).

Can you see them? Can you hear them? This is your tribe! This is your family! These are the ones you will spend all of eternity with. Picture them! Look at their beautiful faces, so diverse, so filled with variety! Watch as they dance, for each one dances in the style of the nation from which they came. As they come together to worship Jesus, the Lord's heart thrills as He looks at each face! He knows and loves each one. He knows and loves them as the unique individuals that they are. He knows their stories and the nations of their birth. He understands their languages and their hearts. As they lift their voices up together, a sound is let loose that is unlike any other. Can you hear it? It is glorious!

For as they stand before the throne, they worship as one. They bring their individual sounds and languages together, and in one accord they lift their voices to sing a song that declares the honor and the glory that is due to the Lamb. As one, they minister together, out of hearts that are set on the One who was slain for their sins. As one, they come together to be the family that the Father so longed for at the creation of the world.

And I hear the Father say: "Oh, how it delights My heart to see them! Oh, how it delights My heart to receive their worship! Their unity, as one Body, with one mind, one heart, and one purpose is like that which the world longs to see. Will you, My child, look and perceive it? Will you allow it to affect your heart and mind? Will you catch My heart for My family, your tribe? Will you let this glimpse of My Kingdom invade your life now? Begin to see your tribe. See your family on earth. Begin this beautiful coming together as one now."

ACTION

This word requires that you truly sit and see by the Holy Spirit. Look now. Let the Father bring this Scripture to life. Let Him show you what He showed the Apostle John in Revelation 7. Watch, listen, take it in, and then allow it to change the way you treat your brothers and sisters in Christ. See them as those you will spend eternity with. See them as your forever family, and ask the Lord to help you treat them accordingly.

Forged in the Fire

"And I will put this third into the fire, and refine them as one refines silver, and test them as gold is tested. They will call upon my name, and I will answer them. I will say, 'They are my people'; and they will say, 'The Lord is my God'" (Zechariah 13:9 ESV).

You have been formed, shaped, and forged in the fire of the furnace of God. The fire of God has brought you to a new place with a renewed vision and a fresh call. The Spirit says, "Allow Me to continue to bring My shape to you. As I hold you in My fire, let Me shape you and mold you in a new way."

Just like a blacksmith, the Lord Himself holds you in the fire and then brings you into the new shape He has fashioned for you alone. Allow Him to do this. Yield to His hand and the fire. Submit to the reshaping. It is for His glory in you and from you that He does this. Yield to His hand and receive your new form.

WORSHIP

Sing your response back to God! Many of you will know "Refiner's Fire," Brian Doerksen's worship song from the 1990s. There's also a more recent song, "Refiner" by Maverick City Music. Find a song about refining fire that you enjoy, sing along, and as you do, meditate on the words, giving Jesus your life again in that moment. Allow Him to take you deeper into the fire of His shaping and burning. Make your song your prayer.

DAY 174

Weapons Forged for You

*The weapons of our warfare are not physical [weapons of flesh and blood].
Our weapons are divinely powerful for the destruction of fortresses* (2 Corinthians 10:4 AMP).

Yesterday we considered the refiner's fire and saw the Lord like a blacksmith, fashioning you into a new shape. And I see that in the furnace He has also forged weapons of the Kingdom, and the King has placed them in your hand and also inside of you. You are on fire, a flaming Kingdom warrior! You are unstoppable and invincible with these fiery Kingdom weapons which the Lord has entrusted to you for this time. See what is in your hands and learn to wield these weapons of warfare.

Align with our warrior commander, the Lord God of the Hosts, *Yahweh Elohim Sabaoth*, and open your hands to learn from Him. He trains you and shows that you have to move with these bespoke weapons of war: God's Word, truth, fire, hope, glory, and so much more that He has given to you, custom fitted for you personally.

ACTION

Open your hands and see what He has put in them. Ask the Lord to open your eyes and senses by His Spirit to see and feel them in the spirit.

Ask the Lord to describe these weapons He has forged in the fire for you and how to use them. See how He moves with you to release His fire power from you! Allow Him to train you. Be diligent in the training. Follow His moves.

DAY 175

Our Responsibility

[Jesus] *told them another parable: "The kingdom of heaven is like a mustard seed, which a man took and planted in his field. Though it is the smallest of all seeds, yet when it grows, it is the largest of garden plants and becomes a tree, so that the birds come and perch in its branches"* (Matthew 13:31–32).

Have we surrendered our responsibility for our nation to a few political, business, media, or religious leaders or personalities? Did we fall into the trap of believing that casting a vote one day every few years was enough to bring righteousness to our nation?

What makes a nation righteous? Its laws? Its leaders? No! It grows from its mustard seed beginnings and spreads, first in the hearts of individuals, then families, then communities, who choose to follow Jesus Christ for themselves. It is never a law or set of laws thrust upon a person or people; it is all about each individual heart's response to their Savior. And from that response we each choose, as individuals and then as communities, to align to biblical morality. We shouldn't need to legislate morality through our nation's laws because if everyone chooses Jesus and follows His ways, His teaching, and His example, then the need for these laws becomes obsolete! Ultimately this is what makes for righteousness within a nation, not setting moral laws.

Of course, we must still boldly and vocally stand against all that is immoral and in opposition to God. We must fight to make right all wrongs and injustices, and we must call our leaders (and ourselves) to account for their (and our) actions or inactions. We absolutely need lobbyists (prophets) who go into the political arena and speak a plumb line of righteousness. But we must each steward the primary responsibility of disciplining those around us. This is not about merely influencing with a vote for a politician who then does the work for us. No! This is about building an alternative every day that shows Jesus as the solution in everything; it's about building His Kingdom.

ACTION

Command the demonic spirit of abdication of responsibility to leave you now, and ask Jesus for ways that you can point the world to Him afresh. Take time to consider Jesus's parable of the mustard seed and be encouraged that you are an agent for the Kingdom that He describes!

Are You an Influencer or Builder?

According to the grace of God given to me, like a skilled master builder I laid a foundation, and someone else is building upon it. Let each one take care how he builds upon it. For no one can lay a foundation other than that which is laid, which is Jesus Christ. Now if anyone builds on the foundation with gold, silver, precious stones, wood, hay, straw—each one's work will become manifest, for the Day will disclose it, because it will be revealed by fire, and the fire will test what sort of work each one has done. If the work that anyone has built on the foundation survives, he will receive a reward. If anyone's work is burned up, he will suffer loss, though he himself will be saved, but only as through fire (1 Corinthians 3:10–15 ESV).

Are you an influencer or a builder? You may be used to thinking, "How much influence can I have?" or "How can I bring the Kingdom of God to the earth by the role I play, the platform I have, or the position I ascend to?" In the Bible we see examples of people who are influencers like this, the leading lights in the Old Testament being Esther, Daniel, and Joseph. They all had a major, significant influence in the life of their nations.

Predominantly, influencers have a mandate to dismantle and will tear down, by their proximity, the world systems. This does require faithful presence in the midst of the world's systems because when you, the salt and light, move out of that world system, it will revert back to its demonic roots. These worldly systems are built on a foundation to honor satan. (It's why satan had them to offer to Jesus when he tempted Him [see Luke 4:5–7].)

But today the Spirit is prompting another question of you. Ask, "What can I build?" In First Corinthians 3:10, Paul likens himself to a skilled master builder and in verse 14 he says that if what has been built survives, the builder will receive a reward.

Know whether you are an influencer or a builder. There is a grace on building that we have not yet truly tapped into in these days. Recently, we have applied any building grace to either build empires of men or megachurches. In doing so, we have fallen back into becoming more fascinated by influence, therefore losing a main biblical thrust to create and build Kingdom of God structures. Are you an influencer or a builder?

ACTION

Spend time with the Holy Spirit, asking the questions: Am I called to be an influencer or a builder? Where am I to influence or build? Have I squandered the grace to build? Do I need to repent of building my own mini-empire?

DAY 177

Building the Kingdom of God

Your Majesty looked, and there before you stood a large statue—an enormous, dazzling statue, awesome in appearance. The head of the statue was made of pure gold, its chest and arms of silver, its belly and thighs of bronze, its legs of iron, its feet partly of iron and partly of baked clay. While you were watching, a rock was cut out, but not by human hands. It struck the statue on its feet of iron and clay and smashed them. Then the iron, the clay, the bronze, the silver and the gold were all broken to pieces and became like chaff on a threshing floor in the summer. The wind swept them away without leaving a trace. But the rock that struck the statue became a huge mountain and filled the whole earth (Daniel 2:31–35).

Yesterday God prompted you to ask, "What can I build?"

The New Testament helps us to understand that the systems of the world (referred to as Babylon in Revelation) will one day be judged. The world systems that we seek to influence are corruptible and unsustainable and will one day come to an end. Therefore, we do not only seek to *influence* world systems, but we also seek to *build* the Kingdom of God, which is permanent and eternal.

Education systems, political philosophies, economic ideologies, the entertainment industry, and so on, are part of the kingdoms of the world and are therefore only temporary. The New Testament urges building the Kingdom of God. It's the very core of the Lord's prayer. "Your Kingdom come" is not solely about the date of the return of Jesus Christ; it's about ushering in the Kingdom of God here and now. It's about creating systems that people can migrate to that will interface with and infect (in a good way!) the world.

"*I will build my church,*" the great statement of Jesus in Matthew 16:18, sets a new tone. We, the people of God, must build the education system, not for the exclusive use of the people of God but rather as a standard of the best education, with a wide-open door to everyone. We, the people of God, must build television studios that tell wholesome, moral stories. We build the new banking system and depopulate the world's banking systems. We use our energy to build predominantly.

ACTION

First, read all of Nebuchadnezzar's dream and Daniel's stunning interpretation in Daniel 2. Then, continue to pray and ask the Holy Spirit, "What would You like me to build of Your Kingdom here on earth?" and "What new things am I to build as a Kingdom alternative to the world's systems?"

Remember, do not despise the day of small beginnings! (See Zechariah 4:10.)

Of One Mind and Spirit

Therefore if there is any encouragement in Christ, if any consolation of love, if any fellowship of the Spirit, if any affection and compassion, make my joy complete by being of the same mind, maintaining the same love, united in spirit, intent on one purpose. Do nothing from selfishness or empty conceit, but with humility consider one another as more important than yourselves; do not merely look out for your own personal interests, but also for the interests of others. Have this attitude in yourselves which was also in Christ Jesus (Philippians 2:1–5 NASB).

Not one of us ever wants to admit to selfishness nor do we purposely try to be selfish. Yet I feel the Spirit of the Lord putting His finger on this Scripture and saying: "You can never be of one mind and one spirit if you are not actively looking to care for the interests of others. This is not just 'others' in reference to those who are in your household or immediate family, but these 'others' are those in your spiritual family, your brothers and sisters in Christ! It's easy to look out for the interests of your family members because you love them. It is not so easy to consider the person across the aisle from you as more important than yourself. Yet this is My desire for My church, for you are My spiritual family!"

The answer to all of the fighting, competition, and striving to be right is found in this Scripture! Yet it begins with you. It starts with each person choosing that position of humility and beginning to ask, "Jesus, whose interests should I be looking out for today? Jesus, in which relationship do I need to choose the position of humility?" For Jesus, who left His seat and position in Heaven to come down and be born as a human baby, knows how to teach you humility. He knows how to prefer or think of someone before Himself; He lived it and gave Himself for us. He's the expert, and He is urging you to ask Him!

ACTION

In your quiet time with the Lord, ask Him if there is anyone that He'd like you to reach out to in order to begin showing interest. Is there someone who needs a friend, needs encouragement, an extra hand, an afternoon coffee time, or maybe even a financial gift? Then ask Him if there is anyone in the Body that you don't particularly like or have never considered. If He highlights someone, ask Him how you need to choose humility and put that person above yourself.

Pledging Allegiance to God

The Lord has established his throne in the heavens, and his kingdom rules over all (Psalm 103:19).

I saw heaven standing open and there before me was a white horse, whose rider is called Faithful and True. With justice he judges and wages war. His eyes are like blazing fire, and on his head are many crowns. He has a name written on him that no one knows but he himself. He is dressed in a robe dipped in blood, and his name is the Word of God. The armies of heaven were following him, riding on white horses and dressed in fine linen, white and clean. Coming out of his mouth is a sharp sword with which to strike down the nations. "He will rule them with an iron scepter." He treads the winepress of the fury of the wrath of God Almighty. On his robe and on his thigh he has this name written: king of kings and lord of lords (Revelation 19:11–16).

My Kingdom is advancing. My government is increasing with peace, with righteousness, and with justice, and My rule is being made known across the face of the earth. But today let Me make My rule known in *your life* afresh.

You have been saved out of one kingdom into another Kingdom. This Kingdom, which is My Kingdom, requires your full allegiance and commitment to Me who rules over it. As one who is part of My Kingdom, your central identity is no longer biological and your central allegiance is no longer national or even global. You have been redeemed and rescued into My Kingdom. Now you have a new paradigm of who "us" is. Your new "us" is the church, extending the Kingdom.

Therefore, know that you're not in the image of one nation or another, but you are in the image of Me. Made in My image and called by My name into My Kingdom, you are to be aligned with My values and are to steward My ways. You have My power ready to release as you extend My Kingdom wherever you go in My name. There must be repentance and freedom from everywhere your heart has wrongly formed an allegiance to anything or anyone other than Me, knowingly or unknowingly. It is time to break free from wrong dependencies and run fully into pledging allegiance only to Me. I am your God, your King, your commander in chief, and under My rule I set you free to proclaim the Gospel of My Kingdom to others who are not yet free.

DECREE

Today say this prayer that pledges allegiance to Jesus: "I belong to You, Jesus. You are my Lord, my King, and I yield to Your reign. My loyalty lies with You. I am a citizen of Your Kingdom. I belong to the Kingdom of God. My allegiance is solely and entirely to Him whose hands are pierced, whose hair is as white as wool, and whose eyes are ablaze with fire."

DAY 180

A Sword and Trowel

After I looked things over, I stood up and said to the nobles, the officials and the rest of the people, "Don't be afraid of them. Remember the Lord, who is great and awesome, and fight for your families, your sons and your daughters, your wives and your homes." When our enemies heard that we were aware of their plot and that God had frustrated it, we all returned to the wall, each to our own work. From that day on, half of my men did the work, while the other half were equipped with spears, shields, bows and armor. The officers posted themselves behind all the people of Judah who were building the wall. Those who carried materials did their work with one hand and held a weapon in the other (Nehemiah 4:14–17).

In this season, it is vital that you know how to use both a sword and a trowel. The sword is for defeating the attempts of the enemy to come in and steal, kill, and destroy. The trowel is for building the things I am calling you to build now. This is not a season of inactivity. Nor is it a season for sitting back and watching. It is a season of advancement. I am on the move! I am building and I am taking ground! I call forth My army of warriors and builders!

As you advance and build, you will need to know how to fight for the future of your sons and daughters. You will need to discern when the enemy is coming after you, and you will need to know how to use the weapon of My Word to strike him down. Have My Word written upon your heart so that it is easily accessible to your mouth! Be a master swordsman by the memorization and active use of Scripture!

Equally, know how to use your trowel. Be a skilled builder. Know the times and the seasons, and through discernment know who to build with and how to put your talents to use. This is the time to make use of those callings and talents that have sat dormant within you. This is the time for those things that you have said that you'll do someday. Now is the time!

ACTION

Memorize a passage of Scripture this week. Write it out, post it where you'll see it often, and begin to build up your storehouse of Scripture. If you already do this, then stretch yourself and memorize long passages, such as full psalms or chapters of the Word.

DAY 181

Occupy the Kingdom on Earth

The Lord had said to Abram, "Go from your country, your people and your father's household to the land I will show you" (Genesis 12:1).

Step into the fullness of your inheritance as a citizen of the Kingdom of God! The fullness of the territory and land in the spirit realm that is open and available to you now is vast. The occupation of your inheritance is there for you to simply step into. You enter by faith and submission to Christ as Lord. There are no extra hoops to jump through, no additional exams to pass in order to enter into your inheritance. It is time to step into the provision assigned to you: your Kingdom of God mandate.

Look and feel, hear and know the fullness of what the Lord has set before you as your territory here on earth. Now you are to occupy in the name of the King and His Kingdom. You have felt at times like you have missed the boat. Perhaps you made a misstep, messed up the timing, or even made wrong decisions that got you to where you are today. Yet the Lord says to you: "I have an inheritance for you now to inhabit. It is yours to live in and abide with Me in. It is tailored and custom-built with you in mind. Step into the fullness of your inheritance in Me. Do not shy away or step back from what I have given you. Surrender to the occupation call of My Kingdom. Subdue your fears and enter into the expansiveness of My Kingdom."

RECEIVE

Pause, quiet yourself, and ask the Lord, "What is the territory, Lord, that You have assigned to me? What is the mandate that You have given me and called me to?"

Hear what the Lord shows and tells you. Take note and pray: "Lord God, please help me understand and navigate what You have given to me to steward at this time. Lord, I thank You for trusting me and for blessing me with all You have given me access to. I ask You to help me navigate and move forward into the fullness of the territory that You have blessed me with. I choose to step in and occupy. I choose to move forward into this new territory and not look back. I choose to walk forward and to be established where You desire for me to dwell."

CHAPTER 7

Encounter More!

Drink Deeply of Me

From now on, worshipping the Father will not be a matter of the right place but with the right heart. For God is a Spirit, and he longs to have sincere worshipers who worship and adore him in the realm of the Spirit and in truth (John 4:23–24 TPT).

Come close! Draw near to Me! Drink deeply from Me; pour out your heart before Me. See Me in both Spirit and in truth. I am so near, closer than you realize. Reach out and perceive My presence. Use your spirit to activate your senses in order to see, hear, and feel My presence. Set your gaze on Me! See Me on the throne! Bow down in awe and wonder as you see, hear, and feel the power of My majesty! As you allow the truth of who I am to overcome your senses, give Me all of your worship and all of your adoration. Drink deeply from My well, and let it satisfy you in spirit, soul, and body.

I have not called you to be a person who operates out of a less-than place. I have never wanted you to feel less than satisfied in Me, yet if you don't come and drink, if you do not pour yourself out as an offering before Me, I cannot fill you up. I cannot satisfy you if you are not hungry for Me. I cannot satisfy your thirst if you are not thirsty for Me!

Come to the place of encounter with a heart that longs to be satisfied in Me. Come ready to pour out your adoration in worship. Pour yourself out and then drink deep for I am here to encounter you. I am here to meet you and to fill you with the deep, deep satisfaction that only I provide.

The Lord is near to all who call on him, to all who call on him in truth (Psalm 145:18).

RECEIVE

Sit in contemplation and reflection of Revelation 19:1–10, and see, hear, and feel what is happening in this passage. What does their worship sound like? How would it feel? What would you see? Join in and add your praise to theirs. Allow your spirit to drink deeply as you worship the King.

DAY 183

Look Beyond!

So we fix our eyes not on what is seen, but on what is unseen, since what is seen is temporary, but what is unseen is eternal (2 Corinthians 4:18).

Do you know that there is more around you than what you see with your physical eyes? Do you know that there are other realms with beings and activities that exist and the way that this world exists? Do you know that you have the ability to see what seems unseen?

God has opened your eyes already so that you can look beyond and see what He sees. Though you may not feel like this is true for you, the Lord is inviting you to contend for what Paul urges and daily make the choice to fix your eyes on what is unseen. The Lord would say to you, "Push beyond this realm of sight, and intentionally seek out the spirit realm. Turn your attention to the pressing reality that the realm of the spirit is always around you."

So, when you feel overwhelmed by a circumstance, stop and ask, "What is going on in the unseen?" When something feels stuck in the natural, stop and ask, "Is there a spiritual blockage that is stopping this from moving forward?" Look and see! You may see with your physical eyes, or the eyes of your heart, you may also feel with your senses such as smell or touch, or you may just *know*. Each of these is just as valuable as the other, as God invites you into the fullness of fixing your eyes on the unseen in this season.

DECREE

- I choose to believe that I can *already* see into the spirit realm.
- I choose to fix my eyes on what is unseen.
- I choose to look for God and His realm.

DAY 184

Access by Faith

Now faith is confidence in what we hope for and assurance about what we do not see. This is what the ancients were commended for. By faith we understand that the universe was formed at God's command, so that what is seen was not made out of what was visible (Hebrews 11:1–3).

Remember, there are new realms of the spirit that God is opening your eyes to in these days. Have no doubt; you have full, unhindered, unrestricted access to see all that the Lord invites you into today.

"It is by faith," the Spirit is saying to you today, "that you receive access to these things. It is by faith," He says, "that you are enabled to feel, sense, see, hear, and interact in the realm of what is spiritual. Allow Me to activate you in this moment to step into that which I have opened to you and for you.

"In this moment know that you are free to move past all fear and doubt about accessing that which is already open to you. You who are born of the Spirit, step into the fullness of what I have laid before you as your inheritance."

DECREE

This invitation God has laid out for you requires activation. Therefore, speak these decrees out loud:

- I choose to trust You, God, that You have given me what I need to access the realm of the spirit.

- I believe that there is an ease for me in seeing, hearing, and sensing You, Your words, Your visions, and all You want to show me in the spirit.

- I choose to activate, by faith, that access. I act now, and by the empowering of your Holy Spirit, I step into encounters and experiences with You behind the veil of the seen realm on earth into the unseen, invisible realm of heavenly things.

Your Body Becomes the Possession of God

How lovely is your dwelling place, Lord Almighty! My soul yearns, even faints, for the courts of the Lord; my heart and my flesh cry out for the living God (Psalm 84:1–2).

Our inner being, inner workings, and inner emotions are meant to desire Jesus and to long for His courts. The Lord says to you today that a new desire for Him is reemerging; your longing for Him is in "surge mode." But this is not all that will happen; this will not remain as only an inner, emotional, heart cry for the one who loves you. It will also break out of your inner world and your whole body; your *flesh* will start to desire Jesus again!

Just as King David in the Psalms saw his internal and external world unite to long for God, the same will happen to you. Your inner world will manifest on your physical frame. Your inner desire for Jesus will easily become a physical action.

Desire for God will *take over* and take possession of your bodily nature. Your aspirations and desires will get cleaned up and aligned, and every part of you will single-mindedly want to commune with God. You will no longer feel fragmented and frustrated over what happens when inside you is a holy thought but it never seems to work out into fully holy actions.

The Lord says that as your desire for Him is restored, there will also be a restoration that comes to brokenness and weakness in your physical frame. You will be healed from the inside out, and wellness will have your heart and your physical being.

Dear friend, I pray that you may enjoy good health and that all may go well with you, even as your soul is getting along well (3 John 2).

This prayer from the Apostle John links the wellness of your physical health to the wellness of your soul. It's a beautiful place to be called, to be so aligned throughout your whole being that every facet of you is well! This is God's plan for you today.

RECEIVE

Take time to open yourself up to the wholeness of God that is rushing toward you. Wiggle your fingers and toes and see God fill you, top to bottom, with who He is, so that *all* you are becomes His possession and not given over to anything less.

DAY 186

Adventures in Higher Realms of Sight

Do not fret because of those who are evil or be envious of those who do wrong; for like the grass they will soon wither, like green plants they will soon die away. Trust in the Lord and do good; dwell in the land and enjoy safe pasture. Take delight in the Lord, and he will give you the desires of your heart. Commit your way to the Lord; trust in him and he will do this: He will make your righteous reward shine like the dawn, your vindication like the noonday sun (Psalm 37:1–6).

"I am carrying you to higher realms of sight," says the Lord. "Grab hold of My hand tightly and I will lift you." And He revealed an image of a young child being pulled up into the blue sky by her right hand. A strong, muscular arm was holding her, pulling her safely higher and higher. Her left arm dangled freely, and in that hand she clutched strings that had been cut loose from their moorings. Soon she let go of the strings and began to grab hold of shining objects that appeared out of the rich blue expanse. The higher she allowed herself to be pulled and the more she reached out, the greater the encounters she had with these bright, colorful shapes and patterns. Before long, the sky was a kaleidoscope of brilliant color and stunning images.

And the Lord says to you, "My child, I have so many adventures for you. Are you ready to be cut free from those things that are holding you down and holding you back?"

It's time to let go of all the ballast, all of the weight that has been grounding you and preventing you from rising into greater revelatory experiences with Christ. Let go of everything that you have made your security and your strength. Property, money, possessions, relationships, position, recognition—none of these aspirations are wrong in and of themselves, but if they come before God in your life, they become limiting weights that are holding you back from soaring ever higher with Him.

ACTION

What things have you made your security or strength? Make a list. Hint: It's often the thing that wakes you up at night or that you talk about a lot when you're stressed. Do you need to ask a spouse or a friend what you talk about a lot? Maybe it's something that you repeatedly pray for or that you have been disappointed not to have.

When you have your list, draw a line through each item, as if you were cutting a string. Repent of holding on to each one, and then tell Jesus that you're ready to go higher and see more with Him. Close your eyes and enjoy what He shows you!

DAY 187

Fight for Sight

One day, as the prophet Elisha and his servant awoke, they encountered a very difficult situation. They were surrounded by one of the greatest armies in the ancient world, the Syrians. What could two people do against an entire army?

> *When the servant of the man of God got up and went out early the next morning, an army with horses and chariots had surrounded the city. "Oh no, my lord! What shall we do?" the servant asked* (2 Kings 6:15).

You probably don't have a hostile army forming a circle around your home, but perhaps you do have a seemingly hopeless situation facing you today and feel similarly encircled by the enemy.

The Bible never pretends that our problems and difficulties don't exist. It simply declares that there is always more to see. Elisha's servant had literally a whole army of reasons to be discouraged! But he only saw half the story. Elisha told him not to be afraid because *"those who are with us are more than those who are with them"* (v. 16) and prayed so that he could see what was actually all around them in the spirit realm:

> *Then the Lord opened the servant's eyes, and he looked and saw the hills full of horses and chariots of fire all around Elisha* (2 Kings 6:17).

As a foundation, we learn to fight for sight by knowing what is in our Bibles well enough to contradict a half-truth with the full truth. This enables us to embrace what is truly real against the lies and deceptions of the enemy. Sometimes, however, the Lord can shut our eyes to the material things in front of us and open them to the spiritual realm, like what happened to Elisha's servant. That same Spirit of the Lord, the Lord of angel armies, is active in you today! It's time to open your eyes to what is really all around you!

ACTION

Praise God for the ministry of His angels. We do not think sufficiently about these spiritual beings. They are still active today, just as they were in Elisha's time! We are surrounded by angels, and they are appointed to look after us, minister to us, and deliver us from danger. Hills full of horses and chariots of fire! You can be absolutely certain that they are ready to be dispatched when required. Do you need to pray for your eyes to be opened to see?

Open Your Heart and See

And [I pray] that the eyes of your heart [the very center and core of your being] may be enlightened [flooded with light by the Holy Spirit], so that you will know and cherish the hope [the divine guarantee, the confident expectation] to which He has called you, the riches of His glorious inheritance in the saints (God's people) (Ephesians 1:18 AMP).

I hear Jesus gently yet firmly say: "You cannot look for Me with the eyes of your mind for you will not see Me in the Spirit if you look for Me with your intellect. Instead, look for Me with the eyes of your heart, your very core, and ask My Spirit to flood you with light so that you may see! Yes, the mind is important, but the things of My Spirit are not understood by mere human intelligence. The things of My Spirit are understood by the spirit. You are spirit, and so you can see in the spirit realm. It is not meant to be difficult, and it is vital that you truly see.

"I come today to help you transition your thoughts to My thoughts. I come to give ease to where you have struggled to see and help you perceive what I am doing in the spirit realm. You have tried hard, and I'm pleased with your desire! But let Me come in and do what only I can; let Me enlighten the eyes of your heart. Let Me teach you how to see. Let Me open the eyes of your understanding. Let Me show you what I want you to see."

RECEIVE

Receive by praying this prayer: "Holy Spirit, help me catch what You want me to see today. It may not be anything that I've seen before or anything that I can think up, so I ask You to help me to perceive Your thoughts and to see Your activity. Open the eyes of my heart and help me to see."

You Will Work Miracles

Then [Jesus] said to the man, "Stretch out your hand." So he stretched it out and it was completely restored, just as sound as the other (Matthew 12:13).

I hear the Spirit of the Lord say, "It is the day of the *reclamation* of the miraculous, and it is the day of the *restoration* of the miraculous."

Reclamation is when the people of God reach up and grab the miraculous. Restoration is when God Himself sends down a new capability in the miraculous.

God says that as you contend and ask for miracles to be worked for you, in you, and through you, He will collide with you. He and you together will overturn brokenness in many. He and you will bring restoration of His order to the circle of lives that surround you.

The Lord says, "It is time for the church to get out of the shallow waters of the miraculous. It is deep-waters time. It is full-power time."

You are being empowered to completely restore lives. As the miraculous power of God pulsates through your being, that which existed before the fall, comprehensive wellness, will be enjoyed again. You will separate people from demonic, negative influences on their lives. You will restore health; you will restore homes; you will restore organizations. God is trusting you liberally with His power. He is saying that it is time to give back and reclaim what has been robbed.

God wants you to enjoy again that which was taken. It is the day of complete restoration!

ACTION

Restoration and reclamation of the miraculous will not happen if you are passive and do nothing. They require you to ask for the miraculous to be manifest in your life. God is reinstating and reestablishing His power in His church. You must ask to be part of this restoration story. Ask for miracles and work miracles. Take time to willingly volunteer and to receive miracle-working power.

Let Me See YOU!

For the Lord is the Spirit, and wherever the Spirit of the Lord is, there is freedom. So all of us who have had that veil removed can see and reflect the glory of the Lord. And the Lord—who is the Spirit—makes us more and more like him as we are changed into his glorious image (2 Corinthians 3:17–18 NLT).

Oh, My Bride, let Me see you, truly SEE you. I know you long to see Me clearly; I know your heart asks why you haven't seen Me as you desire to. I come today to answer this question, and I gently kneel right in front of you to tell you that you've built walls that prevent you from seeing Me. It's time to allow Me to take these down. Do you see the walls? Will you give Me access to those places that you keep well hidden? Those hidden places actually keep Me from fully connecting with you. They keep you from connecting with Me. They cloud your vision, so you can only see Me in a way that is distorted. Yet this is not what I want for you.

So, today will you give Me full access to every part of you? Will you come out of hiding? If it's too difficult, I can help. I just need your yes. It is My joy to bring increased freedom to your life! I want you to access every bit of freedom that I, your Savior, purchased for you! I want you to walk in it! Say yes and give Me permission to deal with these issues that have kept you walled in and contained. Say yes and trust Me.

ACTION

Watch for opportunities to peel back the surface layers in your life in order to give the Lord full access to every part of your heart. Picture it like a child who picks up rocks to see what's underneath or like a gardener who digs past all the topsoil, roots, and rocks to get underneath to where the nutrients and the dark, brown soil is that gives life. When you allow the Lord to get under those surface issues and into the deep, deep places, He can then cultivate the hidden gems in you. Feel the anticipation of allowing the Lord to smooth the rough edges, heal the deep pain, and bring out the treasure that lies inside of you. Look for ways to anticipate His work rather than leaving these areas hidden, unseen, and stuck behind walls.

DAY 191

Exploring for Hidden Treasures

It is the glory of God to conceal a matter; to search out a matter is the glory of kings (Proverbs 25:2).

Seek out the hidden things of God. Pursue Him with all your strength, and do not relent until you have unearthed His treasures. The Lord has hidden precious jewels of revelation that are for you, things that only you and He will understand. There are secrets of His Father's heart for you that will bless you and transform you when you find them.

Search these things out as an archaeologist would uncover ancient artifacts or an explorer would hunt for undiscovered places. Spend time with the map, which is the Word of God, and allow it to illuminate your steps: *"Your word is a lamp for my feet, a light on my path"* (Ps. 119:105). Allow the Holy Spirit to guide you to new places in Scripture, off the well-worn and beaten path, where you will learn new things.

Most importantly, spend time with God, making space for Christ Himself to show you things in your life that He wants to shine His light on. There is no shortcut to searching out a matter that God has concealed. He buries the treasures of His wisdom and knowledge deeply so that we might adventure with Him by His Spirit.

Are you ready to adventure and explore? Are you prepared to put in the time to hunt out the precious things that the Lord has hidden for you? Are you ready to let Him shine His bright light on you so that you can see both what is beneath your feet and on the path ahead of you?

RECEIVE

Pray: "Jesus, I receive the truth that I am a king and it is my glory to search out a matter, just as it is Your glory, as the King of kings, to conceal it. I am ready and prepared to go on an adventure and explore all the treasures You have for me. I trust You, Lord."

Angels and the Prayers of God's People

And I saw the seven angels who stand before God, and seven trumpets were given to them. Another angel, who had a golden censer, came and stood at the altar. He was given much incense to offer, with the prayers of all God's people, on the golden altar in front of the throne (Revelation 8:2–3).

Heaven is a very busy place, with angels and other spiritual beings and creatures appearing before the throne of God and carrying out various functions in the courts of the King. Just as satan, the adversary, appears before the Lord to accuse humans, so also angels speak on your behalf before the throne (see Job 1; 33:23–26).

The angels are not acting as mediators but rather preparing God for your prayers. You are able to go directly to God when you pray, but even so, you should be encouraged to know the angels are already there, speaking for you in the presence of God. It seems angels are doing what we ought to be doing! We appreciate it so much when our friends pray for us, how much more that the angels do so as well.

The Apostle John in Revelation speaks about an angel who offered incense on the altar in front of God's throne (see Rev. 8:3). The smoke of the incense, together with the prayers of God's people, went up before God from the angel's hand. The angel is bringing the prayers of God's people to His attention and in so doing enhances the prayers of the saints. The Lord responds to the angel's action of taking our intercessions and laying them before Him, and verse 5 tells us what happens next:

Then the angel took the censer, filled it with fire from the altar, and hurled it on the earth; and there came peals of thunder, rumblings, flashes of lightning and an earthquake.

This action of the angel unleashes God's righteous justice on the earth. It seems these angels want to act in judgment against evil and injustice and play their part in bringing about the new heavens and the new earth. These angels are some of who you have on your side, fragrancing your prayers with incense! Wow!

ACTION

There is another example worth reading today; in Zechariah 1:8–13 the angel of the Lord prays and brings the good news of God's mercy to the prophet. Knowing that angels are backing up your prayers to God should radically alter your prayer life.

DAY 193

"Shoes Off!"

When the Lord saw that he had gone over to look, God called to him from within the bush, "Moses! Moses!"

And Moses said, "Here I am."

"Do not come any closer," God said. "Take off your sandals, for the place where you are standing is holy ground." Then he said, "I am the God of your father, the God of Abraham, the God of Isaac and the God of Jacob." At this, Moses hid his face, because he was afraid to look at God (Exodus 3:4–6).

I heard the Lord say, "Shoes off!" as He extended to you an invite to come very close to Him. He says to you: "Just as I invited Moses to take off his sandals for the ground upon which he stood was holy, so I say to you, 'Shoes off!' you are on holy ground, the place where encounters and transformation happen as a constant occurrence. In fact, your whole life has become holy ground because of My presence in and around you. So, 'Shoes off!'—position yourself for an encounter, and just like Moses assumed a posture of curiosity and looked to see what was going on, come ready to inquire, to investigate, and press in, and see what I will do as we meet.

"As you take your shoes off as a sign of being at home, know also that as your shoes come off your feet today, you are making a statement that you are at home in My presence, that you belong in this place of intense encounter and transformation. This uncomfortable place of meeting is also meant to be entirely comfortable for you. Don't rush, linger. Don't be hesitant, but come right in and let Me overwhelm you with the weight of who I am."

ACTION

Right now, close your eyes and think about Jesus. Start to focus on the presence of God. Can you feel Him? Can you feel His weight? Can you see and sense and taste and feel Him? Breathe in and breathe out. His presence surrounds you. Let yourself become increasingly aware of His glory on you right now.

Can you feel that stirring in your chest, that comforting warmth, the tingles on your skin as you increase in awareness of the nearness of God?

He is here. He is with you. His presence is on and around you.

You are a temple of the Holy Spirit, and the Spirit of God, the glory of the Lord, rests on and in you.

Born of the Spirit

Jesus answered, "Very truly I tell you, no one can enter the kingdom of God unless they are born of water and the Spirit" (John 3:5).

You are born of the spirit, and you are primarily spirit. You are one who is made to move, breathe, and live in and from the spirit realm. You are born again in Christ, given access to both the seen and unseen. You are fully born and formed in the spirit. It is easy for you to not only encounter God and His angels but also the fullness of the many locations and experiences in invisible places. The unseen spirit realm is open to you because you are one born of the Spirit.

As you begin to realize this truth that you are one born of the Spirit, I see that the Lord has His hand on you, pressing you deeper into that specific revelation and realization.

You are spirit, soul, and body. Your home is as much in the spirit realm as it is in the earth realm in which you currently live and breathe.

ACTION

Ask the Lord to show you what it means to be one who dwells in the spirit with Him.

Make time to quiet yourself. Close your eyes and thank God out loud that you have been born of His Spirit. Ask the Lord to open your heart and mind to this truth. Speak out loud that you desire this truth to be more of a reality for you. Ask God to take you on a journey of exploration. Welcome the Holy Spirit to be your guide and to take you by the hand and lead you in these encounters beyond the veil. Trust God, and say yes to all that He has for you in this moment.

Understanding with God

God looks down from heaven on all mankind to see if there are any who understand, any who seek God (Psalm 53:2).

"Do you not see? Do you not understand, My child? Ask Me for My understanding and My perception at this moment, and surely I will give it to you. I am looking for those who seek My understanding and My perspective at this time. This is not the day for fighting for *your* personal viewpoint or establishing *your* opinion. This is the time when you focus on seeing and hearing My perspective and opinion and reflecting it.

"Move beyond your limited view. Come higher and see what is in front of you. Position yourself next to Me and look where I am watching."

I see Jesus Himself, pulling you up in the spirit to stand next to Him, to gaze and focus upon those things that He has His own eyes on. Choose to allow Him to lift you up and position you in that place in the spirit where you only see and perceive what God Himself is focused on.

Watch with God. Focus with God.

He longs for you to see what He sees and hear His voice to gain understanding.

RECEIVE

Ask Him for His opinion and viewpoint in this moment, and as you watch with Him, take note of what He shows you and reveals to you. Make this a regular practice and habit, and you will train yourself to see every circumstance from a heavenly, not earthly, perspective.

Continual Pursuit

Seek the Lord and his strength; seek his presence continually! (1 Chronicles 16:11 ESV)

Rejoice always, pray without ceasing, give thanks in all circumstances; for this is the will of God in Christ Jesus for you (1 Thessalonians 5:16–18 ESV).

The Lord calls you into a life of continual pursuit of His presence, where not a moment goes by when you are not measurably aware that He is with you.

He says: "Turn your eyes to Me at all times; look for Me in the small and seemingly insignificant moments. My promise to you in return is if you look for Me, you will find Me. If you pursue Me, I will draw near. Do not think that encounters are reserved only for certain moments and places in your diary. No! You can meet with Me in the supermarket, looking after your children, getting ready for work, typing emails at your desk, at the gym, and any other place that you can imagine. I am always accessible to you. Therefore, posture yourself with a level of determination to live in continual pursuit of Me. Seek Me continually, look for Me always, pray without ceasing, and you will find Me and be with Me."

Do not overcomplicate coming close to Christ Jesus. Do not reserve it for a later date in your diary or another day on your calendar. Every waking moment is a seek-His-face moment. Every millisecond is a millisecond you can spend in His presence.

ACTION

Repent of not continually pursuing Him, and recommit yourself to seek Him at all times today and every day. Every time you change location today, for example, if you move rooms or go out somewhere, take a moment to rejoice, give thanks, and pray something like: "Even here Lord, I seek You. I know You are here, and I welcome Your manifest presence here with me. Even as I go about my tasks, I am open to encounters with You and to hearing Your voice."

DAY 197

Miracles on Dark Days

Going on from that place, he went into their synagogue, and a man with a shriveled hand was there. Looking for a reason to bring charges against Jesus, they asked him, "Is it lawful to heal on the Sabbath?"

He said to them, "If any of you has a sheep and it falls into a pit on the Sabbath, will you not take hold of it and lift it out? How much more valuable is a person than a sheep! Therefore it is lawful to do good on the Sabbath."

Then he said to the man, "Stretch out your hand." So he stretched it out and it was completely restored, just as sound as the other. But the Pharisees went out and plotted how they might kill Jesus (Matthew 12:9–14).

The church has been guilty of thinking that it's incredibly difficult to see miracles come to the earth, that miracles are rare and only happen several steps away from us, and that somehow they are not our normal, regular experience. Have you fallen into this thinking? We seem to wrongly believe that to see a miracle requires carefully curated, faith-filled rooms, where the miraculous is fragile and seems to hang delicately in the balance. We worry to ourselves, "We dare not put a foot wrong or the miracle might shrivel up and die and not be seen!"

Yet Jesus heals the man with a withered hand, in the synagogue, on the Sabbath, surrounded by the skeptical and cynical Pharisees. Working miracles was forbidden on the Sabbath. In the place that was most controlled by religion, where His power was despised and feared, at the most contested time, with the religious leaders plotting against His life, Jesus works the miracle.

The Spirit of the Lord says to you today that the atmosphere He will work miracles in is the place of your greatest pain, the season of your greatest opposition, and the moment of your greatest confusion. When you are in total despair and even in hardness of heart and considerable brokenness, *that* is when Jesus will enable miracles to come!

We have set the wrong tone for expecting miracles; we think they must only come when we are faith-filled and feeling good. Jesus says to us today: "Now you must expect miracles at your most broken, when your energy is low and your faith is small, and the walls of oppression seem high around you. That is where you will see miracles, and that is when you can work miracles. When a miracle looks at its least likely and most difficult, when what has opposed you looks as if it is at its most victorious, in that place miracles will be seen!"

DECREE

Speak this out and believe it: "I am in the right place to see a miracle; I am loved by God as much now as I ever will be. I will see the goodness of God in the land of the living. God will make a way where there seems to be no way."

DAY 198

The Beautiful Veil

Now the Lord is the Spirit, and where the Spirit of the Lord is, there is liberty [emancipation from bondage, true freedom]. And we all, with unveiled face, continually seeing as in a mirror the glory of the Lord, are progressively being transformed into His image from [one degree of] glory to [even more] glory, which comes from the Lord, [who is] the Spirit (2 Corinthians 3:17–18 AMP).

I saw a thin veil, a fine, white fabric, that appeared very beautiful to the eye and shimmered in the bright light shining behind it. It rippled in the gentle breeze and folded over your hands and around your body. It was smooth and soft to the touch and made a nice blanket to sit down under, and was a covering for sleep. And that is what happened. The veil became a sheet, covering your head and body. It seemed strong and protective, and it called to you and encouraged you to lie down underneath it and slumber. You settled down and went to sleep underneath it. But it is not the best for you!

Jesus has torn the veil! We have had the veil removed so that we can see His glory full on. Don't be tempted to settle for half sight or living lying down. Jesus won freedom for you so that you can stand, worship, and go further! Stretch yourself, train yourself to want more of an encounter with the Holy Spirit all the time. It is time to stand up, free from all that veil (no matter how pretty or comfortable it seems), and be transformed by degrees of glory to even more glory!

ACTION

Train yourself to drink deeply of God as you worship Him. Push your spirit to go further and with more unveiled abandon every time you come before the Lord in praise and worship. You have been drinking from His fountain with a thimble as a cup, and your spirit has become used to feeling satisfied with these small amounts. You come to Him and He gives you what you ask for, but He has much more for you if you would only ask. Now it is time to drink from a bigger glass. And soon you will come to Him armed with buckets!

In that day you will sing: "I will praise you, O Lord! You were angry with me, but not any more. Now you comfort me. See, God has come to save me. I will trust in him and not be afraid. The Lord God is my strength and my song; he has given me victory." With joy you will drink deeply from the fountain of salvation! (Isaiah 12:1–3 NLT)

A white-tailed deer drinks from the creek; I want to drink God, deep draughts of God (Psalm 42:1 MSG).

DAY 199

Your Church Has an Angel!

In the Book of Revelation John is told to write "what is now" (chapters 1–3) and "what will take place" (chapters 4–22). There are seven prophetic words (seven letters for seven churches) in chapters 2 and 3. These are "what is now" for John's present time and refers to the state of the seven churches of Asia, each of which has a guardian angel, an *angelos* (this Greek word means "messenger").

Carefully read the following excerpts from these seven letters, even though there is some repetition:

The mystery of the seven stars that you saw in my right hand and of the seven golden lampstands is this: The seven stars are the angels of the seven churches, and the seven lampstands are the seven churches (Revelation 1:29).

To the angel of the church in Ephesus write: These are the words of him who holds the seven stars in his right hand and walks among the seven golden lampstands (Revelation 2:1).

To the angel of the church at Smyrna write: These are the words of him who is the First and the Last, who died and came to life again (Revelation 2:8).

To the angel of the church at Pergamum write: These are the words of him who has the sharp, double-edged sword (Revelation 2:12).

To the angel of the church at Thyatira write: These are the words of the Son of God, whose eyes are like blazing fire and whose feet are like burnished bronze (Revelation 2:18).

To the angel of the church at Sardis write: These are the words of him who holds the seven spirits of God and the seven stars. I know your deeds; you have a reputation of being alive, but you are dead. Wake up! (Revelation 3:1–2)

To the angel of the church at Philadelphia write: These are the words of him who is holy and true, who holds the key of David. What he opens no one can shut, and what he shuts no one can open (Revelation 3:7).

To the angel of the church at Laodicea write: These are the words of the Amen, the faithful and true witness, the ruler of God's creation (Revelation 3:14).

Seven churches, seven angels, and one angel per church. Angels care about all that takes place in our cities and churches, and they help reveal God's will to us. What a comfort to know how deeply God has ordered things for our good! Have we failed to listen to the messenger angels who surround and guard us? Do we need to begin to pay more attention to what is happening in the spirit realm around us and our churches and cities?

RECEIVE

What would Jesus say to the angel who watches over your church? Spend time receiving fresh revelation from Him and document what He reveals to you: *To the angel of the church at* [insert the name of your church, fellowship, or city] *write…*

DAY 200

I Am Your Refuge

The Lord will roar from Zion and thunder from Jerusalem; the earth and the heavens will tremble. But the Lord will be a refuge for his people, a stronghold for the people of Israel (Joel 3:16).

This I declare about the Lord: He alone is my refuge, my place of safety; he is my God, and I trust him (Psalm 91:2 NLT).

My children, it is so crucial that you learn to see Me as your refuge. There will be more and more days when you have no one else to turn to, no one to receive words of comfort from, and no one to bring relief. Yet, for you who have learned to see Me as your hiding place, you will know where to turn and where to go for refuge. You will have a sacred space with Me, where you and I commune, and where I comfort, instruct, strengthen, and steady you. This place will allow you to thrive in the days to come, which will be extremely challenging.

So I urge you now, come and truly *see* Me as your place of refuge. Let Me show you what this place looks like. Open your eyes to see how it looks when you and I meet together. See the expression on My face. See My delight when I see you running toward Me! See what I have prepared for you in this place of refuge. There is much to explore!

And not only that, but after you have learned to see and really spend time in this place, I will then ask that you share with others. You will take what you have been given from Me and you will share it with others. For they will need to know how to take refuge in Me, as they will need to know those who truly know Me as the God in whom they are safe.

ACTION

Sit with the Lord and ask Him to show you what your place of refuge in Him looks like. It could be a garden where you meet with Him; it could be a vista where you sit and overlook things from a high vantage point of safety. Or it could be, as Psalm 91 describes, a place that is hidden under His feathers. It will be unique to you and Him, so ask Him to show you what your safe place, your refuge in Him looks like. And then begin to meet with Him there.

DAY 201

"Come Up Here!"

After this I looked, and there before me was a door standing open in heaven. And the voice I had first heard speaking to me like a trumpet said, "Come up here, and I will show you what must take place after this." At once I was in the Spirit, and there before me was a throne in heaven with someone sitting on it. And the one who sat there had the appearance of jasper and ruby. A rainbow that shone like an emerald encircled the throne. Surrounding the throne were twenty-four other thrones, and seated on them were twenty-four elders. They were dressed in white and had crowns of gold on their heads. From the throne came flashes of lightning, rumblings and peals of thunder. In front of the throne, seven lamps were blazing. These are the seven spirits of God. Also in front of the throne there was what looked like a sea of glass, clear as crystal (Revelation 4:1–6).

"Come up here!" calls the Lord, just as He did to John the Revelator. "Come up here and be with Me where I am." And at this I saw an invite being handed to you today, an invitation to join God in the heavenly places and to encounter Him in His domain. Your invite was handed to you, and it was personalized especially for you. You have been invited to encounter God in the heavenly realms and to meet with Him in the throne room! The Lord says, "I have made space for you, and I extend an invitation toward you to come up here to be with Me."

This is not a generalized call to the masses, but a very special and specific call that He makes directly to those who will listen, receive, and accept. Will you accept His invite? As you say yes to God, allow Him to take you in. You may feel the encounter, see it, sense it, taste it, hear it, or you may just know that it is going on. You may need to push past your fears and apprehensions and let God take you in. You may need to lay aside your insecurities and worries, throwing off every weight that could distract you as God calls you to "come up here!"

Do not allow yourself to become distracted by other things—or even by the encounter itself. Your eyes must be fixed on Jesus. He is the reason for the encounter, the reason for your breath, and the reason for your life. He is the focus and He is the agenda! Fix your eyes on Him; let distractions cease; respond to His invite: "Come up here!"

ACTION

As God extends this invitation to you to "come up here," it is important that your mental and physical space is cleared of distractions. Ask God to shine His light on what these distractions are. You may know what they are already, or you may not even realize that they exist. As you receive revelation about your distractions, hand them over to God. Give Him your distractions, and then give Him your undivided attention. Once you have done this, it is time to reply to His invite. God is asking, "Will you come up here?" What do you say in reply?

God Interrupts Our Senses

Our God is in heaven; he does whatever pleases him (Psalm 115:3).

I heard the Lord say, "I will interrupt how you usually hear from Me and how we normally interact. I will cause you to fall into trances and take you up in the spirit to see new things."

A trance is a stunned state, where a person's body is overwhelmed by the Spirit of God. The New Testament Greek word for *trance* is *ekstasis*, from which we get the word *ecstasy*. This should suggest that they are a good thing! Often a person in a trance is stupefied, held, or arrested, and placed in a supernormal state of mind. It is often a visional state, where revelation is received. However, the word *trance* nowadays makes us nervous because it has been hijacked by the occult and New Age practitioners. However, Scripture has many examples of good, important, God-ordained, God-given trances, for example: *"When I returned to Jerusalem and was praying at the temple, I fell into a trance"* (Acts 22:17).

It is in this trance that Paul is given an immediate instruction to leave Jerusalem. God caught him up into the spiritual realm where he could be spoken to with urgency and be given a life-saving action that he might otherwise have missed!

Peter, in Acts 10, is also placed in a trance and receives his instruction to take the gospel to the Gentiles. Had he not had the trance Christianity may not have come to the Gentiles! The entire history of the church was changed by one experience of a trance and an entirely different way of interpreting Scripture was given. Through this trance Gentiles came to faith in Jesus; Christianity was no longer viewed as being exclusively a Jewish faith. Praise God!

ACTION

Do business with God today by giving Him permission to speak to you, challenge you, and even to catch you up in the spirit realm however He sees best. Repent for resisting Him and wanting to be the only one in control of your spiritual encounters. Pray: "God, I want to be led by You and You alone."

DAY 203

Eagerly Desire

Now eagerly desire the greater gifts. And yet I will show you the most excellent way (1 Corinthians 12:31).

It is time to shift your desire to another level. It is time to deliberately and boldly work up your eagerness for God. It is time to make a daily, hourly choice to eagerly desire the gifts of the Spirit in your life.

Watch and listen to yourself carefully today. As you go about your day, check how many times you think or say, "I really want..." or "I'd really like..." or "Today I really must..." or "I need..." or "I'd love..."

As you become more aware and conscious of all these needs, wants, and desires that you already have, begin to work with the Holy Spirit to replace them—or supersede them—with an eager desire for the gifts He has given you.

Step out of bed and say, "Right! Today I want to pursue You, God, and I eagerly, earnestly desire the gifts You have given me to become manifest in my life in greater measure!"

Every time you catch yourself saying, "I want" or "I need," add another request: "But even more I want to use the gifts You have given me, Holy Spirit!"

ACTION

Plan how you will keep a check on yourself today so that you think about the Holy Spirit and His gifts whenever you express another want, desire, or need. Be eager about the gifts, especially prophecy. These are gifts for you! Desire them!

Follow the way of love and eagerly desire gifts of the Spirit, especially prophecy (1 Corinthians 14:1).

Vital Faith

As Jesus was on his way, the crowds almost crushed him. And a woman was there who had been subject to bleeding for twelve years, but no one could heal her. She came up behind him and touched the edge of his cloak, and immediately her bleeding stopped. "Who touched me?" Jesus asked (Luke 8:42b–45).

Four times Dr. Luke uses the Greek verb *haptomai*, "to touch," in the recording of this incident in Jesus's ministry. As a medic, he must have been very interested in how someone, simply by touching Jesus in a crowd, could be amazingly healed.

All that this woman did was touch the edge (or hem) of Jesus's cloak, and from that moment, everything about her life changed! After she identified herself, Luke records that Jesus told her that it was her faith that healed her (see Luke 8:48). Saint Augustine said, "Faith is to believe what we do not see; the reward of this faith is to see what we believe." The woman had spent an enormous amount of money consulting doctors, and none had been able to cure her. Hearing that Jesus was in town, she sought Him out. She must have heard hundreds of testimonies of Jesus's healing miracles, and faith, which comes by hearing, must have welled up in her heart.

It is striking that we are told that she had suffered this bleeding disorder for twelve years. A ruler of a synagogue called Jairus had a daughter who was very sick and near to death. His little girl was twelve years old. While all this had been going on, Jairus had been trying to get Jesus to his house to save his daughter—who had been born in the year that the woman had begun to suffer (with disastrous consequences for her religious and social life). How remarkable—two lives joined by the same number of years, and both lives are wonderfully changed on the very same day.

The faith of this woman was vital for her healing miracle. A holy desperation is so often seen in those who experience longed-for breakthroughs. These are the times that a passive faith simply will not do. One preacher who was greatly used in a major awakening in the United States, Jonathan Edwards, called this kind of faith "pressing into the Kingdom of God." By this he meant that we need an active, dynamic faith that is joined to a regular pursuit of God.

DECREE

Pray about something in your life that you need to be "pressing into the Kingdom of God" for. You must be like the psalmist: "*One thing I have desired of the Lord, that will I seek*" (Ps. 27:4 NKJV). To build your faith, write some decrees or declare out loud what you desire.

DAY 205

Fighting Faith

Now faith is confidence in what we hope for and assurance about what we do not see (Hebrews 11:1).

In attempting to answer the question, "What is faith?," many Bible teachers speak about what they call "conversion faith." This is the faith you had when you acknowledged your sins and first believed that Jesus was your Savior and your Lord. On that day you were justified by faith, declared innocent by God. You cannot be a born-again, saved follower of Jesus without conversion faith.

But that's not the end of the matter regarding faith. A second kind of faith is usually called "continuing faith." It is the kind of faith we read of in Hebrews 11. It is the confident assurance that what we hope for is going to happen or *"the evidence of things we cannot see"* (Heb.11:1 NLT). You must go on believing in Jesus every day. You need *continuing* faith, not just *conversion* faith.

Next is what is called "charismatic faith." In First Corinthians 12, Paul mentions faith as one of the gifts of the Spirit (see verses 7–11). In the following chapter, he describes a faith that can move mountains (see 1 Cor. 13:2). Charismatic faith is mountain-moving-faith! It is a sudden, supernatural, surge of confidence (faith) in God that He is about to do something miraculous. We need to ask for this spiritual gift of faith. The woman with the bleeding disorder in Luke 8 (see yesterday's word), who desired a miraculous healing, had *charismatic* faith.

Today the Spirit of God wants to give you faith like that woman's, and He is calling it "fighting faith." This fighting faith you are being gifted does not ignore anxieties or tears, but it enables you to fight and push through to your place of breakthrough. This fighting faith requires both the divine and the human. It is a gift of the Holy Spirit to us that we must lay hold of and choose to act upon courageously and intentionally. Receive your gift of fighting faith!

ACTION

Put out your hands before God. Say something personal to Jesus such as, "I am ready to receive the gift of Your faith, Lord." Look at your fingertips as you pray and wiggle them to remind yourself that they are there. Now stretch out a finger as the woman who touched Jesus would have done. That finger is a conduit of the same power that Jesus felt go out from

Him. If you have a healing need, put that finger on the place that best represents the issue and say, "By faith I am healed by the power of Jesus Christ in me." Receive your healing now. Are you prepared to exercise that same fighting faith for the healing of others? It's time to go about your Father's business in the authority that He has given you through His Son!

Encounters as You Sleep

Jacob left Beersheba and set out for Harran. When he reached a certain place, he stopped for the night because the sun had set. Taking one of the stones there, he put it under his head and lay down to sleep. He had a dream in which he saw a stairway resting on the earth, with its top reaching to heaven, and the angels of God were ascending and descending on it. There above it stood the Lord (Genesis 28:10–13a).

The Lord is about to saturate your sleep in revelation and in streams of living water. As He does this He is washing off every entanglement that has harmed your sleep, and He is releasing to you an ability to rest deeply and encounter deeply at the same time.

The Lord decrees over you today: "Encounters are waiting for you while you sleep! I have prepared revelation for you to receive only when you sleep. Raise your expectation for dreams of fresh revelation for each new day. Expect encounters with angelic hosts who come and heal you from the pain of the previous day while you are in your bed. Expect transformational visitations of My spirit as you rest that will change and empower you."

As well as this, the Lord is ready and willing to heal night terrors, insomnia, and interrupted sleep. He says, "No longer will you wake up feeling exhausted and weary! I am releasing to you a full night's encounter-filled rest that will ready you for the tasks that are at hand."

Receive His healing now, in the name of Jesus!

ACTION

Pray around your bedroom and welcome God to speak. Welcome the angelic hosts to minister to you as you rest. Before you go to sleep, pray: "Holy Spirit, source of all revelation, I decree that I am open and ready to receive anything that You have for me as I sleep. I invite You to speak to me in dreams so that I might know Your heart better. As I rest tonight, reveal Your ways to me and help me understand them. My imagination is Yours, my mind is Yours; use them to speak to me tonight. Amen."

DAY 207

Doors of Access Are Open

When Jacob awoke from his sleep, he thought, "Surely the Lord is in this place, and I was not aware of it." He was afraid and said, "How awesome is this place! This is none other than the house of God; this is the gate of heaven" (Genesis 28:16–17).

The doors and the gates are open! There are new "access doors" available to you to access the spirit realm. I see the Lord establishing new access points in specific places in your home and even your region.

These access points are doors of access like Bethel was to Jacob, which we read in Genesis 28. They are doors or portals by which the angelic seem to ascend and descend unhindered. They are locations of special revelation and allow even greater access to supernatural encounters, as if these places on earth were fully open to the spiritual realm. I see angels marking specific locations and opening these doors as you partner with Heaven in this hour. I see a flurry of activity as the Lord marks your home and the region you reside in for His glory.

There are doors opening in the spirit in specific rooms in your home.

I see Holy Spirit "water wells" being broken open in the spirit in your home by angels; these have fountains of water springing up from inside your home and in specific locations in your region. In the spirit there is a flourishing orchard of trees that bear much fruit being established; these are growing both in your home and region.

RECEIVE

- Allow the Lord to attune your own spiritual senses to see and hear the doors, wells, and trees.

- Ask Him to show you where in your home and where in your region these are being revealed and established.

- Request that He shows you the meaning and name of the wells (we know from Scripture that all-important wells are given names) and what these fountains of water will accomplish in the spirit.

- Ask the Lord what trees have been planted and what their fruit is there to accomplish.

- Finally, ask the Lord what else you need to hear and understand to fully partner with what He is revealing to you today.

DAY 208

He Stood at My Side

At my first defense, no one came to my support, but everyone deserted me. May it not be held against them. But the Lord stood at my side and gave me strength, so that through me the message might be fully proclaimed and all the Gentiles might hear it. And I was delivered from the lion's mouth. The Lord will rescue me from every evil attack and will bring me safely to his heavenly kingdom. To him be glory for ever and ever. Amen (2 Timothy 4:16–18).

In every circumstance, whether it be a joyful celebration or all-encompassing grief, Jesus desires for you to know that He stands at your side. In times of spiritual warfare, you may see and hear Him as He paces as the Lion of the tribe of Judah. You'll feel the holy fear of His zealous righteousness, and you'll know that He is ready to release His roar over those in the spirit realm who have come to oppose you. At other times, when He is there to be a gentle healer, you may see Him with deep eyes that are filled with compassion toward you. And when He comes as the Revelator, the One who teaches, corrects, and imparts, you might see Him with piercing, burning eyes of fire.

Just as He stood with Paul as his support, strength, and defense, He stands with you, for He never leaves you or forsakes you. Just as Paul saw the Lord and knew that He was there standing with him when no one else would, so can you! He longs for you to see Him and encounter Him today, tomorrow, and every day. Believe this word for it is the cry of His heart for you!

"Encounter Me right where you are! Look around the room and see where I am! Feel with your senses and discover what emotions I am feeling for you right now! Let go of any preconceived notions or man's misconceptions that would say that I cannot be seen. Get rid of any excuses that you may have to give as reasons why you can't see Me. I desire for you to see! It is My will for you! Receive this gift today! Walk in it each and every day! Let Me be the One who stands with you, never to leave or forsake you no matter what may come. Look and see Me in every circumstance of every day!"

ACTION

As a daily practice, begin to look for Jesus in the room with you. See where He is standing. Notice what He is doing. Ask Him what He wants you to know today. Begin to discover the truth that He never leaves you or forsakes you.

DAY 209

Say No to the Counterfeit!

He who was seated on the throne said, "I am making everything new!"
Then he said, "Write this down, for these words are trustworthy and true"
(Revelation 21:5).

We do not want counterfeit encounters with God; we do not want to
be seduced by anything other than *His* voice, *His* ways, and *His* methods.
We do not want to be accidentally or inadvertently led by our own mental
wanderings or curses from our family line.

I heard the Spirit of God say that today there is an opportunity for you
to cleanse your family line and cleanse your own imagination; doors that
have been opened to divination, spiritual pollution, and off-course revelation can be slammed shut and not reopened.

I heard the Spirit say that you have stewarded some revelation that was
not completely illuminated by God. You may have been contaminated by
generational sin and your desire for comfort outside of His Kingdom. But
today the grace of God is poured out on you and your fears, and He is here
now to strip away all counterfeit revelation from you. God is standing right
with you, and He is removing blinders on your eyes and inner-revelation
distortions. He is decreeing that you will see and hear Him clearly and that
you will navigate straight paths of instruction. I see Him bringing a fresh
ability to be separate from your past; His sword moves to detangle you
from webs that keep you confused, misled, and fearful.

It is clean-up day for you! A time of cleaning up where decisions have
been made that didn't start in purity but instead began in fear. God is cleaning up where decisions were made from contaminated revelations that got
you off track. Receive the purification of God today. Allow His weighty
hand of glory to rest on you and to bring separation from your past and the
sins of your family line.

DECREE

Read Revelation 21:5 again and declare: "Lord Jesus, I want to work
with You today, and I agree that in Your holy name that all things in my
life are made new by You." Start the clean-up process with Him; repent of
everything that needs to be cleared out.

DAY 210

The Glory of the Lord

And the glory of the Lord will be revealed, and all people will see it together (Isaiah 40:5).

Be under no illusion that in the years ahead there will be a seemingly constant bombardment of bad news, fearmongering, and a social media news feed that contains every opinion except perhaps the Lord's. Don't be scared by this, as fear only leads to inaction and backing down. This noise of bad news is satan's reaction to the ever-increasing knowledge of the glory of the Lord, which is covering the earth in greater and greater measure year after year, just as Habakkuk prophesied: *"For the earth will be filled with the knowledge of the glory of the Lord as the waters cover the sea"* (Hab. 2:14). It is satan who is running scared, not the people of God!

So, who will counter all that is dark and depressing in this war of words? God's solution is you! You know that you are God's temple and His Spirit dwells in your midst (see 1 Cor. 3:16)! Prepare yourself to shine anew and afresh. Ignore satan's bad news and *be* the good news. You have more tools at your disposal that give you the potential to reach and influence more lives this year than at any point ever in history. What are you going to do to bring the knowledge of the glory of God to the earth?

> *When the priests withdrew from the Holy Place, the cloud filled the temple of the Lord. And the priests could not perform their service because of the cloud, for the glory of the Lord filled his temple. Then Solomon said, "The Lord has said that he would dwell in a dark cloud; I have indeed built a magnificent temple for you, a place for you to dwell forever"* (1 Kings 8:10–13).

When the thick cloud of the glory of the Lord descends on a place, it stops everything; all projects, processes, and schemes have to be put on hold. Even the temple priests, who were schooled, trained, and experienced in the ways of God, had to stop their business when the cloud filled the temple.

DECREE

Make a new commitment to share the good news of the Kingdom of God, which is advancing on the earth: "I am going to be someone who shares good news! I am a glory carrier. There is no temple anymore; there is me! I am going to host the glory of God. It is my job to share the knowledge of the glory of God with those who I can. It's time for me to transform my news feed!"

DAY 211

When God Comes

God came from Teman, the Holy One from Mount Paran. His glory covered the heavens and his praise filled the earth. His splendor was like the sunrise; rays flashed from his hand, where his power was hidden (Habakkuk 3:3–4).

It is the blackest night, yet in a moment dawn will melt the sky into color. The sun-streaked, fiery red rises over the dark silhouette of mountaintops; shimmering light fills the land with gold. It's the picture of God's glory and splendor filling the earth as He comes striding into His world.

Ahead of Him are thunderous, apocalyptic clouds of plague; behind Him, pestilence trails, for He brings judgment. For a moment He stands, a colossus in the land; beneath His feet the earth quakes and gigantic tectonic plates shift. A mountain crumbles into dust at a mere glance from Him.

People, who a moment ago thought they ruled the world, step out of their tents and gasp in disbelief, cowering behind the mud-brick walls of their homes. They know they are doomed. Their pride in their power and achievements now seems pitiable. The ruler of the universe has come to judge, no longer patiently waiting for people to freely acknowledge Him. It is a truly terrible sight. Dumbstruck, the people watch as His glory races toward the horizon, then sweeps beyond it, filling earth and sky. Then they see His hands and realize that this is where His power is hidden (see Hab. 3:4). From His hands intense light flashes outward as if He is the very origin of light itself, the center and sun of the whole universe! Back in the eons of space and time, those hands shaped a universe; now they come to judge it.

Between these two momentous moments, His hands reach out to us:

- Protecting us (see Exod. 33:22)
- Holding our hands (see Isa. 41:13)
- Feeding and providing for us (see Ps. 145:15–16)
- Nailed to a cross (see Mark 15:24)
- One day wiping away all our tears (see Rev. 21:4)

Such tenderness from one who wields such awesome power is truly amazing.

RECEIVE

Meditate on Habakkuk chapter 3. Close your eyes and ask Him to show you His hands and the power contained within them. Welcome any visions that the Holy Spirit gives you.

And don't forget that demons are driven out and people are healed by the finger of God (see Luke 11:20). This is your Kingdom mandate now; it's time to lay hands on people!

Becoming Proficient in Sight

But solid food is for the mature, who because of practice have their senses trained to distinguish between good and evil (Hebrews 5:14 NASB).

The realms of the spirit, the heavens that declare the glory of God, are invisible territories that are open to you.

But just as your eyes take time to get used to seeing in the dark, it will take time for you to adjust and navigate this realm. Allow the Holy Spirit to train your senses as you keep coming back to Him; put on invisible realm lenses, as it were (like a soldier would put on night-vision goggles), and focus your "unseen" spiritual senses.

Repeated exercise of these senses and repetitive activation of your sight gift will enable you to become proficient. If you do not exercise and train, you will not get to the level of being able to run and move quickly in the unseen realm. The more activation and practice you do, the more proficient you will become.

Be like the soldier who trains their senses so that they can operate on night assignments. Acclimatize and allow your senses, particularly your spiritual sight, to adjust and refocus as you do this. This exercise will become more natural the more you repeat it.

ACTION

You can ask the following questions as prompts to help you as you train in seer activations:

- Holy Spirit, what do You want me to see and focus on today?

- What do You desire to tell me today that I need to see for my life?

- What do I need to see that You are wanting to show me that relates to my personal call from You, God?

Write down what you hear the Lord saying and come back to these questions again and again to train your senses frequently. Of course, add in your personal questions as you feel led to.

CHAPTER 8

Strength for the Journey

I Am Redecorating Your Heart

Are you weary, carrying a heavy burden? Come to me. I will refresh your life, for I am your oasis. Simply join your life with mine. Learn my ways and you'll discover that I'm gentle, humble, easy to please. You will find refreshment and rest in me. For all that I require of you will be pleasant and easy to bear (Matthew 11:28–30 TPT).

"I am redecorating your heart," says the Lord, "and all that has become old and dusty, monochrome and lifeless is being removed to make way for abundant life to occupy your insides."

The Lord took me into a vision where I saw your heart as a house. It was filled with furniture and decorations that had become tired and beyond their useful life. These objects represented weary thoughts that have stuck around too long; fears and worries that have occupied your space for years; unforgiveness, bitterness, and offense that have long hung on the walls of your heart as a constant reminder of pain. And yet the Lord said in a voice of triumph, "I am redecorating your heart."

As He said those words, I watched Him rush in like a master renovator and redecorator. Every thought, fear, memory, and root was removed in one sweep, and the house was laid bare, like a canvas ready for a painter to make his first brushstroke. God then began to redecorate. Furniture and décor in an array of lively and bright colors filled each room.

If you let Him, the Lord will release new life to your heart, as He deals with some of the long-held heart wounds that have hung around for too long. Life is coming again to your insides; a vibrancy of thought life, a capacity to look through the eyes of hope, the ability to dream, and more are going to fill your heart today. No more shall your heart be a place filled with weariness and fear, but instead with life and joy!

RECEIVE

Will you let go and let God into those deep places? Begin to take your past wounds to Jesus; you can trust Him with your pain. Ask Him to hold your hand as you repent of holding onto any offense, bitterness, or malice. Choose to forgive those who have hurt you. Allow Jesus to minister healing to your sore places, and then begin to receive new life in those places that are dusty and lifeless.

You Can't Do It by Yourself

Are you so foolish? After beginning by means of the Spirit, are you now trying to finish by means of the flesh? (Galatians 3:3)

John writes: "Me do it Grandad!" says my three-year-old grandson with a determined look when I hold out my hand to help him down some particularly steep steps. So, I remove my proffered hand and applaud his progress. After all, I don't want him to be dependent on anyone's hand by the time he is, say, twelve. And when I'm 90, I will probably want *him* to help *me* down the odd flight of steps! But there are some things that neither he nor I, whatever our age or experience, will be able to do for ourselves.

That is what had gone horribly wrong for the Galatians. They had begun their Christian life in dependence on the Holy Spirit, and then they thought they could go the rest of the way and grow up as believers by doing it for themselves. "No way!" says Paul.

The dynamic of the relationship we have with God is that we will still be totally dependent on Him until the day we die. How you begin your new, born-again life is how you carry on, right to the end. In fact, maturity in the Christian life is through becoming even *more* dependent than you were yesterday, not less.

The Galatians had moved from accepting what God had done for them (through Christ's death on the cross) to attempting to earn God's favor by what they now did for Him (in living lives of religious obedience). The message they heard of *"Jesus Christ...crucified"* (1 Cor. 2:1–5) was to them all about a big "do" not about a big "done." Tearing themselves away from the satisfying feeling they had of thinking that they were contributing to their own salvation was very hard. Every bit as hard as it is for us.

Today Jesus wants us to hear what the Galatians had to hear: Look at yourself. Having started by the supernatural power of His Spirit, do you really think that you can finish the race by your own human effort? And just in case you think that Abraham pleased God by keeping the law, you're wrong. God blessed him because he believed. Faith works! He is always with you in Spirit, and you can expect to see real miracles among you—when you believe in Him, not because you obey laws.

ACTION

Ask yourself some honest questions, allowing the Holy Spirit to convict you where you need it. Ask yourself: "Am I experiencing as much of God's power as I once did? Or have I slipped into partial self-dependence, stumbling, and struggling in my own strength?" Repent and commit yourself into His hands, into the way and power of His Spirit.

The God Who Sees

She gave this name to the Lord who spoke to her: "You are the God who sees me," for she said, "I have now seen the One who sees me." That is why the well was called Beer Lahai Roi; it is still there, between Kadesh and Bered (Genesis 16:13–14).

I am *El Roi*, "the God who sees," and I see you! Do not think for a moment that I have not seen where you are, or where you have had to walk. Do not think that I am somehow a passive God whose eyes are shut. I see and I know.

Will you see Me in this place where you have been? Look around and see where I am. Look for Me in those places where it seems that you cannot find Me. I am there. Look past the distractions, look past your own thoughts, look past what feels dark and even overwhelming. I am here. Does not My Word say that even in the depths I am there? Even in the darkness, I can find you. Look with a heart of faith and know that I am here. I am walking with you, and I have hemmed you in. I go before you and come behind you. I have promised that I will not let you fall; there is no place that you can go that I cannot find you. Will you believe this and reach out for Me?

My desire is that you and I would walk in such close communion that you will always know that I am right with you. With this knowledge of Me at your side, you will walk as one who knows that no weapon formed against you will prosper for I, the Lord, am fighting for you and with you.

DECREE

Read through Psalm 139 and Psalm 121; both are full of promises and assurances from the Lord. Write out the promises that stand out to you; say them out loud and keep them before you.

Laying Down Heavy Burdens

For my yoke is easy and my burden is light (Matthew 11:30).

I hear the Lord asking you to allow Him to take off all the heavy burdens that have weighed you down. He longs for you to walk with the ease that Matthew 11 gives you. An ease and a light burden that is His to carry with and for you. So let go of all those ungodly and unholy burdens that are not yours to carry. These are burdens of false responsibility. You must only carry and pick up the responsibilities that He has given us.

The Lord says: "I long to give you more weighty responsibilities that you will carry lightly. To do this, you must bend over and give Me your burdens so that you carry only what I am asking you to take in this season. Be one who bears the light burdens of the Lord and not the heavyweight burdens of man. Move with Me; move by My Spirit. Watch with Me by the Spirit and carry burdens with Me by My Spirit only. Be sensitive to My leading and My call. Bend only to the burdens I am asking you to carry. Bend, child, bend."

ACTION

First, repent for all false burdens and responsibilities you have knowingly or unknowingly picked up recently or over the years. The Lord is kind and slow to anger. He loves when we confess and repent. Pray this out loud: "Father God, I confess and repent for every way, known and unknown, that I have partnered with false responsibility. I choose now to break agreement with my habits and practices of doing this. I lay down all the heavy weights and burdens I have unwittingly picked up and carried, even those I took on for individuals in my life:—jobs, tasks, roles. I now lay them at Your feet and ask for Your forgiveness and Your healing. Free me, Lord, from all false burdens. I give them all to You in this moment."

You may wish to do a prophetic act of physically lifting weights off your shoulders and laying them at the feet of Jesus. As the Holy Spirit identifies these false burdens with you, name them and lay them down, for example, people, projects, roles, or jobs.

Pray: "I choose in this moment to bend, Lord, to Your burden alone, to bend under Your yolk and weight that is easy and light. I thank You, Lord, that there is ease when I bend to You alone."

As you posture yourself in this way before the Lord, take time to hear, sense, and see what burdens of the Lord that are specific to you. Ensure that all of the false burdens and responsibilities have been laid down at the feet of Jesus.

Rest in My Favor

May the favor of the Lord our God rest on us; establish the work of our hands for us—yes, establish the work of our hands (Psalm 90:17).

The Lord is coming close to you as you read this. As He comes in close, He whispers over you and says, "You are My favored one! I take such delight in you. In fact, I love to just be near you!" He says it in a way that would cause you to take notice as He is so intent in His delight over you. He doesn't need you to do anything; He doesn't want you to even try to be anything. He just wants you to notice Him, to feel His presence, to rest in His delight.

And as you rest and lean back into His presence, He is calming your thoughts. He's silencing the noise. He is putting His hand on the tired muscles, and He is speaking words of truth into your being. He says, "Here, in My presence, you can just rest and be with Me. You don't need to work for it; you don't need to try to do anything—just be. Just be still and feel My delight over you. Rest here in My favor for it is in this place where I can minister to your needs. It is here in this place that I speak value to those places where you feel less than everyone else."

And Jesus says: "I speak clarity to the fogginess that you have felt in your thoughts. I speak wholeness to the parts of your heart that feel so broken. I speak delight and favor over your entire being. In this place I call you into the person that I saw when I planted you in your mother's womb. In that moment I saw the fullness of your life; I saw the real you that I created you to be. And it filled Me with so much delight!

"Today as you read this, allow My words to soak in. Simply believe Me and rest in Me. Choose to let go of the striving, the performing, the effort, the hard work, the constant doing, and just be with Me. I delight over your being. So, rest and be."

RECEIVE

If you find it hard to sit and be still in the presence of God, then take some time today to sit with Him. Or if you find it easier to *do* than to *be*, then take some time to let Him speak to you about how much He values you, not for your doing, but for who you are!

A good way to start is to just pray this prayer out loud: "Father God, I thank You that I am accepted and valued. Because of Jesus, I have full permission to sit in Your presence, to let You pour Your love out on me, and I don't have to do anything because Jesus did it all! I get to just receive; help me to receive Your delight and rest in Your favor today."

DAY 218

Am I Too Defensive?

As iron sharpens iron, so one person sharpens another (Proverbs 27:17).

Dear friends, since God loved us that much, we surely ought to love each other (1 John 4:11 NLT).

We should be in constant reformation, but the church has been guilty of pausing reformation. When reformation is paused, we tend to stagnate and become nominal ("in name only") rather than cutting edge. We fall into a defensive mindset, leading to a church whose dominant objective is to protect and defend at all costs. Without vision and change, we cease to see beyond our own bias and our own small, little world. When you are in protect and defend mode, you lose all sense of risk-taking and the ability to transform. We become reductionists, reducing our beliefs to small, more easily defendable ideals, mere sound bites that don't encompass truth fully. All we do is partially quote isolated Bible verses to make it say anything that we think will shore up our position. We practice fake warfare in our social media posts, defending our version of reduced truths in short and glib posts that don't say much really. We go into our bunkers and silos and practice the art of suspicion of the rest of the body of Christ or those we perceive are on opposing sides.

We have lost the art of dialoguing truth and discussing long swathes of Scripture with those who don't think like us. Instead, we destroy relationships to defend a small version of unresolved truth. But the Bible does not ever tell us to defend the truth; truth is strong enough to stand on its own! Constantly defensive people make enemies easily, just as constantly defensive nations make enemies. However, the Bible *does* teach us to prioritize and defend good relationships. We must therefore hold loosely our inherited orthodoxy and not get stuck in past traditions and under-resolved doctrines of men. We are arrogant enough to believe that we have understood truth, which is like saying, "I comprehend God." But as a wise saint of old once said: "A comprehended god is no god." We must understand that even in eternity we will always keep learning about God!

It is time to learn again from Hebraic culture that regards that any seemingly inconsequential human being may be trusted by God to have key and fresh insight into how Scripture should be interpreted and applied. Therefore, they highly prioritize conversations about truth amongst one another. We have lost this in preference of defense. We have lost the concept of being sharpened by those of different denominations, political persuasions, and international cultures. Defensive people cannot easily steward change. And the church should always be changing from one degree of glory to another!

RECEIVE

With the Holy Spirit prompting your conscience, ask: "Am I too defensive and too reactionary? Am I too quick to shoot something down without listening? When was the last time I had a wholesome, fulsome conversation that allowed me to be challenged and to review my life through another lens?"

Receive the truth afresh from Proverbs 27:5–6: *"Better is open rebuke than hidden love. Wounds from a friend can be trusted."* Then pray: "Father God, would You send friends who will faithfully shape me? Help me be a friend who listens."

Warrior, Are You Prepared for Persecution?
Part 1

Dear friends, do not be surprised at the fiery ordeal that has come on you to test you, as though something strange were happening to you. But rejoice inasmuch as you participate in the sufferings of Christ, so that you may be overjoyed when his glory is revealed (1 Peter 4:12–13; see also verses 14–19).

It is astonishing to discover how much of the New Testament was written to Christians who were suffering or about to suffer persecution. Peter in his first letter, John in Revelation, Luke in Acts, the author of Hebrews, and Jesus Himself were all concerned to warn believers that they would face persecution. Peter, in the above passage, seems especially concerned to prepare the believers living in Asia Minor for the coming storm they would face. Many had just experienced the Great Fire of Rome in AD 64 (which Nero, the emperor, insisted they had started). Popular opinion at the time supported the imprisonment of Christians. At first, Nero simply crucified them. Later he dressed them in wild animal skins and set his hunting dogs on them. Additionally, to light up the imperial palace at night he rolled Christians in tar pitch and set them on fire as living torches. Public opinion eventually turned against Nero because of this cruelty but the "fire" of persecution which began in the middle sixties of the first century continued to burn for the next 250 years.

Open Doors's annual *World Watch List 2021* reports the 50 countries where Christians are most oppressed; forty are classified as having very high levels of persecution, but ten have extreme levels of persecution.[1]

Just as the Holy Spirit is breathing fresh life around the world and renewing His people, so satan is doing horrific things to those he has a strong controlling influence over. As the church grows (and it is!), there is an ever-increasing confrontation between the forces of light and darkness, and our brothers and sisters around the globe are suffering persecution more and more. Jesus said, *"In this world you will have many trials and sorrows. But take heart, because I have overcome the world"* (John 16:33 NLT).

John writes: I remember saying to my mentor during my early years of ministry, "I don't think I could die for Jesus. I often wonder if a crisis really came and I was about to be thrown to the lions, would I give in?" He wisely said, "John, if you are faithful in little things now, He will give you grace when the big challenges come. But if you give in to the little things now, you will never face the big ones."

ACTION

To learn more about the history of the Christian faith, read *Parade of Faith* by Ruth A. Tucker.

NOTE

1. For more information or to receive a copy of *World Watch List 2021*, visit www.opendoorsusa.org/2021-world-watch-list-report/.

Warrior, Are You Prepared for Persecution?
Part 2

Blessed are those who are persecuted because of righteousness, for theirs is the kingdom of heaven. Blessed are you when people insult you, persecute you and falsely say all kinds of evil against you because of me. Rejoice and be glad, because great is your reward in heaven, for in the same way they persecuted the prophets who were before you (Matthew 5:10–12).

You are blessed *when* you are insulted, blessed *when* you are persecuted, blessed *when* you are slandered. With persecution, there is no *if* only *when* in Jesus's words to us. When these things happen to you, don`t be surprised; it is perfectly normal for a disciple of Jesus.

When Jesus sent the Twelve out, He warned them that they would be flogged in the synagogues, handed over to the local councils, brought before governors and kings, arrested and imprisoned (see Matt. 10). Disciples of Jesus will be hated by everyone, betrayed, persecuted, and killed. Jesus told them, *"Do not be afraid of those who kill the body but cannot kill the soul. Rather, be afraid of the One who can destroy both soul and body in hell"* (Matt. 10:28).

In the Book of Acts, we read of Stephen, the church's first martyr. The original Greek word meant "witness," and it has come to mean someone who dies for their faith, which has frequently happened to Jesus's followers. How then do we prepare for suffering and persecution?

- We must expect suffering and persecution and not be surprised when it comes.

- We must endure it patiently and not be resentful. Keep thinking eternally; we will not understand it if we approach it from the perspective of this mortal life only.

- We must rejoice when it comes and not be discouraged. The early Christians rejoiced in the fact that they were counted worthy to suffer for Christ!

- We must overcome it, blessing those who curse us and praying for those who spitefully abuse us.

The Book of Revelation is sent to seven churches. The churches in Smyrna and Philadelphia are not criticized at all. They are the churches suffering persecution, and Jesus has only words of encouragement and comfort for them (see Rev. 2:8–11; 3:7–13).

ACTION

Rejoice that our present sufferings are not worth comparing with the glory that will be revealed in us (see Rom. 8:18). Refix your gaze on the eternal horizon line.

Heart Strength

Nevertheless, I am continually with you; you hold my right hand. You guide me with your counsel, and afterward you will receive me to glory. Whom have I in heaven but you? And there is nothing on earth that I desire besides you. My flesh and my heart may fail, but God is the strength of my heart and my portion forever (Psalm 73:23–26 ESV).

"To the weary and the sad, to those who feel a little worn out inside, today I am inviting you into a journey of receiving strength for your heart," Jesus says. As He speaks, I see Him beckon you to come in close and to be wrapped in His robes, to be covered entirely by His cloak and enveloped by His love. He says, "Come on in, let Me cover you and give strength to your heart."

Jesus is seeking access to you; He wants you to open up your heart and hide nothing from Him. He is not scared of your pain, your anxiety, your loneliness, your desires, or your grief—whatever you may be hiding. He is not afraid of the "stuff" that you try to hide. Jesus longs to see it, heal it, and release you from the power of it.

RECEIVE

Tell Jesus, "My heart is open to You." Let Him see all the "stuff" and confess it to Him. As Jesus looks at everything around, He says, "Give it to Me!" There's no burden too heavy for Him to take, no sin too sour to look at, no brokenness too hard to heal. Let Jesus have it all.

As He takes off every burden and false weight, Jesus wants to give you strength in return. He says to you, "As I wrap you in My cloak and heal you of your pain, I am giving to you a new heart strength and an ability to temper storms, to emotionally process well, to stay connected to Me, and to have communion with Me as your highest priority. Receive strength in your heart today!"

Strengthening for His Glory

Fear not, for I am with you; be not dismayed, for I am your God; I will strengthen you, I will help you, I will uphold you with my righteous right hand (Isaiah 41:10 ESV).

I am strengthening you, My child. In this moment I come to undergird and underpin you in a fresh way. Let Me have access and allow Me to come close to push and build My strengthening structures into you so that they may be more securely established in you.

There may be pain in the moment of underpinning, as I come to expose your areas of weakness and sensitivity. Yet you must allow Me this access so that I may see you shine in the brightness of My glory that is inside you, waiting to be revealed in greater and greater measure. I see it and I look for the fulness to come forth. There is a day coming when you will be brilliant in your shining, and I long for that day. Let Me bring things to the surface that need to be exposed to My love and healing. Allow Me to go where the raw, tender areas are. Let Me bring them into the light so that they may be strengthened for this journey ahead.

You will be strengthened for My glory. My glory is within you, waiting to be revealed.

Allow Me to come close. Will you give Me access?

DECREE

This prayer of response is worth praying out loud. You may have to repeat it until you really mean it!

*I give You access to the tender parts of me, God, those I know of and those I do not. I allow You to expose the raw parts to excise all that is not of You out of me. I give You full right of entry to every part of me, God. Even though I know there will be pain in the process, I recognize that I need this underpinning. I give You permission to do everything it takes to have Your strength built in me to reveal the glory inside me for Your glory and in Your timing. **God, have Your way!***

The God Who Hears

When the Lord saw that Leah was not loved, he enabled her to conceive, but Rachel remained childless. Leah became pregnant and gave birth to a son. She named him Reuben, for she said, "It is because the Lord has seen my misery. Surely my husband will love me now." She conceived again, and when she gave birth to a son she said, "Because the Lord heard that I am not loved, he gave me this one too." So she named him Simeon (Genesis 29:31–33).

Today I want to clear away any and all doubt regarding My care for you. Just as I saw and heard Leah's pain, I have seen and I have heard yours. You are My beloved child; you are part of the Bride of Christ! My love for you is endless! No lack, no hardship, no struggle, no other person could ever separate Me from you. Although Jacob could not see Leah's full value, I did. I heard her cries for love; I listened to her. Because of my heart for her, I honored her and blessed her to be the mother of not just the tribe of Judah, but of six of Israel's tribes! I blessed her! I honored her!

Allow Me to blow away doubt and replace it with My extraordinary love. I desire to bless you and honor you as well, especially in those places where you have cried out to Me. I have heard those cries, and I have kept your tears. Look up and lock eyes with Me. Meet with Me in these places; allow My love to come in to heal, restore, and satisfy. No one else can love you like I do. No one else sees you as I see you. No one else will satisfy as I long to. Never doubt this again; look to Me for I want to bless you. Look to Me for I want to honor you. Look to Me and know that I am the God who hears.

RECEIVE

Reflect on and receive the truth of Psalm 56:

You number my wanderings; put my tears into Your bottle; are they not in Your book? When I cry out to You, then my enemies will turn back; this I know, because God is for me. In God (I will praise His word), in the Lord (I will praise His word), in God I have put my trust; I will not be afraid. What can man do to me? Vows made to You are binding upon me, O God; I will render praises to You, for You have delivered my soul from death. Have You not kept my feet from falling, that I may walk before God in the light of the living? (Psalm 56:8–13 NKJV)

Don't Ignore the Mold

As for any fabric that is spoiled with a defiling mold—any woolen or linen clothing… if the mold has not changed its appearance, even though it has not spread, it is unclean. Burn it, no matter which side of the fabric has been spoiled (Leviticus 13:47, 55b).

It's time to root out everything rotten and moldy. A little mildew will ruin everything.

One of the first things that property developers will do when they buy a new building is to thoroughly survey it for rot, dampness, mold, infestation, and other structural defects. They don't wait for these things to grow and reveal themselves. Instead, they relentlessly and persistently go after every sign of damage and potential threat, and they rip it out before it has any more chance to affect their property. They are not defensive and reactive; they are proactive and go on the attack, and then they seal up and shore up anything that looks like it might be a future entry point for damage. Nothing is left to chance. Nobody who redevelops a building just says, "I'll ignore that dampness in the basement; it'll probably come to nothing."

Be like a savvy developer and shine a torch into all the spaces that you have been given to occupy, including your own body and soul. Don't ignore any dark corners; make sure there are no breeding grounds for the enemy's mold. There are no shortcuts to this process, but if you make yourself available to the Holy Spirit's searchlight, it doesn't have to be complicated.

And Jesus says to you: "Will you allow Me to wash you clean? Will you be vulnerable to My healing touch? Come and confess everything to Me; repent and be free of everything dark and rotten that lurks in the shadows."

Make it a regular exercise to do a "scan" with the Spirit, praying, *"Search me, God, and know my heart; test me and know my anxious thoughts. See if there is any offensive way in me, and lead me in the way everlasting"* (Ps. 139:23–24).

RECEIVE

It's time to confess and receive forgiveness and purification. Pray Psalm 139 and allow the Holy Spirit to bring to mind the first thing to be repented of. It might be something you were aware of, but it could also be something that surprises you. Now confess that thing to God, repent, and make a choice to walk away from it, believing in the truth of First John 1:9: *"If we confess our sins, he is faithful and just and will forgive us our sins and purify us from all unrighteousness."*

Remember the Victories

Every good and perfect gift is from above, coming down from the Father of the heavenly lights, who does not change like shifting shadows (James 1:17).

I hear the Spirit of the Lord say: "It is a time to remember your victories. It is a day to contemplate all the things that Jesus has enabled you to overcome. Just as the children of Israel built a memorial with stones after they had crossed the Jordan, which brought them into a place of remembering God working on their behalf, I am asking you to do similarly."

Take time to list the victories that you have had in your life, even from childhood. For example, did you overcome abuse, bullying, poor education, or verbal undermining? Overcoming these adversities is a victory!

And the Lord says: "Doing this will awaken thankfulness in you, which will help you enter My presence; it will equip you to pour out praise and will strengthen you to face your future as you reflect on My faithfulness.

"It is not a day to lurch from crisis to crisis, but instead to move from gratitude to gratitude. I want you to live a life where you perpetuate the memories of what I have done in you. Review the years and see My hand."

ACTION

Tell someone else of the number of victories you have had. For Father God says, "I want you to give others a new view of Me as the God who works good things in all His children's lives. Your sharing is an important community transaction that will turn others toward hope and away from despair. Do not grieve My Spirit by not remembering. Have a gratitude party in your heart. It is more important that you celebrate right now than allow your default emotions to stay established in you. Celebrate and see your heart and flesh come alive."

DAY 226

Open Heart Surgery

My son, give me your heart, and let your eyes observe my ways (Proverbs 23:26 ESV).

The Lord has planned "open heart surgery" with you today. Will you allow Him full access?

Issues that you have felt stuck in emotionally, some of them for decades, Jesus now comes to remove them from you.

Will you allow Him that access now?

ACTION

Place your hand on your heart and pray: "Lord Jesus, I give You full access to my heart and emotions in this moment. Despite my nervousness, I give You full access and declare that my heart and my emotions are open to You, my Savior. I desire for You to bring freedom and healing to the deep places of me."

Allow Jesus to come close and touch your heart. I see Him in the spirit close to you now. His hand is moving with love toward you and is kindly but determinedly pushing His hand inside your heart. I see that He then pulls His hand back and removes what looks like small black stones from your heart. They are removed in one moment.

Jesus says to you: "Child, as you give Me access to the pain, the grief, and the difficulty held in your heart and emotions, I come right now to remove all that causes discomfort. Allow Me to go deep. Don't resist My touch. Don't resist Me."

Respond to Him: "I give You full access, Jesus. I give You all my pain and grief (specifically name the pains and difficulties out loud). I give You this pain, Jesus; please take them from me now."

Sit back or lie down and allow Jesus to go deep. Let Him press His hand in to remove all the pain and heaviness. Receive that freedom. Don't resist Him.

In that place ask Him if there is anything else that He would like to say to you or do for you. Enjoy this time and receive from Jesus.

Strengthen Yourself in the Lord

And David was greatly distressed, for the people spoke of stoning him, because all the people were bitter in soul, each for his sons and daughters. But David strengthened himself in the Lord his God (1 Samuel 30:6 ESV).

I hear the Lord ask you today, "Do you know what makes you strong and come alive? For in days of trouble and change, you are to know how to steward strength and life on your insides."

Just as David was able to strengthen himself in the Lord even whilst chaos ensued, so the Lord is inviting you to discover what you can do to strengthen yourself in Him. The Lord says to you: "Do not overcomplicate what often is very simple. Your journey to strength is along the path of reading Scripture, feasting on truth, worshipping, speaking in tongues, and being in a place of sharpening community. However, you can get strong by very creative and even very simple ways too."

As Jesus said this, I saw flickers of scenarios that may include some ways that you receive strength. For some, walks in nature will give you strength. For others, laughter with friends will strengthen you. Some need lots of sleep, and some need to feast. Others know that they find God in creative expressions painting, writing, drawing, creating, and singing.

ACTION

Ask the Holy Spirit, "How strong am I in You today?" Let the Holy Spirit reveal a measurement back to you: Are you a 10 out of 10, a 1 out of 10, a 5 out 10, or another rating? Ask Him, "Why am I at this level of strength?"

Don't despair at the answer. Follow this up by asking the Holy Spirit, "What do I do to strengthen myself in the Lord? How can I get strong in You?"

Write a list of the needed activities and actions and start to put them to practice.

Endurance and Deliverance

We do not want you to be uninformed, brothers and sisters, about the trou-
bles we experienced in the province of Asia. We were under great pressure,
far beyond our ability to endure, so that we despaired of life itself. Indeed, we
felt we had received the sentence of death. But this happened that we might
not rely on ourselves but on God, who raises the dead. He has delivered us
from such a deadly peril, and he will deliver us again. On him we have set
our hope that he will continue to deliver us (2 Corinthians 1:8–10).

Take heart for many, many have had to learn endurance, just as you are now. Learn from them and receive comfort from their stories, but most importantly, see how they turned to Me as the Comforter. I endured the cross. I endured the pain, the shame, the suffering of death. I know how to help you endure, for I Myself had to endure.

Endure, but know that it is not the end of the story! I endured the cross for the joy that was set before Me. I knew what was coming. Grab hold of hope in these days; in the days that try your soul, grab hold of My comfort. The days of your life on this earth are short, but the days of eternal life are endless. Those are the days that are before you! So live these days with end-less hope in your Deliverer. Live with hope for I am the God that raises the dead. I am the God who takes every situation and desires to turn it for your good. I long for men and women who will run with perseverance the race that is before them because they see Me. They see the joy that is ahead; they know that there is deliverance coming! They also see those who ran before them and who endured, just as I did, and so they receive comfort knowing that many others have endured, persevered, and finished their race well.

Choose to be one who will learn to endure, who will learn to rely on Me as the Deliverer, who will tap into My joy, and who will, in turn, teach others to also endure!

DECREE

Use Second Corinthians 1 to make decrees over your life that will encourage, comfort, and strengthen you. For example, you can say the fol-lowing declarations:

- I praise the Father of compassion who is the God of all comfort!

- He comforts me in all my troubles!

- My comfort abounds in Christ!

- I am one who patiently endures!
- I do not need to rely on myself but on God, who raises the dead. He will continue to deliver me again and again. I set my hope that He will continue to deliver me from all deadly peril.
- I don't rely on worldly wisdom but God's grace.
- It is by faith that I stand firm!

An Anointed Mandate

The Spirit of the Sovereign Lord is upon me, for the Lord has anointed me to bring good news to the poor. He has sent me to comfort the brokenhearted and to proclaim that captives will be released and prisoners will be freed (Isaiah 61:1 NLT).

Because I love you, so you can love.

Go and show love, without restriction or prejudice.

Because I have anointed you with My Spirit, you can move in miraculous power.

Go and act powerfully under the anointing of My Spirit.

Because I have commissioned you, you can go.

Go and make disciples.

This is not just for those in leadership positions; *you* too can make disciples.

Because I have freed you, you are no longer in captivity.

Go, leave your prison cell, put on new clothes, and tell the other prisoners and slaves the good news that freedom is here for them!

The Spirit of the Lord is upon me, for he has anointed me to bring Good News to the poor. He has sent me to proclaim that captives will be released, that the blind will see, that the oppressed will be set free (Luke 4:18 NLT).

ACTION

Read Isaiah 61:1 and Luke 4:18 at least five times. Isaiah's prophecy was fulfilled first in Jesus Christ, but He has given you His Spirit. These verses are now your mandate! Do you need to pick up your commission again? You can do this. He has anointed you by His Spirit!

Capping Versus Capability

If we claim to be without sin, we deceive ourselves and the truth is not in us. If we confess our sins, he is faithful and just and will forgive us our sins and purify us from all unrighteousness. If we claim we have not sinned, we make him out to be a liar and his word is not in us (1 John 1:8–10).

It is good to have a strong sense of your capabilities, to know what you are good at and what you do well. Today the Lord says, "I want you to know your strengths and know the anointings I have placed on your life."

ACTION

List what sits on your life as a gift of God: What do you excel at? Where do you have real ability? What has He anointed you to do?

The Lord also says: "Today the power from My throne is to deal with the capping of limitation on top of your capabilities. There are many capabilities that have not reached their full potential because of a capping."

He says, "It is time to know both your capabilities and your capping."

What caps you? What limits you? Capping is often from unresolved pain, past church experiences, self-sabotage, or living with rejection or unrepented sin. God says to you today, "See the cap, know the cap, and present it to Me so that together we might smash and remove it!"

RECEIVE

Receive the revelation of what is a capping on your life. Sit with God and be brave enough to ask Him to reveal what you have partnered with that is like a weighted blanket on you, smothering your anointings. Don't resist; be truthful with yourself that there *is* a cap because some things in you have not yet been fully resolved or healed. Present them to God, acknowledge their existence, and let them be removed.

DAY 231

Look to God!

I lift up my eyes to the mountains—where does my help come from? My help comes from the Lord, the Maker of heaven and earth. He will not let your foot slip—he who watches over you will not slumber; indeed, he who watches over Israel will neither slumber nor sleep. The Lord watches over you—the Lord is your shade at your right hand; the sun will not harm you by day, nor the moon by night. The Lord will keep you from all harm—he will watch over your life; the Lord will watch over your coming and going both now and forevermore (Psalm 121).

Look to the Lord, the maker of the heavens and earth, for it is He who also gives you strength.

Look to the Lord, the Alpha and Omega, the beginning and the end, for it is He who rescues you in the day of trouble.

Look to the Lord, the One who reigns above all, for it is He who fights on your behalf and liberates you from bondage.

The Lord says to you: "Do not look to your left and to your right for strength, look to Me! Do not seek out salvation from that which is created and mortal; look to Me, who is Creator. I am here, ready and waiting for you to look to Me and call on Me to come and lift you up. Do not fear; I will not ignore your cries and your prayers for help. I hear and I answer! I see and will intervene!

"So raise your expectations and contend, press in, and cry out for Me. For surely I shall come in and overwhelm that which is seeking to overwhelm you."

ACTION

What is overwhelming you at the moment? What thoughts, fears, anxieties, stresses, or concerns are troubling and invading your atmosphere? Write each of them down on separate notes or pieces of paper. Now write "Alpha and Omega" on top of each note. This action is a reminder that Jesus is above and over all these things. Give Him preeminence; He is superior and surpasses all others. As you do, declare out loud: "Jesus Christ is the Alpha and Omega, the first and the last, the beginning and the end. He created me in my mother's womb, and He will be with me forever and ever. He is above all things, including those things that I thought were going to overwhelm me."

Let Me Love You!

...fixing our eyes on Jesus, the pioneer and perfecter of faith. For the joy set before him he endured the cross, scorning its shame, and sat down at the right hand of the throne of God (Hebrews 12:2).

Jesus comes again to you now and stands before you. Look to Him. Do you see Him? His eyes are filled with love for you; He has such beautiful, deep adoration for you. He comes to gaze at your face and look into your eyes. As you respond to Him, look into His face and fix your eyes on His (intentionally turn your inward gaze toward Jesus). Focus on Him and allow yourself and your senses to become aware of Him.

"Look into My eyes. See My face," Jesus urges you.

As you do this and acclimatize yourself to the reality of Jesus standing before you in the spirit, be aware of what He is saying and what His expression of love is communicating to you now.

I see His eyes burning with love for you as you take this time to allow Him to see you and you to see Him. Watch His face as Jesus loves you through His intense gaze. Allow yourself to go with Jesus, to follow His lead now, and to go with Him where He is inviting you to go. There is a place of rest and refreshment, as you bask in the tenderness and affection of your King. There is no end to the love He has for you. His invitation to follow Him into the place of rest and refreshment is always available, but today there is something specific that Jesus longs to impart to you: a deep, deep rest; a deep reset in rest.

"I am leading you by the still waters. I am making you lay down with Me. Listen to My heart for you in this moment and receive My words of affirmation and love."

RECEIVE

Let Jesus show you this place of rest and reset. Receive His peace and His refreshing, restorative energy of love. Breathe in His presence. Accept the weight of His passion for you. Listen to Him and hear and receive His words of love.

Choose To Be Empowered!

The God of all comfort is coming today, and He's putting His hand on your shoulder. Rest in His presence until you feel the reassurance of His hand upon you.

Read these verses from Paul's letter to the church in Rome. They were also written to encourage and instruct you because God knew that you would read these words and need the simple instruction found in them.

> *Love must be sincere. Hate what is evil; cling to what is good. Be devoted to one another in love. Honor one another above yourselves. Never be lacking in zeal, but keep your spiritual fervor, serving the Lord. Be joyful in hope, patient in affliction, faithful in prayer. Share with the Lord's people who are in need. Practice hospitality. Bless those who persecute you; bless and do not curse. Rejoice with those who rejoice; mourn with those who mourn. Live in harmony with one another. Do not be proud, but be willing to associate with people of low position. Do not be conceited. Do not repay anyone evil for evil. Be careful to do what is right in the eyes of everyone. If it is possible, as far as it depends on you, live at peace with everyone* (Romans 12:9–18).

These instructions of Paul are practical, seemingly small things that will build up to have a great impact on your life if you'll choose to practice them. It's especially important to practice them on days when you don't feel like it. When it feels impossible to honor another, choose honor anyway. In moments when hope and joy feel lost, look again! They're there! When affliction or trials seem to be coming your way without end, choose patience. For you have the Spirit of God within you, the One who produces the fruit of love, joy, peace, and patience. You have been empowered with these in order that you might walk in them, even when your circumstances shout otherwise.

And hear Jesus reassure you now: "I have gifted you with the Helper, your Advocate, who enables you and empowers you to do all that I am instructing you. You are not powerless in or a victim of your circumstances. Choose to receive My encouragement; choose to put these into practice today."

ACTION

Read through this passage and make a list of the areas where you have felt powerless. Then speak with the Holy Spirit. Tell Him how you've felt, and then receive from Him the power fruit of love, joy, peace, patience, kindness, goodness, faithfulness, gentleness, and self-control. These are yours! Choose to put them on and walk in them; He is giving you the strength to do so!

Look Up! God Has Made a Way

With your help I can advance against a troop; with my God I can scale a wall (Psalm 18:29).

If you are feeling stuck or facing a dead end, look up! The Lord says to you: "I saw that you had reached what seemed like an impossible place. I recognize that you did not turn back at this but instead waited for Me. Good! I heard your cry, and I let down a rescue ladder for you, but you did not see it because you kept looking down. But now is the time to look up and begin to climb out of your circumstances. I have given you the means of escape."

As the Lord spoke, I saw a figure representing you standing by a very high concrete wall that towered above everything. The wall was completely smooth; it was physically insurmountable. The person at the foot of the wall had done everything to try to climb it. They had beaten against the wall; they had paced around the foot of the wall; they had lain down before the wall. But then a net made of thick rope was thrown down over the wall. There was now a way to climb, but the figure at the bottom did not notice. They were too preoccupied with where they lay. They adjusted the shoes on their feet as if this would somehow suddenly help them to scale the wall!

If you feel like this figure at the foot of the wall, it is time to dust yourself off and look up to God and the fresh means of ascent that He has provided.

This High Priest of ours understands our weaknesses, for he faced all of the same testings we do, yet he did not sin. So let us come boldly to the throne of our gracious God. There we will receive his mercy, and we will find grace to help us when we need it most (Hebrews 4:15–16 NLT).

ACTION

In the illustration above God is asking you to climb because He has provided the way by which you can climb. Is there something you need to do to change your situation now that God has made a way? Even if you've previously cried out, "There is no way!" look up and try again.

Eternity Must Become Your Reality

*Do not let your hearts be troubled. You believe in God; believe also in me.
My Father's house has many rooms; if that were not so, would I have told
you that I am going there to prepare a place for you? And if I go and prepare
a place for you, I will come back and take you to be with me that you also
may be where I am* (John 14:1–3).

In the moments of loss, in the moment of shaking, in the moments of
uncertainty, how do we anchor ourselves? How do we hold a place of inner
equilibrium?

The Spirit of the Lord says, "Cast your anchors forward."

Throw your hope forward into the certainty of eternity at Jesus's side.
Rehearse the stability of the Kingdom of Heaven, which cannot be shaken.
See your "forever home," and allow that image to hold you in this tempo-
rary realm.

Know that the new Heaven is prepared, with its streets and homes, as
a place that is bespoke fitted for you. Look up! The throne room is waiting
for the sound of your voice to join the angels in perpetual worship. See the
kitchens where the angels are cooking and preparing recipes for the feast
of the marriage of the Lamb! Allow yourself to perceive the trees that bear
fruit monthly that line the streets of the heavenly city. Catch a glimpse of
the twenty-four elders, who cast down their crowns in homage to the King.

Allow the truth of your name being written in the Lamb's Book of Life
to wash over you. Your future, which Jesus paid for, is strong and certain
and unshakable.

RECEIVE

Let the assurance of your future secure you in this moment. Receive a
new stability deep within you; let the truth now become a medication to
all that has a tendency to quiver inside of you. Today you will rise with
strength as eternity is a refreshed reality in you.

The Lion in Daniel's Heart

At this, the administrators and the satraps tried to find grounds for charges against Daniel in his conduct of government affairs, but they were unable to do so. They could find no corruption in him, because he was trustworthy and neither corrupt nor negligent (Daniel 6:4).

Every sphere of life needs to have its Daniels—men and women of integrity and outstanding character. He was a politician with a squeaky-clean reputation in the midst of a terrifyingly corrupt dictatorship. Despite his colleagues and enemies conducting a security check on him, they could not dig up any dirt that they could level against him. There were no gray areas or moral weaknesses in Daniel's life, no skeletons in the cupboard, no double life. The only basis his enemies could find for a charge against him had to do with his faith and faithfulness to God.

Sadly, some of those who have taken the name of Christ over the years have so lived that people have even questioned if they are believers at all. It is a tragedy that words such as *scandal* and *church* are linked in many people's minds today.

But let your life be different! Be like Daniel. And the Holy Spirit says: "My desire for you, whether you work and serve in the area of politics, industry, sports, entertainment, education, economy, health, family, construction, retail, service, family, church, or something else, is that you would be like My servant Daniel, a man of integrity. However, integrity must be cultivated—though it can be lost in an instant. Daniel's integrity was created out of his prayer life and intimacy with Me. He spent time in My presence and allowed Me to search his mind and his heart.

"All of this led to the growth of a strong trust in Me, which never wobbled when his faith was most severely tested. If you want to walk in the integrity of Daniel, I will be gentle and tender as I minister to you and search your soul. Much that has been hidden will come to light and will need to be repented of before you see the transformation that you long for."

ACTION

Read Isaiah 11:3. It was prophesied that the Messiah would *"delight in the fear of the Lord."* Daniel also delighted in the fear of the Lord, and it became the foundation for his life. Will you commit yourself to the discipline of delighting in the fear of the Lord?

Press On and Do Not Give Up

Not that I have already obtained it [this goal of being Christlike] or have already been made perfect, but I actively press on so that I may take hold of that [perfection] for which Christ Jesus took hold of me and made me His own. Brothers and sisters, I do not consider that I have made it my own yet; but one thing I do: forgetting what lies behind and reaching forward to what lies ahead, I press on toward the goal to win the [heavenly] prize of the upward call of God in Christ Jesus (Philippians 3:12–14 AMP).

Press on and do not give up. Shake off the dust of fatigue, the air of exhaustion, and set your eyes on the prize again. Look at Jesus and run toward Him, for fellowship with Jesus is your reward, your high prize, your aim of the race. Do not allow discouragement to set in and demand that you sit down. Take heart and be encouraged that I have given you all you need to run the race.

Feel truth infuse your innermost being with new life and vigor; receive strength from the breath of My Spirit filling your lungs; see the cloud of witnesses cheering you on, and start to press forth toward the prize. Persevere, oh child, persevere and do not give up or stop. Persevere and let perseverance produce in you its full work.

Know that you do not persevere in your own strength. It is not by thinking really hard or by trying with all your might. It is by the strength of My Spirit in you that you are able to persevere. It is by the life of My Spirit in you that you are capable of pressing on. Perseverance is not an activity you do devoid of Me but because of Me! You do it because I am in you enabling you to do it.

Let perseverance finish its work so that you may be mature and complete, not lacking anything (James 1:4).

RECEIVE

Receive strength today to persevere as you read our prayer over you: "We release Holy Spirit strength to persevere to you right now. Where you are weary, now receive life! Where you are discouraged, receive strength! Where you are worn out, now receive energy! Feel the Spirit of God start to bubble up in you, like a fountain in your deepest place. He will enable you to push on, press on, and keep going. Start to rest into the power of the Spirit to persevere, and let perseverance produce its work in you."

Lay Regret Down and Receive Joy

Sing praises to the Lord, O you his saints, and give thanks to his holy name. For his anger is but for a moment, and his favor is for a lifetime. Weeping may tarry for the night, but joy comes with the morning (Psalm 30:4–5 ESV).

You were made for endurance and not just for short bursts of success. Your strength comes each day from the living God. You gain all your determination from Him and through Him. No matter what the previous day held, there is joy in the morning of the new day.

So in this moment let go of all regret for yesterday. Allow yourself to be delivered of everything that has caused you to be held back. Let go of the "if onlys" and the remorse, guilt, shame, the process of pilgrimage that is tied to religious performance, and the systematic repeat of false responsibilities.

Step into the freedom of allowing God to be your strength in weakness; push through and allow the muscle of perseverance to be strengthened.

ACTION

Lay down before Jesus all the heavy burdens in this moment. Lay down the regrets of yesterday, the people, the projects, the promotions, the breakdowns, the breakups. Lay them down at the feet of Jesus.

You may find it helpful to speak each specific theme or burden out to Him: "Jesus, I give You this weight which is (list the person/relationship/issues) and speak through each one."

In choosing to speak them out and lay them down at Jesus's feet, you let them go, speaking out loud to say, "I lay this down at Your feet, Jesus, and let it go!"

Once you have gone through all of these heavy weights, be sure to linger with God to receive the joy that comes in the morning. Step into His joy, and declare that the joy of the Lord is your strength and that you now come to fasten yourself to joy and not be separated from it.

Remember each morning to step into the joy of the Lord that is new for you each day!

DAY 239

Join in His Rebuilding

*O storm-battered city, troubled and desolate! I will rebuild you with precious
jewels and make your foundations from lapis lazuli* (Isaiah 54:11 NLT).

Take courage, My children, and live in good hope, for I am the restorer
and the rebuilder. Do not rest in the ruins of what was once great but instead
join in the rebuilding program. It is time to get on with it because waiting
for the good days that you remember or that you have read about will not
turn the clock back. I will not turn the clock back because this is a new day,
and in this day I am restoring much that was not there before.

Join in with My building work. Spend time with Me, and I will show
you the part of the wall that I want you to work on. And do not stint on or
hold back the resources that I have given you to use and that I am going to
give you, for I am the Lord your God and I have unlimited supply for those
who are ready to go about the task that I have appointed for them.

*Enlarge your house; build an addition. Spread out your home, and spare
no expense! For you will soon be bursting at the seams. Your descendants will occupy other nations and resettle the ruined cities* (Isaiah
54:2–3 NLT).

ACTION

God may speak to you through this word in very specific, personal
ways. For others, the most obvious interpretation is that this is a word
about co-laboring with Christ as He builds His church. Do you need to
repent of looking backward with longing and not to the future with hope?
What projects could you do or what ministry could you help to expand.
What part of the "wall" (think of Nehemiah's rebuilding of Jerusalem) is
God calling you to help rebuild?

Breaking Out of Stagnant Waters

Deep calls to deep in the roar of your waterfalls; all your waves and breakers have swept over me (Psalm 42:7).

I hear the Lord say, "I am breaking you out of stagnant waters." The Holy Spirit is releasing a river of life over you; it's a fast-moving river that will break the bank of your current place of containment. There is a people release happening right now, and you will be displaced from your captivity.

The waters of the Holy Spirit will cause you to know a new place and a new glory. This can be unsettling because, although we want to move into the fullness that God has for us, we have become used to the frustrations of the current, familiar ways that we live. Even though we know we are not in fullness, we get stuck in delayed hope and in partnership with lesser journeys. But God is calling over you, "Life! LET GO OF THE LESSER PLACES."

DECREE

Break agreement with the lesser place you find yourself in. This means speaking out loud that you no longer will settle in the lesser life experiences when God made you for more. Make a declaration: "I am over and done with this place I stand in. It is no longer my home. I break agreement with stagnant waters being what I know."

Today God is releasing a grace for change along with His waters. He's releasing a grace for adapting to the new; a grace for moving with Him.

And the Spirit of the Lord says, "The process of shifting and changing will be one that brings life."

Wisdom for Today

The proverbs of Solomon son of David, king of Israel: for gaining wisdom and instruction; for understanding words of insight; for receiving instruction in prudent behavior, doing what is right and just and fair; for giving prudence to those who are simple, knowledge and discretion to the young.... The fear of the Lord is the beginning of knowledge, but fools despise wisdom and instruction (Proverbs 1:1–4, 7).

In desperate need of God's help, King Solomon went to Gibeon to sacrifice one thousand burnt offerings. The Lord responded to him in a dream, saying, *"Ask for whatever you want me to give you"* (1 Kings 3:5). The Lord was so pleased with Solomon's request for a *"discerning heart to govern* [God's] *people and to distinguish between right and wrong"* (v. 9) and what Solomon did *not* ask for (revenge) that He gave him both a wise and discerning heart and great wealth as well. Solomon's wisdom outclassed all others, and he became so famous that people traveled the length and breadth of the land to hear his wisdom (see 1 Kings 10:23–25). Solomon had witnessed the damage caused by his father's adulterous affair with Solomon's mother, Bathsheba, and had seen three of his older brothers (Amnon, Absalom, and Adonijah) destroy their lives by ignoring God's Word. He was determined, at least during the opening years of his reign, not to follow their example.

God gave wisdom to Solomon so that he might pass it on to people like us so that we might learn to live wisely and with discernment too, even in the twenty-first century. For example:

- We can learn about sexual faithfulness from hot coals: *"Can a man scoop fire into his lap without his clothes being burned? Can a man walk on hot coals without his feet being scorched? So is he who sleeps with another man's wife; no one who touches her will go unpunished"* (Proverbs 6:27–29).

- We can learn about making money from the flight of an eagle: *"Do not wear yourself out to get rich; do not trust your own cleverness. Cast but a glance at riches, and they are gone, for they will surely sprout wings and fly off to the sky like an eagle"* (Proverbs 23:4–5).

- We can learn about handling anger from churning butter: *"For as churning cream produces butter, and as twisting the nose produces blood, so stirring up anger produces strife"* (Proverbs 30:33).

ACTION

Why not commit to reading a chapter of Proverbs each day? Some mighty men and women of God make this a habit—one chapter for every day of the month. Billy Graham did this for many years. Such a habit can be very beneficial. You will soon find yourself thinking with God's wisdom before you act.

Athlete, Run Harder!

Therefore, since we are surrounded by such a great cloud of witnesses, let us throw off everything that hinders and the sin that so easily entangles. And let us run with perseverance the race marked out for us, fixing our eyes on Jesus, the pioneer and perfecter of faith. For the joy set before him he endured the cross, scorning its shame, and sat down at the right hand of the throne of God. Consider him who endured such opposition from sinners, so that you will not grow weary and lose heart (Hebrews 12:1–3).

You are God's athlete! He is assembling a huge team from all around the world, one like the world has never seen, both in size and spiritual fitness. In every corner of the globe, His athletic superstars are limbering up to run their races. The work continues in the training camps of everyday life, where God's athletes are going through the disciplines, the exercises, the diet, the workouts, the teamwork, and the races.

"Team Christ" is emblazoned on their running vests; they bear His name, these elite athletes. They make Him proud. On every track and in every gym where His athletes are going through their training routines, He is there, shouting constant encouragement and direction.

These athletes are really quite something to behold! When they run, whether a training exercise or a full-on sprint, they run with purpose and determination. They are supernaturally strong, and every day they become stronger, leaner, and more able. They know their goals; their focus is fixed. They listen for and hear their coach's encouragement over the noise of the stadium's roar, and it helps them speed up, spurred on by His delight and pleasure in them.

This is you. You are God's athlete.

RECEIVE

Don't allow doubt to creep in. Allow the truth of what this word is saying to seep into you. Begin to believe it. Look at the author's words in Hebrews 12:1: *"Throw off everything that hinders."* No matter your age, no matter how athletic (or not!) you feel, you have the same Spirit your biblical heroes had. They ran their race; so can you! Ask God to renew your mind so that you think differently about your spiritual walk—your spiritual race! Wherever you are, whatever you are going through, may you run with perseverance today.

Inheritance Returns

But on Mount Zion there shall be deliverance, And there shall be holiness; The house of Jacob shall possess their possessions (Obadiah 17 NKJV).

We serve a God who restores. His desire is to bring you back into His blessing and realms of abundant life. He desires you to possess your possession, just like He said to Israel's descendants in the Book of Obadiah.

DECREE

Speak to your inheritances that have been captured. Think about what has been promised but you have not yet seen. Speak life and the returning of that which has been assigned to you by God. Speak to those things that never fully worked out, that never got resolved, that never came to pass. For it is time for that which never came into fullness to come back out of captivity. Shout "Restoration!" over that which is yours.

Today is a turning point for restoration. It is a turnaround time for what looked like it had been lost or had been taken from you.

I remain confident of this: I will see the goodness of the Lord in the land of the living (Psalm 27:13).

CHAPTER 9

Dressed to Conquer

Live Victoriously!

*There is therefore now no condemnation to those who are in Christ Jesus....
Who then is the one who condemns? No one. Christ Jesus who died—more
than that, who was raised to life—is at the right hand of God and is also
interceding for us. Who shall separate us from the love of Christ? Shall trouble or hardship or persecution or famine or nakedness or danger or sword?
As it is written: "For your sake we face death all day long; we are considered
as sheep to be slaughtered." No, in all these things we are more than conquerors through him who loved us* (Romans 8:1, 34–37).

Have you sat and taken in the truth of this passage of Scripture? It says
that there is no condemnation to you who are in Christ Jesus. That is you!
So why do you listen to those who condemn? Even more so, why do you
believe that Jesus and the Father condemn you? These voices of condemnation have to be named for what they are: arrows of accusation sent to keep
you from living victoriously. Until you see them for what they are, you will
stay bound in victimhood.

And yet the goodness of God is that He is coming to pull you out and
away from these condemning voices. He is covering you, embracing you,
equipping you, and sending you back out as a victorious one! Shut your
ears to all voices that condemn, and tune in to the sound of Jesus, who is
interceding on your behalf! What is He praying? Why is He interceding?
He wants to see you walking in the victory that He purchased for you! Will
you listen to Him? Will you believe His voice over the enemy's?

If your heart cry is yes, then ACTIVATE this word by saying out loud:
"Jesus, I receive the truth that You are FOR ME! Your blood has wiped
away all condemnation. And in Your name, I speak to those voices that
accuse and condemn, and I tell them to be silent! I declare this passage of
Scripture over myself now for I am a conqueror in Jesus's name!"

ACTION

Ask Jesus what He is praying for you today? Begin a journey of partnering with Him and seeing yourself as He does. You are not a victim; you are
living and walking victoriously as a conqueror.

Warrior Worship

Gideon and the hundred men with him reached the edge of the camp at the beginning of the middle watch, just after they had changed the guard. They blew their trumpets and broke the jars that were in their hands. The three companies blew the trumpets and smashed the jars. Grasping the torches in their left hands and holding in their right hands the trumpets they were to blow, they shouted, "A sword for the Lord and for Gideon!" While each man held his position around the camp, all the Midianites ran, crying out as they fled. When the three hundred trumpets sounded, the Lord caused the men throughout the camp to turn on each other with their swords (Judges 7:19–22).

Raise your voice, Oh mighty warrior, and start to praise God! Praise Him for the victory, for He has triumphed over death and the grave. I hear the Lord say: "It is time for warrior worship to arise in the earth, and it is time for you to begin to steward praise as a weapon that destroys the enemy. Just as Gideon stood on a mountain, raised a sound of praise and worship, and started to overcome the enemy, so can you watch the giants fall as you worship Me with passion and conviction.

"Do not hold back in your worship; do not give half-hearted praise. Instead, give Me your all. As you pour out your all in worship, the enemy will begin to be destroyed. Your worship shall cause the enemy to take himself out, and the sound you release shall cause destruction in the camp of the one who opposes Me."

So, wake yourself up today and worship until the enemy does not just retreat but is completely and utterly destroyed. Worship your way through the battle! Sing on the battlefield! Praise your way through the war, and watch as giants fall.

ACTION

Pick a battle that you are currently facing, whether that be relationally, financially, geographically, or physically. Look at it, and then look to God. Start to sing and worship out loud declaring who God is. You may want to pick a worship song, psalm, or hymn that is filled with decrees about God or even step out and sing your own song. Begin to let out a radical song of worship, and watch as giants fall, walls move, and enemies retreat.

DAY 246

A Sword for the Lord!

So David went to Baal-perazim and defeated the Philistines there. "The Lord did it!" David exclaimed. "He burst through my enemies like a raging flood!" So he named that place Baal-perazim (which means "the Lord who bursts through") (2 Samuel 5:20 NLT).

You have prayed, you have begged, you have pleaded for Me to act on your behalf. I have heard your cries for help, and I delight in being the One who comes to your aid. And yet, I do not do things based on what *you* think. I do not see your situation as *you* do. I come in *My* way to do what is best for you.

Begin to raise your expectations. Ask Me to show you how I do things. Look through Scripture and note that I never did anything the same way twice. I am full of endless possibilities. Even more than that, do not look for the solution, instead *look to Me as the solution.* Begin to see Me as the One who is your solution in every single circumstance. I have ways to do things that you cannot even fathom; I have answers that you cannot think up or dream of.

Even yet, I do not want to just be the One who you come to when you are in trouble or need help. I want to be the One who you look to at all times. I want to show you who I am, not just what I do.

ACTION

Get out and take a walk with Jesus; if possible, get away from anything man-made. Don't walk and think about the busyness you've left behind. Walk with Him, listen for His voice, and set your gaze on Him. Ask Him to show you something new or forgotten about who He is. Enjoy His presence, and be present with Him.

The Lord Is a Warrior

The Lord is a warrior; the Lord is His name (Exodus 15:3).

When we follow Jesus, we follow Him into a war zone. From Genesis through Revelation we encounter God engaged in a great, cosmic battle against the powers of evil. It's no surprise, therefore, to find God described as a warrior in the Hebrew Bible.

Paul was no stranger to Roman armor, having even been chained to soldiers whilst he wrote. However, his explanations of the *"armor of God"* in the famous passage of Ephesians 6 come straight from Old Testament verses that described either God Himself or the coming Messiah (Jesus). In his letter to the Ephesians, Paul seems to have been picturing God Himself clothed in a warrior's battle armor.

When Paul says, *"Put on the full armor of God,"* he doesn't simply mean bits of equipment that God hands out to His followers. He also implies that these are actually what *God* wears! We fight under the protection of the character and attributes of God Himself. He is the God of truth, righteousness, peace, salvation, and the Spirit-inspired Word.

It is *who* you need not *what* you need that will enable you to stand firm in this battle. There is a war on, and no one in this war is a civilian. We are all soldiers on active duty, and the whole church of Christ Jesus is on the front line of God's cosmic battle.

The enemies of God and the church are many, and Paul gives us a comprehensive list of the spiritual forces of evil (see Eph. 6:12). They may be a defeated enemy, but they still fight with flaming arrows against God and His people. Therefore, put on the armor of God. Put on Him! He is a warrior; the Lord is His name.

RECEIVE

Take time to picture God as a mighty warrior. If you normally only view Him as Shepherd or Friend, you may need to meditate on this warfare aspect of who He also is. You could use a Bible dictionary or concordance to look up verses from Scripture that describe Him as a warrior. See also the appendix for a list of warfare Scriptures.

DAY 248

The Full Armor of God

ACTION

What greater protection could we hope to have but to put on God? Study again Ephesians 6:10–17. Although you may know it well, there is much, much more that Scripture says about the armor of God. It is worth reading each verse in its context in your own Bible.

THE BELT OF TRUTH:

Righteousness will be his belt and faithfulness the sash around his waist (Isaiah 11:5).

The belt of righteousness speaks of the Messiah's mission of justice and good government. Putting on Christ's belt of truth means that we will seek to speak the truth in love. We won't cover our sins; we will confess them. We will not speak falsehoods; we will speak truthfully. We will resist the urge to be a liar like the devil. The truth of the Gospel holds everything together in the Christian life and warfare.

THE BREASTPLATE OF RIGHTEOUSNESS AND THE HELMET OF SALVATION:

He put on righteousness as his breastplate, and the helmet of salvation on his head; he put on the garments of vengeance and wrapped himself in zeal as in a cloak (Isaiah 59:17).

The saving, righteous acts of God in the Old Testament and the righteousness we have through our faith in Christ are our spiritual protection in our war with the powers of darkness and even death. Add to this the righteous integrity of the life Paul calls us to live in Ephesians 4:24; 5:8–9, and we can be confident that living righteously makes the devil's work harder!

THE SHOES OF THE GOSPEL OF PEACE:

How beautiful on the mountains are the feet of those who bring good news, who proclaim peace, who bring good tidings, who proclaim salvation, who say to Zion, "Your God reigns!" (Isaiah 52:7)

There's nothing particularly beautiful about feet—unless they are wearing the running shoes of the messengers of the good news of God's peace for those who need to hear it (see Rom. 10:14–15).

THE SHIELD OF FAITH:

"You make your saving help my shield, and your right hand sustains me; your help has made me great" (Psalm 18:35; see also Psalm 28:7).

The psalmists put their faith in God to be their shield against all kinds of nasty attacks. We must do the same.

THE SWORD OF THE SPIRIT—THE WORD OF GOD:

He will strike the earth with the rod of his mouth; with the breath of his lips he will slay the wicked (Isaiah 11:4b).

He made my mouth like a sharpened sword, in the shadow of his hand he hid me; he made me into a polished arrow and concealed me in his quiver (Isaiah 49:2).

Jesus used the Scriptures to resist the temptations of the devil. And we can likewise fight back with the Word.

Extinguishing the Enemy's Arrows

In addition to all this, take up the shield of faith, with which you can extinguish all the flaming arrows of the evil one (Ephesians 6:16).

The Lord says: "Warrior, I have given you a shield of faith that will extinguish every effort the enemy makes to cause harm, destruction, and death. A shield is not just defensive; it is used by advancing armies. It is time for you to thwart the adversary's evil plans before his minions have even had an opportunity to launch them. Therefore, advance with your shield pointed right at him and crush his attempts to invade the spaces that you occupy. Snuff out his fires and trample on his schemes!"

Why do you cower in fear over where his next attack or counterattack might come from? Do not wait for him to tear into you; go after evil and root it out from everywhere that it seeks to take hold. Your shield of faith reflects the glory of the Lord God Almighty so use it to expose darkness. Advance and allow the glorious light that you reflect to illuminate every dark corner where death, sickness, and immorality festers. Shine! You are clothed in the armor of God; as long as you tread where He tells you to tread, you cannot and will not be harmed.

The faster you go on the offensive, the more you close down his plans and limit his ability to spread his flames. Courageous warriors, clothed with the armor of the Lord, filled with His Spirit, and carrying His shield of faith, will outmaneuver devils and further establish the Kingdom of Jesus Christ in your area, community, city, and nation. For too long we, the *ecclesia*, have allowed the sin to swarm like a forest fire that is out of control. It's time to extinguish the flames and force our defeated foe into his rightful retreat!

ACTION

By now you should realize that putting on the armor of God (see Eph. 6:10–17) is a command, not a suggestion! As a prophetic act, stand up and "put" each item on as if you were a soldier of old preparing for battle. As you act out getting dressed with each item, speak out a declaration, such as, "I am placing the helmet of salvation on my head so that my mind is reminded of what Christ has done for me." When you pick up the shield of faith, make sure you brandish it boldly and shout, "By faith I will extinguish every fire of the enemy in my life and in the places God takes me to!"

Activated Faith

And without faith it is impossible to please God, because anyone who comes to him must believe that he exists and that he rewards those who earnestly seek him (Hebrews 11:6).

"Everything that you need to conquer all things is inside you and given by Me," says the Lord. As you go in His name, He reminds you of the weapons of His Word, the power of His anointing, and the authority inside you. He asks you to recall the faith that moves mountains and the insight by the Spirit of God that is in you.

- You are not lacking. You are "fully loaded" and ready to advance!

- You are made for victory and overcoming.

- You are not small or insignificant.

- You are made to be a giant of faith and power in the Holy Spirit.

In this moment God's finger is pointing specifically at the gift of faith inside you. It looks like the power button of an electronic device, and I see Him draw attention to it, and then press it at the same time as He says: "I have activated your faith before, and now I do so again. This weapon of faith is the one thing you need to overcome your obstacles. You are empowered through and by faith in Me and My abilities, not your own. Faith enables you to move beyond your own perceived limitations and into my limitless abilities."

And Jesus said: "I activate the gift of faith inside you again so that you become one who goes beyond your own boundaries. Allow Me to expand you by receiving this activated faith."

So, in this moment, as God Himself pushes that power button of faith again, watch and see how expansion comes to your thinking and to your approach to life and the challenges that will inevitably arise.

In every situation and with each challenge, allow the faith of God Himself to take you beyond your perceived issues and borders. Allow faith to move you beyond, into a spacious place of expectation and possibility.

ACTION

Receive your new perspective with the lens of faith—and act. Activated faith really only works if you apply it to something. In other words, now action is required from you. What are you going to do differently? How are you going to change your prayers?

The Lord Gives Victory

Now this I know: The Lord gives victory to his anointed. He answers him from his heavenly sanctuary with the victorious power of his right hand. Some trust in chariots and some in horses, but we trust in the name of the Lord our God. They are brought to their knees and fall, but we rise up and stand firm. Lord, give victory to the king! Answer us when we call! (Psalm 20:6–9)

Who have you put your expectations on? Who have you looked to for help? Have you looked to leaders, friends, and family rather than trusting in Me? Have you relied on your finances to get you through when I have been asking you to trust Me rather than your bank account? Take the time to consider these questions that I, Yahweh Jireh, am asking. Each of these things will fail or disappoint at some point in time. Yet I will never fail. And if your trust is truly and fully in Me, then I don't disappoint either.

Begin to trust Me in all things. Allow Me to be the One that you stand upon. Stand firm in Me! I am the One who both gives you victory and enables you to go from victory to victory. That is My gift to you; it is My desire for you. I, the Alpha and the Omega, know fully well how the temporary things of earth fade away. I also know your beginning from your end, and I desire the absolute best for you. I love you with an endless love. Put your trust in Me. Stand upon My promises; be strengthened as you stand firm upon My Word. I am a strong tower; run to Me and find safety. Trust Me as your mighty warrior who fights for you and has already given you the victory.

ACTION

Go through the questions at the beginning of this word. Have an honest conversation with yourself and the Lord about where your trust is. If He highlights a specific area, then write that worry or anxiety down. Along with that, write down where your trust has been in regards to that worry. Then declare over that situation: "Lord, I know that if I rely on myself and my abilities or people and their abilities to solve this worry, I am choosing to trust someone other than You. I repent for that! And I ask You to help me trust this situation into Your hands. I know that You are trustworthy and far more capable than me or anyone else. I choose to trust You above all else."

Speak with Power

"Is not my word like fire," declares the Lord, *"and like a hammer that breaks a rock in pieces?"* (Jeremiah 23:29)

The tongue has the power of life and death, and those who love it will eat its fruit (Proverbs 18:21).

"I have given you bold words to break chains. Do not hold them back! Your words go even to the places your feet cannot, and they release Kingdom light that destroys darkness. So do not hold your words back!"

God has placed in you a force of power so that when you speak Holy Spirit words, they go forth as weapons of war that demolish strongholds and release life. This force is as much a mindset and expectation as it is an action. Do you expect your words to be used by the Spirit to win battles? Do you know that when you speak, you create havoc for the enemy while releasing life for the Kingdom of God?

The Lord says: "Stand up and begin to speak My words into atmospheres. Let Me train you in the daily art of decrees and show you how to use your words as Holy Spirit weapons. Ask Me for the right words for each situation you face, and listen for what I will say to you from within. Speak them forth with confidence, and expect real change to occur, with tangible results that will glorify Me."

ACTION

Write a list of daily decrees that you can begin to use that are specific to some warfare situations that you are facing. You can use the following as a guide, but ultimately ask the Holy Spirit to tell you what they should be as He is the ultimate source of revelation:

- I decree that God has already overcome (name it) _____.
- I decree that this situation (name it) _____ shifts in Jesus's name!
- I decree victory over (name it) _____ in the mighty name of Jesus!

Occupy for Jesus

So he called ten of his servants, delivered to them ten minas, and said to them, "Do business till I come" (Luke 19:13 NKJV).

For do I now persuade men, or God? Or do I seek to please men? For if I still pleased men, I would not be a bondservant of Christ (Galatians 1:10 NKJV).

"I have given you space and territory to advance into and occupy in My name," says King Jesus. "So now, advance and occupy for My Kingdom!"

Each area that God has given into your hands is yours to steward, for example, your relationships, your work, your home, and your family. Be one who "oversees" what God has given to you for His glory and for the continued expansion of His Kingdom. It is time to acknowledge this role you have and put your responsibilities into action each day.

Questions to ask Jesus:

- What places have I been specifically called to occupy and steward?

- How am I to advance Your ways in these places?

Bring these questions before the Lord, and wait on Him for the answers to enable your advancement. And in the meantime ensure that you occupy all that He has already given you to influence. Everyone has somewhere they can influence for good.

ACTION

Build an altar to God. This doesn't have to be a pile of stones like in the Old Testament. An altar is somewhere where God is worshipped. Because of Jesus, this can be anywhere that you are. Practically speaking, this will look like worship, praise, and prayers of dedication in your places of occupation. By your prayers, decrees, and declarations you can consecrate your home, business, or place of work (for example, your desk or office), and in doing so, you set up an altar to the Most High God.

Example prayer: "I commit and give this work/business/home to You, God, in the name of Jesus Christ. I say that this place belongs to You, Jesus, You alone, and what happens here will be worship to You."

Then, anoint the building's wall or furniture with oil; this can be any oil that you have prayed over and set apart for this purpose. By marking boundaries in this way, you are making a sign that it is set apart for God and His work. Anoint the doors of access to your property and buildings, decreeing, "Nothing but what furthers the Kingdom of God and glorifies God may enter here." Maintain regular worship and adoration to Father, Son, and Spirit in these places. These places have been given to you to occupy.

DAY 254

Deal with the Unfruitful Areas

You, my brothers and sisters, were called to be free. But do not use your freedom to indulge the flesh; rather, serve one another humbly in love....So I say, walk by the Spirit, and you will not gratify the desires of the flesh. For the flesh desires what is contrary to the Spirit, and the Spirit what is contrary to the flesh....But the fruit of the Spirit is love, joy, peace, forbearance, kindness, goodness, faithfulness, gentleness and self-control. Against such things there is no law. Those who belong to Christ Jesus have crucified the flesh with its passions and desires. Since we live by the Spirit, let us keep in step with the Spirit (Galatians 5:13,16–17, 22–25).

You are to speak truth to power, just as Jesus did. Be filled with the Holy Spirit of Jesus Christ so that you do as He did with boldness, courage, and wisdom.

But as you step forward to advance His Kingdom by speaking truth to corrupting power, make sure that you have indeed been fully set free by truth and that you know God's truth by walking in step with His Word.

If there are still areas of your life that are in bondage, deal with these before you go speaking before others. Be mindful of those areas in your life that are not yet bearing the fruit of the Spirit and in step with the Spirit (see Gal. 5). Are there any unfruitful areas of your life? Apply God's truth to them and be set free!

ACTION

Take time to do the following steps:

- List the nine fruits of the Holy Spirit that Paul mentions in Galatians.

- Now, beside each one write down what it would look like to not have that fruit (for example, not having joy will look like a joyless life).

- Then, go one step further and write down what the opposite of each fruit would be (for example, the opposite of joy might be misery or despair).

- If you are struggling with this, you can search online for antonyms (opposites) of each word.

- Now, circle any of the words that you've written that you recognize in your own life.

- Confess those areas of your life that are unfruitful (missing fruit) or that are bearing bad fruit.

- Tell the Holy Spirit that you're ready to walk more in step with God's Word and that you need His help to cultivate fruit in your life.

Dressed to Conquer

I delight greatly in the Lord; my soul rejoices in my God. For he has clothed me with the garments of salvation and arrayed me in a robe of his righteousness (Isaiah 61:10).

All of you...have clothed yourselves with Christ (Galatians 3:27).

In the Bible, people wore clothes that were often an indication of their destiny in life. For example, the boy Samuel wore a linen *ephod* (see 1 Sam. 2:18) because one day he would function a bit like a priest. Also, each new year his mother made him a little robe (see 1 Sam. 2:19). This robe represented Samuel's prophetic authority. Later, when Samuel rips Saul's robe, he prophetically signs that Saul's kingdom will be "torn" away from him and given to David (see 1 Sam. 15:27–28). On another day David refuses to kill Saul but instead cuts off a corner of his robe (see 1 Sam. 24:4–5). Although David spares Saul in this moment, Saul's kingdom is eventually "cut off" and given to David. In due time the entire nation of Israel was to be torn apart like a garment, into twelve pieces (see 1 Kings 11:30–32).

Today's fashionistas like to wear designer fashions with brand names clearly visible. Most sportswear is emblazoned with the maker's label or mark. It sometimes seems that it's not the color or the style of clothes but who designs and makes them that really matters.

It's the same in the spiritual realm. We are wearing Christ. We are covered by His design label; in fact, *we* are His designer label. Even if you are in financial poverty, you are clothed in Christ. If you are affluent beyond words, you'll still be no better dressed spiritually because you are already wearing the very best—you are clothed in Christ. Whether you are a teenage girl in the latest fashions or an old man in shabby clothes, you will be what Christ clothes you in—beautifully dressed in Himself. When we wear Christ, our background, social status, and worldly wealth mean nothing; these things have absolutely no significance. You are dressed in the robe of His righteousness and the garments of salvation (see Isa. 61:10), and you are ready to conquer!

RECEIVE

Are you guilty of noticing someone's social status or worldly worth before you see that they are "wearing Christ"? Repent. Are you too focused on clothes, fashions, brands, labels, and appearances? Ask the Holy Spirit to shine His light on this area of your life and help you to see yourself as your heavenly Father sees you—beautifully dressed in His Son.

More Than a Conqueror

No, in all these things we are more than conquerors through him who loved us (Romans 8:37).

We are more than conquerors! What does that mean?

This is an odd phrase, isn't it? Surely we are simply just conquerors and overcomers, and most of us would like to feel that we live in successive victories more than we do.

Emma writes: My sporting hero Andy Murray, the all-time greatest Scottish tennis player, is a conqueror because he has won Wimbledon (twice), two Olympic gold medals (and a silver), and a US Open. Andy is the conqueror, so he rightfully takes home the conqueror's prize money for his victories.

After Andy has a victory, I assume that his wife goes to the most expensive, upmarket shops and spends his winnings. Andy Murray is a hero and a conqueror. His wife is *more than a conqueror*. She lives out the blessing of his victorious place. She spends the winnings he achieves.

Do you get what this means for you? You don't have to fight the enemy as Jesus did. He won that victory. You get the easy part of choosing how to apply His winnings. You are more than a conqueror! The foe is defeated, and now your Messiah asks you, "What do you want to do with the victory that I bought for you?"

You are more than a conqueror. Greatness was bestowed on you by the resurrection of Jesus.

ACTION

Apply the victory of Jesus to situations that you are currently in that require a major breakthrough. This means you speak with the confidence that situations will turn around in the name of Jesus. Receive the truth that you are more than a conqueror and that victory is something already secured for you. Decree the victory of Jesus with ease!

All Kinds of Prayer

And pray in the Spirit on all occasions with all kinds of prayers and requests. With this in mind, be alert and always keep on praying for all the Lord's people (Ephesians 6:18).

Oh, My warrior, how I long for you to increase in prayer! Many of you know how to pray and pray well, but you have been limited in the type of prayer you have known. You have not understood how to pray in the Spirit with all kinds of prayers. In the core of your being, you have cried out as you have longed to go to a new height and a new depth in prayer. I am here to answer that cry, and My Spirit is here to teach you. There are incredible heights and wonderful depths to be explored in prayer. There are things in the Spirit to discover, and there are even new languages to utter as you pray.

Take the limits off and begin to pray in a new way today. I am giving you new tongues as you open your mouth and trust Me to fill it. I am shutting off the mental clutter that distracts you when you attempt to pray in the Spirit. I am tuning your hearing so that you will begin to hear the various sounds of intercession and know when to use them. And I am increasing your understanding of prayer so that you will begin to pray into the areas in which I direct you strategically.

These are crucial days that require a new level and a higher standard. The old was good, but this new level is even better. So, come today and begin to learn the new ways that I have for you.

ACTION

Ask the Lord who you can join in prayer. Is there a local prayer group or an online group of prayer warriors that you could learn from? Are there areas of prayer that you've not explored and need to study? Are there new tongues that the Holy Spirit wants to give you? Could you increase your time of praying in tongues? Have a conversation with the Holy Spirit about these things and ask Him for a new strategy and a new impartation of prayer today.

Agree and Decree

Again, truly I tell you that if two of you on earth agree about anything they ask for, it will be done for them by my Father in heaven (Matthew 18:19).

Though one may be overpowered, two can defend themselves. A cord of three strands is not quickly broken (Ecclesiastes 4:12).

I hear the Lord say, "It is a day to agree and to decree!"

The Lord is highlighting to you two often-overlooked but immensely powerful weapons of warfare today: agreement and decrees. By agreement and decrees, you are able to shift darkness and release light. The Lord says, "Agreement and decrees are good partners for war. You need others you can pray and agree with and then decree together."

The Lord is encouraging you to pursue warfare relationships with those you can bond with authentically and agree with in intercession, warfare, and prayer. These people may be known to you already, but they may likewise be still currently unknown to you. Pray and ask God to shine His light to reveal who they are or pray and ask Him to send the right people to you.

As you find these people and start to agree and decree, the Lord says: "You shall release breakthroughs in the atmosphere like an unstoppable force that destroys the enemy, liberates captives, and breaks chains. Your agreement, partnered with your decrees in My name, will be a wrecking ball to the plans of the enemy and the prison walls of the captives."

RECEIVE

Pray: "Jesus, I recognize that You have given me the weapons of agreement and decrees. I choose to pick them up and use them. Lord, would You reveal to me the people I am meant to partner more intentionally with to agree in prayer and intercession. Who have You positioned around me that I need to pursue? If there isn't anyone around me, God, would You bring into my life those who I can agree and decree with in prayer and warfare."

DAY 259

Tongues—the Heavenly Power Engine

But you, beloved, building yourselves up in your most holy faith and praying in the Holy Spirit (Jude 20 ESV).

There is a power source inside of you that is like a turbocharged engine, and it needs your attention. It is set up and ready to go and will provide full-throttle power from Heaven that will propel you forward into the fullness of the missions God has for you. It is a way by which you can move with ease into the fast-flowing movement of Heaven's "jet stream"!

This "heavenly power engine" is ignited and charged by the Spirit languages God has put inside you and connected you to. Do you use these? Do you build yourself up in your most holy faith by praying in the Spirit? If not, it is time to turn the ignition and allow the engine to build up to full power!

This means practicing your heavenly tongue languages and exercising this spiritual muscle regularly. As you do, the spiritual power and energy you tap into from Heaven will increase and become more manifestly noticeable in your life of service to the Kingdom.

RECEIVE

If you already speak and pray in tongues, be encouraged to practice this more. Increase your daily time speaking, singing, and praying in tongues from at least ten minutes by increments of five more minutes each day. Build up as much investment of time as you are able to. Get used to speaking and praying in tongues when you are doing routine tasks or activities, such as walking, gardening, showering, and household chores. Make it part of your daily routine and see how supercharged you become!

If you don't yet speak in tongues, take time to ask the Holy Spirit to activate the gift within you, and make yourself available for that to happen. This can be easier to activate during worship as you will feel a deep connection with God in that moment. Find space and time to be uninterrupted by anyone, and allow the Holy Spirit to awaken this power gift.

If you have ever spoken *against* tongues or the gift of interpretation of tongues in your life, ask the Holy Spirit to highlight where and how you need to confess and pray. If you have said, "I don't want this gift because of…," again you will need to confess this and ask for God's forgiveness. If you don't deal with this first, it will be a block to beginning this journey. Allow Him to convict and illuminate where any blockage might be. Pray:

"Please show me, Holy Spirit, if I have offended You in any way concerning the gift of tongues. Please shine Your light on this because I desire to fully access the force of power that you have gifted and placed within me."

To Those at the Threshold

Be strong and courageous, because you will lead these people to inherit the land I swore to their ancestors to give them. Be strong and very courageous....Have I not commanded you? Be strong and courageous. Do not be afraid; do not be discouraged, for the Lord your God will be with you wherever you go (Joshua 1:6–7, 9).

A *threshold* is the strip of wood or stone that goes across the bottom of a doorway and is crossed when entering a house, building, or room. In science it's defined as the magnitude or intensity that has to be exceeded for a certain result or reaction to happen or manifest. New homeowners step across the threshold together as a sign that they are entering their new dwelling place; it belongs to them now. An airplane will have to reach a certain threshold speed on the runway in order to be able to take to the air.

Have you been waiting at the threshold of the new or the next thing?

The Spirit of the Lord says to you, "It is good to step forward. Go through the doorway and into what you have been waiting for." God has heard your prayers; He has watched you in your place of waiting. You asked Him for this, and you chose to trust God, and He has brought you to this place of the threshold of the new.

But now you need to take an act of will and make the step through to take the inheritance of what you have waited and prayed for. God will not push you through, nor does He want to carry you through. This is for you to cross. This is your time to gather what you need, do what needs to be done, put down what needs to be put down, invest what needs to be invested, and walk over the threshold, through the doorway, and into that promise. This is not the time to start to get fearful or anxious. Remember that you desired and prayed to get this far. So be bold and be strong for the Lord your God is with you. Be blessed as you enjoy what is next!

DECREE

I decree and declare today that I am strong and courageous. I decree and declare that the Lord my God is with me. He is the God of Joshua and the Israelites, who crossed out of the wilderness and into their promised inheritance. I will not be anxious or afraid. I will put my trust in the Lord my God. It is time for me to cross the threshold!

Now, what steps do you need to take?

Worship Ascending

When he had led them out to the vicinity of Bethany, he lifted up his hands and blessed them. While he was blessing them, he left them and was taken up into heaven. Then they worshiped him and returned to Jerusalem with great joy. And they stayed continually at the temple, praising God (Luke 24:50–53).

Jesus was *"taken up to heaven"* precisely forty days after He was raised from the dead and ten days before the feast of Pentecost when the Spirit was given in the Upper Room. The biblical text seems to imply that Jesus journeyed (literally was "carried up") on a cloud, which eventually hid Him from the disciples at ground level. This was in accordance with the Psalms: *"He makes the clouds his chariot and rides on the wings of the wind"* (Ps. 104:3). The disciples were still gazing into the sky when two men in white clothes (the uniform of angels) spoke to them. *"Why do you stand here looking into the sky? This same Jesus, who has been taken from you into heaven, will come back in the same way you have seen him go into heaven"* (Acts:1:11).

After Jesus disappeared but before they returned to Jerusalem, the disciples worshipped Him together. They must have raised their hands and voices as they praised and glorified their risen and ascended Lord, the God-man, Christ Jesus. This must surely have been the most animated, enthusiastic, joyful, and spontaneous time of worship they had ever had! Here were Jewish men who all their life had believed there was only one person called God and that to use divine titles of anyone else was sacrilege and blasphemy of the worst kind. But now they knew that everything Jesus had said, especially about Himself, was true. Everything He had done was His Father's will, and the cross was a triumph, not a tragedy. They now knew that Jesus *would* be coming back as He had promised and they were about to embark on a worldwide mission of telling everybody that God so loved the world that He had sent His only Son to die and that whoever believes in Him will not perish but will have everlasting life (see John 3:16)! It is no wonder that they returned to Jerusalem with *"great joy"*!

ACTION

You are probably very used to worshipping Jesus as Lord, but take time to check if any note of familiarity has crept into your worship. Think of the reasons the disciples had for their liberated and unrestrained praise. Could you be more full of joy and freedom in your worship of your ascended Savior?

You Need to Act Prophetically

Then he said, "Take the arrows," and the king took them. Elisha told him, "Strike the ground." He struck it three times and stopped (2 Kings 13:18).

The Bible is full of stories of people who acted out prophetic signs, men and women of faith who knew that the power of action in the natural earth realm would cause something spiritually significant to happen. Prophetic acts catch the attention of Heaven and show just how serious you are in pursuing God's solutions.

In the Old Testament, Naaman, full of leprosy, had to bathe in the Jordan seven times to be healed. He could not just receive his healing by standing still. He had to act for Heaven to open and give him what he desired. In the New Testament, Jesus asked His disciples to gather two fish and five loaves of bread to feed five thousand. The first step of gathering the small amount of food was a prophetic act that enabled Heaven to respond with a mass-feeding miracle.

Perhaps the most lackluster, disappointing prophetic act is found in Second Kings 13. In this story the prophet Elisha gave a king instructions to strike the ground with arrows to secure a military victory. Unfortunately, the king did not grasp the need to act with determined passion and high faith, and he struck the ground limitedly and stopped prematurely. Elisha explained to the king that he would not have victory because of his lack of ability to act out a prophetic sign.

ACTION

Ask, "What do I need to act out to secure a victory, God?" Let God lead you creatively and do whatever He says with eagerness and enthusiasm!

Emma writes: Some personal illustrations from my own life might help your thinking. We have taken tent pegs and used them as stakes in the ground of land and buildings that God has said He will give us. We have anointed our home, doorframes, and windows with oil as a sign that only things of the Kingdom of God are allowed access to our property. We have laid hands on people's car keys and house keys and blessed them into safety when they have been threatened. And we have marched around the outside of buildings where poor but significant decisions were being made as a statement that the kingdom of hell cannot advance beyond where we set our feet.

In fact, acting out prophetically what God says should be a regular part of our lives as we grow in the understanding of the connection between the natural and the supernatural realms. What we act out in one realm impacts and releases the Kingdom of God to present itself in the natural.

DAY 263

Partner with the Angels

See, I am sending an angel ahead of you to guard you along the way and to bring you to the place I have prepared. Pay attention to him and listen to what he says. Do not rebel against him; he will not forgive your rebellion, since my Name is in him. If you listen carefully to what he says and do all that I say, I will be an enemy to your enemies and will oppose those who oppose you. My angel will go ahead of you and bring you into the land of the Amorites, Hittites, Perizzites, Canaanites, Hivites and Jebusites, and I will wipe them out (Exodus 23:20–23).

My angels have been dispatched to go into the areas that I am redeeming for My Kingdom. Be alert to them as they move and advance and seek for partnership. Follow the angels where they go, for they are moving according to My plans for your life and for the areas you are called to bring freedom into.

- Angels are moving in your workplace. Can you see them?

- Angels are moving in your family. Can you sense them?

- Angels are moving in your geography. Are you aware of them?

- Angels are moving. Will you follow them?

These angels are sent and designated for entering new territory and new wine. They are angels that bring you into promised land and wide spacious places. Follow them and they will teach you how to fight, show you how to war, and bring you in to occupy this new place. This may cause fear for some of you, and yet I say to you, "Fear not!" These hosts are of Me and from Me. They are moving according to My plan, and I will bring you on a journey of sight and of partnership that you are able to navigate. Look to Me first always, and I will reveal the angelic hosts as and when required.

RECEIVE

Respond by following these steps of asking questions that will help you see Jesus and angels in the spirit:

1. Where is Jesus in the room? Look in the spirit. Where do you sense Him most?

2. Come near to Him.

3. Ask Him, "Jesus, would you let me see the angels that I need to be aware of for battle right now?"

4. Look at what they are wearing, their colors, the weapons they are carrying.

5. What are the angels called?

6. What is their role?

7. Ask: "Lord, how should I respond to them?"

DAY 264

I Will Not Be Silent!

My heart may sing your praises and not be silent. Lord my God, I will praise you forever (Psalm 30:12).

You have a determination and a voice within you that must be released. You are filled with power and authority from Heaven that must be charged and deployed. God did not make us like "spirit bombs" to be left undetonated. We must not be silent! It is time to release your voice, and in doing so, detonate the spiritual weapon that you are. Open your mouth and God will fill it! Be willing to speak out and so be used for transformation and for God's glory. Be ready to speak when He asks you to, and you will enforce the victory in Christ by releasing your words.

I see the Lord using your bold, power-filled, Holy Spirit–inspired words, both written and spoken, to bring transformation and to blast a way through religiosity, humanism, lethargy, apathy, and so much more. You are to release words that in the spirit create a way through where there seems like there is none, like a tunnel blasted through an impassable mountain range. Your words will provoke, irritate, and create a way through the places of captivity, both for the people of God and for those who do not yet know Him.

"Enforce My victory with your words, My child!" The Spirit of God encourages you today, "Enforce the victory! Release the weapons of warfare from your mouth and your writing hand. Speak! Write! Release your weapons of hope, breakthrough, and challenge. Make a way through with the words that I have given you!"

RECEIVE

Ask the Lord where your words should be directed. Ask for Holy Spirit–inspired words. Speak where He says to speak. Send your written words where He says to send them. Is there an issue or a challenge that needs to be addressed? Know that the Holy Spirit has put the words in you to be directed and released to bring transformation. Wait before the Lord and hear the vocal and written solutions that you are to bring. Act on them, and let your words be weapons that cause breakthroughs!

Enabled with Great Boldness!

"What are we [the Sanhedrin] *going to do with these men?" they asked. "Everyone living in Jerusalem knows they* [Peter and John] *have performed a notable sign, and we cannot deny it. But to stop this thing from spreading any further among the people, we must warn them to speak no longer to anyone in this name." Then they called them in again and commanded them not to speak or teach at all in the name of Jesus* (Acts 4:16–18).

The same spirit that was at work amongst the Jerusalem Sanhedrin in the first century is at work around you in these days. It seeks to shut your anointing down and prevent you from doing what you have been gifted to do. It uses fear, intimidation, law, mockery, religion, and even trends such as correctness or being relevant to shut down believers from fulfilling the resurrection mandate given by Jesus.

Peter and John were bold in their reply to the religious leaders: *"As for us, we cannot help speaking about what we have seen and heard"* (Acts 4:20). Nevertheless, when they were released from jail, they still beat a hasty retreat back to the relative safety of their own people.

But the company around them would not let them stay in hiding or retreat for long and rose up in courageous, encouraging prayer:

Now, Lord, consider their threats and enable your servants to speak your word with great boldness. Stretch out your hand to heal and perform signs and wonders through the name of your holy servant Jesus (Acts 4:29–30).

Today we make this prayer over you, whether you are part of a great company, a really strong church fellowship, or even if you feel you are on your own and surrounded by many threats: "Lord, enable your servant (put your name here) to speak Your Word with great boldness. Stretch out Your hand to heal and perform signs and wonders through the name of Your holy servant Jesus."

DECREE

Hear this prayer for yourself, and would you also please join us in praying it out loud over everyone else who reads this book? And then go! Go and speak with great boldness! Go and heal and perform signs and wonders by the name of Jesus!

After they prayed, the place where they were meeting was shaken. And they were all filled with the Holy Spirit and spoke the word of God boldly (Acts 4:31).

DAY 266

Arrayed in Splendor

The Lord will extend your mighty scepter from Zion, saying, "Rule in the midst of your enemies!" Your troops will be willing on your day of battle. Arrayed in holy splendor, your young men will come to you like dew from the morning's womb (Psalm 110:2–3).

I delight greatly in the Lord; my soul rejoices in my God. For he has clothed me with garments of salvation and arrayed me in a robe of his righteousness, as a bridegroom adorns his head like a priest, and as a bride adorns herself with her jewels (Isaiah 61:10).

The Lord is coming today to give you a new perspective of yourself. He's coming to show you how He sees you. Some have seen themselves as always dressed for battle, but never in the royal robes of one who is a child of the King. Is this you? Have you never seen yourself dressed as one who rules and reigns? On the other hand, some see themselves in their royal dress but never clothed as the Bride of Christ. Is this you? Have you not yet known Jesus in an intimate, face-to-face way? There are still others yet who have never seen themselves seated at His banqueting table, with His banner of love waving over them. What about you—is this you?

The Lord God says to you: "I see you in the fullness of who I am. I am God who is mighty in battle, but I am also the lover of your soul. I am a fierce warrior who brings vindication and who fights for you! Yet I am also that gentle Shepherd who picks you up and carries you on My shoulders. I am the One who prepares a table for you to feast in front of your enemies! I am the One who dresses you to rule and reign for you are arrayed in My splendor and My glory! Hear Me as I say, 'Rule in the midst of your enemies! Rule as one who knows who I am and knows who you are!' Your enemy knows who you are and he knows who I am, so he does all he can to keep you from seeing fully. Yet I come to show you the fullness today!"

RECEIVE

Take time to look at yourself in the spirit. Ask the Holy Spirit to hold up His mirror to you so that you see yourself as He sees you. It may not be easy to overcome what you have previously thought about yourself, so invest time and don't give up! Do you see the beautiful crown that sits upon your head? Do you see the color-filled garments that God has dressed you in? Do you feel the rich quality and the care that has been put into how He has clothed you? Even when you go to battle, you go as one who is washed clean, well-equipped, trained, and armed as royalty! Take the time today to see yourself as He does.

DAY 267

Out Loud

So faith comes from hearing, and hearing by the word of Christ (Romans 10:17 NASB).

What is the best way to read the Bible? The answer is out loud.

Reading Scripture inwardly, meditatively, and silently is vital, but the Word of God tells us that faith comes from *hearing*.

Faith comes when we hear. Therefore, your ears must open to receive truth, and that truth must be the Word of God. So, when we read the Bible out loud, we stir our faith levels. We take hold of our inner world and strengthen it by hearing truth wash over us. When we hear our own voice speak truth, we are able to take greater ownership of the truth.

If life and death are in the tongue (see Prov. 18:21; Matt. 15:11; James 3), how much more will the Word of God on our tongues build us into new levels of vibrancy and goodness?

ACTION

Start reading the Psalms out loud. Read until you feel your inner world shift and strengthen. Practice this discipline daily, and measure how much more alive you are from hearing the Word of God resonate around you. Speaking the Word of God will revolutionize how you spend time with God and transform your atmosphere. Devils will fly away as they hate hearing the Word of God.

Resist the Devil

Submit yourselves, then, to God. Resist the devil, and he will flee from you (James 4:7).

You were made to overcome satan daily. Victory is not something that happens on an occasional basis. As you resist satan, he knows he must flee. However, access to your victory only comes after you have submitted to God. This is the biblical order which cannot be altered. Read James 4:7 again and notice this.

Our yes to Jesus, our submission to Him, comes *before* we can overcome. This means that in our hearts we must grasp that His will is better than ours. Jesus may not make our desires or lusts for wrong things suddenly disappear; God may not change our fleshly instincts. But our yes to Jesus and our obedience to His ways enables us to resist the devil, to resist temptation.

Our lives are to be a story of increasingly deeper yeses to Jesus and trusting that when we say no to what is *not* Him, it further deepens our yes to Him too. It is in this heart place of yielding to all He says that we can overthrow satan because satan has no part of us.

ACTION

Spend time today looking at all the ways you say no to Jesus, for example, perpetual sin, willful ideas, unforgiveness, and stubborn independence. Review each of them and hand them to Jesus, allowing your heart to increasingly say yes to holiness and His leading. Release forgiveness to others; let go of offense and become truly dependent on Him. Then you will be a stable, successful spiritual warrior, who will gain authority over yourself and set others free.

DAY 269

Make Your Home a Kingdom of God Zone!

Then he poured some of the anointing oil on Aaron's head and anointed him, to consecrate him (Leviticus 8:12 NASB).

You prepare a table before me in the presence of my enemies; You have anointed my head with oil; my cup overflows (Psalm 23:5 NASB).

The Lord is inviting you today to partner with Him in praying around your house to create a Kingdom of God atmosphere and a no-go zone for the enemy. The Lord says, "My desire is that you have a glory-filled home, where encounters and intimacy are easy. Pray around your home with Me today and anoint your home with oil, releasing My glory on every wall, in every room, and to occupy every space."

As you go around your home, ask the Lord to highlight anything specific that you need to deal with. It may be a room that needs specific prayer, or it may be an object or piece of decoration that needs to be anointed or perhaps even thrown out. The Lord will reveal and shine His light as you inquire of Him. Ask Him what to pray and let the Lord lead you by His Spirit to create a "glory-filled zone" in every part of your house.

The Lord says: "You get to determine the atmosphere you live in. You get to determine the atmosphere you sleep in. You get to determine the atmosphere that visitors encounter when they come to your home. So partner with Me, shift demonic atmospheres, deal with darkness, and release a Kingdom of God atmosphere that makes encountering Me and being intimate with Me easy."

ACTION

Get some anointing oil and pray over it. Ask God to bless it, and then move throughout your house praying as you feel led by the Spirit. Remember that this is about partnership, so ask the Holy Spirit, "How would You like me to pray in this room?" or "Is there anything specific I need to anoint or pray for in this room?" Then move throughout your house until you feel settled with the atmosphere.

DAY 270

Your Life As an Altar

When they came to the place of which God had told him, Abraham built the altar there and laid the wood in order and bound Isaac his son and laid him on the altar, on top of the wood (Genesis 22:9 ESV).

"Build an altar of worship to the Most High God alone!" is the cry of Heaven. Do you hear it? Earlier in this chapter, you were encouraged to consider creating a physical space that would be an altar of worship to God. Now, spend yourself on setting foundations and establishing an altar of worship to Him in *every* aspect of your life.

Worship at this altar alone, and allow God to build and make what He desires from your life through that worship: songs, praise, proclamations, and decrees; sacrifice, honor, and glory—give all this to God Most High. Let your worship be your words and your song but also ensure that it is your life and work on the altar, building glory only to God, not to man and not for yourself.

"Build an altar for Me and for no other," I hear the Lord say. "Build Me an altar and allow Me to have your worship!"

Make room in your life, in your everyday, to worship God alone. Ensure you are aligned to Him. Have no idols in your life. Give no other the worship that He alone is due.

ACTION

Ask yourself searching questions: Have I built altars of worship for myself or people? Have I worshipped and looked to another for my salvation and strength; do I have an idol before God? Have I put money, success, position, or fame ahead of God?

It is time for a reset of your worship, making it point to God alone. Approach God in reverence and holy fear as you confess where you have knowingly or inadvertently established foundations of worship that are contrary to God in your life. Allow the Holy Spirit to convict you and bring to attention those areas where false altars and idols have been given room. Demolish those altars in your life and refocus your heart, mind, work, and life goals to build only for Him. Ask for the Lord's forgiveness and reset your foundation of worship to Him.

DAY 271

Calling Worshipping Warriors

Hallelujah! Praise God in his holy house of worship, praise him under the open skies; praise him for his acts of power, praise him for his magnificent greatness; praise with a blast on the trumpet, praise by strumming soft strings; praise him with castanets and dance, praise him with banjo and flute; praise him with cymbals and a big bass drum, praise him with fiddles and mandolin. Let every living, breathing creature praise God! Hallelujah!
(Psalm 150:1–6 MSG)

A draft notice has been sent out to worshipping people throughout the earth. A call to arms has been sent out from the heavenlies to worship leaders, singers, musicians, and songwriters around the world. Worshipping warriors arise—this is your time! You are needed for the harvest!

But this is not just to those who are in established positions and roles; this is also to those potential conscripts to the worshipping army of the Lord, as He even calls upon the reservists in this time. Bedroom worshippers arise! Those of you who sing in your car, your shower, or as you take a walk, this is your call-up time too!

I saw a vision of a gladiatorial arena, where worshipping warriors would do battle for the spiritual atmospheres of their lands. Worshippers were coming out from gates around all sides of the arena. Some had guitars strapped to their backs, others had loud hailers, others had banging drums, and others carried armfuls of words, notes, chords, and rhythms!

And God is calling on young people to rise up in worship across their areas of online influence. You are to broadcast the goodness of God and the desirability of Jesus Christ across the channels where your friends are watching. Video makers, arise! Social networkers, take your place of worshipping warfare! Messengers, influencers, and communicators, spread the good news! Dancers, writers, artists, and creatives, now is the time to be bold and brave with what God has put on your heart. Learn how to broadcast your worship. Practice singing a new song. Make your decrees and declarations before the nations for the glory of the Lord!

DECREE

Instead of making a private decree or declaration like you usually do, your challenge today is to record something and put it out on one or more of your channels! Nowadays nearly everyone has the ability to record a video or type a message and broadcast it to a wide audience. Imagine if every believer flooded the online networks with their true worship! You could write a status update or blog post. You could record a song, a dance, or a short message on video, or you could draw or make something and then take a photo. Even if you're feeling short on inspiration, there is more than enough song and poetry in the Book of Psalms that you can freely use and share.

DAY 272

Quenching the Spirit

Who could imagine that the all-powerful Spirit of God could ever be quenched, limited, or restricted in what He wants to do in our lives and our churches. Surely this would be beyond the realm of possible. But it is in the Bible:

Do not quench the Spirit (1 Thessalonians 5:19).

Fan into flame the gift of God, which is in you through the laying on of my hands. For the Spirit God gives us does not make us timid, but gives power, love and self-discipline (2 Timothy 1:6).

Do you ever stop to think of ways in which you may be quenching the work of the Spirit? The Holy Spirit wants to work in your life and in your church. He wants to turn up the heat of His presence among us. He wants to fill our hearts with the warmth of His indwelling power. But we must not pour a bucket of cold water over what the Holy Spirit wants to ignite.

Here are six examples of ways that we can quench the Holy Spirit:

- Partnering with a spirit of fear.

- Having misguided theology—I don`t believe cessationists intend to quench the Spirit, but by not believing in the miraculous gifts today, this is the outcome. By prohibiting what the Spirit can and can't do, such as the miraculous gifts, in our lives and in our churches, we quench the Spirit, whether we intended to or not.

- Despising prophecy—don't treat it as if it were unimportant or trivial but test everything (see 1 Thess. 5:20–21) and eagerly desire the gift of prophecy (see 1 Cor. 14:1).

- Partnering with a spirit of legalism leads to the creation of man-made rules, doctrines, and traditions that do not permit spontaneity and the special leading of the Spirit.

- Not recognizing the Spirit as a person in the godhead. *Never* just think of Him as an "it" or an "influence." He is God!

- Failing to lead people into the conscious, felt awareness of their adoption as God's children (see Rom. 5:15–16; Gal. 4:4–7).

ACTION

Search your heart for any possible ways that you may have quenched the Holy Spirit in your life and in the life of your church.

Pray: "Oh, Holy Spirit, please work in my life that I will never quench the fire You have caused to burn. Let me never pour water on what You want to ignite. Will You come, unquenched, into my heart as a burning flame, and may I never be a hindrance in the work of Your Kingdom."

Decrees

You will also declare a thing, and it will be established for you; so light will shine on your ways (Job 22:28 NKJV).

God and satan listen to what you say. Each of them looks at your decrees and declarations—your words—and wants to use them. God wants to inhabit your praises and ensure that blessing is established for you as you speak according to His Kingdom. However, satan wants to harness your words to back you into a corner and allow death to partner with you. He wants you to have death of friendships, finances, and spirituality.

When Queen Esther was facing a death edict against her people in chapter 3 of the Book of Esther, the entirety of the children of Israel were under a decree of limitation. But Esther knew that a righteous decree would overturn any decree that had gone before.

Speaking according to the will of God and the Kingdom of God overturns any other curses or words previously spoken. Child, it is time to undo what has been spoken by you and to you over many years that opened a door for satan and death. It is time to revoke all previous words that stand against you, words about your looks and abilities, your call and intelligence, your education, your destiny, and your strengths.

ACTION

Pull down, tear down, like pulling bill posters down from a wall, all previous decrees and word curses. This means that you will need to speak in the name of Jesus that all previous word curses and limitations are now rendered null and void over your life. Break their hold by decreeing that their power now ends. Then speak in the name of Jesus a new and more powerful decree that what Jesus has for you will now be made manifest in your life.

CHAPTER 10

Alive in Christ

When the Wilderness Comes

Therefore I am now going to allure her; I will lead her into the wilderness and speak tenderly to her. There I will give her back her vineyards, and will make the Valley of Achor a door of hope. There she will respond as in the days of her youth, as in the day she came up out of Egypt (Hosea 2:14–15).

The wilderness season can feel tough, as though you are in the middle of nothing. And yet I hear the Lord say: "The wilderness is not an empty or a pathless region. Instead, it is brimming with new life and opportunity. I extend an invitation to you who find yourself in the wilderness to find Me and encounter Me and be overwhelmed by the magnitude of My desire and love for you." Instead of complaining, thank God for the wilderness and trust that He knows what He is doing here.

"Do not despise the seasons of wilderness, for it is in the wilderness place that I form you, heal you, equip you, and launch you." The wilderness is like a womb that forces the new to come forth from you. Just as Jesus went into the wilderness filled with the Spirit and then came out of it in the power of the Spirit, so as you journey through these days know that the Lord is activating the fullness of His Spirit in you.

He says to you, "As you trust Me in the journey, I will wake up power from within, and you shall emerge raised and ready to steward power and transformation as you leave the wilderness. So thank Me for the wilderness! Choose to love it, to linger in it. Do not rush the seasons when wilderness comes. Instead, let Me perfect My work in you. For it is in the wilderness that you are formed, healed, equipped, and launched. Are you ready?"

ACTION

Ask the Lord:

- What are You achieving in me in this wilderness season?

- How can I partner with Your work as I am in the wilderness?

- What can I expect as an outcome for this season?

Start to thank God out loud for everything He is going to do when wilderness comes. Set your expectations high for what will be a highly formational season.

Praise Is Your Weapon

They spread a net for my feet—I was bowed down in distress. They dug a pit in my path—but they have fallen into it themselves. My heart, O God, is steadfast, my heart is steadfast; I will sing and make music. Awake, my soul! Awake, harp and lyre! I will awaken the dawn. I will praise you, Lord, among the nations; I will sing of you among the peoples. For great is your love, reaching to the heavens; your faithfulness reaches to the skies (Psalm 57:6–10).

To you who have dealt with shock, trauma, disappointment, or betrayal, the Lord God is saying to you now: "Your praise is a weapon! Praise Me when it hurts! Praise Me when it stings! Praise Me when you feel that you have nothing else to give this life. Praise Me. Offer it up as a sacrifice. Yes, it is costly. Yes, it does require something of you; yet your praise has a destructive effect upon the spiritual enemies coming against you. So, praise Me on the days when you feel least like it. Put your dance shoes on and dance! Pull your flags out and wave them as your banner of victory! Open your mouth and sing! Why? Because you are not defeated! You have not lost the battle! It may look like you have, but this is not the end!

"When you make the choice to praise Me, even in the most horrific circumstances, you choose to live by faith and to declare with your praise that I will carry you through. You elevate the truth of who I am, and by doing so, you open up the heavens so that I can pour down on you all that you need. You create space for Me to come in and do what is needed to turn your situation around. I take your praise seriously. Will you do the same?"

ACTION

Put on a good praise song and praise Jesus today! Be intentional and do what you least feel like doing. Dance! Sing! Wave your hands or flags as a banner of His love and goodness over you. Offer your praise as a beautiful sacrifice to your King. Once you've done that, you can go even further by intentionally praising Him over specific situations that need to turn around or choosing to praise Him for specific attributes that speak about who He is rather than just what He does for you.

DAY 276

Hold Onto Me

I have told you these things, so that in me you may have peace. In this world you will have trouble. But take heart! I have overcome the world (John 16:33).

"Although there will be hardship, trial, and challenge, I am with you and I am for you," promises Jesus Christ our Lord, who is standing with you and is holding you, and all that you are, together in Him. You are not abandoned. You are not bereft of help and support.

"Hold on to Me as I hold onto you, My child. There are times now and times to come that will be dark and turbulent. There will even be days when you will ask, 'Why must it be so difficult?' And yet, I am working My purpose in you and through you. You will get through all things in and through Me. Do not forget that you are a signpost that points to Me for the salvation and hope of others.

"Make your stand in Me today and allow Me to press you forward in the fullness of My life in you. For there is more of Me in you than you have fully seen or even understood. Step forward with boldness and remember that I am in you. And you are in Me. With Me, nothing can hold you back!"

DECREE

Determine that you will stand in Christ in all circumstances and not allow the turbulence of the world and your life to overwhelm or submerge you. Decree and declare this out loud so that you hear it—and so that the world hears it too:

- I am not moving from the position of determined faith because of Christ in me!

- I will stand on the Rock and will be immovable from that place of trust in all circumstances, knowing that my Lord Jesus Christ has overcome the world and all trouble in it!

- I have this because Jesus Christ has this!

DAY 277

Alert and Supersensitized by His Spirit

Be alert and of sober mind. Your enemy the devil prowls around like a roaring lion looking for someone to devour (1 Peter 5:8).

God has given you spiritual senses that enable you to be watchful and sensitive to all that He is doing, as well as alerting you to the enemy who comes with the intention of slowing you down and interfering with you.

He has supersensitized you by His Spirit!

Be aware of how your spiritual atmosphere feels each day. Be alert to changes in your mood and how your surroundings feel to you. This will help you to be alert to combat where the enemy tries to come in and interfere with your life. Realize that you already have the ability and gifts to do this by the Holy Spirit of God. It's time to sharpen your senses with the Lord.

RECEIVE

Ask the Lord to awaken your senses in the spirit even more than they already are. Know that you have the ability to see, feel, hear, smell, and taste in the spirit as much as you do in the physical. The gift of the discerning of spirits (see 1 Cor. 12) helps you to determine which spirit is at work: Is it your own spirit or another human spirit? Is it a holy spirit (such as the Holy Spirit or an angelic being), or is it an enemy spirit, a demon? Your spiritual senses are alive with the possibility of assessing when God is moving and when the enemy has come to disrupt you.

Take time each day to assess what you are feeling and ask the Holy Spirit, "What is this? Is it my emotion? Is it You, God, or is this the enemy?" Practice trying this each day, and you will soon find that you are easily able to determine from the moment you wake up what is happening in the spirit. Practice this throughout your day, becoming more aware of shifts and changes in the atmosphere around you. Take time to respond, pray, and acknowledge these changes to ensure that you are moving with the Lord more than you are being moved or making decisions by your emotions (or the demonic). Pray in the Spirit on all occasions to help you stay sharp in this.

DAY 278

No More Mediocrity!

I know your deeds, that you are neither cold nor hot. I wish you were either one or the other! So, because you are lukewarm—neither hot nor cold—I am about to spit you out of my mouth. You say, "I am rich; I have acquired wealth and do not need a thing." But you do not realize that you are wretched, pitiful, poor, blind and naked. I counsel you to buy from me gold refined in the fire, so you can become rich; and white clothes to wear, so you can cover your shameful nakedness; and salve to put on your eyes, so you can see. Those whom I love I rebuke and discipline. So be earnest and repent (Revelation 3:15–19).

Heed the Lord's pep talk to you today as He pulls you up from a place of spiritual mediocrity and puts you on a platform for your true potential to be unleashed. Be uncompromising in your pursuit of righteous and bold Christianity. It is time to repent, be refined, and to shine.

And He says to you, "I desire to be your influencer. I desire for you to model yourself on Me and not on the world. Be shaped and clothed by My Spirit, not by the spirits of the age."

This is a time for self-denial and making a deliberate decision to not take part in all that the world offers. Make a daily choice to let go of all that is mediocre and instead pursue God's very best for you. Allow the Holy Spirit to influence you and every part of your life, and you will become *truly* rich.

ACTION

Read Christ's words to three of His seven churches in Turkey (see Rev. 3). Repent of any ways in which you've been like the Laodicean church. Confess any ways that you have been lukewarm. Ask Him to make you burn for Him and be like those in Sardis and Philadelphia.

DAY 279

Wilderness Experiences

Then Moses led Israel from the Red Sea and they went into the Desert of Shur. For three days they traveled in the desert without water (Exodus 15:22).

All the tests they endured on their way through the wilderness are a symbolic picture, an example that provides us with a warning so that we can learn through what they experienced (1 Corinthians 10:11 TPT).

When you go through tough times, you may ask, as the Israelites of old did, "If God is with me, why is this happening?"

And Jesus beckons to you, "Come to Me for understanding since I experienced forty days in the wilderness while on earth. I know the dry places through which our lives must pass. I am ready to help when you suffer as a believer, so be patient in your distress, for I will never cease to show you My loving-kindness."

Sometimes fear is overwhelming and our faith falters, like the Israelites' faith did, or Peter's when he sank beneath the waves as he tried to walk on water. Like us, his faith was small but what matters about faith is not the amount you have but the object of your faith. Jesus Christ is the object of our faith. In Him we trust, and that is what makes the difference. Though our faith may be small, we have a great God. Though our faith may be weak, like Peter's on the water, the hand of Jesus is strong to save. No matter how small your faith, you can rely on Jesus to hear your prayer for help.

In the case of the Israelites, their leader, Moses, cried out to God, and He showed him the branch of a tree, which Moses threw into the water. The water became sweet and the Israelites were all able to drink. Miracles do happen in the wilderness; bitter waters can become sweet.

ACTION

Thank God that miracles do happen in our wilderness experiences. Ask Him for a greater gift of faith and recommit to making Him the object of your faith. Make nothing else the object of your faith. Submit yourself to God's wise plan for your life, and you will see Him perform miracles for you. Perhaps His greatest miracle will be the one He performs in you!

Sovereignty, Mystery, and Goodness

As for God, his way is perfect: The Lord's word is flawless; he shields all who take refuge in him. For who is God besides the Lord? And who is the Rock except our God? (Psalm 18:30–31)

God's ways are perfect. What a challenging biblical statement. This is a truth that we often wrestle with as we navigate situations that on the surface look anything but good and perfect. How do we resolve this dilemma of the perfect ways of God and the real, tangible struggles that we face? How do we walk the line between the God who works all things for our good, when what we are facing shows little signs of measurable goodness?

We tightly grab hold of three words: *mysterious, sovereign,* and *good.*

God is mysterious. We are not always going to be able to understand His processes, His order, and His overarching view of our lives.

God is sovereign. He possesses the ultimate plan for us all, and He gets to choose the timings of our lives; He knows when to give and when to take away.

God is good. His goodness is utterly reliable and constant, and although His goodness might not look like we want it to look, His goodness is always the underpinning of all that He does.

DECREE

I acknowledge that You are a mysterious, sovereign, and good God. I hold to these foundational truths about You that are present throughout the Bible, and I step into the comfort and support that they give my life, even when from my vantage point it looks like the enemy has had a victory. Your goodness and sovereignty will never fail.

Naked I came from my mother's womb, and naked I will depart. The Lord gave and the Lord has taken away; may the name of the Lord be praised (Job 1:21).

Life in Abundance

The thief comes only in order to steal and kill and destroy. I came that they may have and enjoy life, and have it in abundance [to the full, till it overflows] (John 10:10 AMP).

You have believed a lie that your life will have a *little* growth but not a *lot* of growth. You have expected a fraction of life but not the fullness of life and a little bit of space for expansion but not a lot of space for expansion. This is just not true. Jesus says: "I have not given you My life in small measures. You don't have a little bit of life, a mere portion of life, only a fraction of life. I have given you life and life *in abundance*. You are made to steward life, to have it flow through you and from you to others."

Right here, right now you can be and feel fully alive in Christ! You can feel the life of Christ pulsate your entire being, giving vibrancy to your being, joy to your thoughts, capacity to your emotions. This is not a future expectation but a present pressing reality for you!

As life starts to fill you, do not forget that this life that He has given to you is not just for you but for others. You are a life-giver to others by the power of Christ from within. You will resurrect hearts, thoughts, dreams, talents, gifts, and the futures of those you encounter. As God has given you excessive and abundant life, so He says, "Give it also to others. Let them feel it, encounter it, and be changed by it."

DECREE

*I am fully alive in Christ! God has not given me a small amount of life but rather an abundance of life. **I am made to bring life to others by the power of Christ.***

DAY 282

A Spacious Place

He reached down from on high and took hold of me; he drew me out of deep waters. He rescued me from my powerful enemy, from my foes, who were too strong for me. They confronted me in the day of my disaster, but the Lord was my support. He brought me out into a spacious place; he rescued me because he delighted in me (Psalm 18:16–19).

My sons and daughters, this dry, barren place that you are in is not My plan for you. This place that you have dwelt in, that feels like an endless rut from which will never get out, is not My best for you. You have circled round and round in cycles that just continue to repeat, and I have had enough of it. Have you?

Together, let us put an end to this place, for I have a wide, open, spacious place for you to dwell. It is a place that is full of life, joy, freedom, color, and fruit. In other words, there is no limit to what can grow in this place that I have for you. Just as I promised Israel a land that was flowing with milk and honey, so I have a fruitful place for you. It is a place where you will see growth, change, and the fruit of a mature vine. It is a place that you have longed for. It is a place where you will feel alive rather than squashed and silent. It is a place that stirs up your vitality, your creativity, and your purpose. It is a place where you will come alive in Me. Do you see it? Do you want to see it?

Cry out for My help today! I always answer those who say, "Jesus, I need help!" So, ask Me! Ask Me to be your Deliverer! Ask Me to do what only I can! You need My help to move you from this barren place and to end these cycles, so cry out for Me to do so. I delight to do so. I am delighted to be your help. It is My delight to rescue you.

RECEIVE

Ask the Lord to show you where you are dwelling in fruitless cycles and dry places. Take note of them and acknowledge the truth that they are not where you are meant to be. Then cry out for His help. Acknowledge that He truly is the only One who can move you out of them. Let Him show you what your spacious place, the place where you will bear much fruit, looks like. Allow Him to be your Deliverer.

DAY 283

"Yes, Lord!"

Then Jesus was led by the Spirit into the wilderness to be tempted by the devil (Matthew 4:1).

When you pray, continue to ask God to keep you from temptation, for there will be times when you come close to falling foul of the desires for the world's pleasures and quick fixes. Yet there also will be occasions when the Spirit of God Himself may lead you into trials and wilderness times in order to bring you into the fullness of your call and destiny, just as He did to Jesus in Matthew 4.

Trust God, so that if He leads you through a wilderness time, you will go in led by the Spirit and come out in the power of the Spirit, just as Jesus did. You will come out of desert places with greater trust and determination in what the Word of God decrees; you will stand in faith because Christ within you will enable you to hold ground and advance.

And so this is an invitation to give your yes to God again today, to give a resounding yes to follow the Spirit's leading in all times, into the glorious riches of all that God has for you and also the tough and challenging places. Know that as you go in and out of these places and times, you will ultimately bear great fruit and glory for God in your life.

PRAYER

I give You my yes again today, God. I say to You that I will go wherever You lead me, wherever You call me, and I will do whatever You ask of me. Because of Christ within I can go where You lead me, and I say that I am willing to go anywhere You lead. Have Your glory from my life, God. Have Your harvest from my life, God—whatever that looks like, each day I say yes to You.

DAY 284

Endure the Unpicking Process

He lifted me out of the slimy pit, out of the mud and mire; he set my feet on a rock and gave me a firm place to stand (Psalm 40:2).

Have you been wondering why some of your plans and aims haven't gone quite as smoothly as you expected? You had sought God for vision and strategy, and you thought you had put in the necessary prayer time, yet things haven't worked out as they should have. In fact, it feels like some parts of the plan are going backward. Does it feel like the plan is unraveling?

God says to you in this place of confusion, "Do not fear and do not give up." Know that His hand is still on you, and He sees your circumstances. He is unpicking where you have gone off course, just as a tailor or seamstress might unpick some stitches that had been sown at the wrong angle or along the wrong path.

"I will set your feet back on the right track," says the Lord. "In My mercy, I have corrected your course. Endure the short time of the unpicking process, and I will show you how to reset things. Your new path will be ablaze with My fire."

DECREE

In the next verse of Psalm 40, David is given a new song to sing:

He put a new song in my mouth, a hymn of praise to our God. Many will see and fear the Lord and put their trust in him (Psalm 40:3).

Open your mouth and begin to sing, speak, or whisper a new hymn of praise to God. Sing or speak out the opposite of your circumstances. For example, if things are uncertain, declare His steadfastness and His rocklike nature. If you feel like your plan is unraveling, sing a song of praise to the Alpha and Omega, the Beginning and the End, the one who knows the end from the beginning. Don't worry about getting your lines perfect; this is a personal song of praise, private between you and your precious Savior, who knows you so well.

DAY 285

Testing Times

In all this you greatly rejoice, though now for a little while you may have had to suffer grief in all kinds of trials. These have come so that the proven genuineness of your faith—of greater worth than gold, which perishes even though refined by fire—may result in praise, glory and honor when Jesus Christ is revealed (1 Peter 1:6–7).

We all have different ways to describe when things get tough. The most positive of us might simply be able to say, "Things are challenging." But then there are those moments of inexpressible, gut-wrenching grief that cannot be explained away with a smile and a few words. None of us are immune to having to travel through those valleys. If anyone tells you that following Jesus means an end to all your troubles, they have not read the Bible.

Apostle Peter touches on an aspect of God's loving work in our lives that we occasionally forget: the fact that God does use times of testing to purify our faith (see 1 Pet. 1:7). It is one of God's blessings, although you may not count it as such at first. Sometimes God arranges our individual circumstances to test and strengthen the areas where our faith is weak (see Ps. 11:5; Job 23:10; Isa. 48:10; Exod. 16:4). He wants to make sure that our faith is the real thing so that when Jesus returns, we won't be left looking foolish with a substandard, weak faith that is not worth having. He wants us to be overcomers.

Remember, temptation is different from testing. Satan tempts us to bring about failure and seeks to attack us to destroy our faith (see 1 Peter 5:8–9). On the other hand, God lovingly *tests* to bring about *trust*. With every test He wants you to grow in faith. He won't do anything to cause you ultimate harm. His exercises are faith stretching, not faith crushing. If you have a strong faith today, it is because it has been tested by trials and troubles. There were times when you could have thrown in the towel, but you didn't. Why not? Because although your faith was small, you hung on, and God, with His great, big hand, hung onto you.

Faith is more valuable than gold. No matter how personally traumatic the trials you face are, through them things begin to take on a different value. What becomes precious is the gold of your strong, refined faith. Faith tested by fire becomes much purer and stronger and will see you through anything. What is more, genuine faith in Jesus Christ is rewarded. Both He and you receive praise, glory, and honor when Jesus returns.

ACTION

Look up the Scriptures listed above and read them carefully. Thank God you are not alone as you face trials. He is there supporting you.

The Danger of Sustained, Relentless Change

Come to me, all you who are weary and burdened, and I will give you rest (Matthew 11:28).

We are a people called to a lifestyle of growth, moving from glory to glory, from faith to faith. This means that we often live in a state of change and transformation, walking out our salvation, straining to be like Jesus.

It requires real maturity and skill to navigate the change and personal development that is integral to successful Christian living. Today the Lord says: "I want you to know the difference between the rhythms of change that I ask you to walk, which are steeped in kindness, where you are led into transformation, followed by a restful consolidation of the driving relentlessness that you often demand of yourself. You have forgotten the value of restful consolidation, which allows you to reflect on and review where you have been and what has been asked of you."

Sustained change without restful consolidation can lead to sustained stress, which lays on you grief, weariness, low mood, and deep down, debilitating fatigue. The Lord says, "You are not to be in a constant endurance mode."

"Remember," He says, "that you need to receive My blessing of reflection and recovery. Furthermore, when you have walked through catastrophic change, you need to enter not just reflection and recovery, but reconstruction times as well."

"I am not your taskmaster," says the Lord, "I do not ask for you to be worked until you are fragmented. I am your emotional and spiritual champion who asks you to steward emotions well. Your body and your spirit need to be in cycles of repair as much as in cycles of growth."

RECEIVE

Take time to receive the revelation of your deep need to have moments of reflection, consolidation, and recovery. Ask God to show you how to walk into these successfully.

Today I pray for you that you might grasp the battlefield rhythms of rest and war, confrontation and retreat. I also pray that you might know when to push forward and when to sit in reflection.

Drink in Christ's Lavish Blessings

Praise be to the God and Father of our Lord Jesus Christ, who has blessed us in the heavenly realms with every spiritual blessing in Christ. For he chose us in him before the creation of the world to be holy and blameless in his sight. In love he predestined us for adoption to sonship through Jesus Christ, in accordance with his pleasure and will—to the praise of his glorious grace, which he has freely given us in the One he loves. In him we have redemption through his blood, the forgiveness of sins, in accordance with the riches of God's grace that he lavished on us. With all wisdom and understanding, he made known to us the mystery of his will according to his good pleasure, which he purposed in Christ, to be put into effect when the times reach their fulfillment—to bring unity to all things in heaven and on earth under Christ (Ephesians 1:3–10).

I saw a parched explorer walking through a desert. He appeared very weary, worn out, and thirsty because of his journey. Suddenly the explorer found a small pool of water, full to the brim with fresh, clear water for drinking. As he started to drink from the pool, I heard the Lord say: "Do not think that you are like this explorer, who only comes across refreshing and nourishment once or twice in the duration of a long journey. You have full-time access to living water, springing up like a well from within. You are never without, you are never lacking, and you are always able to drink deep and receive renewal inside."

And I hear the Lord say for you: "Drink deep! Drink in My blessings that I have lavished upon you and receive a deep infusion of strength. Drink deep today; as you do, allow any fatigue to flee, all fear to cease, every anxious thought to disintegrate, and every limitation to dematerialize as the weight of My spiritual blessings land on you and in you. So drink deep today, My child, and let Me lavish who I am upon you. It is always time to drink of Me. Do not put off taking a drink of My Spirit to a later time or think it is something that can only happen at an event or in a special moment. You can access all of who I am right now! So drink deep, My child."

RECEIVE

Sit where you are right now; get comfortable and start to focus on Jesus. Meditate on John 7:37–38:

On the last and greatest day of the festival, Jesus stood and said in a loud voice, "Let anyone who is thirsty come to me and drink. Whoever believes in me, as Scripture has said, rivers of living water will flow from within them."

Say out loud, "I choose to drink deep." Keeping your eyes fixed on Jesus, be aware of living water filling you up with everything you need. Feel yourself get fuller and more alive and even freer as you sit and drink deep.

Made Alive

But because of his great love for us, God, who is rich in mercy, made us alive with Christ even when we were dead in transgressions—it is by grace you have been saved (Ephesians 2:4–5).

There is a delicious fullness and abundance to the concept of being made "alive with Christ." It sings of wholeness and inner settled security. Made "alive with Christ" expresses the power of God, cascading over all we are and establishing us in a manner of doing life that is superior to the ordinary, everyday internal wrestles we have.

His life enables us to feel the emotions of freedom and to collide with deep, consistent, applied redemption. We feel the joy and reality of our salvation, and we are so certain of His love and so established in His life-giving abilities that we steward inner solidity.

Yet today the Spirit of the Lord says: "You are pushing away the fullness of life that I want you to know because your version of mercy is different from Mine. You are yet to fully grasp how *My mercy will give you what you do not deserve*. My mercy triumphs over My judgment! My mercy is stronger and more potent than you have yet accepted. I do not score you on the mechanics of your personal devotion. But My mercy is actively practiced so that you get to receive a lifestyle of being made alive in Me! You delight in sacrificing for Me, but I delight in mercifully making you alive."

Come, receive another level of what it means to be made alive in Christ, and experience how that feels.

ACTION

Take time to receive the life of Jesus in every part of your being. Work methodically from the top of your head to the end of your toes, and allow the life of Christ to touch every sinew and tissue, every emotion, and every unsettled portion of your being. Watch in the spirit realm as your body takes on the fullness of what it means to be alive in Christ.

The Eternal Versus the Ephemeral

Therefore we do not lose heart. Though outwardly we are wasting away, yet inwardly we are being renewed day by day. For our light and momentary troubles are achieving for us an eternal glory that far outweighs them all. So we fix our eyes not on what is seen, but on what is unseen, since what is seen is temporary, but what is unseen is eternal (2 Corinthians 4:16–18).

"Do not lose heart!" The Spirit of the Lord is reiterating this passage of Scripture because it is so key to the victorious life. Trials come and go; difficulties arise out of nowhere. Yet every single day He says to you: "Do not lose heart! You are living for an eternal purpose. Look ahead, not just to five years from now or ten years but to eternity. Your life on earth now is but a moment, a blip on your time line. You were created to live for eternity, and what you do in this life matters to your eternal life. So, look ahead, persevere, allow these moments of hardship to be those that mold you into My greater glory. You are spirit, soul, and body. Only one of these is temporary; the rest will live into eternity. Focus on that which will last."

You may read this and ask, "How? How do I do that?" And the Lord responds: "Take a step back from all that is pressing in on you. Step back and put some space in between you and the matters of today. Look at the time line of your life, and then put it out in front of you at a distance. See yourself in the perspective that I have—wide, vast, endless. See the crisis you face today; see how it is gone tomorrow. Yet see how you are still here today, tomorrow, the next day, and on it goes throughout eternity. You matter; the circumstances around you will fade in the light of eternity. Let your trials be what they are, temporary afflictions that will not last. Even if you have been given a bad diagnosis, what does tomorrow hold? Eternity!

"I hold your days; I know your years; I long for you to live with eternity in mind because it will prepare you for a glorious, full life with Me in glory. I have given you what you need to help you live this life in the best way possible, so do not lose hope. All you need is found in Me, and I am your living hope."

RECEIVE

Pray this prayer of Peter aloud over yourself today:

Praise be to the God and Father of our Lord Jesus Christ! In his great mercy he has given us new birth into a living hope through the resurrection of Jesus Christ from the dead, and into an inheritance that can never perish, spoil or fade. This inheritance is kept in heaven for you, who through faith are shielded by God's power until the coming of the salvation that is ready to be revealed in the last time. In all this you greatly rejoice, though now for a little while you may have had to suffer grief in all kinds of trials. These have come so that the proven genuineness of your faith—of greater worth than gold, which perishes even though refined by fire—may result in praise, glory and honor when Jesus Christ is revealed (1 Peter 1:3–7).

DAY 290

You Make God Glad

God is our refuge and strength, an ever-present help in trouble. Therefore we will not fear, though the earth give way and the mountains fall into the heart of the sea, though its waters roar and foam and the mountains quake with their surging. There is a river whose streams make glad the city of God, the holy place where the Most High dwells. God is within her, she will not fall; God will help her at break of day. Nations are in uproar, kingdoms fall; he lifts his voice, the earth melts (Psalm 46:1–6).

Listen to what your heavenly Father says to you today: "You make Me glad. I smile at your name, and everything you do is important to Me. I care deeply about you, more deeply than you could ever comprehend. I am always there, surrounding you as your refuge and your strength. Do not fear man; pay little attention to those who strut around as if they hold all power. Fear Me, for I am the Lord your God. I am a mighty fortress, and I am with you always. Amidst the proud noises and haughty bluster of the world's powers and powerful people, still yourself. Quiet any anxiety inside you for there is only one God, and I will be exalted among the nations, exalted in the earth."

See what great love the Father has lavished on us, that we should be called children of God! And that is what we are! (1 John 3:1)

RECEIVE

You make God glad. Spend time settling yourself in this. Begin to speak it out so that you can believe it. Say it: "I make God glad." Say it again: "I make God glad!" Thank Jesus for what He has done for you.

Three Great Promises

Jesus answered, "I am the way and the truth and the life. No one comes to the Father except through me. If you really know me, you will know my Father as well. From now on, you do know him and have seen him" (John 14:6–7).

Could there ever be another like Jesus? Actually, yes—the Holy Spirit.

We might sometimes think, "If only Jesus were here right now." But remarkably Jesus promised His followers that after Him the Holy Spirit would come in such a way that it would even be *for our good* that He was going away.

> *But very truly I tell you, it is for your good that I am going away. Unless I go away, the Advocate will not come to you; but if I go, I will send him to you* (John 16:7).

Bible translations use different words for the name Holy Spirit: Helper, Advocate, Comforter, Counselor, Friend. Why would this be to the disciples'—and our—advantage? Well, the only thing better than having Jesus *with* us is to have Jesus *within* us. And that is what we have, wherever we go, if we are united in Christ.

This is why Jesus could truthfully promise His followers three things:

- *"I am with you always"* (Matt. 28:20), just before He ascended.

- *"Do not let your hearts be troubled....I will not leave you as orphans"* (John 14:1;18), on the night that He told them that He would be leaving them.

- *"Whoever believes in me will do the works I have been doing, and they will do even greater things than these, because I am going to the Father"* (John 14:12).

During His short life here on earth, Jesus's presence was restricted by His physical body. But now He dwells within His followers—within you—by His Spirit. This means that His ministry, His power through us, is multiplied exponentially!

ACTION

Read all of John 14 and be encouraged. You are not alone. Paul says in Colossians 1:27, *"Christ in you, the hope of glory."* This is how Paul summarizes in just seven words (both in English and the original Greek) the privilege of being a Christian in its entirety. What excites you about this summary of the Gospel message? Someone has said that when Christ looks at each of us, He does not simply say, "Mine!" He also says, "Home!" Enjoy thinking about this, and let the truth change you.

Carrying the Burden

I want to know Christ—yes, to know the power of his resurrection and participation in his sufferings, becoming like him in his death (Philippians 3:10).

It is time to pick up your cross with full knowledge that there are times and days in your life when you will be asked to walk the road bearing the cross as Christ did, carrying the weight. There will be moments when you will fall on the road and need help to get up. There will be trials and tests that will cause you to bend, but you will say, "Not my will, God, but Yours be done." There are days coming and there are days even now that you will need to count the cost and bend.

Say yes to dying to self and dying to all that you once knew and pursued. Die to it all for the sake of Jesus Christ. Say yes to Him and take up the weight of His cross. Sufferings and trials are real, and although they are momentary in eternity, they will leave their mark and bring you into a new shape. And the Lord says to you now, "Bend to Me and pick up what I ask you to carry in this moment. Bend and carry what I am going to give you. Remember, with Me you will find that My burden is light."

ACTION

Think of moments in the past when you knew you had an opportunity to fulfill something God asked of you but you chose to decline, saying, "Please, I would rather not do this, God. This would cost me too much time, focus, effort, courage, or emotional or physical energy."

Think of a time when you did not bend to carry that burden for someone or something because you were already holding and carrying enough already. Now, do not get caught up in self-condemnation and cursing, but rather see this moment as a fresh grace opportunity to say, "Lord, I want to be one who stoops down to let You put the burden and Your cross on me when You choose, however and whatever that may be. I choose at this moment to bend. I am ready for You to lay Your burden on me for exactly what You are calling me to at this moment and every day. Lord, I choose to be obedient to the call, and I enter into the fullness of life following You."

Take time to write down what you sense the Lord is asking you to carry. Perhaps it is another person, through relational, emotional, or financial support? A prayer burden? A care burden for a particular people group or nation? Perhaps the Lord is asking you to be generous beyond anything you have given before; it could be money, resources, or time. Be that person who gives as the Lord instructs, in the time He asks you to. Step into the grace of the burden bearer. Listen to what He is asking of you now.

DAY 293

His Restoring Light

When Jesus spoke again to the people, he said, "I am the light of the world. Whoever follows me will never walk in darkness, but will have the light of life" (John 8:12).

Has the enemy stolen your joy and dulled your determination? By the Holy Spirit I saw you surrounded by the enemy, who celebrated, saying, "Didn't we do a good job at deterring them from moving forward at the speed God had set for them. Haven't we done well to steal and kill hopes and dreams? Well done, us!"

But then I saw Lord Jesus enter and cause the demons, who had been gleefully dancing around at their success over your life, immediately become silent and still. I saw Jesus standing in front of you and smiling. His gaze penetrates your eyes, and He wipes away the tears, brushes off the dust, tends to the wounds, and then opens His arms wide to you. As He holds you now, His light, which is the *"light of life,"* penetrates and permeates every part of who you are and illuminates you with such ferocity that nothing else within a wide radius in the spirit realm can look upon it without being blinded. The demons are indeed blinded and run away screaming, knowing that in an instant, all they thought they had achieved in destruction has been restored!

Life! The life that is the light of Christ floods every part of you both in the seen, earth realm and in the unseen, spirit realm. The light of life brings restoration to all that was damaged, hurt, and stolen and brings what was dead or shut down back to life!

RECEIVE

"Let Me fully saturate you with My light, right through your whole being," I hear the Lord say. Let Jesus wash His light over you and through you now. As He does, feel yourself coming alive again. Sense as your dormant emotions, dreams, and hopes are reignited. Hope is renewed and born again. You are being filled with light. I can hear the resonance of it begin to occupy you now. It is somehow weighted at the center of your being and is oscillating out from you into the space you now stand or sit in.

I hear the Lord say, "Now let there be light." As He speaks these words, I can no longer see you in the spirit because you have become a moving, encircling structure of light waves that make sounds like *"the whirling wheels*" seen by Ezekiel the prophet (see Ezek. 10:13), as they move as one force.

"Let there be light!" the Lord commands once more as He establishes this light movement and sound in you and through you, radiating outward, touching all around it. No darkness can exist next to this fire of light. No demon is anywhere near you now. You are fully restored and alive in light, ready to transform the world you inhabit. "Be full of light," Jesus says to you now. "Shine and be light."

Healing from Trauma

The Lord God is my strength [my source of courage, my invincible army];
he has made my feet [steady and sure] like hinds' feet and makes me walk
[forward with spiritual confidence] on my high places [of challenge and
responsibility] (Habakkuk 3:19 AMP).

The Lord is healing warfare trauma right now and lifting off from you
shock that has come from unexpected warfare.

I saw in the spirit a bungee cord strapped to your back. This bungee
cord lets you advance so far, only to pull you back to the beginning. This
cord represents trauma and its effect in your life. It lets you get only so far,
but then you're pulled back to the beginning.

And yet, the Spirit of the Lord says: "I am sovereignly and supernaturally washing trauma and its effects off of your life today. Coming to you is
an ability to turn and settle the active trauma from your past so that it will
no longer hold you back. You will find it easier to let go of the trauma that
has long attached itself to you and find a fresh ability to move forward with
freedom and bravery, unhindered and unhooked from your past.

"As trauma disintegrates and goes, I am releasing to you an ability to
scale high places. You will be wise and skillful in your navigation of the
spiritual realms, of decision making, of life, and no longer will you feel like
your past is prophesying trauma into your future."

Be free from the spirit of trauma in Jesus's name! Let Him lift it off you
right now and receive your deliverance, healing, and wholeness by the
Spirit of God, as He begins to overwhelm you, starting from the inside out.

RECEIVE

Breathe in and out. Start to become aware of the presence of Jesus that
surrounds you. He is with you; He is for you; He is ready to heal you. Tell
Jesus out loud, "I want to give You my trauma right now. I no longer want
to live life hindered by it."

You may want to prophetically act out the process of handing Jesus
something, especially if you feel or see trauma on your body somewhere.
Give it to Jesus, and let Him take it from you.

I Am Rebuilding You

Afflicted city, lashed by storms and not comforted, I will rebuild you with stones of turquoise, your foundations with lapis lazuli. I will make your battlements of rubies, your gates of sparkling jewels, and all your walls of precious stones. All your children will be taught by the Lord, and great will be their peace. In righteousness you will be established: Tyranny will be far from you; you will have nothing to fear. Terror will be far removed; it will not come near you. If anyone does attack you, it will not be my doing; whoever attacks you will surrender to you (Isaiah 54:11–15).

Arise, My beloved! You who have felt like a victim for so long, stand up. I am rebuilding you. I am forming you into an impenetrable tower. You will no longer be easily overwhelmed or overcome by your enemies. You will no longer be defenseless and easy prey. In the past seasons, you have walked through storm after storm, trial after trial, and yet you never quit. You kept walking! As you kept going, I was doing a deep strengthening work inside you. I have built you up to a level of endurance that you have not even known that you possess. You, My mighty one, now stand tall above your enemies. They see your growth; they know what you are becoming. It is now time for you to know!

Let Me show you how strong your foundations are in Me. Look how your roots have gone deep down into who I am; you are a mighty oak of righteousness. You have been fortified, built to last, ready to thrive. You are now a fortress, a strong tower, a defense for others to come to; you will provide rest, sanctuary, a safe space to teach others how to endure with endless faith. Stand tall and see how far you have come! Stand tall and give thanks for the work that has been done in your life! Stand tall and shout, "I am who God says I am!"

ACTION

Grab a sheet of paper and some pens and draw a tower, a fortress, or a mighty oak tree. Sketch out what one of these looks like, and let the Lord give you a picture of who you are in Him so that you have a visual to keep.

Hearing from God Part 1

My sheep listen to my voice; I know them, and they follow me (John 10:27).

How do you know that you are actually hearing from God rather than just hearing your own thoughts?

John writes: As I review decades of pastoral experience, a number of tough questions come to the surface. It seems that we can all hear from God on many fairly spiritually trivial matters: Which job should I take? What church should I go to? Where should I live? But on some of the big issues dividing the church today, or even on issues of what God is saying to whole nations, structures, and institutions, we seem to hear less clearly or we all seem to hear something different from our brothers and sisters! The more voices that are added to the mix, the more it seems that human opinion takes over and the actual voice of God becomes lost.

For example, why do Anglicans hear God telling them to baptize their infant children, yet Baptists hear God telling them not to? What about when believers say painful things such as, "God has told me the reason you are divorced/infertile/unemployed is because of this thing that you did wrong." Are they *really* hearing from God when they say this? It can be easy to take all of this and conclude that we don't hear from God anymore, and some have even taught this and made it a doctrine of the church. But this is not what our Bible really says. We may get ourselves in a muddle of confusion and uncertainty over if and how we hear from God, but we must put all doubt behind us and believe that as followers of Christ we are those who *do* hear the voice of God.

We need to be crystal clear: Christians hear from God. We worship a God who speaks; He speaks from Genesis to Revelation. He never stops speaking, and because He is *the Word*: *"In the beginning was the Word, and the Word was with God, and the Word was God"* (John 1:1). We are the sheep of our great Shepherd, and sheep know their Master's voice.

RECEIVE

Over the next couple of days we will keep considering these questions about hearing from God. For now, repent of any ways that you have allowed your own opinions and thoughts to cloud or influence what should have been the voice of God on a matter. Meditate on John 10:27, and thank Jesus that He knows you and speaks to you. Do you quiet yourself to listen to His voice enough? Do you follow the sound of His voice or your own? Do business with Jesus over this.

Hearing from God
Part 2

Consider Jesus, the Word made flesh. The writer to the Hebrews talks about Jesus as God's climatic and definitive act of speaking:

In the past God spoke to our ancestors through the prophets at many times and in various ways, but in these last days he has spoken to us by his Son, whom he appointed heir of all things, and through whom also he made the universe (Hebrews 1:1–2).

We are those to whom God has spoken in these last days through His Son! To put it another way, our primary method of hearing the voice of God should be through encountering Jesus. Realizing this is tremendously important, for it makes Jesus central rather than any subjective thoughts and impressions that we might have.

How do we do this? We hear from God by reading about Jesus and listening to His words throughout the whole Bible, by listening to Him all the time, by praying in the Spirit, by obediently living the way He taught us, by being baptized, by laying down our thoughts and opinions and truly dying to self, by regularly sharing in bread and wine with other believers, and by putting others first and Jesus at the center. Encountering Jesus regularly in these ways causes us to hear the voice of God.

As this process continues, something else happens over the days, weeks, months, and years. We begin to think about things in a Christlike way. We might watch a political debate on the TV news, and instead of joining in the partisan debates, we find Jesus's words from the Sermon on the Mount are foremost in our brains, helping us think afresh about the issue under discussion from His perspective, not ours.

The daily ongoing renewal of our minds through worship gives us the ability to hear what God wants us to do. We have been given what Paul calls, *"the mind of Christ"* (1 Cor. 2:16). And so we can teach Scriptures, preach truth, counsel by the Spirit, and disciple one another in Jesus's name. We become a body in which people prophesy, speak words of wisdom and knowledge, and use other spiritual gifts to edify, encourage, and comfort one another.

DECREE

Declare again over yourself, "I have the mind of Christ!" And pray: "Heavenly Father, help me to be persistent in developing a relationship with You so that I can truly hear and discern what You are saying. I commit myself to keep talking and speaking out, but Holy Spirit please help me to hear Your words first so that I represent You well and speak Your glory opinion on every matter."

Hearing from God Part 3

This is what was spoken by the prophet Joel: "In the last days, God says, I will pour out my Spirit on all people. Your sons and daughters will prophesy, your young men will see visions, your old men will dream dreams. Even on my servants, both men and women, I will pour out my Spirit in those days, and they will prophesy" (Acts 2:16–18).

The New Testament describes a community of people who not only hear from God through Scripture, prayer, and sharing bread and wine, but also through prophecy, known and unknown tongues, and words of wisdom and knowledge. Ordinary people, not just special people like priests or apostles, prophesied. Some of them predicted global events. Others spoke in earthly languages they had never learned. Several had visions that were crucial to the rest of church history. On the Day of Pentecost, Peter said this happened because the Scriptures said it would, referring to Joel (see Acts 2:14–21).

We know God speaks, so when His Spirit is poured out, everyone starts hearing from God. To Luke, the writer of Acts, this is *normal* Christianity! Hearing from God about things, even major life decisions, is quite ordinary. For example, a church prays together, and God speaks to them (see Acts 13); a missionary decision has to be made, and a man pops up in a vision and sends Paul and Silas to Greece (see Acts 17); a prophet predicts a famine and the capture of leaders (see Acts 11; 21). The gifts of the Spirit radically changed the decision-making process in the early church. At the start of Acts, everyone draws lots to make decisions, but after Pentecost, they stop doing this. Instead, they listen to God's voice.

For those who are in Christ, hearing from God is one of the most natural things in the world, like children hearing their parents' voices or two friends talking with each other. We have a God who speaks. What a delight!

ACTION

Read God's Word to hear God speak. Does reading Scripture sometimes seem dry and remote? Try using your Holy Spirit–sanctified imagination to read and step into the story as if you were there. Don't just read about other people being involved with Jesus; read as if you were there and involved with Him. Try this while reading the following passages:

- Jesus feeds the five thousand (see Mark 6:30–44).

- Jesus heals a crippled women in the synagogue (see Luke 13:10–13).

- Jesus stills the storm (see Matt. 8:23–27).

To Those on the Rim

Now this I know: The Lord gives victory to his anointed. He answers him from his heavenly sanctuary with the victorious power of his right hand. Some trust in chariots and some in horses, but we trust in the name of the Lord our God. They are brought to their knees and fall, but we rise up and stand firm (Psalm 20:6–8).

You are one of the many faithful followers who have been climbing high with God, climbing above your earthly circumstances to catch a better view of what is possible with Him. And now you have come to a point where you feel like you are on the edge of things, and you are a little bit unsure about your next move, not sure what the safest next move is.

But this is only the next stage in an amazing adventure! You are on a rim, like the rim of a giant bowl. The rim edge is curved and smooth and does not have obstacles that will trip you. You are not in peril; you have not climbed this high only to fall back down. Instead, the Spirit of God is urging you to take the plunge and to begin to slide down the steep inside curve of the bowl, into the great lake of adventure that lies below.

Others are also sitting around the same rim and are beginning to launch themselves down the side of the bowl; some are going down carefully, edging their way down; others are careering down the slope with great abandon. But the speed of descent is not the important thing because the slope has its own momentum. Everyone who has climbed up high and chooses to press on forward and down the slide toward the great lake of adventure is going to plunge in deep at the same pace.

God has so much in store for you. You've come this far and climbed this high. It's time to let go of the edge and slide into the deep adventure that He has for you!

RECEIVE

This vision is just one way that the Holy Spirit has chosen to show the next step in the adventure with Him. Close your eyes and ask Him to paint a picture on the canvas of your imagination of some of what He has in store for you. As He does, ask Him to name some things that are holding you back from taking the plunge. If there is anything holding you back, release it to Him and be free!

The Gift of Sustainability

Stand up and praise the Lord your God, who is from everlasting to everlasting. Blessed be your glorious name, and may it be exalted above all blessing and praise. You alone are the Lord. You made the heavens, even the highest heavens, and all their starry host, the earth and all that is on it, the seas and all that is in them. You give life to everything, and the multitudes of heaven worship you (Nehemiah 9:5–6).

I heard the Lord say to you for today, "There is prayer that is more fundamental than your prayers for breakthrough and advancement, and it is this: 'Make me sustainable.'

"I am looking for those who will fight to receive and hold onto a gift of sustainability. I want you alive. In fact, I want you alive and kicking, full of energy and vibrancy. I do not want you burnt out or worn out; I want you to be sustainable.

"I am not the God of the boom and the bust, the hot then the cold, the one day on fire and the next day not. I am the God who is consistently constant in every way, and I am inviting you to contend for greater sustainability in your life today.

"You are to be a living sacrifice, not a half-alive or a worn-out sacrifice. You are to be a fully alive sacrifice that is poured out toward Me. Ask Me for the gift of sustainability."

ACTION

It is important to know what drains your life and what gives you life. Therefore, go on a journey with Jesus and ask Him about the practical applications of this word in your life. What brings you alive? What steals your life? Who brings you alive? Use the following questions to prompt your discussion with the Lord:

- Is there anything in my life that is currently limiting my sustainability?

- What do You want me to do that will help me grow in sustainability?

DAY 301

Compassion That Raises the Dead

Soon afterward Jesus went with his disciples to the village of Nain, and a large crowd followed him. A funeral procession was coming out as he approached the village gate. The young man who had died was a widow's only son, and a large crowd from the village was with her. When the Lord saw her, his heart overflowed with compassion. "Don't cry!" he said. Then he walked over to the coffin and touched it, and the bearers stopped. "Young man," he said, "I tell you, get up." Then the dead boy sat up and began to talk! And Jesus gave him back to his mother (Luke 7:11–15 NLT).

"When the Lord saw her, his heart overflowed with compassion." This is still who Jesus is today. His heart overflows with that same compassion toward you. He sees; He hears; He understands like no one else can or ever will. Just like He brought life back to this woman, He desires to bring life back to you today.

To every place that looks dead within you, He brings the sparks of life. Will you let Him touch those places with His fire? Will you let Him ignite that hope again? Under the ash of the things that have been burned, there are new shoots of life. Do you see them? Do you want to see them? There is so much life left to live, and there is no qualification or standard for you to meet in order to access this. He came to give you life in all its abundance as a free gift. Run and meet with Him today!

RECEIVE

Today look right at Jesus and speak to Him about the areas of your life that need His life. Truly look at Him and speak to Him as the source of all life. Nothing is too difficult for Him! Do you believe that? If you need help believing, then it's as simple as praying: "Jesus, I want to believe that nothing is too difficult for You. I need help to believe that You can bring every part of me back to life! I desire to thrive! Come and touch me with Your fire today! Awaken every dead place within me."

Let Jesus Untangle You

And do not set your heart on what you will eat or drink; do not worry about it. For the pagan world runs after all such things, and your Father knows that you need them. But seek his kingdom, and these things will be given to you as well. Do not be afraid, little flock, for your Father has been pleased to give you the kingdom (Luke 12:29–32).

When a wire, electrical cable, or hose becomes over-coiled or tangled up in a tight mess, the best solution is not to keep twisting and turning, hoping for a miraculous undoing. Instead, it is good to stop, pause, and lay the cable out somewhere warm (like in a spot of sunlight or beside a radiator) to allow softening and flexibility to return. After doing this, you can often hold one end of the wire up high and allow the kinks and coils to naturally unwind and fall out of it.

This is how the Holy Spirit would have you be as you review and take stock of the past season. When you look back and see that you have become forced into knots and the path is not as straight or straightforward as you thought it would be, don't keep trying to navigate your way out of the tangled maze, hoping for a miraculous intervention that will smooth everything out. All you will do is stress, tighten, and entangle yourself all the more!

God is perfectly able to intervene in an instant, but He has a better way: Stop, pause, and lay yourself out as flat as you can and allow yourself to be in God's light, His presence. Make yourself available to the radiance of His truth, love, and revelation. Then, fix your gaze as high as it can go to the high King of Heaven. Ask for the high-up, heavenly perspective on things. As you keep your focus high, everything else will begin to supernaturally uncoil and unwind.

RECEIVE

Take the time with Him to sort things out before you proceed any further. You'll make the time back (and much more) once you are in a place to advance with a fresh, heavenly perspective. In your place of stress and tension, it may feel counterintuitive to stop and rest; our natural inclination is to keep going round and round, trying harder. But God's Kingdom is upside down compared to ours! Stop, rest, pause, spend time with Him and you will find that things begin to remarkably, even miraculously, unwind.

DAY 303

Shout Yourself Free!

When the trumpets sounded, the army shouted, and at the sound of the trumpet, when the men gave a loud shout, the wall collapsed; so everyone charged straight in, and they took the city (Joshua 6:20).

The Spirit of the Lord says: "Meet your yesterday, whether you like it or not. Face the unfinished business in your history. Do not ignore where you have been. Face it, close the door to your past, and do not let your yesterday hold you in a wounding."

God cannot fully use us if we do not close the account on the past.

Turn and face yesterday; bar it from negatively impacting today. Claim your healing from it. Some days we do need the specialist hand of a deeper healer; other days we need a fresh determination and a shout that will stop the lies of our history.

I heard the Lord tell you: "Turn physically where you are right now and look at your past. Where there are lies, make a decree right now that they are not true. Crush your old thoughts, and do not pet the demons of your past or entertain the lies of your history."

Today the Lord is enabling you to ROAR! He is increasing your sense of righteous indignation about your previous seasons where you have been a captive. The way you conquer tomorrow's enemies is by conquering your past today. Your past cannot speak again to you, otherwise you will not have the strength to overcome tomorrow.

ACTION

Literally roar yourself free. Just as the children of Israel roared, cried, and shouted and the walls of Jericho came falling down, so today you are to follow their example. Just as God anointed their cry to physically bring down the opposition's walls, so also your determined shout will bring down the lies and entrapments of your history! LET OUT YOUR ROAR!

DAY 304

He Allures You in the Wilderness

Therefore I am now going to allure her; I will lead her into the wilderness and speak tenderly to her. There I will give her back her vineyards, and will make the Valley of Achor a door of hope. There she will respond as in the days of her youth, as in the day she came up out of Egypt (Hosea 2:14–15).

Wilderness is being somewhere you don't want to be. Are you somewhere you don't want to be physically, geographically, relationally, spiritually, or emotionally? Wilderness often features at critical moments in the biblical story. Elijah, Moses, Jesus, and the children of Israel were subjected to the transformation of wilderness days. When we stand in the wilderness, we come under the care of a loving God, and we feel the storms of transformation swirl about us.

It is in the wilderness that Jesus allures us, speaks tenderly to us, and begins a new love story with us. It's there that we find the rod and staff of Christ to lean on. When we have been going in our own strength and ways, Jesus loves to get us back to a level of dependency on Him, and wilderness enables that.

We are the results of our testing. We are the shape of the battles we have endured and won. Wilderness is like a blacksmith's hammer and anvil where we are forged and formed.

When Isaiah speaks of new ways coming in wildernesses and springs in deserts, it teaches us that new beginnings are birthed in the places of barrenness (see Isa. 43:19). The promise of a fresh momentum of life is given in hard places. It is in the wilderness that we steward our own death—death to self—and with greater clarity the new creation that we are meant to be rises.

In the wilderness there is evening, and then there is morning, which brings a new day.

RECEIVE

Open your hands and receive the comfort of God as you reflect on the aspects of your life that look and feel like wilderness. Receive the ability to perceive the new springs of life, and allow yourself to smile today, knowing that God makes new life come even in the most difficult of places. A desert becomes an oasis in His hand. Let that encourage you.

CHAPTER 11

Ruling and Reigning

Advance My Kingdom

Now the seventy-two returned with joy, saying, "Lord, even the demons are subject to us in Your name!" And He said to them, "I watched Satan fall from heaven like lightning. Behold, I have given you authority to walk on snakes and scorpions, and authority over all the power of the enemy, and nothing will injure you. Nevertheless, do not rejoice in this, that the spirits are subject to you, but rejoice that your names are recorded in heaven" (Luke 10:17–20 NASB).

"Rejoice that your names are recorded in heaven." As we rejoice over this fact, I feel the Spirit of the Lord shifting our gaze and turning us to look out over the neighborhoods, towns, cities, and nations in which we live. He's asking us to look at the individuals who live where we are. Look at them and see them; truly see them! He longs for them just as He longed for you to know Him.

He says to you: "I gave you authority over all the power of the enemy so that you would win souls for My Kingdom! And as you win souls, you win nations. Oh, I long for the nations to know Me! I long for every family to come into *My* family! I have equipped you and given you the authority to take these families for My name! Go and rebuke the devourer who has sought to destroy them! Set them free from demonic oppression! Show them that I am the Mighty One who heals, delivers, and saves! Go and advance the Kingdom for their sakes and Mine!

"For what a day of rejoicing it will be when we all come into the fullness of time and each one stands before Me to see that their name is written in My Book of Life. You will rejoice; they will rejoice; My angels will rejoice! That is the purpose for which I have called you. So, rejoice that you know Me and that I have given you authority over the enemy, but never forget those around you who also long to rejoice. Go and find them. Bring them into My Kingdom, and let's advance together!"

ACTION

Today take some time to pray for your neighbors. Take a walk and pray for the souls of those who live in your neighborhood or community. Ask the Lord to open your eyes to truly see those who live around you. Ask Him, "Lord, what can I do?" And like the seventy-two, go and advance His Kingdom.

Entrepreneurial Creativity

Then the Lord said to Moses, "See, I have chosen Bezalel son of Uri, the son of Hur, of the tribe of Judah, and I have filled him with the Spirit of God, with wisdom, with understanding, with knowledge and with all kinds of skills—to make artistic designs for work in gold, silver and bronze, to cut and set stones, to work in wood, and to engage in all kinds of crafts. Moreover, I have appointed Oholiab son of Ahisamak, of the tribe of Dan, to help him. Also I have given ability to all the skilled workers to make everything I have commanded you" (Exodus 31:1–6).

I heard the Lord say: "I am raising you up with entrepreneurial creativity to steward Kingdom ideas and solutions in the earth realm. Little or large, global or local, for the masses or the one, each is valuable and each needs Kingdom entrepreneurial works to be released into them. Do not doubt yourself and think, 'Not me,' for just as I anointed Bezalel to create and steward building, so also I can anoint you with skill even beyond your natural capabilities as part of My Kingdom plan in your life."

I saw God put in your hands massive blueprints that were rolled up like scrolls waiting to be unwrapped and read. The Lord then said, "Look at what is in your hands."

And so He asks: "Do you see what is in your hands right now? Are you aware of the blueprints, the mandates, the exploits, the solutions, and the ideas that I have placed in your hands for such a time as this? See, you are both anointed and equipped to partner with Me in entrepreneurial creativity. Your lack of training doesn't bother Me; your lack of experience isn't a concern. I have anointed you, and My grace is on you to steward Kingdom solutions into the world that surrounds you."

So, do not doubt yourself today. Look in your hands; see what God has given to you, and believe that He knows what He can do through you.

ACTION

Ask the Holy Spirit, "What have You put into my hands? Reveal to me what You have given to me to steward."

God Is a Broadcaster

The heavens declare the glory of God; the skies proclaim the work of his hands. Day after day they pour forth speech; night after night they reveal knowledge (Psalm 19:1–2).

God loves spreading good news. He is a good news broadcaster! Today He is anointing you as a herald, one who will make public proclamations; and a forerunner, one who speaks, leads, and shapes with vocal clarity. You are to become a herald who cries aloud with a powerful, valiant shout and a proclamation of truth.

Your voice will have a megaphone anointing put on it so that the truth can travel far and wide as you broadcast. God says to you today, "As you receive the herald, broadcasting anointing, you will put the devil on mute, and you will overturn the cacophony of chaos he has been used to getting away with."

Today the Lord says: "Receive a new ability for clarity; receive a new ability for fresh revelation. I am ending the days of contested communication, of muddled relational interaction, and I am releasing to you a specific ability to be effective in disseminating and stewarding truth verbally. I am ending the days of the people of God giving uncertain words, for now comes the days of distinct, clear communication and statements of truth. Let the communicator, broadcaster, and herald anointing now rest on you."

ACTION

Think of some of the key issues the church faces today, and rather than mull internally what a solution might be, stand up and speak truth and solution over the muddied waters of church challenges. In this, you will be preparing yourself to steward in more visible places of communication, and you will have done your "due diligence" to practice what God is asking of you. Being a broadcaster and herald requires the discipline of private practice. Make the case for the truth of God plain and clear and decree it now.

DAY 308

The Lion Roars Over You

Then one of the elders said to me, "Do not weep! See, the Lion of the tribe of Judah, the Root of David, has triumphed. He is able to open the scroll and its seven seals" (Revelation 5:5).

The Lion of the tribe of Judah is roaring over you. His breath is sweet, hot, and stronger than a hurricane. His roar will set you free. It will melt away all hardness and will warm even the cold, dark corners of your soul. The fragrance that comes on the wind of His voice will plant new seeds in you, seeds of trees that will bear fruit. The power of His mighty shout will tear off all the dirty grave rags that still hang from your shoulders—*"put off your old self"* (Eph. 4:22).

The Lion is ready to roar over you. Will you stand before Him? He is passionate about you and is jealous for your attention. Are you prepared to let your guard down and walk into the throne room of this majestic King? Will you kneel before Him and allow the vibrations of His voice to thunder through you?

It is time to come into a new appreciation of the King of kings, the Lion who reigns over all of Heaven and earth. It is time to stand before Him in awe and wonder and allow Him to breathe on you. He is welcoming you into His presence and beckoning you to look into His eyes, even those eyes that blaze with a burning fire! Let Him gaze on you; let Him look into your depths; you are His creation, after all. No matter how uncomfortable the prospect of being fully looked upon feels, please don't flinch or run away from His invitation. You can trust Him. He will not be afraid, shocked, or intimidated by anything you show Him. He loves you with a holy affection that is unmatched by any other. This is your time with Him, one-to-one with the Lion of Judah. Allow Him to roar over you.

RECEIVE

The Bible tells us that we were created to walk in true righteousness and holiness (see Eph. 4:24). A key to this is to take our eyes off ourselves, our failings, and our problems and spend more time with and looking at Jesus Christ, the Lion of Judah. Deliberately set some time to stand or kneel before Him. He has beckoned you to come into His presence. What will your answer be? Will you allow Him to look at you eye to eye? Will you allow Him to roar over you? If it is uncomfortable or difficult to do, you will need to repeat this over and over. Spend time worshipping His glorious power and majesty, His might, and His strength. Being this close to the Lion will transform you!

Do It Again, Lord

Lord, I have heard of your fame; I stand in awe of your deeds, Lord. Repeat them in our day, in our time make them known; in wrath remember mercy (Habakkuk 3:2).

There's something poignant about Habakkuk`s words, *"I have heard of your fame."* What? Only heard of it? Never experienced it yourself? Do you believe only because of the great stories of Yahweh's meetings with Abraham and Moses? That was centuries ago! As a faith-strengthening exercise, memory is good, but the past alone is not enough. Like Habakkuk, we need a God who does something *today.*

Therefore Habakkuk says, "Do it again, God. I've heard You speak and now we need to see You act." And there is a difference. Asking questions and getting answers from God is an incredible privilege, but Habakkuk longs for action, not fading memories from the past. Habakkuk knows what Yahweh did in the past and what He is going to do in the future (at the end of history, when Jesus comes again). But in his day, right there in the middle, he wants to see the Lord operating.

Do you ever pray like Habakkuk? God is not a God of nostalgia, idly reminiscing about what He used to do. Nor should we be. Stop harking back to old memories of revivals and awakenings of previous generations. Don't get stuck in how things *used to be.* Like Habakkuk, we need to cry, "Lord, please, we want to see You *now.* Do these things in our day, in the middle of the years. Don't just be the God of the beginning and the end. Lord, You have done it in the past. Would You do it now?"

Of course, God is always sustaining us and answering our prayers, dramatically at times. We praise Him that there is a fresh breath of His Spirit blowing among the nations. Let us be like Habakkuk and ask God for more. Now!

ACTION

Make the words of Isaiah 64:1–2 your prayer for today:

Oh, that you would rend the heavens and come down, that the mountains would tremble before you! As when fire sets twigs ablaze and causes water to boil, come down to make your name known to your enemies and cause the nations to quake before you!

Advance!

The Lord our God said to us at Horeb, "You have stayed long enough at this mountain. Break camp and advance into the hill country of the Amorites" (Deuteronomy 1:6–7).

Advance! Advance! Hear the call to advance and move out!

The Lord is speaking to you about the particular "how" and "when" that He is calling you to move into, including the places of occupation that He has marked out for you now and as part of your legacy on the earth.

Move and shift with the Lord in these days and in this time, for the Lord comes to call you into the place of momentum and forward advancement. Expect invitations for promotion, possible locality or geographical shift, and even change of career and focus in these days to come, as the Lord calls time on some unfruitful areas or specific projects and tasks that have come to an end in His perfect timing.

You are now in your mobilizing season, where the Lord is saying with great determination over you and to you, "Advance into the specific areas I am opening up to you now in this moment." These may be a particular role or job, vocational ministry, or missions. Be sensitive to the Holy Spirit's leading, and stay close to how His gentle but determined breath leads you forward and moves you on into greater fullness and focus of your personal call, for these are your *days of advancement*.

RECEIVE

Wait on the Lord in silence so that He can lead you as you hold this prophetic word before Him in your heart. Ask, "Where are You leading me and calling me to advance, Lord?" Pray and ask God for His divine appointments, divine conversations, and divine communications to show you the way ahead. Ask for confirmation from God; expect it to come through Scripture and from other people. Speak to your spiritual leaders about any major changes you are feeling that the Lord might be leading you into. It's good to have a mature, seasoned sounding board to talk to about what you are sensing.

DAY 311

Now Occupy!

Go to all the neighboring peoples in the Arabah, in the mountains, in the western foothills, in the Negev and along the coast, to the land of the Canaanites and to Lebanon, as far as the great river, the Euphrates. See, I have given you this land. Go in and take possession of the land the Lord swore he would give to your fathers—to Abraham, Isaac and Jacob—and to their descendants after them (Deuteronomy 1:7–8).

The Spirit of the Lord says to you, "Now occupy the places that I have called you out into!" Occupy the places you live, work, and inhabit in the seen, natural realm and also the unseen realm of the spirit. There should be a determination rising up inside you in this moment to advance and occupy like never before, with a warlike fortitude and resolve. It's a choice between life and death for the many people and areas that you have influence over and come into contact with. You are bringing Kingdom transformation; you are making a difference. You are establishing the Kingdom of God where you are in a more tangible way.

I see your contact and habitation in these areas being an impactful reality, like walls coming down, like the infiltration of colored ink in water that increases and spreads as you move out and inhabit all the Lord is opening up to you. The cry from Heaven over you is, "Choose life and occupy, both for you and for those you influence in your daily life." I hear the Lord say, "By My Spirit you are empowered. By My Spirit you are called and given the strength to hold ground. In My timing you are made ready to advance and occupy." Therefore, agree with the word of God that is strong on you and over you today for the occupation of the territory God has given you. Advance and occupy! It's yours.

DECREE

Speak this out loud today: "I step forward today to possess my possessions and the territory You have marked out for me, Lord, in accordance with Obadiah 1:17. I choose to occupy the ground that You have opened up and given and assigned to me. I take hold of it by faith, knowing that You are with me."

Now take time to listen to the Lord and seek Him for the specific areas God has given you to particularly occupy. Write them down and ask for occupation strategies, Heaven's methods and ways. Request clarity from the Holy Spirit on timing and the particular people that God is asking you to connect with to bring the occupation to fullness.

Be resolute, knowing that what God is calling you to is a life call; it is not going to be achieved fully in months or perhaps even in a few years. Advancement and occupation begin now but are for an entire generation. And it leaves a legacy for the next generation.

DAY 312

Heavenly Viewpoint

It is a land the Lord your God cares for; the eyes of the Lord your God are continually on it from the beginning of the year to its end (Deuteronomy 11:12).

There is an invitation from the Lord Jesus to come and stand with Him as He stands in a high place overseeing your territory. From here He sees all the territory that He has asked you to occupy. He invites you today, "Come and stand with Me and see what I see. Come and glean from My perspective at this time for what you are made to engage and conquer. There will be an ease from this high place of oversight."

Come and see all the terrain the Lord has called you to dwell in and engage with from His vantage point.

Just like a general in the army, Jesus gives you a view of the field of battle and shows you that the way is open to you to move into position. It is easy to see all that He has given you from here. Step up next to Lord Jesus, and watch with Him as He shows you how much ease there is when you take His perspective.

RECEIVE

Take time to watch in the Spirit as Jesus invites you "up here" to see and look at all that is currently under your feet. Pray: "Lord Jesus, I choose to step up to where You are and see as You see and see what You see. Show me, Lord, what it is I need to see today to be assured that You have made a way for complete conquering and habitation of all You have given me."

Allow Lord Jesus to show you and lead you into the territory that He has assigned to you; watch as He watches, listen to what He is saying, and follow His lead.

Defend!

Watch and pray so that you will not fall into temptation. The spirit is willing, but the flesh is weak (Matthew 26:41).

"Defend! You must defend. What I have given you is yours to defend and watch over," says the Lord. "Be intentional in the watching. Be observant in the areas of growth and opportunity. Push through to establish that growth with Me. Be observant to where the enemy attempts to storm your 'gates' to overrun and conspire against you. Call others to watch with you and assume the position together of those who are faithful stewards at this time. For I have called you as a faithful one. I have called you as one who will defend what I have put into your hands, and you will have consistent victory over your enemies!"

As you defend and steward what He has given you, He assures you of the victory. Watch over all the Lord has said is yours to steward in both the seen realm and unseen realm. So now is the time to watch and pray over what He has asked you to take righteous responsibility for. Secure it. Shield it in prayer and guard it. Be a good guardian of all the Lord has given to you. Do not do this in fear, but do it in joy, as this is what the Lord Himself has given to you to be the righteous custodian of.

ACTION

Bring the following questions before the Lord. Await His answer:

- Who do you bring together to shield in prayer what God has given into your hands (your family, business, property, ministry, work, influence—whatever you have been given to occupy you must now defend)? Who are your people/team for this defensive call? Who will be there to stand with you, to pray, and to watch?

- How do you grow and expand that which God has given you in His timing? Ask the Lord for Heaven's strategies and blueprints.

- Where are the "weak spots" that need to be shored up to prevent enemy access?

- What are the God-ordained opportunities that you have been given favor for, to push through to expansion and another level of agreement with those you relate to in this area of oversight?

Seek the Lord, receive His direction for defense, and then put that plan into action. Wisdom comes from the Lord, and it is available when we ask. Do not be afraid to ask the Lord more questions as you feel led, and await His answers. There is no limit to the questions! Asking questions opens up more wisdom and heavenly strategy to you. Remember, the Lord wants you to succeed and has all that you need to be a success in this—just ask.

Satan Falls

God says: "I have seen, planned, actioned, and already written about the downfall and judgment of satan. I want you to remember this and see, like I see, what has been achieved and planned for the forces of darkness."

And the devil, who deceived them, was thrown into the lake of burning sulfur (Revelation 20:10).

The Lord says: "Do not magnify what I have minimized and defeated. Today I want you to see the scale and magnitude of My Kingdom, its power and its victory, and then I also want you to see the *limited* power and containment of the kingdom of darkness that I already have victory over.

"Do not empower the enemy by rewriting him into your life story as a more dominant character than I want him to be. Do not fear him; do not give him any credit. When you fear him, you empower him. Your fear is opening a door to assist him. It is time to have a healthy opinion of demons, which is to understand that their only legitimate position is under your feet!

"The church has an unfortunate tendency to give satan a throne created by fear. I want you to dethrone him by seeing his end and by breaking agreement with your fear of demons, satan, and all of the kingdom of darkness. Your spiritual reality is that satan and his hordes are absolutely terrified of you and are especially fearful that you will regain a biblical balance in understanding how incapacitated they really actually are."

The God of peace will soon crush Satan under your feet. The grace of our Lord Jesus be with you (Romans 16:20).

ACTION

Today it's important that you walk out a prophetic act where you grab hold of your fear of demons and lay it at the feet of Jesus, decreeing that you will not pick it up again. Then, you need to set down the magnifying glass that you have long carried that made the power of darkness bigger and scarier in your world than it ever was in reality.

DAY 315

Moved by Faith

By faith Noah, when warned about things not yet seen, in holy fear built an ark to save his family. By his faith he condemned the world and became heir of the righteousness that is in keeping with faith (Hebrews 11:7).

God says to you, "Be moved by faith." Stir up your faith. Begin to pray prayers, make declarations, and write decrees that are motivated by your faith.

If you have been feeling unsure or have been in need of confirmation about the next step that God requires for you, or if you have been praying for something for a very long time: STOP. Stop and ask for faith. God already knows your need; He has heard your prayers. Now it is time to work on your faith so that you can actually start to move. You do not need another confirmation or another prophetic word in this moment; you need the gift of faith.

Get close to God so that you pray and act out of faith alone. Be moved by faith! It is time to move.

By faith Abraham, when called to go to a place he would later receive as his inheritance, obeyed and went, even though he did not know where he was going (Hebrews 11:8).

ACTION

Stir up your faith by reading the Hebrews 11 Hall of Faith. Be inspired by your biblical heroes, who had many flaws and were very human, but also had faith.

What declarations and decrees of faith do you need to make today? What one movement, one step of faith can you make today? Big or small, God will work with those who move with faith in Him. He loves it when we do!

Reign with Him!

Death once held us in its grip, and by the blunder of one man, death reigned as king over humanity. But now, how much more are we held in the grip of grace and continue reigning as kings in life, enjoying our regal freedom through the gift of perfect righteousness in the one and only Jesus, the Messiah! (Romans 5:17 TPT)

Freedom is yours! He whom the Son sets free is free! This is you! As if that wasn't enough by itself, you are also now free to enjoy your freedom! Any king would have fully understood this truth because kings had full rights and full freedom! This is such an amazing truth! This is a truth that is worth dwelling on every single day until you also begin to see yourself as one who rules and reigns with Christ Jesus!

Everything about the Kingdom and godliness is yours. The Father God, as the incredible Father that He is, is inviting you to enjoy this freedom of reigning over life. He's welcoming you to take your place, your heavenly seat next to Jesus, and to see the position from which you reign. You are above and beyond every trial, every attack, every tribulation that comes your way. Your right and privilege are to walk through this life in righteousness, peace, and joy! These are yours!

And so today He says to you: "I hold you in the firm grip of My grace; now walk out the life that My Son purchased for you with His blood. Explore the depths of My love; soar in the freedom that is yours! Set your eyes on the heavenly realm so you're not distracted by the things of this earth that try to keep you from your rightful position and perspective. Enjoy the view from up here, but also let it put your view into focus. See things as I see them. Seek Me for understanding. Let Me give you the wisdom and instruction to rule and reign well for this is your purpose and your destiny!"

ACTION

The Book of Romans provides so much freedom to those who study it. Take some time this week to really read and take in the truths of this book. Your life will be changed by it.

Leadership

Here's what I want: Give me a God-listening heart so I can lead your people well, discerning the difference between good and evil. For who on their own is capable of leading your glorious people? (1 Kings 3:9 MSG)

Just as you have grown in revelation, discernment, and spiritual sight over the last seasons, now I can entrust to you a new level of leadership. I have called you to influence atmospheres and hearts toward Me and My purposes. And to you who have grown in discernment, I now trust into your hands a greater level of influence this day. Feel the weight of this influence rest on you right now; as it lands, expect all to change. I have trusted you to shift atmospheres and people, to create a "glory space," a miracle zone wherever you go. This is what leadership is.

You are going to know what it is to be led by My Spirit to take charge and release Kingdom principles on the earth. Underpinning your coming seasons is going to be an acute awareness of My presence pressing on you that will enable you to lead people and atmospheres well.

Receive this marking of leadership today! Let it fall on you. Do you choose to accept it? Do you say yes to receiving it? As I connect you to it, so I am connecting you to opportunities to shape and shift the spheres I'm positioning you in. This is who you are; this is your call and mandate. You are trusted because you have learned to steward revelation and discernment.

RECEIVE

Receive the weight of leadership that God is putting on you. As you receive this in the spirit, you may even feel the press of hands on your shoulders as you are commissioned into a new level of leadership. This should not feel like a heavy burden that will weigh you down. Rather, you should feel taller, stronger, more able. Keep receiving and listen to the encouraging things that Jesus has to say to you as one of His leaders on earth.

DAY 318

The Gate to the Field

I see a vision of God opening a gate to you so that you can move out into the new. Jesus Christ is the gate, the waymaker.

I am the gate; whoever enters through me will be saved. They will come in and go out, and find pasture (John 10:9).

And He says to you, "See, I am the gate, and I make a way for you to enter into the new place that I have allotted to you and your family. Walk through and remain in Me as you enter into this new place of flourishing and fruitfulness."

I see such a beautiful, spring green field of long grass, gently moving in the breeze in a wave. Jesus is the gate to this field, opening Himself wide as He invites you to "step through the gate and enter in." Your field and its fruit are unique to you. Both represent where the work and focus of your hands are to be. You will likely have numerous interconnecting fields of work and fruit; continue to look and hear from the Lord on these. Focus your heart and senses on Jesus now as He invites you to ask Him about these fields and what they represent.

RECEIVE

Ask the Lord Jesus what your fields are called, what type of fruit they bear, and what your role is. Spend time receiving from Him as you enter into this field He has for you.

DAY 319

The Kingdom and the Spirit

After John was put in prison, Jesus went into Galilee, proclaiming the good news of God. "The time has come," he said. "The kingdom of God has come near. Repent and believe the good news!" (Mark 1:14–15)

We know the Kingdom of God is here because Jesus said it repeatedly. From the beginning of His ministry, He announced its coming, and it was central to almost all of His teaching and ministry. The reason this centrality soon became obvious: Jesus is the King. When He comes, His Kingdom comes. But in another sense, the Kingdom is *still* to come because Jesus is coming again to reign in the full authority of His risen glory.

We live in this Kingdom tension between the "now" and the "to come," between its start-up inauguration and its full consummation when Jesus returns. Today as we submit to His lordship and sovereignty, we live the Kingdom life. This means that the Kingdom is wherever we live, work, worship, and play insofar as we live under His lordship as the King's subjects.

Right from the beginning of His ministry, Jesus linked the Kingdom and the Spirit together: *"No one can see the kingdom of God unless they are born again"* (John 3:3). Jesus also linked the Kingdom and the Spirit when He cast out demons: *"If I cast out demons by the Spirit of God, surely the kingdom of God has come upon you"* (Matt. 12:28 NKJV). The truth is that Jesus was only able to bring the Kingdom as He did because He had been anointed by the Holy Spirit at His baptism (before this He did not perform a single miracle). So even Jesus Himself could not have established the Kingdom of God on earth, in power, without the Holy Spirit.

When Jesus left earth at His ascension, the disciples might have thought, "Well, that's goodbye to the King and goodbye to the Kingdom." But Jesus had other plans!

ACTION

Rejoice! The Kingdom of God is being established. We don't see headlines in the newspapers or on social media about the Kingdom. In fact, a lot of our headlines seem to come from the kingdom of satan. But rejoice that the Kingdom of God is absolutely spreading across the face of the earth.

DAY 320

Under-Realized Expectation

Our Father in heaven, hallowed be your name, your kingdom come, your will be done, on earth as it is in heaven (Matthew 6:9).

We continually live with the tension that the Kingdom of God is here and now, but it's yet not fully established. What can Christians receive right here, right now, and what only comes to us at His return? If we're honest with ourselves, most of us have under-realized ideas of how much Kingdom is for now; in other words, we expect too little. Is this you?

The Lord's Prayer in Matthew 6 urges us to call for the manifestation of the Kingdom of God. I hear the Spirit of the Lord say, "You have under-realized what is for you *right now*, and this has been measured by a lack of daily expectation."

Hebrews 6 explains that we have tasted of the powers of the age to come. This means we should know the taste of the Kingdom of God and its force. It should not be unusual to us; it should be recognizable and ingested regularly. We have fully received it inside. God uses the sense of taste to express how we interact with His power. Just as we know the taste of our favorite meal with its familiar seasonings and distinct aromas, this is also how we are to know the power of the Kingdom of God. When we eat an unknown meal, we might scrunch up our face because of the unfamiliar taste. But the Kingdom of God and its power is meant to be like a familiar meal to us.

Become familiar with the power of the Kingdom of God; taste with bigger expectations. You should be shocked when miracles don't happen rather than when they do happen. You should be shocked when demons wrestle with you rather than stay away from you because you've tasted the power of God. You should be shocked when you don't see regularly in the spirit realm rather than shocked when you occasionally do. You should be shocked when your spirit language, speaking in tongues, is familiar because new dimensions of the language of Heaven should be regularly yours.

The Lord says that He wants you to allow Him to inflate your ideas of what is possible. He wants you to taste the power of the age to come. What you think is reserved only for the future is meant to sustain you in *this* age.

RECEIVE

Open your mouth, and let the powers of the age to come to be poured in. Ask Jesus to help you become familiar with the taste of the Kingdom of God; continually receive and increase your expectations!

Seek My Kingdom

But first and most importantly seek (aim at, strive after) His kingdom and His righteousness [His way of doing and being right—the attitude and character of God], and all these things will be given to you also (Matthew 6:33 AMP).

Come back to this Scripture. Come back to this truth. It is a foundational passage that gives you a key for Kingdom living. It's a Scripture that requires you to plumb the depth of it, study it, and discuss it with My Spirit. It requires that you come and know *Me*! Ask Me what makes up My character. What attitudes do I have? Who am I? How does My Kingdom reflect what I value?

Many have learned about Me or have pursued what they thought was My Kingdom. Yet they wrongly pursued man's idea of Me; they wrongly pursued ideas of My Kingdom. And they have wasted their lives in striving and in good works because they did not know Me. Do not fall for the same trap that they have! I desire to teach you who I am, to show you My values, and to instruct you on Kingdom living. Learn from Me!

It's time to explore My Kingdom, and that begins by first knowing Me, the KING! You will never be satisfied by anyone else except for ME. You will never find fulfillment in striving after anything else except MY KINGDOM. Get the first things first; until you do, you will always feel that there is an emptiness and a void. I created you with a void, a hunger, a deep well within that can only be satisfied by ME!

ACTION

Here are some ideas to help you.

- Read the story of Mary and Martha as it shows a great picture of who had her priorities in order.

- Read Scriptures with the phrase *"the kingdom of heaven is like."* What do these Scriptures teach you about the Kingdom?

- Ask the Lord to give you a revelation of where your concept of the Kingdom doesn't line up with His. Ask Him to show you how to start to align your life with the Kingdom.

DAY 322

The Kingdom and You

Everyone was filled with awe at the many wonders and signs performed by the apostles (Acts 2:43; see also verses 14–47).

It was always Jesus's plan that His disciples would have the same anointing with power in the Holy Spirit and would repeat what He had done: heal the sick, raise the dead, release people from demons, and demonstrate the Kingdom with power. If a person can be filled with the same Holy Spirit that enabled Jesus to do what He did, is there anything that person cannot do? No! It is a breathtaking reality that is available to us! Jesus said, *"Whoever believes in me will do the works I have been doing, and they will do even greater things than these"* (John 14:12). What He had begun to do and teach was not going to stop, and now He would do it through the disciples, through us, through *you!* The Kingdom is wherever the Spirit is, and to discover the Spirit is to discover the Kingdom.

In the New Testament after the Gospels, the emphasis is on finding subjects for the Kingdom. It's almost as if Jesus said, "Now that you have the Spirit, you must go everywhere in the world and do what I have been doing. You must set people free from satan and bring them into the Kingdom. Go into all the world, make disciples, baptize them, and teach them everything I have taught you."

The goal of evangelism is to produce people who are able to do everything Jesus commanded. What an amazing task! To do so, we must introduce everyone to the power of the Holy Spirit.

ACTION

- Are you suppressing any spiritual gifts that God has given you?
- Have you stopped developing what the Spirit is wanting to do in your life?
- Are you living in a community of the Spirit where together you can keep in step with the Spirit?

What are you going to do with your answers to these questions? Take responsibility and play your part in the Kingdom of God.

Prophetic Evangelists for the Harvest

Then I heard the voice of the Lord saying, "Whom shall I send? And who will go for us?" And I said, "Here am I. Send me!" He said, "Go and tell this people..." (Isaiah 6:8–9).

"My food," said Jesus, "is to do the will of him who sent me and to finish his work. Don't you have a saying, 'It's still four months until harvest'? I tell you, open your eyes and look at the fields! They are ripe for harvest. Even now the one who reaps draws a wage and harvests a crop for eternal life, so that the sower and the reaper may be glad together. Thus the saying 'One sows and another reaps' is true. I sent you to reap what you have not worked for. Others have done the hard work, and you have reaped the benefits of their labor" (John 4:34–38).

"I am raising you up to bring My voice to those who do not know Me, to liberate those bound in sin, and to bring My salvation to the lost. You are a prophetic evangelist, one who stewards harvest and revelation."

Call out to release prophetic words that bring people into communion with Jesus, as He did with the woman at the well. And just as Jesus's words of revelation saved not only the woman at the well but her entire community, so what you steward prophetically shall go forth and release revival fires for the ones, the twos, the threes, and the mores!

And He says to you, "Do not hold back in these days of shaking and chaos. You are My Kingdom agent, called to introduce My ways into the world around, called to expand My domain throughout the earth. Yes, you! This is who you are."

RECEIVE

To those who receive this word today, the Lord is giving a gift of *consistently radical bravery*. You are not going to find yourself brave one day then filled with fear the next. Instead, you are going to know daily bravery to share the Word of God and prophetically speak to those who need to be introduced to Jesus. You will know by the Spirit who to speak to and who to strike up a conversation with, but you must partner with the Holy Spirit's bravery in order to step out and speak.

A Row of Archers

"Before me every knee will bow; by me every tongue will swear. They will say of me, 'In the Lord alone are deliverance and strength.'" All who have raged against him will come to him and be put to shame (Isaiah 45:23b–24).

One single archer is powerless against a whole army, but a row of archers will put dread fear in the hearts of the enemy. Be righteously aligned.

Find your row of archers and take your place amongst them. You will be no less for doing so, but you immediately shift from *largely ineffective* to *highly effective* for the Kingdom.

There is no place for lone archers on the frontlines of the Kingdom. Kneel alongside the sharpshooters, and know that God is with you. He is the Lord of all victories.

ACTION

The Kingdom of God is all about working as a body, as a community of believers, as the church to be highly effective in advancing the Kingdom. Have you found your fellow archers yet? Is your expectation that someone else needs to make the first move, or are you prepared to do whatever it takes to find your place on the frontline alongside the sharpshooters of the Lord's army?

Overcome Evil with Good

On the contrary: "If your enemy is hungry, feed him; if he is thirsty, give him something to drink. In doing this, you will heap burning coals on his head." Do not be overcome by evil, but overcome evil with good (Romans 12:20–21).

I am coming to put a fiery determination within you for these days in which you are living are not for the faint of heart. Receive this determination. It is a determination that says, "I will not live at the level or behavior of those in the world around me. Instead, I will live as one who knows the God in whom I serve. With Him, I can overcome any evil that comes my way. With Him, I can face my enemy with compassion for I know that my God wins! I will live as one who knows that He is for me and never against me! I will overcome for greater is He within me than he that is in this world!"

In every situation where you face an evil agenda or an enemy fueled by demonic opposition, resist the desire to respond out of a defensive, reactive position. Instead, choose to overcome by living in a way that glorifies Me. Live out of an offensive, overcomer position that is fueled by My fire and the determination to be one who overcomes evil with good!

ACTION

Pick a territory in your life that the enemy is trying to conquer. Ask the Lord to show you how to stand firm in His determination to not be overcome. Ask Him to show you how to gain back that territory. Stake a claim in love, listen to His timing, be conditioned to win the fight! Stand and overcome for the battle belongs to the Lord!

Shine My Light

You are the salt of the earth, but if salt has lost its taste, how shall its saltiness be restored? It is no longer good for anything except to be thrown out and trampled under people's feet. You are the light of the world. A city set on a hill cannot be hidden. Nor do people light a lamp and put it under a basket, but on a stand, and it gives light to all in the house. In the same way, let your light shine before others, so that they may see your good works and give glory to your Father who is in heaven (Matthew 5:13–16 ESV).

Arise, shine, for your light has come, and the glory of the Lord rises upon you. See, darkness covers the earth and thick darkness is over the peoples, but the Lord rises upon you and his glory appears over you (Isaiah 60:1–2).

The Lord says to you, "I have called you to rule and reign with Me, extending My goodness into the territories of darkness and despair. Every place of bondage and limitation is an opportunity set before you to bring an explosion of My power to liberate and release."

I see the Lord equipping you with massive torches in the spirit to release light into darkness. As the torch is turned on and the light is released, the enemy retreats and leaves.

The Lord says, "You are a territory taker, a light releaser, and a captive liberator for My Kingdom! Shine My light into the darkness and watch the enemy retreat. Shine My light into the areas in your family that are under oppression and see liberation come. Shine My light into financial turmoil and watch My breaking come. Shine My light into ill health and watch My healing come. Shine My light into every place of darkness and confusion and watch those situations turn around. Shine My light and see My Kingdom of God!"

DECREE

Respond in prayer: "Jesus, I am ready to be a light for You and to make a difference. I am ready to be a presence of light in the lives around me. Even now I decree and declare that light will flood areas of darkness."

Think about areas that are in darkness, and decree: "I release the light of Christ into (list the areas) in Jesus's name!"

Under Your Foot

You will tread on the lion and the cobra; you will trample the great lion and the serpent (Psalm 91:13).

Who is your God? Remember that He is your great champion and defender, your refuge and mighty fortress! Jesus has won every battle; He has conquered, and you are more than a conqueror.

Why are you allowing the great lions and snakes to restrict and limit you and stop your forward momentum? Why have you allowed them to become a dead end, a cul-de-sac, on the journey of your destiny? You are supposed to walk over them and trample them under your feet!

Jesus says to you: *"I have given you authority to trample on snakes and scorpions and to overcome all the power of the enemy; nothing will harm you"* (Luke 10:19).

Some of you have been stopped in your tracks by sickness, others by a spirit of poverty, and yet more of you by cursing words of limitation that have deceived you as to the real goal and prize in your life. Today it is time to put on your walking boots and walk all over the head of the serpent! Walk over them; walk onward out of that dead-end street without even looking back.

DECREE

Read Psalm 91 a few times and then turn it into some declarations that you can make over your life. Adapt them to your circumstances. Write them down and make them regular decrees.

Deliverance Anointing

And these signs will accompany those who believe: In my name they will drive out demons; they will speak in new tongues; they will pick up snakes with their hands; and when they drink deadly poison, it will not hurt them at all; they will place their hands on sick people, and they will get well (Mark 16:17–18).

Sometimes we think that to display our faith we must manifest only kindness and love, and that is true, but that is only a part of the biblical picture. The Gospel of Mark clearly states that those who believe will drive out demons in the name of Jesus. This is not for a small minority of deliverance specialists; it is the command to the entire Body of Christ!

The Spirit of the Lord is waking up the warrior, military, and deliverance aspect of the Kingdom in the hearts of His people in this era. God wants to anoint and commission you today into the army of deliverance ministers. He wants you to look demons in the eye and cast them out. He wants you to talk to them and displace them in His name. He wants you to be a demon confronter. He wants you to be a demon terrorizer! You are being called into the ministry of deliverance today, especially the ministry of mass deliverance, where many demons go with ease as you bring the Kingdom of God.

Will you hear the call and accept the challenge? Will you receive and reflect this aspect of biblical truth?

DECREE

It is time for God to hear your yes regarding His call for you to be a freedom enforcer. The out loud yes must now pour from you, even if you initially feel apprehensive.

The people who know their God shall be strong, and carry out great exploits (Daniel 11:32 NKJV).

Advancing Out of the Trenches

But small is the gate and narrow the road that leads to life, and only a few find it (Matthew 7:14).

In addition to all this, take up the shield of faith, with which you can extinguish all the flaming arrows of the evil one (Ephesians 6:16).

I saw believers in battle trenches, keeping low to avoid enemy fire. The trenches circled one side of the battlefield, opposite enemy territory. Some believers were huddled together, others walked around the trench network. Everyone seemed busy and occupied by the stresses of war.

The Lord is pleased that you are on your feet, willing to fight, and ready to move. But now listen to the Holy Spirit as He urges you on, up, and out of the trenches and onto the battlefield.

He says, "My warrior, I did not ask for you to stay in the battle trench, going around and around in the mud and enduring the stress of constant fire. The trench is on your side, and so you will never truly see a breakthrough in this battle if you remain embedded here. If you want to enforce the victory, you will need to go up and out.

"So, mighty warrior, it is time to remind yourself that you wear the armor of God and that Jesus Christ goes ahead of you. You can climb out of the trench and step up onto the battlefield. Advance and do not fear your foes, for their fiery darts will be extinguished. Do not heed the enemy's shouts and taunts; take no prisoners as you walk forward on the path that God will illuminate for you."

RECEIVE

Our battle is not against flesh and blood; we are to be engaged in daily spiritual warfare. What are the spiritual strongholds that are oppressing you and keeping you huddled in the trench? Does the enemy have you on the retreat in areas of your life? It is he who is supposed to be on the retreat from you! Take time to receive courage from the Lord, courage to take to the battlefield and win some spiritual victories in the name of Jesus Christ, who overcame it all for you!

Find Me Every Day

It is the glory of God to conceal a matter, but the glory of kings is to search out a matter (Proverbs 25:2 NASB).

And you will seek Me and find Me when you search for Me with all your heart (Jeremiah 29:13 NASB).

I am coming today to give you a new, fresh desire to seek Me. I long for you to seek Me like a child who is on a treasure hunt, full of excitement and expectation. Come and seek Me with the delight of knowing that when you find Me, you will be so surprised and delighted by what you find.

As you seek Me, let Me brush off the old dusty ways that you have used to approach Me. Let Me shake off the old thoughts that say that I am too hard to be found or that everyone else easily finds Me but you do not. Let Me reassure you that I am not hard to find. In fact, I love when you look for Me. I enjoy the treasure-hunting process as much as you do.

So, look for Me when you are at your desk working. See where I am when you are standing in the kitchen and washing dishes. Notice Me when you are playing with your children. I am here! When you choose to seek Me, you will always find Me. What you will discover is that I may not look the way you expected. I may not do what you think I will do, but that is the joy of the discovery. I am infinite and marvelous in all My ways. Let Me surprise you each day! Let Me bring deep, deep delight to your life. Let Me take you on a treasure hunt that will both thrill your heart and sustain your days.

Today receive this new desire to seek Me and take on the attitude of a king who loves the thrill of investigating and digging deep.

ACTION

Spend some time looking for Jesus today. Be intentional and focused. Start by sensing His presence in the room with you. Then look to see Him. What is He doing? How is He dressed? What mood is He in? When you've done all of this and have locked eyes with Him, ask a simple question: "Jesus, what do You want me to know today?"

DAY 331

Marching Shoulder to Shoulder

For our struggle is not against flesh and blood, but against the rulers, against the authorities, against the powers of this dark world and against the spiritual forces of evil in the heavenly realms (Ephesians 6:12).

I hear the Lord say, "You are not a lone soldier, an isolated troop thrown into battle and just expected to get out alive on your own. I have grafted you into an army, and you march shoulder to shoulder with all who have said yes to service."

So do not be dismayed. You are surrounded not only by heavenly armies but by sons and daughters of God, the church, the Bride of Christ, who form a glorious army, imbued with power from on high. There is no such thing as a lone soldier or an isolated troop in God's family. Everyone fights shoulder to shoulder with one another. The enemy may try and convince you that you are alone, but this is a lie. Tell this lie to disintegrate in Jesus's name. Whether people are present with you physically, the truth still stands: You are not alone!

Ephesians 6:12 doesn't say *"my* struggle" or *"your* struggle" but *"our* struggle."* The wrestle and the battle are a family affair that the people of God achieve together.

ACTION

Repent of when you have behaved independently or partnered with a spirit of isolation. Banish the lies of the enemy that have told you that you are totally alone. God always likes us to be in community, in relationships. Who are you to work alongside? What do you need to do to form a shoulder-to-shoulder regiment?

Beware Social Action without Spiritual Power

For the kingdom of God is not a matter of talk but of power (1 Corinthians 4:20).

The action of doing good and bringing justice to society (sometimes called "social action gospel" or "social justice") must not be devoid of spiritual power. Do not split and separate doing good from the power of God.

We clothe the naked, befriend the lonely, home the homeless, feed the hungry, and love the unlovely, but we also work miracles, heal the sick, raise the dead, strip out demons, and bring the resurrection power of God into lives.

Today the Spirit of God lays a charge against us: We have valued *either* the miraculous gospel or the social gospel. But we don't get to choose. One without the other is an undermining of the full picture of Jesus. The Lord is cautioning us today to keep both community transformation and miraculous power side by side, woven together, both highly functioning.

Good social activities without the presence of the miraculous are an impotent version of Jesus. The miraculous without compassionate action and justice is ripping the heart out of Jesus. His Kingdom is power, love, action, impact, transformation, supernatural, and just.

No longer are we to feed somebody in need without also laying on hands and commanding the miracles. No longer are we to clothe somebody without also laying on hands and kicking out demons first.

The social gospel has failed to solve the problems of wickedness and oppression; it has emptied the Gospel of the Kingdom of its spiritual power. We cannot make the world a better place by our own efforts. We need the power of God to war against the spiritual forces that oppose us.

RECEIVE

Today should be an internal course correction for us. We must now receive a rebalancing to our thinking. Allow yourself to be led into a place where the Gospel of the Kingdom of power and action can flow from you.

DAY 333

Fear Not

So this is what the Sovereign Lord says: "See, I lay a stone in Zion, a tested stone, a precious cornerstone for a sure foundation; the one who relies on it will never be stricken with panic" (Isaiah 28:16).

"Fear not, for I am with you," says the Lord. "I will never leave you and I will never, ever betray you. Let Me be your rock and do not make men your cornerstone. Men and women will fail you, even those you put hope and confidence in. But I, the Lord your God, am your sure foundation. So, shift your feet from the shoulders of men onto Me."

Are there people, even those in leadership or authority in your life, you need to release as your place of hope? Is there offense that needs to be set down? Is there forgiveness that you can show to those who have not measured up to expectation, which was possibly wrongly allocated in the first place? Can you forgive those that you perceive as having betrayed you? Allow God to be the judge and do not take on this burden yourself.

But know that you have someone who will never let you down and who is always consistent, true, and keeps His word. He is the Lord God Almighty, who was, and is, and is to come.

ACTION

Begin by meditating on Jesus Christ, your faithful Lord, your solid rock, your sure foundation. He never changes and will never fail you. Praise Him for this. Do this until you find your security in Him and Him alone.

Next, repent of putting your faith and security in anyone other than your King. Make Him your King once again, and release everyone else from this responsibility.

Now, ask the Holy Spirit to give you names of everyone you need to forgive who has let you down, offended you, disappointed you, failed you, and has not measured up.

King Jesus, You alone have proven Yourself worthy. Jesus, You alone are the one who never fails and in whom I can place my hope. Jesus, I list all those who have failed and fallen short. In doing so, they hurt, disappointed, offended, limited, abused, and let me down. Some of them didn't do anything wrong, but I put expectations on them that I shouldn't have. Lord, I say now to each one of these people, 'I forgive you.' Jesus, You are my healer, and I need Your healing now. I receive Your healing balm on my wounds. Thank You, Jesus.

Living Water Rivers

Now the Lord God had planted a garden in the east, in Eden; and there he put the man he had formed. The Lord God made all kinds of trees grow out of the ground—trees that were pleasing to the eye and good for food. In the middle of the garden were the tree of life and the tree of the knowledge of good and evil. A river watering the garden flowed from Eden; from there it was separated into four headwaters (Genesis 2:8–10).

Streams of life are found at the heart of what God does. A river flowed from Eden and watered the garden before spreading to the four corners of ancient civilization. The river brought life and blessing, watering the dry earth. Throughout the Old Testament Scriptures, streams, rivers, and wells are found alongside many moments of deliverance or blessing; they serve as reminders of the life that the Creator brings. In Ezekiel's vision of the temple (see Ezek. 47) he saw a river coming out of the temple and bringing life and refreshing to even the Dead Sea, the most lifeless place on earth. John the Revelator saw a *"river of the water of life…flowing from the throne of God and of the Lamb"* (Rev. 22:1–2).

We are meant to inhabit and occupy the earth and be like rivers of life wherever we are established. We are to bring blessing, life, and refreshment to the land around us. Even when we are in exile, strangers in a foreign land, we are to bring Heaven's life to earth. Like Israel in Babylon or Egypt, we are a different people, with a different purpose and a different source. We are to be like a river of life in Babylon, bringing the blessing of the living water.

Jesus said: *"Anyone who believes in me may come and drink! For the Scriptures declare, 'Rivers of living water will flow from his heart'"* (John 7:38 NLT).

Let the living water bring refreshment and life wherever you go. Everywhere is spiritually dry and barren without the water of life; it needs irrigation. Cultivate the Garden of Eden wherever you are; bring Heaven to earth.

RECEIVE

Take time in Scripture; read Isaiah 12:3, 35:6, 44:3, 55:1; 58:11; Ezekiel 47:9; John 7; and John 4:14. Are you dry and thirsty? Get refreshed, and then begin to water the land around you. Where can you bring blessing and life? What is dry and in need of a river?

CHAPTER 12

Daily Victory

Choose Movement

Then we turned back and set out toward the wilderness along the route to the Red Sea, as the Lord had directed me. For a long time we made our way around the hill country of Seir. Then the Lord said to me, "You have made your way around this hill country long enough; now turn north" (Deuteronomy 2:1–3).

You are presented daily with the choice to move forward or stay stuck, to continue in cycles of bondage and delay, or to *"set* [your] *face like flint"* and keep going (Isa. 50:7).

The Lord says to you: "Break the cycles. Break the going around and around. Do not consider your life as one that will always follow the same, cyclical patterns always. See it as a mountain you are ascending, a river you are sailing down; a wild adventure I am taking you on. Every day there are new realms to experience, new moments of intimacy to encounter, and new levels of My love to be washed in.

"So, decide today to break the patterns and cycles that are keeping you bound both in your thoughts and in your actions. From your sleeping patterns to your thought life, from your timekeeping to your emotions, set yourself this day to break out of containment and into forward movement."

ACTION

Recognize the areas of your life that have kept you in cycles of "stuckness." Recognize the places where you have been bound to wrong habits or routines and start to decree:

- Demonic cycles are ending in Jesus's name!

- Routines of stuckness are ceasing in Jesus's name!

- I am not going around the mountain of (name the issues) anymore.

- I am advancing!

- I am moving forward.

- This is a day of decisive change for me.

From Strength to Strength

What joy for those whose strength comes from the Lord, who have set their minds on a pilgrimage to Jerusalem. When they walk through the Valley of Weeping, it will become a place of refreshing springs. The autumn rains will clothe it with blessings. They will continue to grow stronger, and each of them will appear before God in Jerusalem (Psalm 84:5–7 NLT).

Blessed are those whose strength is in Him! Although you may not realize it, He sees you as one who goes from strength to strength, glory to glory, victory to victory. You may not feel this, but He is saying it loudly over you!

"You are called to find your strength in Me! Do not worry or fret when you feel tired, unable to cope, or weak. In those moments I come in like a flood to strengthen you, to lift you up, and to put you back on your feet! These are the moments through which I can and want to work in your life. Even if you pass through the Valley of Weeping, I can turn that into a spring of refreshment. Even in the autumn seasons when things feel as if they are dying and fading away, I come with blessings. Look and see!

"When you open your eyes to catch what I am doing, when you set your gaze on Me rather than on what you face, I can turn things around and give you a new perspective. I am the God who clothes you with strength; I am the Lord who arms you for battle. I am the champion who goes before you to lead you from victory to victory. See Me. Walk with Me; dwell with Me."

ACTION

Read from the Psalms, and meditate on David's heart of thankfulness, even in his trials. For example: Psalm 7; 34; 44; 92; 95; 100; 111, and so on.

Notice how the Lord is always the answer in every situation. Ask the Lord to help you remember times when He has brought you through the wilderness and into His joy. Give Him thanks for these moments in your life and appreciate who He is! He is the God who can do anything!

Break the Cycle

The one who breaks through goes up before them; they break through, pass through the gate, and go out by it. So their king passes on before them, And the Lord at their head (Micah 2:13 NASB).

Choose this day to move forward and not go back! Choose this day to say no to all that has held you back before, all the regrets, the pain of broken relationships, the unresolved history of offense, and the cries for justice that feel unanswered. Let these go now, and choose to walk forward in this moment, for the way is open. There is an opportunity now to move up and out of the places that you have been stuck in before, repetitive cycles of behavior, doubt, and unnecessary caution.

Today the Lord says to you: "Child, let it all go. Let the disappointment, grief, and unanswered questions go, and simply trust Me with it all. Step forward into the path that I have opened up to you now. This is the day of forward movement and momentum. You will not move out from the restrictive cycle without first agreeing to let go and move forward. So say yes to Me today, and I will pull you out from where you have become stuck in repetitive cycles."

DECREE

As the Lord gives you this choice here today, say yes to Him. Trust Him in this moment that He knows all your history and will bring resolution in His timing and His way. Press forward into moving beyond what previously had you in a holding pattern.

Say yes to God, and move past all that has hindered you.

Say yes to going beyond.

Say yes to the path the Lord is opening up for you.

Say yes to His ways and methods.

Give Him your yes today.

DAY 338

Embrace Holy Discontentment

You will live by the sword and you will serve your brother. But when you grow restless, you will throw his yoke from off your neck (Genesis 27:40).

When God moves in an individual, it often starts with a deep sense of discontent.

I hear the Spirit of the Lord say today: "I bless you with spiritual discontentment and an appetite for more. This will include dissatisfaction with selfish things, which will open your heart to long for more of Me.

"Restlessness enables you to break out of the place you are in. I do not call you to live in continual ease, but rather I allow moments of deep, gnawing frustration because in that place of frustration and dissatisfaction it enables you to be catapulted forward."

When Jacob is blessing Esau in the Book of Genesis, he explains that when restlessness grows, it will enable him to throw oppression off his life. Restlessness becomes a gift that you can use to break heavy yokes. Restlessness and holy discontentment become the doorway to freedom and your next level of glory. God enables frustration to come when we plateau. The Spirit of the Lord says, "You have done well to get to where you are today, but there has been a plateauing. Now I will help you break into a more rewarding, higher space."

ACTION

The Holy Spirit of the Lord says, "Acknowledge with Me your plateaued state (where you have leveled out and settled)." Allow your plateaued state to frustrate you. Feel the emotions that come from having plateaued. Have an honesty moment, so that you can receive the gift of discontentment and restlessness that will move you and shift you.

DAY 339

Get Free!

These signs will accompany those who have believed: in My name they will cast out demons, they will speak with new tongues (Mark 16:17 NASB).

Jesus is highlighting the need for His people to pursue a new depth of personal freedom from demonic oppression.

Do not allow the enemy to linger on your doorstep or even to sit across your threshold any longer. Ask the Holy Spirit to reveal areas of your life that are still shadowed by the demonic and the unholy, for example, habitual sins and failings. Have these areas remained in the dark despite your repeated confessions and prayers of repentance?

It is time to clear these areas once and for all! It is time to rebuke the enemy in your doorway.

ACTION

1. Repent of your sin; repent of allowing the demonic this access to you. Yesterday gave an example of a simple prayer of repentance.

2. Say out loud, "I completely break agreement with this sinful area of my life and any effects of the demonic that have been shadowing my life. The enemy is not welcome in my life. Jesus Christ is Lord of my life, and I am completely surrendered to Him."

3. Now develop an authoritative language for rebuking the demons that are oppressing you in this area. Tell them to get out of your life in no uncertain terms! Let them know that you belong to Jesus Christ.

4. By His authority cast them out! Blow them right out of your life. You might want to physically blow, yawn, or cough them out at this point. Do you feel freer? Keep going until you know by the Holy Spirit that you are free of whatever demonic influences have been oppressing you.

5. Finally, welcome the Holy Spirit to fill that area of your life with His light, life, and goodness.

Begin to walk in the fullness of your freedom. You have just been delivered!

Rhythms of Repentance

Repent, then, and turn to God, so that your sins may be wiped out, that times of refreshing may come from the Lord (Acts 3:19).

Produce fruit in keeping with repentance (Matthew 3:8).

I heard the Spirit of the Lord say, "It is time to become reacquainted with daily rhythms of repentance. The enemy wants to keep you locked in shame over sin, where you feel paralyzed and capped. He wants to disarm you by keeping your past unresolved and untouched. Yet I have given you a weapon to destroy this enemy tactic and it is called repentance.

"Repentance releases victory. Repentance kills shame. Repentance releases overcoming. Repentance destroys bondage to sin. Repentance heals you of fear. Repentance releases life.

"Daily you can come before Me in both repentance and worship; as you do, daily victory will be yours. As you worshipfully repent, you will find new fruitfulness. Repentance releases fruitfulness and causes you to live in My favor; it pulls you into a dance of grace and glory with Me. As you repent, My face shines on you."

ACTION

We tend to overcomplicate repentance to the point that we feel like we don't actually know how to do it. But repentance is simply recognizing your sinful ways, exposing them before God, saying sorry, and then choosing to turn around and walk away from those ways.

Here is a simple prayer you can use for yourself, and be led by the Spirit as you go: "Lord Jesus Christ, I come to You and recognize that I have sinned. I repent for (name what comes to mind) and now say that I am sorry. I know that this did not reflect Your goodness, and I choose now to ask for Your forgiveness and turn away from it. Thank You that You are faithful, good, and kind, and You choose to wash me clean from the sting of sin. Amen."

See the Glory of Christ

The Word became flesh and made his dwelling among us. We have seen his glory, the glory of the one and only Son, who came from the Father, full of grace and truth (John 1:14).

The Spirit gives life; the flesh counts for nothing. The words I have spoken to you—they are full of the Spirit and life (John 6:63).

How can we see the glory of Christ if we have never seen Jesus physically as the first believers did?

Jesus points us to the answer to this question: in the way that the Holy Spirit ministers to us:

The Holy Spirit, whom the Father will send in my name, will teach you all things and will remind you of everything I have said to you (John 14:26).

When he, the Spirit of truth, comes, he will guide you into all the truth. He will not speak on his own; he will speak only what he hears, and he will tell you what is yet to come (John 16:13).

These two verses tell us that the writers of the Bible put what they saw of Christ and His glory into words and wrote them down for us to read. This recording of what they saw enables us to see the glory of Christ as clearly as they did.

ACTION

Read First John 1:1–4. Again and again John emphasizes what he and others had seen and heard was revealed to them as they walked and talked with Jesus, so that we, as a later generation, would see the glory of Christ by reading what they wrote down. The glory of Christ shines through the pages of our Bibles!

Knowing that seeing the glory of Christ awaits you as you read the words of God's Word will encourage you to avidly read the Bible every day.

Start reading through the four Gospels of Matthew, Mark, Luke, and John, together with the Book of Acts. Not just once, but repeatedly, and you will see the glory of Christ every day.

Your Daily Bread

Then Jesus declared, "I am the bread of life. Whoever comes to me will never go hungry, and whoever believes in me will never be thirsty" (John 6:35).

I am your daily bread. I give you nourishment; I fill you with great satisfaction. When you eat from Me, you no longer desire anything else. Let Me fill you! Let Me satisfy the deep, deep places of your being. Let Me be the One you run to first thing in the morning and the One you speak to as you fall asleep each night. Let Me express My delight over you. I am so generous in My outpouring of love, understanding, peace, kindness, patience, wisdom, guidance, direction, finances, and all that you need!

Come and eat from My banqueting table. Sit and fellowship with Me. Partake of My joy. Laugh with Me. Talk with Me. Eat your fill! I'm not a God who gives sparingly. I am lavish in My giving, especially of Myself.

Will you grab hold of My offer? Will you come and partake? Will you let Me fill the places where lack, poverty mentality, self-focus, and victimhood have stolen from you and left you raw and empty? Let Me nourish and heal. Let Me fill you to overflow! Make the time to eat from My table.

RECEIVE

Make a point to feast on the Word every day as much as possible. Let the association with nourishment in the physical truly resonate with the spiritual. Every snack time, snack on the Word. Every mealtime, feast on the Word.

Let him lead me to the banquet hall, and let his banner over me be love (Song of Songs 2:4).

Freedom from a Sick Heart

Hope deferred makes the heart sick, but a longing fulfilled is a tree of life
(Proverbs 13:12).

Is there a sickness of deferred, unfulfilled hope inside the core of who you are? Is there pain, discomfort, or grief sitting in the midst of you that has come from fruitless dreams or delayed hopes? If you have felt this, know that God now has His hand on the core of your being, pressing on this place of sickness.

In the spirit, I see Jesus coming close to you, putting His hand on your belly. He is looking at where the pain is—right into the core of who you are. His look is tender, filled with compassion and deep love. Then, He looks at you and says with His eyes, "Allow Me to press My hand into your core and excise the sickness." He pauses for your response. Jesus is here now, close to you, to remove the infection that has come from this condition of dreams and hopes deferred. He comes to bring healing to all of the sicknesses.

RECEIVE

As Jesus asks you to let Him in to heal these raw places, would you intentionally allow Him close to see and touch the places of disappointment and pain, and the place where your questions remain unanswered (the whys and what-ifs)? He knows that this is raw and sore. Ask for His help if you are struggling. Give these over to the Lord and allow Him access to the painful places in your memories and reflections.

Write down a list of hopes and dreams that you feel have been pushed back unfulfilled and have made you sick. Take time to hear and sense with the Holy Spirit what these are, some may be elusive and not so obvious. He desires to bring deep, full healing to the inner places of your heart and mind today.

After writing each one down, give it over to the Lord. Speak out loud whatever words come with the intention of saying, "Jesus, I give you this pain/grief/disappointment. I let it go and trust You with the outcome."

If unforgiveness or issues of offense with individuals come to mind, bring these people to Jesus and release forgiveness. If you are unable to forgive or let go of offense, be willing to go on a journey with the Lord to be able to release forgiveness and let go of offense.

Pray: "Help me, Lord, to let go of offense and pain in this situation. (You can name it and the people involved if that helps you.) I am finding it so hard to forgive this person and let go of this situation. I am willing to go on the journey, and I ask You to help me get there so that I can wholly forgive with all of my heart. Please help me do this, Jesus. I say yes to Your healing and the way You want to do it."

What God Wants

Then turning toward the woman [Jesus] said to Simon, "Do you see this woman? I entered your house; you gave me no water for my feet, but she has wet my feet with her tears and wiped them with her hair. You gave me no kiss, but from the time I came in she has not ceased to kiss my feet. You did not anoint my head with oil, but she has anointed my feet with ointment. Therefore I tell you, her sins, which are many, are forgiven—for she loved much. But he who is forgiven little, loves little" (Luke 7:44–47 ESV).

What does God want from us? What does He really want? Most would probably say something like, "To do good" or "To believe in Him." Of course, God indeed wants both of these things, but we can fall into the trap of assuming that God will *only* be pleased if we get all our *doing* or *thinking* right.

This was how the Pharisees thought. All that mattered was getting it right, doing your duty. But the focus in Luke 7 is on a woman who has lived an utterly immoral life.

> *A woman of the city, who was a sinner, when she learned that he was reclining at table in the Pharisee's house, brought an alabaster flask of ointment, and standing behind him at his feet, weeping, she began to wet his feet with her tears and wiped them with the hair of her head and kissed his feet and anointed them with the ointment* (Luke 7:37–38 ESV).

The Pharisee didn't appreciate or understand the embarrassing display of love. But Jesus responds with forgiveness and praise.

He loves us. He wants us to love Him back. It is that simple. When you have been forgiven and have felt the breathless wonder of leaving your wrongs behind, knowing that God will never bring them up again, you respond in love.

DECREE

Lord, I don't want to stop with only my forgiveness and with my debt cleared. I want to go much further and respond to Your love for me. Lord, I want a relationship with You, daily intimate contact with the God who longs for me and loves me. I want to respond to Your love with my poured out love every moment of my day and night.

Shun the Words of the Accuser

Then I heard a loud voice in heaven say: "Now have come the salvation and the power and the kingdom of our God, and the authority of his Messiah. For the accuser of our brothers and sisters, who accuses them before our God day and night, has been hurled down" (Revelation 12:10).

Where you have felt like you have been on trial, remember that your accuser is without authority. *All* authority in Heaven and on earth belongs to Jesus Christ. That means that satan, the accuser, has no authority. His words carry no weight.

The words of the accuser, designed to weaken your perception of who you are, may be numerous in your mind, but they are weak and without basis or authority and shall not shake those who hold on to the truth of the Lord.

Jesus, your Savior, is extending His strong arm to you at this time. Grab hold of it. Feel the strength of His grip on you. Even though you stand in the midst of accusations and trial-like circumstances, know that the King of kings has a strong hold on you. You will not come to harm if you remain close to Christ, the One who has all authority, and turn away from the voice of the accuser. Do not heed that liar and deceiver any longer.

ACTION

Though his words are weak and without authority, satan has probably thrown a lot of words at you, and some of them may have stuck and become something that you believe about yourself.

Picture these ungodly words, phrases, sentences, or beliefs like sticky notes that are covering your head and body. Every single one of these sticky notes needs to be thrown in the fire. Tell Jesus that you are ready to throw every word of satan into His holy furnace. As a prophetic act, peel off every note that has been stuck to you. Peel them off your head, your ears, your body. If the Holy Spirit reveals what some of the words or phrases are, speak them out. For example:

- I renounce the accusation that I am stupid.

- I tear the word *ugly* off my body. It is a lie. The truth is that I am a child of God, and He says I am lovely.

The Macedonian Anointing

And now, brothers and sisters, we want you to know about the grace that God has given the Macedonian churches. In the midst of a very severe trial, their overflowing joy and their extreme poverty welled up in rich generosity. For I testify that they gave as much as they were able, and even beyond their ability. Entirely on their own, they urgently pleaded with us for the privilege of sharing in this service to the Lord's people. And they exceeded our expectations: They gave themselves first of all to the Lord, and then by the will of God also to us (2 Corinthians 8:1–5).

God is calling the church to be a radical community. He is shaping us to no longer be isolated individuals but to be unified, marked by love and forgiveness, the collective expression of Jesus Christ, the tangible community of the King.

A significant part of this is radical generosity, where we no longer pander to the selfishness of the culture around us but are instead compelled to give extravagantly. This is typically called the Macedonian Anointing after the example of the church in Macedonia, who were commended by Paul in Second Corinthians. Something remarkable happened to the Macedonian churches. In the midst of their poverty and trials, they stewarded an ability to give beyond what anyone thought was possible. Paul writes of them giving *"even beyond their ability."*

We think that if we give 10 percent of our income we are doing well, but that is an Old Testament concept and falls far short. The New Testament instructs us to give everything, thus pulling us to a higher standard. A good starting point toward coming into alignment with the New Testament standard of giving and generosity is to aim to join the 51 percent group, giving away more than half your income.

Would you like to receive the Macedonian giving capability?

ACTION

Repent for any partnership with the culture of stinginess or financial selfishness. Ask God for His mercy and then receive a Macedonian capability for extreme generosity and for being able to model the radical community of what church should be. Write a giving list for those you would like to sow into over the next handful of months. Make sure your giving list is more fulsome and longer than your own aspirational list of things you would like to purchase and own!

DAY 347

Truth from the Outside In

Behold, You desire truth in the inward parts, and in the hidden part You will make me to know wisdom (Psalm 51:6 NKJV).

So then faith comes by hearing, and hearing by the word of God (Romans 10:7 NKJV).

The Lord says to you, "I am working truth deep inside you, but it may not be in the way that you expect. Scripture is not just meant to be read but to be *said*; it is not just to be thought about but to be spoken out loud."

When you speak out Scripture, you stir up your faith and it increases to explosive levels. Your faith goes from being *minute* to *monumental*, from being little to big, from being reserved to overflowing! Reading truth aloud causes a tidal wave of glory and power to crash over you. Declaring Scripture from your mouth makes the enemy flee and his chains break. When you read truth aloud, it fills you up and expands in your insides.

Reading the Bible out loud is a secret weapon that is often overlooked. It is the sword that you need when the chains of bondage try to keep you down; it is the artillery you need when the arrows of the enemy's lies are fired at your mind. Read out loud and watch as your interaction with truth and your inner being change radically.

ACTION

Ask the Holy Spirit, "What key passage of Scripture do You want me to work with today?" Let Him reveal a chapter or even a whole book that He wants you to read.

Open your Bible to the pages and start to read it out loud—not internally—the words on your tongue, your breath, and out of your mouth. Measure the changes and transformations inside of you, and see your faith increase exponentially.

DAY 348

Straight Ahead!

Listen carefully, my dear child, to everything that I teach you, and pay attention to all that I have to say. Fill your thoughts with my words until they penetrate deep into your spirit. Then, as you unwrap my words, they will impart true life and radiant health into the very core of your being. So above all, guard the affections of your heart, for they affect all that you are. Pay attention to the welfare of your innermost being, for from there flows the wellspring of life. Avoid dishonest speech and pretentious words. Be free from using perverse words no matter what! Set your gaze on the path before you. With fixed purpose, looking straight ahead, ignore life's distractions. Watch where you're going! Stick to the path of truth, and the road will be safe and smooth before you. Don't allow yourself to be sidetracked for even a moment or take the detour that leads to darkness (Proverbs 4:20–27 TPT).

My Word, the whole of it, brings life and health to every part of your being. Just as you would take your time to savor every delightful bite of an expensive, gourmet meal, it is vital that you do the same with My Word. Every day, treat it as a cherished gift, and as the passage from Proverbs 4 says, take the time to unwrap My words. Eat from them; let them nourish your very being. As you do so, allow Me to set your priorities straight; let Me give you focus and purpose for your very being. I desire for you to be one whose gaze and focus are set straight ahead.

Much in this life distracts, detracts, and keeps you from the path I have designed you to walk. This path is for your safety, your delight, and the fulfillment of all you were meant to be and do. Yet the guidebook, the nourishment, the sustenance required to stay on this path is all found in My Word. Take it, savor it, enjoy it, feed from it. Let it bring health to your bones and life to your soul. Let it keep you on the path you were meant to journey—straight ahead, fully focused on Me.

Remember that you become what you behold!

ACTION

Know your why! Write in bold, capital letters the reasons why the Word will bring fruit in your life. Write in concrete terms, including specific fruits that are tangible and that you expect to manifest.

Walk Out into Victory!

But thanks be to God! He gives us the victory through our Lord Jesus Christ
(1 Corinthians 15:57).

There is a way of walking in daily victory for you. There is a prescription from the Lord to ensure a victorious mindset and positioning with Him, no matter what the circumstances of life that you face.

The Lord is setting out three particular elements for victory that will help you to follow through into triumphant life. He says:

- "Give Me your yes." The Lord is asking for your yes each day. This can be an unspoken agreement in your heart as much as it can be a verbal declaration, such as, "You have my huge yes, God, whatever it takes and whatever this means for my life."

- "Surrender your will to My will." The Father says: "Let your heart say, 'Your will be done in my life always. I surrender my heart and my will to Yours, knowing that Yours is the best for me. I stop fighting for my will and my choices and instead choose Your ways above all of mine. I surrender.'"

- "Trust Me," the Lord says, "in all circumstances trust Me. In all outcomes trust Me. In all storms look for Me, for I am there. I have you and the situation, whatever that might be. Trust Me and see My face in the storm. I have this for you. All is well. Look at Me."

Walk in the way of surrender and trust, knowing that you are choosing God's best for you and not your own version of life. In full submission you will walk through trials and challenges yet in victory every time. There will be challenges, but you will overcome in surrender to God.

RECEIVE

Take time to pray this through with the Lord. Give Him everything. Speak each of the three points above out loud. Ask Him for His help to get you to the place of full surrender. If you can't say yes wholeheartedly yet, ask the Lord to get you to your huge yes. He will hear you, and He will help you to get there.

Root Out Idols

"Do not forget the covenant I have made with you, and do not worship other gods. Rather, worship the Lord your God; it is he who will deliver you from the hand of all your enemies." They would not listen, however, but persisted in their former practices. Even while these people were worshiping the Lord, they were serving their idols (2 Kings 17:38–41a).

To those who feel destroyed and spiritually emaciated, the Holy Spirit says: "Place your trust in Me again. Trust in Me alone and no other god. Repent of taking other idols alongside or in place of Me. The sin that has beset you found an opportunity to torment your life when you bowed low to something you should not have kneeled before."

With this sobering message comes fresh hope for you: repent and root out the idols and the things that have followed in behind them.

There is a way back for those who feel totally wiped out and destroyed. Jesus's victory on the cross was your moment of Exodus, your escape from slavery and bondage, and the beginning of your journey to discover the full extent of your new identity in Christ.

Place the Lord your God as preeminent in your life once more—no competition—and you will see that the destroyed places are rebuilt and that your spiritual emaciation is replaced by a healthy satisfaction in the One who provides for your every need.

ACTION

Have you felt spiritually emaciated or weak? It could be because God is not first in your life. Have you been serving idols, even whilst worshipping the Lord?

Take time to ask the Holy Spirit to convict you of any things in your life that come before God. Are you in bondage to something or someone that is not Christ? Repent and recommit yourself to Him, the Lord of lords.

Who is like You among the gods, Lord? Who is like You, majestic in holiness, awesome in praises, working wonders? (Exodus 15:11 NASB)

DAY 351

Rebuilding Your Battered Walls

Take courage My children, and live in good hope, for I rebuild, and when I do, it is with much finer materials than before.

O storm-battered city, troubled and desolate! I will rebuild you with precious jewels and make your foundations from lapis lazuli (Isaiah 54:11 NLT).

Do not rest in the ruins of what was once great but instead join in the new building program. It is time to get on with it because waiting for the "good old days" that you think you remember or that you have read about or that others talk about fondly, will not turn the clock back. I will not turn the clock back because this is a new day, and in this day I am restoring much in ways that you will not recognize from before.

Join in with My building work. Spend time with Me, and I will show you the part of the wall that I want you to work on. And do not stint on the resources that I have given and will give. I am the Lord your God, and I have unlimited supply for those who are about the task that I have appointed for them.

Enlarge your house; build an addition. Spread out your home, and spare no expense! For you will soon be bursting at the seams. Your descendants will occupy other nations and resettle the ruined cities (Isaiah 54:2–3 NLT).

RECEIVE

How many of your church programs are a celebration of the past or attempts to recreate what was successful before? Move forward, not backward. Don't look to the past and the history of men but work with God now. You must begin to listen prophetically, working with the Holy Spirit to know what is possible and at what scale you need to plan. What prophetic words have you or your church received? Did you assess them through lenses of the past, adding limitations that are not God's limitations? And if you are not working to prophetic blueprints, it's time to get some!

Forgive or Be Limited

And when you stand praying, if you hold anything against anyone, forgive them, so that your Father in heaven may forgive you your sins (Mark 11:25).

We often feel justified in keeping a record of other people's sins against us. Our tendency toward indignation, offense, and unforgiveness blocks us from the fullness of life in Christ. The Kingdom of God has its own unique culture: those who live by its standards will sound different, look different, and think differently. We are to have a Kingdom vocabulary that represents and reflects our heavenly citizenship. What comes out of our mouths will reflect the mercy, tenderness, and kindness of the Kingdom of God.

Let's be real. Releasing forgiveness to someone is incredibly difficult, especially in cases of genuinely deep abuse, violence, and rejection. It is often easier to keep a strong sense of indignation to protect us when we have been wounded. The thought of releasing our grip and letting go of our judgment and hurt can seem insurmountable. Willingly coming to the table to release forgiveness is often hard.

Today God says: "I need you to unfurl your hands and let go of your unforgiveness, for it has become a weapon that you are using against yourself. See that your unforgiveness has become your own limitation; it hardens your heart and establishes an internal numbness and puts walls of defensiveness up between you and Me. I am bound by My Word to forgive you as you forgive, so today I am releasing a grace to you and a strength to let go and speak forgiveness."

ACTION

Step forward and come to the table of exchange before God. Here you will give Him your unforgiveness, and He will give you back the ability to come alive. Physically open and unfurl your hands as a sign of release and a sign of a receptive posture. Speaking out loud, release forgiveness to those who have deeply, negatively wounded you. Watch as doing this enables numbness to leave you.

The Proximity of My Power

He went down with them and stood on a level place. A large crowd of his disciples was there and a great number of people from all over Judea, from Jerusalem, and from the coastal region around Tyre and Sidon, who had come to hear him and to be healed of their diseases. Those troubled by impure spirits were cured, and the people all tried to touch him, because power was coming from him and healing them all (Luke 6:17–19).

Come close enough to feel My power. Come close enough to touch Me. Your healing is found in Me. Come and learn from Me. I want to walk so closely to you that you can reach out and touch Me at any time. I want to walk so closely with you that you feel My power. I want others to see Me in you!

In that close proximity to Me, your mind is at peace; your heart is untroubled. In walking so near to Me, your body is healed. Come and learn the lifestyle of living in My presence! I will never leave nor forsake you. Stay right by Me. Learn from Me and listen to My words. Take delight in My teaching and My companionship.

I have seen as you have wondered where the power-filled life is. You have wondered if My power truly exists and if you will ever see it manifest through you. Let Me tell you now that if you will you do this, you will naturally reflect My power and My presence to those around you. Others will come to be close to you because they see Me in you. And you will know Me so well that you will never wonder again about My power. You will know Me as the One who flows in power.

DECREE

Pray this out loud over yourself today: "Lord Jesus, I want to walk so close to You that I feel Your presence and Your power! I want to become one who reflects both! Help me to determine to be a person who walks right next to You each and every day. Help me to dwell in the place of Your habitation. I want to be right where You are."

A Lifetime of Faith

So Abram went, as the Lord had told him; and Lot went with him. Abram was seventy-five years old when he set out from Harran. He took his wife Sarai, his nephew Lot, all the possessions they had accumulated and the people they had acquired in Harran, and they set out for the land of Canaan, and they arrived there (Genesis 12:4–5).

In Genesis 12 we first meet Abram, who later became Abraham. He lived by faith in God for his whole life. The key to understanding how Abraham lived revolves around the term *friend*. He knew that God was his friend and he responded as God's friend. God was for him, and Abraham lived in that assurance.

Abraham is referred to as the friend of God three times in Scripture:

- The first time is in the middle of a prayer. King Jehoshaphat was threatened by an invading army. In his prayer to God for help, he identified the nation of Judah with *"Abraham your friend"* (2 Chron. 20:7).

- Isaiah spoke the word of God to the people that identified Israel as the descendants of *"Abraham my friend"* (Isa. 41:8).

- The third mention of Abraham as *"God's friend"* is in the New Testament letter of James (James 2:23).

What a title to have! Abraham was God's friend when everybody else was His enemy and rebelling against Him. Even the gods Abraham grew up knowing about were distinctly unfriendly and continually needed to be appeased. But God was not like one of them. Abraham knew God was his friend, and he lived each day, not perfectly, but in an atmosphere charged with the goodness of God. He lived and responded as God's friend.

What about us? On the night before His crucifixion, Jesus had a deeply moving conversation with His disciples:

Greater love has no one than this: to lay down one's life for one's friends. You are my friends if you do what I command. I no longer call you servants, because a servant does not know his master's business. Instead, I have called you friends, for everything that I learned from my Father I have made known to you (John 15:13–15).

ACTION

In our culture today we hear a lot about developing a healthy self-esteem so we can live an enjoyable life. We are encouraged to find our satisfaction within ourselves. However, today as you ask the question, "Who am I?" consider the answer "friend of God" and think deeply about the amazingly good news encompassed in those three words. Remember Jesus's words: *"I have called you friends."*

Permission to Go at It Again

Jabez was more honorable than his brothers. His mother had named him Jabez, saying, "I gave birth to him in pain." Jabez cried out to the God of Israel, "Oh, that you would bless me and enlarge my territory! Let your hand be with me, and keep me from harm so that I will be free from pain." And God granted his request (1 Chronicles 4:9–10).

"Go again. Go at it again. Have another go. Pick up and restart." Heaven encourages you today!

Can you feel a weight on these phrases and their relevance to your life? The prospect of "going again" might not fill you with an immediate and abundant joy, but if you feel even a slight resonance with the idea then know that God has hold of you and wants you to make a restart to the project that He gave you.

For some, this will seem as simple as a reboot of a computer or machine, an opportunity to clear out some things, and you will be able to pick up where you left off, albeit with a fresh spring in your step.

But for many more, this is a case of ending your sitting under the tree with bare branches, the tree where the fruit dried up long ago. Chop it down and plant what God has put in your hand now. The seeds may look similar but new things will grow from there. "And if you do this, if you go again with what I give you and you plant where I tell you to plant, I will surely water the sapling and will supply what you need," says the Lord.

ACTION

What objective, project, or idea did you shelve because it didn't bear fruit? Write it down. Write down some of the reasons it failed. Now ask God if this "go at it again" word is for this project. Is He encouraging you to go again now that it is a new season? What things does He want you to do differently? What supernatural help do you need to make this a power project, full of life, one that will bear fruit?

DAY 356

Scriptural Authority

For the word of the Lord is right and true; he is faithful in all he does (Psalm 33:4).

The Spirit of God reminds you once again to allow Scripture to become your absolute guiding authority. It must become increasingly informative to how you think and act. No longer can cultural norms trump biblical principles; no longer can you merge and fuse Scripture with culture. Become accountable to biblical standards.

"I want you to be a good cultural tourist, where you see what the world does and then you come home to My Kingdom and step in the holy fire of cultural decontamination. What you think must be more rigorously subject to the fire of God. You are not right to think that what happens in your own logic is always accurate. Rigorously interrogate yourself and put your own emotions and judgments under My spotlight. I want you to think My thoughts. Holiness is not a posture that happens only in a church service, nor is it occasionally good decision-making. Rather, it must be your aim to live according to the standard of Scripture and not to merge your political or cultural opinions with biblical truth. You have no right to be offended by Scripture! I need those who will think, feel, and understand *above* the accepted cultural status quo and who will challenge the spirits of the age with the standard of truth that I outline in My Book, My Word."

God is releasing and raising up a new generation of biblical, prophetic theologians who will have the capacity to steward truth and rigorously understand the arc of Scripture.

DECREE

It is time to decree out loud that you believe in the absolute truth of Scripture and to say that you want to live to its standards only.

If you want to be part of the generation of biblical prophetic theologians, then use the words of Isaiah when he responded to God's call:

> Then I heard the voice of the Lord saying, "Whom shall I send? And who will go for us?" And I said, "Here am I. Send me!" (Isaiah 6:8)

Deliverance Lifestyle

So Jesus said to them, "Because of your unbelief; for assuredly, I say to you, if you have faith as a mustard seed, you will say to this mountain, 'Move from here to there,' and it will move; and nothing will be impossible for you. However, this kind does not go out except by prayer and fasting" (Matthew 17:20–21 NKJV).

One day the evil spirit answered them, "Jesus I know, and Paul I know about, but who are you?" (Acts 19:15)

The Lord says to you, "I am calling you to develop a deliverance lifestyle that builds your reputation as a destroyer of darkness; the demons are scared to even touch you because of the lifestyle of freedom and warfare that you have created around you."

Authority is not just an action or a moment or a prayer. Authority is not just saying, "Get out in Jesus's name." Authority is a recognition of identity and will affect your whole posture and approach to life. Authority is how you stand; it is who you are. It is where you can say with great gusto and confidence, "I am a destroyer of darkness."

Do not partner with a spirit of negotiation with darkness instead of standing in the fullness of your authority. Do not convince darkness to leave; tell it to go! You are not in this war to fight back and forth. You are in this war to win!

The Lord is calling you to build a life of prayer and fasting because it is this sort of lifestyle that prepares you to face and destroy *any* work of darkness. It is this lifestyle that deals with institutionalized demons and breaks their hold. It is this sort of lifestyle that causes demons to say, "Jesus I know, Paul I know...and you I know too! I am getting out of here!"

RECEIVE

Pray and receive from the Holy Spirit: "God, what do I need to do that will create a deliverance lifestyle? Is it more prayer? Is it more fasting? Is it more practice? Reveal Your ways to me, God, as I seek to use the authority that You have already given me."

All in for Jesus

"No," said Peter, "you shall never wash my feet."

Jesus answered, "Unless I wash you, you have no part with me."

"Then, Lord," Simon Peter replied, "not just my feet but my hands and my head as well!" (John 13:8–9)

The Lord asks you, "It is all or nothing. Are you all in with Me or not?" You may respond today, "I am all in with You, God, and I am completely for You in this moment," knowing confidently deep inside that, whatever happens, you will always be full-on in faith and full-on in following God. That is remarkable!

But in this, also acknowledge that there will be occasions of great challenge to your faith. Even Peter had to confront his own lack of faith when it was challenged. His faith had been seemingly so assured and so solid. He walked so closely with Christ Jesus, and yet he had a momentary but significant wobble in who he was following. When confronted, he went from, "I am all in Lord" to "I don't know this Man at all." In a moment it seemed like it was all over.

But then God! His grace abounds, and Peter is loved, accepted, and chosen to be the foundation the early church is built upon. Despite the bottom dropping out of Peter's faith, his life is not over—he is chosen!

Know that there will be challenges to your faith and yet you are chosen. You will have momentary wobbles, yet there is grace. His grace is there for you when your faith is as solid as rock but also abounds when your faith is more like Jell-O! The Lord is with you in all these times. He is consistent and unchanging. He is always saying over you, "You are Mine" and "You are chosen."

Don't give up in those faith-challenge moments. In these times the Lord will remind you who you are and that no matter what happens, you were made for love and relationship with Him. He will remind you that you are chosen and that you were created for winning spiritual battles that advance the Kingdom of God in the places He has set you. He will carry you through, even in the wobbly, small-faith moments. You will be carried through.

DECREE

If you are in a moment of strong faith, write down some decrees about your unbreakable relationship with God that you can read when you're feeling low, challenged, wobbly, or discouraged. If you are feeling like your faith is in a season of challenge and you're hanging on by a thread, read the story of the transformed Peter in the early chapters of Acts. He made it, and so will you!

He Is Here!

Yet to all who did receive him, to those who believed in his name, he gave the right to become children of God—children born not of natural descent, nor of human decision or a husband's will, but born of God. The Word became flesh and made his dwelling among us. We have seen his glory, the glory of the one and only Son, who came from the Father, full of grace and truth (John 1:12–14).

He is here! The King is here! He is alive and He is near. He is with you. Emmanuel is near. He is with you right now.

Quiet the voices in your head and listen to Him. Listen to His gentle breath as He sits close to you. Jesus loves you so much that He went on a miraculous mission for you. Though He is fully God, He became flesh and blood, fully human, a newborn baby, so that you might believe in Him and know that He won the victory over death for you.

And He is here with you now. He desires friendship. He desires your listening ear, for He has much to whisper in it. He desires your stillness because He wants to sit near you and comfort you. The King has come, and He is with you today.

RECEIVE

What a miracle—the Word became flesh and made His dwelling among us! And now by His Spirit, He dwells *in* us! Is there any greater gift that you can receive than to hear the voice of Jesus, our Emmanuel, which means "God with us." But we so often fill our lives, our ears, our eyes with noise, busyness, images, and films that we miss out on His friendship and His voice.

Find a moment of peace and stillness amidst the busyness of your life and allow Him to speak to you. Don't fill the silence with your voice and your questions. Wait on Him.

How To Be a New Covenant Warrior

These were all commended for their faith, yet none of them received what had been promised, since God had planned something better for us so that only together with us would they be made perfect (Hebrews: 11:39–40).

The letter to the Hebrews was written to Jews who had become believers in Christ. They had come out of Judaism but not fully; they had come into Christianity but not fully. And so this letter needed to be written to show its readers that even the finest acts and deeds of the old religion must be left behind. Christ is all we need, and we must run the race looking to Him alone as our Savior and the way.

The word *better* occurs twelve times in the letter. Christ is better than the angels, better than Moses, better than Joshua, better than Aaron. In Jesus, we have a better sacrifice than bulls and goats. He has made a better covenant than the old covenant. Better, better, better—it's all better for us. It's the best! The new way in Christ is better than the old way for Christ Jesus the Messiah is so much better than any previous leader, deliverer, hero, king, prophet, or priest.

Below are six of the twelve things described as "better" or "superior." Meditating on these will open your eyes afresh to the newness of the new covenant and the joy and freedom of living under the best covenant in the whole Bible.

> *After making purification for sins, he* [Jesus] *sat down at the right hand of the Majesty on high, having become as much superior to angels as the name he inherited is more excellent than theirs* (Hebrews 1:3–4 ESV).

> *Though we speak in this way, yet in your case, beloved, we feel sure of better things— things that belong to salvation* (Hebrews 6:9 ESV).

> *It is beyond dispute that the inferior is blessed by the superior* (Hebrews 7:7 ESV).

> *A former commandment is set aside because of its weakness and uselessness (for the law made nothing perfect); but on the other hand, a better hope is introduced, through which we draw near to God* (Hebrews 7:18–19 ESV).

> *This makes Jesus the guarantor of a better covenant* (Hebrews 7:22 ESV).

As it is, Christ has obtained a ministry that is as much more excellent than the old as the covenant he mediates is better, since it is enacted with better promises (Hebrews 8:6 ESV).

ACTION

Read and meditate on all the things that are better in Jesus. Ask the Holy Spirit to shine His light on the areas of your life that are based on an inferior, religious mindset, and not that of the better—best—new covenant.

DAY 361

The Benefits of Pursuing Holiness

And we all, who with unveiled faces contemplate the Lord's glory, are being transformed into his image with ever-increasing glory, which comes from the Lord, who is the Spirit (2 Corinthians 3:18).

Pursue holiness and do not wander from this. You are called to be holy. You are part of a holy people, and you will stand out from the crowd because of this. It will set you apart from others around you, but you must retrain yourself to embrace the joy of being one of God's set-apart people. Do not believe the misguided notion that you must be like everyone else in order to be winsome and attractive for Jesus. You are not supposed to blend in. After all, how can a shining light ever blend in?

Pursue holiness and purity. Clean out everything that is unfit or dishonorable to someone who professes to follow Christ. If you do, God's promise to you is that you will be used by Him for honorable use and every good work. Isn't that what you desire so much and ask of Him often?

It is not true that a life lived in holiness will make you have a religious spirit or make you legalistic or pharisaical. The way of holiness is the way of true joy. Follow Jesus! It's the best way!

ACTION

Make it your determined aim to be like Timothy, who Paul urged to *"flee the evil desires of youth and pursue righteousness, faith, love and peace, along with those who call on the Lord out of a pure heart"* (2 Tim. 2:22).

Search Me, Know Me, See My Path

Search me, O God, and know my heart; test me and know my anxious thoughts. Point out anything in me that offends you, and lead me along the path of everlasting life (Psalm 139:23–24 NLT).

Are you ready to be led along the path of everlasting life? Do you want to avoid the pitfalls, the traps, the things that cause unnecessary pain and heartache? This is My heart for you. I desire to lead you along the path of My righteousness. Will you yield? Will you yield your heart as David did? Each and every day there is a choice to yield or not. There is a choice to go down the path that I want to lead you on or to choose the path that looks best to you. One is full of error, stumbling, and heartache. The other path is narrow and far from easy, but it is where I am. It is filled with abundant life because I fill it! Which do you choose?

Allow Me to search your heart. I am the One trustworthy enough to do a fair search; I have your best in mind. I know that the things that offend Me are the things that hurt you. So, will you open your heart and let Me see deep inside? King David was a man after My own heart; he yielded to this process. Because he did, his life was blessed. I desire to bless you, to keep you, to shine My light and My love upon you. I desire to see you walk the path that brings you abundant life. Today make the choice to choose Me!

ACTION

This choice is one that we make every day in a variety of situations. Allow the Lord to teach you the lifestyle of yieldedness. Allow Him to do this daily search of your heart. Just say, "Yes, Lord, I yield. I want to walk Your path. Search me, know me, and lead me down Your path. I choose You before all else." If He reveals any area where you've not yielded, simply repent and yield.

DAY 363

Delight Delivers the Promises of God

Delight yourself in the Lord, and he will give you the desires of your heart (Psalm 37:4 ESV).

Blessed is the one who does not walk in step with the wicked or stand in the way that sinners take or sit in the company of mockers, but whose delight is in the law of the Lord, and who meditates on his law day and night. That person is like a tree planted by streams of water, which yields its fruit in season and whose leaf does not wither—whatever they do prospers (Psalm 1:1–3).

I heard the Lord say: "Delight delivers My promises to you. Delight is the express way of bringing good things into your daily life. Delight in Me and see your day marked by breaking-ins of My sovereign plan for your life. Delight, delight, delight in Me."

He asks, "Where does your daily delight come from? Does it come from that which is temporary, material possessions, finances, food, entertainment, worldly pleasures? Or does it come from Me, the eternal One, the Desire of Nations, the Ancient of Days, who knows what you need at every turn? For your delight will determine the degree of your overcoming. Your delight in Me determines the measure that you walk in fulfilled promises. Your delight in Me determines the measure of your fruitfulness. Delight in Me every day and see My manifest presence invade every aspect of your life."

The Lord is inviting you into a lifestyle of delighting yourself in Him, where He is the supreme pleasure of your life, high above everything else. He is convicting you, even now, to show where your delight is out of balance, where worldly pleasures have inadvertently ascended to a higher place in your life than God. He says, "Let Me recalibrate your desires today."

ACTION

Come to the Father with an open heart and pray, "Father, I recognize that I have often delighted in worldly pleasures more than I have delighted in You. For this, I am sorry." Let the Holy Spirit reveal pleasures that have ascended higher than God, whatever they may be. Pray, "Father, I give to You the pleasures of (name what comes to mind) and declare that You are my supreme pleasure, the One that all my delight is in."

Start to pray out loud to the Father all that you are delighting in Him for. "I delight in Your never-ending mercy. I delight in Your overwhelming holiness. I delight in Your overflowing joy."

Don't rush ahead when you pray this. Sit in the emotion; sit in the delight. Let delight bubble up from within and overflow your being. Feel all your delight start to center on God, your good, good Father. "All my delight is in You!"

DAY 364

Show the Way

I will give you every place where you set your foot, as I promised Moses (Joshua 1:3).

The Spirit of the Lord says, "Well done, for you have cultivated resilience. See, you are not as you were even a few months ago. You have been forged like steel in My fire. Now I require you to lead. Many will need your honesty and your insight. The battlefields of the future of the church will be messy, dirty, and confusing places. My church can easily get lost in conflicts, but if you seek Me and speak My words and receive a new leadership mantle, you will be able to show the way and navigate many people through the storms of the next few years."

The Lord shouts in a loud voice, "Show the way! Show the way! Become a signpost, go ahead. Today a grace is put on you to cut through the opposition that stands in the way of My people advancing. I need you to receive, with serious sobriety, the mantle to shape, form, and lead in the Body of Christ.

"You are resilient enough to stand as Joshua did before you and to bring new and creative strategies to My people. The promise I gave to him is the promise I give to you: wherever you put your foot it shall be yours."

DECREE

I receive the call to lead afresh. I will not set down this mantle, but I will honor the trust that God is putting in me.

DAY 365

Walk with Me Daily

He has shown you, O mortal, what is good. And what does the Lord require of you? To act justly and to love mercy and to walk humbly with your God (Micah 6:8).

There is no end to your faith journey with the Lord, only new beginnings. Maturity in faith comes over years of giving your yes to God one day at a time, week by week, month by month, season by season, year by year. Be consistent in your desire to go further and deeper, one step after another, one step at a time.

Jesus says to you, "Take My hand and walk with Me today. Walk with Me every day. Remember to consciously take My hand for I am with you in all things. I am right here with you.

"I am growing you up in Me. You are taking on increased maturity with every yes and amen you give Me. You are exercising your faith every time you talk to Me and respond to My voice. With each decision you make to obey what I ask of you and follow My teaching there is increase and advancement in your life.

"You are Mine and I am yours always. Walk with Me into greater depths of maturity. We are on a journey that never ends. Let us continue our walk together."

ACTION

Respond to Him in prayer (use your own words if you are able): "Lord Jesus, I take Your hand, open my ears, and choose to walk with You into increased faith and an ever-growing, ever-deepening relationship with You. I choose to walk forward into the greater depths of my connection with You, God. I desire more than I currently experience right now, and so today I am deciding to walk on with You and to never stop listening to Your voice. I choose to daily venture further than I have been into the unknown with You because I trust You, Father God. I love You, Jesus, and I am ready for more adventures with Your Holy Spirit."

APPENDIX

Warfare Scriptures

The Lord is a man of war; the Lord is His name (Exodus 15:3 NKJV).

Praise be to the Lord my Rock, who trains my hands for war, my fingers for battle (Psalm 144:1).

Behold, I have given you authority to tread on serpents and scorpions, and over all the power of the enemy, and nothing shall hurt you (Luke 10:19 ESV).

"No weapon forged against you will prevail, and you will refute every tongue that accuses you. This is the heritage of the servants of the Lord, and this is their vindication from me," declares the Lord (Isaiah 54:17).

Through You we will push down our enemies; through Your name we will trample those who rise up against us (Psalm 44:5 NKJV).

For You have armed me with strength for battle; You have subdued under me those who rose up against me (Psalm 18:39 NKJV).

Put on the full armor of God, so that you can take your stand against the devil's schemes. For our struggle is not against flesh and blood, but against the rulers, against the authorities, against the powers of this dark world and against the spiritual forces of evil in the heavenly realms. Therefore put on the full armor of God, so that when the day of evil comes, you may be able to stand your ground, and after you have done everything, to stand. Stand firm then, with the belt of truth buckled around your waist, with the breastplate of righteousness in place, and with your feet fitted with the readiness that comes from the gospel of peace. In addition to all this, take up the shield of faith, with which you can extinguish all the flaming arrows of the evil one. Take the helmet of salvation and the sword of the Spirit, which is the word of God (Ephesians 6:11–17).

Truly I tell you, whatever you bind on earth will be bound in heaven, and whatever you loose on earth will be loosed in heaven. Again, truly I tell you that if two of you on earth agree about anything they ask for, it will be done for them by my Father in heaven (Matthew 18:18–19).

The Lord will cause your enemies who rise against you to be defeated before your face; they shall come out against you one way and flee before you seven ways (Deuteronomy 28:7 NKJV).

Fight the good fight of the faith. Take hold of the eternal life to which you were called when you made your good confession in the presence of many witnesses (1 Timothy 6:12).

The weapons we fight with are not the weapons of the world. On the contrary, they have divine power to demolish strongholds. We demolish arguments and every pretension that sets itself up against the knowledge of God, and we take captive every thought to make it obedient to Christ (2 Corinthians 10:4–5).

Emma Stark

Emma Stark is an Irish prophet known around the world for her authority and authenticity. A fifth-generation Bible teacher, she communicates with a rare clarity, humor, and Celtic boldness. Emma is author of the best-selling books, *The Prophetic Warrior* and *Freedom from Fear*, is a regular TV and radio guest, and is host of her own live-streamed broadcasts and podcasts. Since 2020 *Power Hour!* has become essential viewing for those who are seeking trustworthy prophetic revelation and profound Bible teaching.

Emma leads one of Scotland's fastest growing churches, Power Church, and in 2009 she founded Glasgow Prophetic Centre. This apostolic hub of experienced prophetic ministers has given tens of thousands of man hours of face-to-face personal prophecy, freedom and healing appointments, ministry events, and training conferences. Now known as the Global Prophetic Alliance, this large and rapidly growing network is one of the primary ways that Emma and her teams train, equip, and disciple believers in the core essentials required of Spirit-filled ministers.

Emma is a founding core leader of the British Isles Council of Prophets. She leads, mentors, and consults with groups of prophets and prophetic roundtables across the nations and is regularly invited to prophesy into the lives of senior leaders in church, business, and government.

Emma and her husband, David, live in the heart of the historic city of Glasgow, just around the corner from her father, John Hansford, and have three remarkable children, Jessica, Peter, and Samuel.

David Stark

David is passionate about combining his fascination with technology, new media, and digital marketing and communication, with his love of Christ Jesus and His church. At 6am on Monday 3 January 2011, he sent out the first *Lion Bites* emails to Glasgow Prophetic Centre's growing database of people hungry for a fresh, authentic, and personal prophetic word. Tens of thousands now read Lion Bites every day: online, in their inbox, on social media. The total number of individual emails sent out numbers in the many millions and it is a joyful thought that these have helped to strengthen and encourage believers around the world, including in some of the darkest places on earth.

David was born and raised in Glasgow, Scotland, and studied music and technology in York, England, where he met and fell in love with Emma. After graduating and working as a freelance trumpet player, David had a ten-year career as a highly sought-after arts marketing leader and consultant, specializing in turning around the fortunes of struggling orchestras. In 2009 he and Emma were ordained as Christian ministers and soon after he turned his back on Bach to join his wife in establishing the ministry that she had founded the previous year, Glasgow Prophetic Centre. David has found that, whether writing, teaching, administrating, editing this book, designing flyers, building websites, fixing tech, totaling accounts, fundraising, prophesying, producing broadcasts, strategizing, or serving teams, all can be done to the total glory of God and enjoyment of Him! And he's still in love with Emma.

John Hansford

As a teenager in London, John Hansford had his mind excited by the expository teaching of Dr. John Stott and his heart warmed by the impassioned preaching of Dr. Martin Lloyd-Jones. Ever since, John has had a ministry characterized by a commitment to both Word and Spirit.

Pastor John, as he is affectionately known, has been in church leadership for nearly fifty years and is a beloved Bible scholar and teacher. After a short career in the city, John moved to Northern Ireland to study at the Irish Bible College. He pastored Baptist churches in Coleraine and Belfast for thirty years, before emigrating to lead an international church in Javea, Spain. He has served as a university chaplain, lectured at Bible colleges at home and overseas, and served on the board of many charities, missions, and church organizations.

In 2015 John and his wife Liz "retired" to Glasgow, Scotland, where they were immediately put to work by their daughter and son-in-law! John continues to regularly teach, advise, and bring his remarkable shepherding wisdom to the Global Prophetic Alliance team.

John was married to Liz for 41 years before she went to be with the Lord in 2016. John has four children (Emma, Nathan, Philip, and Charis) and six grandchildren. If he's not on an adventure with them, he can be found reading a book— or three!

Sarah-Jane Biggart

Sarah-Jane is Director of Prayer at the Global Prophetic Alliance and the organization's lead *seer* prophet. She spends much of her time leading and equipping strategic prayer teams and watchmen in the UK, Europe, and internationally. Sarah-Jane is leader of the British Isles Prayer Watch, a group associated with the British Isles Council of Prophets— of which she is also a member.

The author of *Seeing Beyond*, Sarah-Jane's heart is to make all believers aware of the ease by which they can meet with Jesus Christ in the Spirit. She introduces them to the reality that seeing, sensing, and engaging in the Spirit can be a daily lifestyle and her passion is releasing the body of Christ into the fulness of "normal," biblical Christianity, so that the Kingdom of God is advanced on the earth.

Much of SJ's work is hidden and "under the radar," including partnerships with senior leaders in various spheres, supporting their reformation call through prophecy, strategic prayer, and spiritual warfare.

Sarah-Jane lives in the beautiful countryside of central Scotland with her amazing husband, Alastair, and they have two wonderful adult children, Thomas and Sophie.

Sam Robertson

Sam is a prophet to nations who loves Jesus, truth, and the church. He travels extensively, preaching, teaching, and prophesying in churches, ministries, and to leaders, raising up a prophetically equipped church who knows how to influence culture and advance the Kingdom of God.

Sam joined Glasgow Prophetic Centre in 2014 as a voluntary project worker and intern. Now, Sam is Director of the organization's Raising Prophets department, running the Global Prophetic Alliance's three-year mentoring program for prophets, as well as overseeing its global network of "Prophetic Nests."

Sam is an anointed and dynamic communicator and prophetic teacher and is passionate about equipping the church to walk in the supernatural, have a hunger for biblical truth, and understand the times and seasons, knowing what to do (1 Chronicles 12:32). He is currently studying theology as well as serving full time for the Global Prophetic Alliance.

Micah Hayden

Micah is from the Rocky Mountains of Colorado where she grew up in a ministry family. She carries a deep love for Jesus, His church, and the nations of the world. From a young age, she knew that she would one day be a missionary. She has a double degree in Spanish literature and theology, and while at seminary, Micah met an Englishman who would become her husband. Together, they live and serve in Scotland where they also homeschool their three children.

Micah has spent the last 20 years traveling to many nations and serving in a variety of ministry roles, including over two years spent as leader of the amazing *Lion Bites* team at Glasgow Prophetic Centre. Today, Micah can be found sharing her heart for Jesus with others, studying history, teaching her children the Word, and writing at haydenmissions.com and wisdom-calls.co.uk.

Printed in Poland
by Amazon Fulfillment
Poland Sp. z o.o., Wrocław
11 July 2023